Clientelism and Economic Policy

With its deep economic crisis and dramatic political developments Greece has puzzled Europe and the world. What explains its long-standing problems and its incapacity to reform its economy?

Using an analytic narrative and a comparative approach, the book studies the pattern of economic reforms in Greece between 1985 and 2015. It finds that clientelism – the allocation of selective benefits by political actors (patrons) to their supporters (clients) – created a strong policy bias that prevented the country from implementing deep-cutting reforms. The book shows that the clientelist system differs from the general image of interest-group politics and that the typical view of clientelism, as individual exchange between patrons and clients, has not fully captured the wide range and implications of this phenomenon. From this, the author develops a theory on clientelism and policy making, addressing key questions on the politics of economic reform, government autonomy and party politics.

The book is an essential addition to the literatures on clientelism, public choice theory, and comparative political economy. It will be of key interest to scholars and students of European Union politics, economic policy and party politics.

Aris Trantidis is F.A. Hayek Fellow at George Mason University, the Mercatus Center, USA, and a Visiting Lecturer in the Department of Political Economy, King's College London, UK.

Routledge Advances in European Politics

For a full list of titles in this series, please visit http://www.routledge.com

118 **The Moral Economy of EU Association with Africa**
Mark Langan

119 **European Space Policy**
European integration and the final frontier
Edited by Thomas Hörber and Paul Stephenson

120 **Policy Making at the Second Tier of Local Government in Europe**
What is happening in Provinces, Counties, Départements and Landkreise in the on-going re-scaling of statehood?
Edited by Xavier Bertrana, Björn Egner and Hubert Heinelt

121 **The Politics of Trauma and Peace-Building**
Lessons from Northern Ireland
Cillian McGrattan

122 **Eurozone Politics**
Perception and reality in Italy, the UK, and Germany
Philip Giurlando

123 **Politics of Identity in Post-Conflict States**
The Bosnian and Irish experience
Edited by Éamonn Ó Ciardha and Gabriela Vojvoda

124 **Unequal Europe**
Social divisions and social cohesion in an old continent
James Wickham

125 **Generations, Political Participation and Social Change in Western Europe**
Maria T. Grasso

126 **Clientelism and Economic Policy**
Greece and the crisis
Aris Trantidis

Clientelism and Economic Policy

Greece and the crisis

Aris Trantidis

Routledge
Taylor & Francis Group
LONDON AND NEW YORK

First published 2016
by Routledge
2 Park Square, Milton Park, Abingdon, Oxon OX14 4RN

and by Routledge
711 Third Avenue, New York, NY 10017

First issued in paperback 2017

Routledge is an imprint of the Taylor & Francis Group, an informa business

British Library Cataloguing in Publication Data
A catalogue record for this book is available from the British Library

Library of Congress Cataloging-in-Publication Data
Names: Trantidis, Aris.
Title: Clientelism and economic policy : Greece and the crisis / Aris Trantidis.
Description: Abingdon, Oxon ; New York, NY : Routledge, 2016. | Series: Routledge advances in European politics ; 126 | Includes bibliographical references and index.
Identifiers: LCCN 2015046996 | ISBN 9781138101401 (hardback) | ISBN 9781315656953 (ebook)
Subjects: LCSH: Patronage, Political—Economic aspects—Greece. | Patron and client—Economic aspects—Greece. | Political planning—Economic aspects—Greece. | Economic development—Political aspects—Greece. | Financial crises—Political aspects—Greece. | Greece—Economic policy. | Greece—Politics and government.
Classification: LCC JN5147 .T73 2016 | DDC 324.2/495—dc23
LC record available at http://lccn.loc.gov/2015046996

ISBN 13: 978-1-138-48823-6 (pbk)
ISBN 13: 978-1-138-10140-1 (hbk)

Typeset in Times New Roman
by Apex CoVantage, LLC

Contents

Figures

Tables

Preface

If social scientists should explore the phenomena in human societies that matter, either because they improve or because they upset our lives, I have chosen to study how political power interferes in economic activity and affects the decisions of actors regarding the allocation of scarce resources. As a researcher, I have focused on clientelism – namely, the distribution of benefits by politicians and political parties to their supporters in return for their votes, campaign contributions and political loyalty. I discovered that clientelist relationships extend beyond the personal exchange of favors between patrons and clients, and have broader implications for the design of economic policy. I soon began working on a research project on clientelism in Greece a little while before the Greek crisis broke up, which affected my parents and my friends, as well as millions of other residents in Greece. The evidence I had collected suggested that clientelist politics had played an important part in shaping the fate of previous efforts to reform Greece. With this book, I wanted to shed new light on what had caused the crisis in a way that advances our understanding of the relationship between politics and the economy.

Years before the crisis, while I was a student in Athens, Professor Panos Kazakos introduced me to public choice theory, a body of work in economics that displaced the assumption that public policy is oriented towards the 'public interest' and, instead, considers politicians and bureaucrats to be driven, like any other economic actor, by their subjective perceptions of 'utility' which often means re-election to office and special economic and financial benefits. Public choice led to a vast literature that has offered an account of 'politics without romance', in the words of its founding father, James Buchanan. Yet, this body of – mostly – formal analysis, like any other in social sciences, is not without fault. Many analyses of public policy tend to overlook that political and social actors interact with one another in nuanced institutional settings under recurrent relationships and specific norms of behavior. These settings shape regular preferences, generate interdependences among the actors involved and limit strategic behavior to a narrower set of options. These settings can only be explored in depth by empirical analysis that is qualitative and historical. Once we observe that the practice of clientelism generates a unique institutional setting, it should not be long before we ask the question: does clientelism have a distinctive impact on policy reform compared to typical interest-group activity and party politics?

The purpose of this book is to put forward a theory on the impact of clientelism on economic reform and explain the Greek case. Greece offers an excellent opportunity to test and refine a number of hypotheses and contribute to the general literature on economic reforms. Using an analytic narrative and a comparative approach, the book casts light on the distinct properties of the clientelist system and explains why resistance to reform is likely to be stronger here compared to other settings. It shows that the clientelist system has properties that substantively differ from established premises about electoral competition and interest-group activity. Clientelism creates a relationship of interdependency between parties and clients that relies on the ongoing supply of clientelist benefits. This explains why client groups are the most important social groups for the political parties, and why clientelism has a unique impact on the bargaining power and relative autonomy of clients and patrons. Unlike the typical context of interest-group competition, the government's autonomy to shift social alliances or forge new ones over proposed policies is expected to be considerably limited in a clientelist system, given that placing limits on the supply of patronage will primarily affect relations inside the party and, ultimately, its cohesion and mobilization capacity.

It is the main finding of the book that exchange relationships between political parties and client groups introduce a *systemic bias* in the design of economic reforms in favor of preserving clientelist supply. This policy bias is resilient even when a country faces rapidly deteriorating economic conditions and has undertaken strong international commitments for policy reform. It is on that basis that the book argues that the Greek crisis is a crisis of politics intersecting with the economy that can occur anywhere else in the word.

Besides a theory on clientelism, the book covers a large historical period, including the Greek financial crisis (2009–2015), and can be a useful source of reference for those interested in Greece's economic history. I also hope that readers with no particular interest in Greece may find other noteworthy claims and findings. The book points to the political party as the main rent-seeking organization. It also demonstrates the pitfalls of state intervention in the economy, which rational politicians and other actors will seek to turn into rent seeking, corruption and patronage. The book seeks to highlight the value of historical research, which the current trend of quantitative analysis and formal modeling has overshadowed. The book also develops a refined view of rational choice by incorporating the role of asymmetrical information, ideological predilections, risk aversion and network dynamics. It shows how empirical information can be translated into analysis and how incentives and preferences can be inferred from empirical observations. The book also illustrates that institutional settings are dynamic and complex systems, and that the adaptive behavior of actors leads to changes in the rules of the game, which are often unanticipated and unintended. Finally, the book aspires to be a good example of how useful within-country comparative analysis can be.

The book builds on my PhD thesis at King's College London. I owe a great deal of gratitude to a number of people who have been supportive of this research project. I would like to warmly thank the two PhD examiners, Professor Andrew Hindmoor and Dr. Stella Ladi, as well as Dr. Scott James, for their insightful comments during that stage. Special thanks to Dr. Faidon Zaras, Dr. Rainbow Murray, Dr. Catherine Needham and Mr. Nick Cowen for their substantive comments to several drafts and chapters. Any errors are my own. I would also like to thank the Mercatus Center at George Mason University and Professor Peter Boettke, in particular, for the opportunity to discuss the book's findings and methodology. With its F. A. Hayek program in politics, philosophy and economics, Mercatus is a unique workshop of ideas that advance the epistemology of economics and social sciences.

I am immensely grateful to Professor Mark Pennington for his continuous support as my mentor, colleague and former supervisor. His scholarship and work ethic have been a source of inspiration and a benchmark for me. The book would not have been possible without his mentorship.

I dedicate this book to my family in Greece and in London. Their unconditional support has made it possible for me to prepare for, embark on and insist in following a very challenging career path.

1 Introduction

Clientelism and economic reforms: the case of Greece

With its deep and prolonged economic crisis and dramatic political events since 2009, Greece found itself at the forefront of worldwide attention. The crisis left a profound impact on the Greek economy, society and politics. The country experienced a downward spiral of economic recession and rising debt levels, which led to high unemployment rates, rising poverty and workforce emigration. The Greek party system underwent seismic shifts – most noticeably, the electoral collapse of the Greek socialists (PASOK), the shrinking of the Greek conservative party (New Democracy) and the rise of the radical left-wing party SYRIZA.

We cannot understand the Greek crisis without looking further back into the country's political and economic history. Greece's substantial growth rates in the late 1990s and most of the 2000s proved to be unbalanced and unstable, given the rising level of public debt throughout that period and the structural weaknesses of the economy. For over three decades, growing macroeconomic imbalances constituted sufficient reason for the Greek governments to introduce bolder and more comprehensive reforms.[1] On many occasions during that period, the country faced the prospect of a fiscal collapse and came close to experiencing a serious economic crisis. Moreover, as a member of the European Union (EU, known as the 'European Community' until 1993), Greece was part of an institutional environment that offered national governments specific prescriptions and general directions for economic reform, either in the form of 'hard-law' directives or as recommendations of 'best practices' in several policy areas. Greece's candidacy for entry to the euro in the late 1990s was an additional pressure for the country to reform its economy and fix its finances in order to meet the macroeconomic criteria of the Maastricht Treaty. Membership in the Eurozone later established new mechanisms monitoring the country's fiscal performance next to a framework for policy coordination. In addition, the European Union allocated

1 The notion of 'economic reforms' refers to policies of fiscal stabilization and structural reforms that change the terms under which markets operate (labor reforms, privatization, deregulation/re-regulation, tax reform, etc.), as well as administrative reforms related to the operation of economic activities.

fiscal resources that were thought to help a reform-minded government in its effort to stabilize its finances and restructure the economy (Marks 1992; Sandholtz 1996). The governments could have also taken a strong initiative to communicate the case for reform to the Greek public (Antoniades 2003). This setting could have strengthened the capacity of consecutive Greek governments to promote a reform agenda, even in the presence of recalcitrant domestic interests.

Why did Greek governments fail to implement the necessary economic reforms that might have prevented this crisis from happening? To explain Greece's long-standing fiscal and economic problems and its incapacity to restructure its economy, most of the literature made use of two frameworks of analysis: interest-group theory and cultural accounts, often in a combined way. Since the 1990s, research on Greece added the dimension of 'Europeanization' as 'a process by which domestic policy areas become increasingly subject to European policy-making' (Börzel 1999: 574).[2] The interest-group framework was transferred in the study of Greek politics as a clash between modernizing and recalcitrant political and social forces in view of reform prescriptions and recommendations from the European Union. The literature introduced the notion of *informal veto players* to refer to domestic interests in Greece that were hostile to comprehensive and deep-cutting reforms (Featherstone 2005a: 232; Featherstone and Papadimitriou 2008). This literature explored specific cases in which reform initiatives were launched, and observed clashes between the government and interest groups, which seemed to confirm its group-centered view.[3] These recalcitrant groups sought to defend 'the current privileges and protection, fearing the risks of more open competition and the consequences of low state welfare provision' (Featherstone 2008: 27; Featherstone and Papadimitriou 2008: 19, 62 and 192; also, Featherstone 2005a: 225 and 2005b). The reform agenda had weak support from other social and economic groups (Featherstone, Kazamias and Papadimitriou 2001; Matsaganis 2002: 119; Vourloumis 2002: 74–5, 77, 110–111).

These studies can be situated in the broader analytic framework in the literature on economic policy, which focuses on how interest groups seek to influence economic policy and associates policy change with their relative influence (cf. Stigler 1971; Krueger 1974; Buchanan, Tollison and Tullock 1980; Becker 1983; Tullock 1993 and 2005). On these accounts, when economic reforms are under consideration, interest groups lobby the government in order to gain benefits and avoid the costs of the reforms which the government considers or is about to

2 See also Vink and Graziano (2007). Applications of this framework in the Greek case include the work of Lavdas (1998); Featherstone, Kazamias and Papadimitriou (2001); Sotiropoulos (2004b); Featherstone (2005b); Featherstone and Papadimitriou (2008); Zartaloudis (2014). For a discussion of issues concerning causal analysis in the Europeanization studies, see Exadaktylos and Radaelli (2009).

3 See Featherstone (2005a; 2005b and 2008); Allison and Nicolaidis (1997); Sotiropoulos (2004a); Featherstone, Kazamias and Papadimitriou (2001); Spanou (2008).

enact.[4] The influence of each group largely depends on the group's ability to organize and undertake collective action (Kaempfer and Lowenberg 1992: 132). Well-coordinated groups are likely to exert more influence on government policy (Callaghy 1990; Evans 1992; Waterbury 1992; Haggard, Cooper and Moon 1993). For part of the literature, politicians often yield to the demands of strong interest groups at a significant cost to the rest of the population, which does not have the capacity to engage in collective action (Denzau and Munger 1986; Bates and Krueger 1993). In that regard, policy outcomes are endogenously determined by competing interest-group dynamics (Kaempfer and Lowenberg 1992: 9–10).

This analytic framework, however, must pay due attention to the degree to which governments and political parties can be autonomous from interest-group pressures and enjoy a room for maneuvering and a wider menu of strategic options, such as co-optation, realignment, compromise and compensation, versus these groups (Evans 1992; Waterbury 1992).[5] According to this view, a group-centered approach can miss important factors that explain why policy changes that harm powerful groups sometimes occur (Geddes 1994: 4). Far from being a neutral arbiter, the government can play a powerful role in shaping the terms and the outcome of domestic competition (cf. Evans et al. 1985; Scharpf 1992; Hall and Taylor 1996). Political entrepreneurship strengthens the autonomy of the state from interest groups, and state officials have greater freedom in choosing how to respond to economic crises and changes in the international economy (Haggard and Kaufman 1992; Geddes 1994). If a latent public interest lacks 'voice' through collective action, political entrepreneurship can use its own resources, which are quite significant, to mobilize broader support.

In Greece, the government's autonomy in the design and implementation of a reform agenda should have been facilitated by key properties of the country's institutional and political setting: the fact that the country was governed, most of the time, by one-party governments with comfortable parliamentary majorities, strong executive powers and a politically subservient bureaucracy (Sotiropoulos 2012: 10). However, the literature has suggested that the Greek state had weak capacity to enact and implement reforms (Petmesidou 2000: 317; Ladi 2005; Monastiriotis and Antoniades 2009; Featherstone and Papadimitriou 2012). This is a paradox. Without any formal veto players and under strong pressures for reform, it is logical to ask the question why the reform capacity of the Greek governments was so limited. How autonomous were the Greek governments from the groups that opposed a bolder reform agenda? Why were these groups powerful enough to block much-needed economic reforms? What is the nature of their association with political power?

4 See Geddes (1994); Schamis (1999). Group-centered and formal analysis includes the work of Stigler (1971); Becker (1983); Velasco (1993); Tornell (1995); Alesina and Drazen (1998); Labán and Sturzenegger (1994 and 1998).

5 For a discussion of the role of compensation to groups expecting losses – when this is possible – see Martini (2007).

Cultural accounts have sought to propose an alternative explanation that stresses the resilience of a political culture hostile to reforms, which is associated with a historical division within Greek politics and society between 'modernizing' political forces and 'traditionalist' political forces – a division that cuts across political parties (Diamandouros 1994). According to this view, the roots of a 'cultural dualism' can be found in two contrasting cultural and historical traditions: on the one hand, the 'backward' East (with references to the Ottoman past and the Balkans) and, on the other side, the 'rationalist' West (with references to Enlightenment and the Industrial Revolution) (Diamandouros 1994 and 1997). Cultural accounts can be seen as additional explanations of the tensions and controversies in the design and implementation of economic policy (Featherstone and Papadimitriou 2008: 41 and 192; Featherstone 2005a: 225; Triantafyllou, Gropas and Kouki 2013). From a broader perspective, this sociological approach brings center-stage the impact of norms on the domestic policy arena as effectuated through a process of socialization.[6] However, norms and ideas are not shielded from change and will evolve following social interactions and the choices of the actors involved. It sounds reasonable to expect that domestic actors, including the government, will choose a set of norms which they think best serves their interests.

From the perspective of public choice theory,[7] a government will choose a policy if the gains it expects from this move will outweigh the anticipated costs. This benefit-and-cost calculation gives a specific meaning to how government autonomy versus groups plays out. It accommodates the possibility that government decisions will favor the political coalition that provides the main support for the government (Stallings 1990: 114) or that the government will be a recalcitrant reformer itself, driven by its desire to win the election or preserve its commitments to its own supporters. External institutional pressures (such as in the context of Europeanization) may lead governments to change their policies, but their response is still conditioned by typical domestic factors: government preferences and interest-group relative power and competition.[8] More broadly, social actors will also follow a rational process and assess competing policy ideas and proposals against a perception of *utility*, for example, re-election for the government, career advancement for a politician or the preservation of special benefits for a group, such as jobs for the unemployed, profit increases for business, job security, higher wages or extra benefits for groups already in employment, etc. What constitutes utility in politics may differ among politicians, too, depending on their position in the party system: the prime target of party leaders may be the preservation or advancement of their leadership position, which

6 See Hall (1986); Ikenberry (1988).

7 The general assumption is that politicians, just as actors in the economic field, aim at utility maximization which primarily regards re-election and the advancement of their careers and that they make a calculation of costs and benefits in view of alternative policy choices.

8 In the EU context, the degree to which European integration affected party politics was found to be very small (Mair 2000).

primarily depends on their party's electoral success. For middle-ranking and career-aspiring politicians, their 'utility' may be more related to the ongoing support and loyalty of party members and sympathizers, as this could be more important for their political survival in the long run than the next electoral victory. Perceptions of 'utility' may include other considerations which, as the following chapters will show, are traceable in a given empirical context.

How does a case study like Greece fit in any of these analytic frameworks? Using these approaches mechanically comes with the risk of assuming away, or assigning less importance to, key properties of the political and economic system under review. Instead, rational and sociological approaches offer complementary models of explanation (cf. Bulmer 2007: 51) that call for a synthesis. In this combined approach, preferences and the relative autonomy of the political and social actors can be inferred with reference to their assumed *roles* and *positions* in a given institutional context, and with reference to their recurrent *interactions* with others in that environment: the kind of commitments and responsibilities these actors have undertaken, the type of relations they are engaged in and the structure of incentives and norms that guides their decisions. Different environments have distinct sets of norms, routines, roles, power relations and institutions that can be associated with recurrent patterns of political behavior. In a rational choice analysis, these sets delineate the preferences of the social and political stakeholders, and limit the range of options for strategic behavior.

Attention to a given empirical setting will also indicate that formal and informal institutions, as well as recurrent social relations, give rise to distinctive *systems*.[9] The literature on comparative political economy has sought to cluster these properties into typologies based on the role of the state in the economy (Shonfield 1965; Schmidt 2007), the model of interest organization – whether corporatist or not (Schmitter 1979), the type of welfare state (Esping-Andersen 1990), and patterns of intrafirm and interfirm relations (Hall and Soskice 2001). On that basis we can identify types of political and economic systems as clusters of cases with common institutional properties which define the nature, intensity and range of political intervention in the economy: *distinct types of political economy*. In each type we can identify the *dominant pattern* by which political power regulates economic activity and allocates economic resources, as well as the stable social and political *relations* and *interdependences* it creates and the impact these relations have on the preferences and strategic behavior of the actors involved. These institutional structures are dynamic and complex systems. They emerge from the interactions of political and social actors whose behavior they condition, but they also evolve thanks to the intended or unintended effects of the adaptive behavior of these actors.

In Greece, the active role of the state in the allocation of economic resources and social opportunities has been a core characteristic of the country's political

9 Informal institutions and norms are defined as 'socially shared rules, usually unwritten, that are created, communicated and enforced outside of officially sanctioned channels' (Helmke and Levitsky 2006: 5).

and economic system. Distribution via state intervention has markedly taken the form of *clientelism*, a term that describes the distribution of resources by political power through an agreement in which politicians – the patrons – make this allocation dependent on the political support of the beneficiaries – their clients.[10] This agreement creates mutual obligations of reciprocity between the patrons and its clients – a 'clientelist exchange', which distinguishes clientelism from other types of political allocation of resources (Piattoni 2001; Robinson and Verdier 2002).[11] When clientelism becomes the predominant mode of resource allocation, a *clientelist system* emerges as a distinctive system of interest intermediation at the crossroads of politics and the economy. A clientelist system intersects with formal or more publicly conspicuous processes of collective bargaining such as labor unions' activity, and, in fact, as the book indicates, it may merge with elements of corporatism or with a pluralist setting of state–society relations, generating *hybrid* systems of interest intermediation. Although it is plausible to say that there is no standard threshold beyond which a country – or any other constituency – will be considered clientelist, this characterization can be a matter of degree: the term can be assigned to countries in which clientelism has a predominant presence in its politics and economy.

Given the prominence of patronage politics in Greece, the country can be said to be a clientelist system. Various studies of Greek politics have pointed out clientelism as a core systemic property of the Greek political system.[12] The literature has associated clientelism with the so-called Mediterranean or Southern model of political economy characterized by extensive state regulation, legal formalism and uncertainty, and an underdeveloped welfare state system.[13] Greece's' state–society relations since the fall of the military junta in 1974 were integrated in a system of party-led patronage (Pagoulatos 2003). Clientelism generated *sui generis* properties in the processes of social dialogue and collective bargaining ('disjointed corporatism' for Lavdas 2005 and 'parentela pluralism' for Pagoulatos 2003: 162). Research has pointed to the clientelist organization of the state (Lyberaki and Tsakalotos 2002; Mitsopoulos and Pelagidis 2011) and found that patronage politics was a key obstacle to structural reforms and fiscal consolidation (Trantidis 2014; Afonso, Zartaloudis and Papadopoulos 2015).

10 The book uses the terms 'clientelism' and 'patronage' interchangeably.

11 Lemarchand and Legg (1972: 150). See also Scott (1972: 92); Eisenstadt and Roniger (1984: 48); Stokes (2005); Lyne (2008); Kitschelt and Wilkinson (2007); Stokes (2007); Kitschelt et al. (2010).

12 Among other authors, Mavrogordatos (1984); Lyrintzis (1984); Kazakos (1993); Tsoukalas (1993); Sotiropoulos (1996); Tsoukalis (1997); Zambarloukou (1997); Sotiropoulos (2001); Lyrintzis (2002); Lavdas (2005); Spourdalakis (1998); Pappas (1999 and 2009); Pappas and Assimakopoulou (2012).

13 Kazakos (1993: 133); Andreou and Koutsiaras (2002: 162); Sotiropoulos (2004a: 11); Featherstone and Papadimitriou (2008: 56). See also Maravall (1993; Ferrera 1996).

Nevertheless, these accounts have not produced a solid explanation of Greece's reform record that is alternative to the prevalent view that emphasizes the clash between pro-reform and anti-reform forces in the context of Europeanization. We have yet to gain an understanding of how clientelism, as an institutional setting with unique properties, shapes strategic behavior and policy making. Do the ties and linkages which clientelism creates in the party system and across society make a clientelist system different from the typical structures of interest-group and interparty competition? This question requires a shift from descriptive accounts that present clientelism merely as a feature present in a country's political landscape towards a deeper analysis of how this phenomenon affects the preferences and relative autonomy of the policy makers and other key social actors with a stake in public policy. This shift will permit a more systematic account of how clientelist politics relates to the conceptual frameworks of interest-group competition, government autonomy and political-electoral motivations.

Clientelism is a key strategy for political mobilization and a distinctive mode of interest accommodation that creates dense interactions and mutual commitments between patrons and clients. It is plausible to expect that policy making in a highly clientelist economy may not be adequately captured though the lens of typical interest-group analysis that assumes that interest groups are independent actors who spent resources lobbying the government, or through a reductionist view of party politics that assumes that politicians and political parties are primarily sensitive to voters' preferences and may, for this reason, overlook the demands of powerful groups if it is in their electoral interest to do so. Instead, the input of clientelism in policy making must be shaped by the web of interdependences connecting the party leadership with its client groups, the special position of these groups in the party system, the constrained autonomy of the governing party from its client groups and the special terms of interparty competition around the supply of patronage. This setting may significantly skew the policy preferences of the government towards the preservation of patronage supply to their client groups, creating a *systemic bias* in policy making that gives priority to the demands of their clients and their organizations.

The study of the clientelist system requires empirically backed analysis that brings the political party center-stage. The focus is on the political party as an organization that seeks to gain access to decision-making power and is, at the same time, entangled in dense and stable ties with its clients that feed back into its decision making. For this purpose, research must go beyond the study of a few selected reform episodes and must cover a longer period of time and the broader context of party politics and government–society relations with regard to:

1 The interparty arena
2 The intraparty arena
3 The interaction between the governing party and key social stakeholders
4 Public opinion and general electoral popularity
5 The interaction between the national government and the EU.

An analytic and historical look at the linkages that connected the Greek political parties with its client groups may better illustrate the dilemmas faced by political leaders and the resulting inconsistencies in the reform policies which Greek governments followed. It may be found that, compared to the general interest-group schema, Greece's predominantly 'rent-seeking character of interest mobilization' was less fragmented and pluralistic (compared to what Pagoulatos thought, for instance, 2003: 161) and that the so-called recalcitrant groups were closely linked to party structures in recurrent exchange relations, which explains the source of their remarkable informal 'veto' power.

It is in this light that the book offers a single-case comparative analysis of economic reforms by consecutive Greek governments (Andreas Papandreou 1985–1989, Constantine Mitsotakis 1990–1993, Andreas Papandreou 1993–1996, Costas Simitis 1996–2004, Costas Karamanlis 2004–2009, George Papandreou 2009–2011, Lucas Papademos 2011–2012 and Antonis Samaras 2012–2015). These time periods are organized into different sets of *observations* or *cases* (Eckstein 1975: 85), which show variation in the dependent variable (economic reforms) over time, given the presence of strong clientelist commitments in the party system. Across these phases, observed patterns of policy change are associated with other pertinent variables, most notably, the presence or absence of institutional pressures for reforms and their degree of authoritative force, the breakup of crisis events, the input of party ideology and the general popularity of the selected policy measures. These 'push' and 'pull' factors have been incorporated in the narrative in ways that advance the book's main objective: to track the linkage between clientelism and economic reform. The aim here is not to assess the relative causal *effect* of each factor but, instead, to offer a comprehensive explanation of the *process* by which clientelism has shaped the pattern of reforms in interaction with these factors. With this comparative approach, the book tracks policy changes in areas where external pressures were absent, as well as in areas where they were present and strong. It covers cases where the government tried to change a policy but its effort was unsuccessful, as well as cases where the government made no attempt to tackle a chronic economic problem.

Besides the interest in understanding Greece itself, the country offers a good case for the development of theory on how clientelism affects economic policy. This is because Greece can be seen as a prototype of a political system permeated by clientelism. Throughout the period under study, it exhibited 'extreme' values of clientelist politics (a strong pull factor away from reform) and, in addition, faced rounds of economic crises that pushed for economic reform (strong push factors for reform). Since the 1970s, and particularly during the 1980s, mass patronage appointments in the broader public sector led to the colonization of the state bureaucracy and the trade unions by party clients. However, by the mid-1980s, deteriorating macroeconomic conditions and institutional pressures from the European Union pushed Greek governments to consider implementing widespread and deep-cutting economic reforms. Some of these prescriptions ran counter to the preservation and development of clientelism in Greece.

Successive Greek governments found themselves under pressure to implement policy reforms, at a time when clientelist policies offered them significant gains in political mobilization and party cohesion. Structural and institutional pressures varied across time and had an escalating degree of urgency and variation in terms of the imminent sanctions for noncompliance across different time periods. An exogenous shock in the aftermath of the 2008 global financial crisis threatened the very foundations of Greece's fiscal and distributional system. These push factors for economic reform create a 'tough' empirical setting which allows us to explore how resilient the clientelist system is and how skillful and creative political actors can be in their policy responses.

In developing a theory of clientelism and economic policy from a single-country comparative study, we can capture how patron–client relationships define regular patterns of behavior, recurrent relations and norms of reciprocity inside the party and across the party system. A case study can offer information about the causal processes at play, which a large-n study may be ill suited to discern (Ragin 1997; George and Bennett 2005: 81).

In this light, the remaining part of this chapter offers a critical review of the literature on clientelism and economic reforms and puts forward a number of hypotheses about the impact of clientelism on economic policy, which the empirical chapters will help us explore, confirm or refine. Although this research design benefits from an empirical setting that is highly typical of the phenomenon under study, 'a pilot case' (cf. Eckstein 1975/1992; Ragin 1997; Rueschemeyer and Stephens 1997; Gerring 2004), any findings are presented as 'contingent generalizations' (George and Bennett 2005: 84) which new studies of larger samples can further explore (cf. Gerring 2004: 349).

Three views of clientelism

Clients as atomized individuals

The typical view of clientelism refers to the exchange of benefits between politicians and individual voters 'where the criterion of distribution that the patron uses is simply: did you (will you) support me?' (Stokes 2007: 605). This definition suggests that clientelism is distinguished from other forms of particularistic politics by the fact that clients offer their political support to their patrons *as reciprocation for* the received benefit (Piattoni 2001; Robinson and Verdier 2002). Clientelism emerges at the intersection of two competitive processes: competition among economic and social actors for access to resources distributed by political power (which creates prospective clients), and competition among politicians for access to political power (which creates prospective patrons). Under these competitive conditions, the very process by which the government distributes scarce resources inevitably requires selection by politicians of a limited number of recipients from the whole population. Not surprisingly, politicians whose political survival and success depend on election to office have a strong incentive to make the allocation of these resources conditional on the recipients' political support. In that context, clientelism is part of distributional politics that resemble an auction mechanism in which politicians bid for the government's right to monopoly by providing a number of goods and services in order to incentivize political support (Tullock 1965), this time by rewarding their loyal clients. From this perspective, clientelism can be seen as a particular *subset of rent seeking*, distinguished by the presence of an agreement of reciprocity between the patron and the client. Prospective clients find it in their best interests to take part in a clientelist exchange with the patrons, but they are the weakest part of this relationship. They have a 'vertical' relationship with their patrons defined by power asymmetry.

Clientelist networks and party structures

The second view of clientelism goes beyond the one-off exchange of votes and the view of clients as atomized or isolated, and observes recurrent clientelist exchanges that create regular and established relations and often lead to the formation of networks of clients (Weingrod 1968, Roniger and Güneş-Ayata 1994; Kitschelt and Wilkinson 2007; Stokes 2007). As an aggregate effect, iterated reciprocation in a clientelist exchange enables a party or a politician to recruit active supporters in order to strengthen their campaign.[14] In essence, clientelism serves as a solution to a collective action problem of the type described by Mancur Olson (1971), this time concerning *the organization and mobilization capacity* of political parties and campaign networks (Trantidis 2013: 6). This also suggests that clientelism works in parallel with ideology and electoral pledges to affect voters' choices (Trantidis 2012: 76). Political mobilization is, therefore, not driven 'either by clientelism or by ideology', and clientelism should not be seen as a political choice that is alternative to campaign strategies that seek to attract voters with programmatic commitments and ideology. In addition, clientelism must not be seen simply as a strategy of vote buying. Instead, the systemic role of clientelism is visible in the way in which it strengthens the capacity of political parties to recruit groups as campaign resources in order to appeal to voters via the conventional means of programmatic and ideological messages (Figure 1.1). Through this indirect effect on voters' preferences, a clientelist exchange generates 'increasing political returns', as the benefit for the patron exceeds the value of the single vote of his or her client, making the selection of some – and the exclusion of others – a rational political strategy. Moreover, because the practice of clientelism affects the distribution of campaign resources among competing parties, we can hypothesize that the unequal distribution of patronage among two or more parties may be partly associated with the unequal distribution of electoral success.[15]

14 See Chubb (1982); Epstein (1986); Kitschelt (2000); Brusco et al. (2004); Robinson and Verdier (2002); Wantchekon (2003); Calvo and Murillo (2004).

15 Next to other parameters such as political divisions and social cleavages, charismatic leadership, ideology and resources/financial endowments.

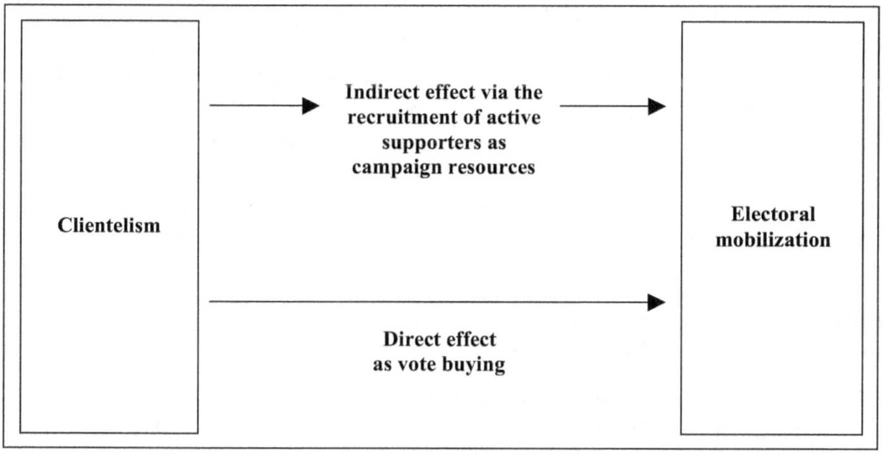

Figure 1.1 Direct and indirect effects of clientelism on electoral outcome

In the existing literature, clientelist networks are seen as dissimilar to typical interest groups. Compared with typical interest groups that claim collective goods for their members, clients inside the party network are engaged with their patrons as individuals who ask for favors to be delivered as private goods. Client groups are simply networks of rent-extracting clients, each of whom is separately accountable to their patrons (Kitschelt 2000: 849; Kitschelt and Wilkinson 2007). Each client's record of contribution to the patron's campaign is the basis upon which the client will continue to be entitled to special benefits. Because clients are expected to reciprocate in public by making visible contributions to the party or the politician's campaign, patrons can monitor their behavior. Like the isolated client, clients who are members of a broader clientelist network are equally vulnerable to threats of exclusion by their patron in case they fail to behave as expected (Medina and Stokes 2007). The individual accountability of each client is the way through which patrons tackle the free-riding problem inside the clientelist network.

Moreover, compared with typical interest groups, clientelist networks are situated in hierarchical party structures (Scott 1972: 92; Eisenstadt and Roniger 1984: 48). We can imagine that, unlike typical groups, clients lack the means to overcome collective action problems. There is no shared purpose for which to organize collective action. Clients do not aim at a 'club good', that is, a collective benefit that is excludable for nonmembers but is shared equally by members. Instead, clients have heterogeneous and even antagonistic preferences. In that regard, clients are thought to have both little reason and limited capacity to engage in collective forms of political expression independently of what the patrons require from them.

Nevertheless, client groups are valued by the patrons and the patron party as vital resources for their political campaigns. This strengthens the degree to which the party as a whole and patrons individually are committed to the demands of their clients and strategically rely on the uninterrupted supply of patronage. Both patrons and clients are tied in a relationship of *interdependence*, where the election of their patron party to power is an objective shared by patrons and clients alike. Hence, it can be argued that although individual clients are, more or less, powerless, the structural ties between the patrons and the clientelist network make the latter an important and valued social group for the former.

The colonization of interest groups by clients and the clientelist-collective system

Clients may be members of formally autonomous social institutions such as labor unions (Graziano 1978: 297; Mouzelis 1978; Spourdalakis 1998: 210). Through this membership, they undertake overlapping roles: they are both political clients claiming individual patronage benefits and members of an organization claiming 'collective' or 'club' goods like any other interest group with formal autonomy from the patron party (Trantidis 2015). Clients organized in party organizations, trade unions or other professional organizations are distinguished from typical clients by their capacity to overcome collective action problems more effectively. Rather than isolated individuals in what is typically portrayed as an asymmetrical power relationship with patrons, organized clients can find in these organizations the infrastructure by which they could hold patrons accountable in certain circumstances.

This observation points to a 'third' view of clientelism in which the incorporation of clientelist networks inside formal organizations gives rise to a *clientelist system* of interest intermediation (Trantidis 2015). In this hybrid system, rent seeking is closely integrated in the broader party structure, and the context of collective negotiations is shaped by the close interaction of client groups with the party leadership and other party cadres on the basis of reciprocity. For organized client groups, a stable relationship with a political party reduces the cost of lobbying when it comes to promoting their collective demands as formal organizations. However, their political behavior as individual clients is still monitored and has to be approved by the patrons. Conversely, for the political patrons, the professional organizations and unions colonized by their clientelist networks become a valuable and stable political ally. They are now expected to accommodate the interests of the groups that constitute their political clients.

Typical interest-group analysis pays scant attention to the distinct properties of the clientelist system and its policy implications. The limited view of clientelism as exchanges between patrons and atomized clients conveys little information on the way clientelist politics drive government policy and how clientelist linkages intersect with other structures of interest accommodation, such as the negotiations between labor unions and the government. First, although the typical view of clientelism is that of a hierarchical and power-asymmetrical relationship between patrons and clients, clients organized in formal associations may restore some degree of symmetry in terms of bargaining power. Unionization could offer clients a collective action structure and a considerable degree of empowerment versus the government. Second, associations such as unions and other professional organizations, when colonized by party clients, cannot be seen as the 'typical' interest groups of the general literature. Situated within a broader party network, they differ from typical interest groups in terms of autonomy, independence of preferences, political importance for the party leadership and centrality in the decision-making process.

The merging of a clientelist exchange with a formal structure of interest intermediation changes the terms of collective action (Trantidis 2015). In that setting, the clientelist relationship between patrons and clients erodes the relative autonomy of the unions or professional organizations whose members are individually linked to political parties via the clientelist exchange and are subject to the controls of the party organization. However, organized client groups and their patron parties are tied in a relationship of interdependence and have to act in coordination for mutual gains. The symbiotic relationship between the government and the political party changes the parameters of the rent seeking that takes place in that system, creating a bias towards supply of benefits to organized client groups under a hierarchical party structure. By the same token, the clientelist ties reduce the autonomy of formal organizations from the patron party, and these associations may not be able to switch political alliances with the same ease that an autonomous interest group may do during negotiations and lobbying in a typical pluralist context.

Given the importance of client groups as campaign resources, it is plausible to expect that this distinctive system affects how a governing party deals with typical political parameters of policy making, such as electoral considerations, the general popularity of the proposed measures and intergroup advocacy of reforms. Policy making may no longer be an open-ended game of interest-group antagonisms, relative power and electoral popularity, as it appears to be the case in general models of government behavior. Instead, because of the informal commitments generated by the extensive practice of clientelism, policy making may be systematically skewed to cater for the interests of client groups, and this bias may also hold when governments have to choose to enact a set of reforms under pressing economic conditions.

The resilience of clientelism was pointed out in the study of African economies by Van de Walle (2001). The poor reform record in most African countries that faced economic crisis was attributed to the combined effect of 'neopatrimonial' political systems,[16] weak state capacity and predominant economic ideas inimical to the proposed reforms. African leaders implemented reforms just enough to secure the continuation of donor funds without undermining their hold of state

16 A term synonymous with patron–client relations.

resources, regardless of the dire consequences which this option had for the general state of the economy. Although Van de Walle placed emphasis on the interests of predatory political elites in authoritarian or semiauthoritarian systems, the resilience of clientelism and its input in policy making must be studied more analytically in societies with higher levels of socioeconomic development, and in the context of stable parliamentary systems where political parties freely compete for voters without having recourse to political violence.

Clientelism and economic policy

Key scholarly work

One of the most systematic efforts to capture the impact of clientelism on economic policy is Barbara Geddes' notion of the 'politician's dilemma' (1994). With regard to the supply of patronage, Geddes contended that when patronage is equally distributed between two parties and politicians would gain even a small amount from a pro-reform vote that would limit clientelist supply, legislators from the larger party have a reason to vote for reform (the good scenario). This is because the losses from reducing clientelism will be evenly distributed between the two parties, whereas the gains in popularity from reform will accrue to those who voted for it. In contrast, if patronage is unequally distributed, legislators of the party that has greater access to patronage have no incentive to vote for reform, unless the gains would again outweigh the costs by the loss of patronage, in rare cases such as that of a public outrage over bureaucratic incompetence (Geddes 1994: 95).

Geddes' account entails a view of clientelism as a practice predominantly employed to attract voters (the direct effect) and, in that sense, overlooks the role that clientelism plays as a method of party organization, which serves political parties primarily to recruit active supporters and build the necessary infrastructure for electoral mobilization (the indirect effect). As already discussed, the value of clientelism as a strategy of party organization – despite its inherent nature of being selective and exclusionary – lies primarily in the fact that it skews the allocation of campaign resources favorably towards the patron party and could significantly reduce its exposure to political contestability and the risk of defections. By helping the political parties and candidates solve a collective action problem, clientelism can be said to have a multiplier effect on how parties attract other voters. As a result, clientelism is complementary, not antagonistic, to other strategies and practices in an electoral campaign, such as the projection of political ideology and the making of (popular) programmatic pledges. Because clientelism has such a strong effect on the clients' loyalties and plays such a central role in party organization, instances in which the political gains from reforms that reduce patronage supply will outweigh any losses in terms of party organization and cohesion are likely to be rare. Moreover, the context of intra-party relations makes such reform less plausible: in cases where the leadership and individual politicians have undertaken direct commitments to their party base, upon which their personal careers depend, it is unlikely that any party of this exchange will be keen to sacrifice these ties due to the high personal cost. For patrons, their career advancement in the longer term depends on their capacity to defend and promote these commitments inside the party and build strong alliances for future promotions. They may consider the preservation of clientelist ties to be more significant than the party's electoral victory and, together with their clients, will react against any initiative by the party leadership to reduce the pool of clientelist supply available for distribution. These within-party dynamics make Geddes' good scenario even less possible.[17]

Besides interparty and intraparty competition, timing matters, as the losses from reducing clientelism will not be distributed evenly between the governing party that takes a reform initiative and its opponent, if the latter keeps promising to resume patronage once elected to power. Even when clientelist networks are symmetrically distributed between two parties, the supply of patronage is not, most of the times, simultaneous, as the party in government has disproportionately larger access to patronage supply for its clients.[18] The party in opposition has fewer opportunities to actually deliver patronage, and maintains its client base mostly by promising future patronage supply. Hence, reducing supply will hurt the governing party more than the opposition party, especially if the latter pledges to resume and restore patronage supply when it comes to power. This case makes it actually *less* probable for reform to be enacted when patronage is equally distributed between two parties. In that context, coordination between the two parties to reduce patronage is likely to be difficult, first, because of the time lag associated with alternation in power and, second, because clientelism is primarily a tool employed by parties and politicians to incentivize and mobilize loyal members and supporters, thereby solving a collective action problem regarding party organization, as described earlier.

Mona Lyne (2008) also makes a systematic attempt to capture the issue of political accountability from the standpoint of voters who receive selective (clientelist) benefits. Her concept of the voter's dilemma reverses Geddes' analytical framework of the politician's dilemma and focuses on the demand side of clientelism: voters' choices. According to Lyne, under some conditions, voters face high risks in using their vote to reward good public policy. In the presence of patronage gains, they would opt for clientelist benefits in a quid pro quo exchange to avoid exclusion from clientelist benefits. Therefore, it becomes problematic for voters to hold politicians accountable for general policy record and failure, as it is almost always preferable to vote for patronage politicians (Lyne 2008: 4). For Lyne, when resources for clientelism are exhausted, politicians would try to adjust policies to continue to supply patronage (clientelist adjustment), but they

17 The view of clientelism as a separate factor behind voters' choices is taken by (mostly quantitative) studies of voting behavior, such as the one by Lindberg and Morrison in Ghana (2008).

18 The opposition party may still offer patronage in the local constituencies and in the social or professional organizations it controls. It can also promise future patronage to its supporters.

may not always meet the reservation price of voters as clients (Lyne 2008: 229–230). At that point, voters are liberated from this dilemma and can then demand accountability on the basis of public goods provision and general policy performance (Lyne 2008: 61–62).

Lyne's addition to Geddes' dilemma from the standpoint of voters again focuses on the role of clientelism as a strategy for attracting votes. However, given the nature of clientelism as the distribution of selective benefits to a few, it appears somehow problematic to anticipate that all voters are placed in the same position (dilemma) against the same level of available clientelist benefits, relative to a promised or envisaged allocation of 'public goods'. Because clientelist resources are limited, they cannot be offered to all equally and evenly by their very nature. Scarcity requires *selection* and *exclusion.* Exclusions draw a line between the insiders (the selected party supporters) and the outsiders of the clientelist system. In that context, other social divisions could define the upper boundaries within which parties and politicians recruit their clients. Because parties tend to occupy part of the political-ideological spectrum across societal cleavages, the supply of clientelism may be distributed to a particular ideological spectrum, or in some societies, to a particular ethnic or religious group. Moreover, by systematically offering supporters special benefits via clientelist exchange along ideological and partisan lines, the exclusion of others may exacerbate divisions on the basis of political identity. These divisions do not allow us to treat 'voters' as one single pool of clients, equally likely to be susceptible to patronage at all times and by all parties indiscriminately.

Moreover, we must again recognize that clientelism is primarily a tool for political mobilization and party organization and plays a complementary role for other campaign tactics that target voters. Because the resources available for distribution are limited, politicians will prefer to enlist as clients those willing to make an active contribution to their campaign on a stable basis. This was found to be the case even under tight fiscal conditions (Cf. Kemahlıoğlu 2012: 13) As clientelist benefits incentivize a group of clients to form an active support base of a political party, clientelism becomes a politically effective strategy despite being offered to a subset of the population.

Finally, we should study how clientelism infiltrates and redefines existing pluralist structures of interest intermediation. First, membership in collective associations, such as labor unions, in political parties allows clients to demand and extract selective benefits on a regular basis. Clients are the 'insiders' who can secure long-standing access to individual benefits. Second, clients do not just undertake an obligation for reciprocity for the benefits they individually enjoy, but they also develop a sense of entitlement to patronage via membership in organized groups, through which they may be in a position to bargain collectively for preferred policies. They will remain loyal to their party as long as economic resources and opportunities are reserved and allocated to them as members of a group. Third, the reproduction of the clientelist system is secured by the party system's requirements for entry and political advancement. Aspiring politicians commit themselves to clientelist supply and must be imaginative and skillful enough to design economic reforms aiming at the survival and renewal of the clientelist system.

A new outlook on clientelism and economic policy

A broader view of the clientelist system will differ both from the image portrayed in the general literature on interest-group activity and the view of clientelism as a practice targeting voters directly. The presence of stable client groups and their integration in formal rent-seeking associations suggests that patronage politics is a more nuanced setting, in the sense that 1) it extends beyond one-off exchanges between the patron and the voters, 2) it primarily involves how political parties are organized and therefore becomes a matter of the internal politics of the party and 3) it may cover instances of collective action, when formal associations have been colonized by clients. Clientelist relations that develop between political and economic actors give rise to a widespread and strong nexus of interdependences between political leadership and client groups. The central position of clients in the party system and the patrons' dependency on clientelism are factors that help secure the reproduction of the clientelist model of political economy, and can be integrated in the following hypothesis:

> H1. *Clientelist bias in policy making:* clientelism as a method of political mobilization creates a strong preference for a political party in government to preserve economic policies that cater to clientelist demands and avoid policies that could limit the allocation of resources to their clients.

This means that the government's autonomy to change alliances with interest groups is expected to be considerably limited, as shifts in the allocation of rents shall primarily affect relations inside the governing party. It will be difficult for the political patrons in government to reduce the supply of rents to client groups, as this move could alienate supporters and trigger defections and internal grievances and, subsequently, a loss of control over the party organization. We can expect that clients organized within party structures or in affiliated labor unions may use their leverage on the patron party to demand and attain preferential treatment in receiving rents by the patron party in government. Political strategies inside the clientelist network must be largely skewed to preserve and expand the supply of patronage.

This view does not preclude policy reforms when there is a strong economic case. It simply indicates that the interplay between clientelism and electoral considerations is more nuanced and explains why clientelism may be very resilient even under pressing economic conditions. It also suggests that economic reforms that could undermine patronage supply will be a suboptimal action for the political party if it chooses to implement them, because 1) they will weaken the cohesion of the party in government as active supporters recruited by clientelist exchange become dissatisfied and dispirited, and this can undermine its mobilization capacity in the election campaign; and 2) they will give the opposition party an electoral advantage if it promises to resume patronage to current or prospective supporters.

In that regard, the allocation of clientelist benefits in a two-party system can be depicted as a 'clientelist game', in which no party has an incentive to unilaterally reduce its commitments to client groups for fear that it would alienate its clients and would undermine its mobilization capacity, giving its opponent an electoral advantage. Because both the success of the party as a whole and the politicians' personal success depend on rewarding loyalty and deterring defection by means of patronage, in a system with two parties or two coalitions of parties competing for power, the leaders are locked in a *political equilibrium* that dictates patronage supply. In the longer run, however, as client groups and political patrons exploit the available rents, a 'tragedy-of-the-commons' situation may emerge when the country's fiscal resources are exhausted via taxation or heavy borrowing that has been employed to fund the supply of patronage:

> H2. In a bipartisan clientelist party system, patronage supply is a Nash equilibrium for the two parties. Any unilateral move by the party in government to implement reforms that reduce the scope and intensity of clientelism will give a competitive advantage to the opposition party in terms of political organization and electoral mobilization. This equilibrium lays the foundation for a fiscal crisis that could affect the overall sustainability of the clientelist system at some point in the future.

Even a slight unilateral reduction in clientelism by the governing party could undermine its own cohesion and mobilization capacity versus the opposition party, who could retain its own party base by promising to resume patronage. Both parties have a strong incentive to continue fiscal profligacy, as this is *nested* in the clientelist equilibrium described earlier.[19] The continuous supply of patronage may lead to further fiscal expansion and, potentially, a fiscal or economic crisis.

19 When patronage is unequally distributed between a dominant party in government and a minor party in the opposition (with a very unequal distribution of votes and access to patronage), the party with a large share or near monopoly of patronage already has a strong mobilization advantage versus its opponent (Trantidis 2012). This suggests that if this party initiates a widespread package of reforms that considerably reduces the supply of clientelism, the opposition may still gain some electoral advantage by promising patronage, as this move can cause a crack on the governing party's advantage or (near) monopoly over patronage supply. This also implies that promising patronage will yield politically 'increasing returns' for the minor party in opposition in the form of signals that will invite new clients. However, it has a long way to go to match the governing party's patronage capacity and credibility. Limiting patronage is more likely to undermine the governing party's cohesion, potentially leading to factionalism, internal conflicts, defections and splits (Trantidis 2012: 59, 75). The greatest challenge to the government may then come from developments within the dominant party.

Clientelism and external pressures for reform

When a crisis hits the economy, the dilemma between launching reforms and preserving patronage becomes much more pressing. Unlike other interest-group settings when the government may have some room for shifting its alliances with interest groups in pursuit of policy change, the political parties in a clientelist system cannot abandon their client groups for the simple reason that they *are leading* these groups and they depend on their support. Clientelist linkages are internal to the party system, whereas pressures for reform are exogenous. Any attempt to limit the scope and practice of clientelism will cause reactions, not merely from the demand side of clientelism, from the part of the recipients of the selected benefits, but also from actors on the supply side within the ranks of the political party. As new and old politicians are engaged in competition for office, some will be better off if they pledge to resume patronage supply. Hence, the clientelist equilibrium is still at play and supports the systemic bias in favor of preserving clientelist supply even under pressing conditions (H1, *clientelist bias* in economic reform). In other words, policy response to external pressures for reform such as a crisis is again nested in the clientelist game played by the two parties and in dynamics internal to each party. A party leadership that breaks its clientelist promises loses credibility and may instigate a within-party reaction or rebellion. It is, again, rational for political leaders to safeguard embedded commitments to party clients. We can hypothesize that when economic conditions deteriorate and reform is inevitable, similar strategic calculations will dictate alternative reform strategies that involve a great deal of political creativity and astuteness in the distribution of its costs across society. The effort is now to tailor a reform agenda that spares the client groups from the costs of economic adjustment as much as possible. The same set of embedded incentives that secured systemic reproduction during the 'good times' defines the nature of policy response in times of crisis. In view of these systemic traits, the *hypothesis* regarding economic reform can be formulated as follows:

> H2a. In response to external pressures for reform, politicians in a highly clientelist system will seek to mitigate the cost of its policies on client groups and will design a reform package that preserves clientelist supply as much as possible. (*clientelist bias in economic reforms*)

Rather than a critical juncture signaling the demise of clientelism, the crisis is an invitation for the party in government to be creative in designing a pattern of policy adaptation that protects its clientelist commitments. To safeguard core embedded clientelist relations from the pressure of the exogenous shock, political parties can choose strategies such as delay in the introduction of reforms, the gradual adaptation of reforms, compensation to clients for losses, rhetorical inconsistency, delay in the implementation of reforms and a shift of patronage to residual areas where the pressure for reform is less pronounced or where new resources have been found. In that context, the case for reforms in a clientelist system faces a collective action problem: clients and patrons inside the party and the opposition benefit as 'systemic' free riders when economic reform succeeds in prolonging the sustainability of the clientelist system, but primarily the outsiders of the system bear most of the adjustment costs.

Finally, it is in the long run that patronage supply can be seen as a 'collectively irrational' outcome (the term used by Rodrik 1996: 10). This is the case in which previous reform efforts have failed to strengthen the economy and prevent an unprecedented exogenous shock from triggering a serious economic crisis. If the imminent crisis is so severe such that the economy is at risk of immediate collapse, the government may take drastic measures to prevent this from happening during its tenure. This may include deep-cutting economic reforms that could reduce patronage supply. Although this move places the governing party in a suboptimal position, at this point, it may still be a less costly option than systemic collapse during its time in government.

A historical and analytic approach

This chapter has put forward a number of initial hypotheses on the impact of clientelism on policy making which the following empirical chapters will test and refine. This method follows a *deductive-empirical cycle*, in which logical deduction is grounded in historical-contextual observations. The hypotheses on clientelist bias in policy design will be strengthened if a pattern is found in which the observed record of reform does not conform to the policy prescriptions of international institutions and the epistemic community *and* it is not just a random set of policies, *but* one that reflects a conscious effort by the party in government to protect its core client groups from the pains and costs of economic adjustment. The strength of clientelism as an explanatory factor is also gauged *in interaction with* other 'push' and 'pull' factors' for reform, such as external pressures, crisis events and party ideology. In the end, the empirical evidence informs the analysis and contributes to the reformulation of the initial hypotheses into a new set of testable hypotheses for further inquiry.

Moreover, a focus on the strategic interactions between political parties and within parties will seek to unearth the causal processes by which clientelist commitments shape the design of economic policy. In several places, the strategic context can be translated into game-theoretic analysis to illustrate the prevalent incentives that drove political behavior and policy making. The book uses an *analytic narrative*, which blends narration and rational-choice analysis to interpret observed behavior (Bates et al. 1998). The strength of this approach lies in its combination of the logical structure of rational choice (game theory in this study), with a data-rich historical, institutional and cultural context (Boettke 2000: 377). A rational-choice approach identifies key actors and maps out their strategies with reference to observed incentive structures. From a rational-choice perspective, individuals 'respond rationally to the incentives they face, and these incentives are a function of the institutions that are effectively operating in that context' (Boettke, Coyne and Leeson 2005: 290). Although the interaction between actors can be presented in a game-theoretical framework, evidence is not subsumed to theory.

We can have greater confidence in explanations of 'the outside' world if we have empirical evidence about the preferences, beliefs and mental states of actors (Hindmoor and Hampsher-Monk 2010). The book makes no thick assumptions on the preferences of actual actors; it does not, for instance, presume that all politicians are seeking office and are primarily interested in preserving and developing patronage relations. Assumptions are kept at a minimum: actors are considered rational, but their rational calculations are bounded by cognitive and informational constraints (Ostrom 1998: 9).[20] 'Internal' or interpretive evidence on the mental states of actors can be independently verified through empirical observation (cf. Elster 2000: 694). We cannot rely on the actors' publicly declared intentions because there is the danger that they will not reveal genuinely their true preferences and motives (cf. Kuran 1995). For instance, when political leaders publicly pledge to reform the economy, they are not presumed to be 'reform minded', unless there is behavioral and factual evidence that supports this claim. It is important to treat these public statements as cases of purposive communication in which actors may want to offer their preferred account of reality in order to produce 'a self-serving historical record' (George and Bennett 2005: 101).

A better understanding of preferences and behavior can rely on the 'contextualization' of actors. We can empirically infer the preferences and mental states of actors from the cognitive context and the strategic environment in which actors are situated. Stable preference orderings can be deduced by exploring the roles assigned to the actors in specific political and social organizations under established norms of reciprocity, with prevalent informal routines, ties and role expectations. Preferences are reconstructed contextually, in connection with 1) the cost–benefit structure that is drawn from the institutional context, in our case, the political returns generated by the practice of clientelism versus expected costs and gains from a different policy trajectory, and 2) the actors' roles, relations and engagements, which reveal their position in the structure of incentives: what constitutes benefit and cost for each set of actors. In this study, the payoffs which the players expect are drawn by the observation of the properties and workings of the clientelist system in which actors' are situated. Norms and incentives related to the practice of clientelism are observed and translated into options and pay-offs for the actors involved. Information on this environment and its embedded party routines, roles and interpersonal linkages is again derived from factual data.

Game-theoretic analysis can incorporate prevalent norms, power relations and the specific roles of actors in the expected pay-offs or the rules of the game, as presented in preference schedules for each actor and the range of outcomes in

20 The assumption is that an actor's rationality is *bounded* by the information received and by other cognitive limitations; behavior is thus 'adaptive within the constraints imposed *both* by the external situation and by the capacities of the decision maker' (Simon 1985: 294).

each game. In an interpretative rather than deterministic mode, *empirically observed* patterns of behavior can be seen as reflecting the *subjective calculations* of rational actors, which may lead to behavior different from our initial predictions. It remains an empirical question to discern whether key players have indeed moved to the equilibrium strategies. Seeking to adapt optimally to their environment, actors often rely on formal and informal norms (the rules of the game) to get to know the options available and the payoffs to each option. If 'the rules of the interaction are known to the interacting agents' (cf. Tsebelis 1990: 32), equilibrium arguments may help explain the optimal behavior of the actors. However, the analysis must not overlook cases in which actors make choices under conditions of uncertainty and without full information of other actors' preferences or expectations. With a degree of uncertainty and, often, with incomplete information, strategies or even preferences may vary because actors may have erroneously or imperfectly understood the rules of the game and the other party's payoffs. In politics, suboptimal and nonequilibrium strategies may be the result of political miscalculations, ideological predilections, biases and incomplete information. Human fallibility often leads to behavior that deviates from what the theoretical analysis would consider best strategy. Behavior is sometimes improvised and cannot be fully captured by a rigid 'rational-choice explanation' *ex ante*, which assumes perfect information. This further relaxes determinism in the analysis. Actors may partially mitigate informational limitations by learning from past experiences (often by a process of elimination of past erroneous moves from the menu of future strategies) and by acquiring information from observing other actors' behavior and interactions.[21]

Moreover, political and social settings are dynamic across time, as actors learn from interactions with one another, acquire new identities, re-evaluate their position in view of new conditions and adjust their behavior, and this process often leads to the emergence of new behavioral patterns (Root 2013: 31). Hence, analysis should rely on historic observations of the dynamics of the institutional context (as shifting structures of norms, roles, relationships and power) in what can be labeled an 'open-form' public-choice analysis (Wagner 2012b). As rational choice trails empirical evidence, the analytic narrative can build, in a way, a historical projection with different trade-offs and pay-offs that can be paralleled to a sequence of moving pictures (Pierson 2000: 72). This implies that we can expect change when there are important shifts in the institutional setting, which can be translated in rational-choice terms as change either in the rules of the game or in the set of pay-offs (Tsebelis 1990: 41). External factors, such as a crisis or pressures by international organizations, may bring about changes in actors' observed responses. It may be the case that actors withstand these pressures and craft creative responses, or manage to gain information and cooperate

21 A good discussion about the limitations of the 'homo economicus' model of behavior and the role of the institutions and norms in helping coordination and cooperation can be found in Boettke and Candela (2015).

with others to make only a few behavioral adjustments. An external event may or may not have a decisive impact on behavior even when others believe that the optimal course of behavior has changed. However, an external event may also trigger a cascade of adaptive behaviors that could generate unintended and unforeseen developments.

With this approach, this book builds a bridge between a *positivist* approach – showing what has happened – and an *interpretist* approach, which explains the observed patterns and their change over time by tracing the structure of incentives, the actors' roles and the patterns of relationships that develop in a clientelist system. The construction of a narrative from both factual evidence and subjective commentary creates *a context of interpretation* for the reader, who is positioned as the observer of unfolding public events and assesses the evidence that the book has assembled.[22]

As the author of this book, I collected data from varied sources such as press releases and commentary, political speeches, party manifestoes and leaflets, public records, policy documents, statistical reports, legislation and economic reports, news, interviews, parliamentary minutes and reports by international organizations, as well as secondary resources such as books and journal articles.[23] Valuable contextual information from labor-intensive archival research allowed the creation of a 'thick' description of events, processes and relations that surrounded the decisions and actions of the actors involved. In weighing the evidentiary value of each type of data source, I gave priority to publicly available data that have been previously exposed to public scrutiny and criticism. To ensure the accessibility and transparency of data, I gave considerable space to footnotes with direct citations to evidentiary sources, including newspapers (cited in italics) with specific page references when physical copies were available. Extensive and full citations allow the reader to have direct access to the original sources.

Contents of the book

The next chapter takes an analytical look at how the model of Greece's political economy evolved in the post-war period until the mid-1980s. A state-led development policy opened the way to the extensive practice of clientelism, which became the predominant form of political mobilization and interest accommodation in Greece. Following the fall of the military junta, clientelism enabled the two main parties, New Democracy and PASOK (Panhellenic Socialist Party), to occupy a dominant position in the center-right and the center-left part of the political spectrum, respectively, creating a bipartisan system with high barriers to new entries. This political landscape had important implications for the design of economic policy in the years to come.

22 This allows a 'look and judge for yourself' access to data (Harris 2012: 80).

23 Unless stated otherwise, economic figures are taken from the Bank of Greece's annual reports or data from the Greek Ministry of Economy and Finance.

Chapter 3 looks at the microfoundations of clientelism as an incentives structure. It shows that clientelism served the two main parties as a solution to a collective action problem regarding how to recruit active supporters in political campaign, predominantly via appointments to the public sector, and created stable political loyalties inside the labor unions. The two main political parties developed *permanent ties* with their client groups and, as a consequence, undertook *political commitments* to them, which generated a context of policy making different from the typical framework of interest-group activity and party-electoral considerations. As clientelism became the prevalent form of political mobilization, the two main political parties were locked in a *clientelist game*, whereby no party would have been better off by a decision to unilaterally reduce the supply of clientelism. Instead, the political equilibrium dictated expansive fiscal policies. This finding suggests that, given the linkages and interdependences between patrons and clients, when economic reform is necessitated, the government must fine-tune its economic policies to preserve and expand its commitments to its client groups. What the book names 'clientelist bias' in economic policy is further illustrated in the following chapters.

Chapter 4 focuses on the macroeconomic crisis of 1985, which was the first test for the resilience of Greece's distributional system. The second socialist government of Andreas Papandreou (PASOK 1985–1989) implemented unpopular policy measures that diffused the costs of adjustment across the population by increasing taxation and imposing a general wage freeze. However, it abstained from enacting structural reforms such as the restructuring or privatization of the ailing public-sector companies, which would have hurt the party's main support groups in the broader public sector. Although this policy mix still triggered confrontation and defections by several party unionists, PASOK managed to contain the reactions and retained its strong mobilization capacity for the following election.

Chapter 5 studies the reform program of the center-right administration of New Democracy under Constantine Mitsotakis (1990–1993). Faced with a deteriorating macroeconomic crisis, Mitsotakis announced sweeping structural reforms and privatization plans. This agenda threatened to cut established channels of clientelist supply and triggered the vocal reaction of unionized public-sector employees with the support and sponsorship of the opposition party (PASOK), as well as segments of the New Democracy party. The Mitsotakis policy agenda departed from the clientelist equilibrium, and the government suffered a heavy political penalty. Mitsotakis was eventually deposed when a group of members of parliament defected from New Democracy. His political fate served as a useful lesson to ensuing governments about the costs of departing from the clientelist equilibrium. Because Mitsotakis chose a politically 'suboptimal' course of reform, this case highlights the role of incomplete information and political miscalculations in political decision making.

Chapters 6 and 7 revisit fiscal policy and structural reforms under the PASOK governments of Andreas Papandreou (1993–1995) and his successor, Costas Simitis, between 1996 and 2000. The focus here is on the first Simitis administration (1996–2000), which coincided with the period when Greece was bidding for entry to the Economic and Monetary Union (EMU). Entry was made conditional upon meeting a number of criteria for macroeconomic performance (the famous Maastricht Criteria). Simitis' prospects of winning the next election were tightly linked to the success of his macroeconomic stabilization program. The stakes were high, because Greece's failure to join the euro would have possibly triggered a 'punishment-by-the-markets' effect with rising borrowing costs for the government.

Chapters 6 and 7 explore economic reforms under PASOK between 1993 and 2004. Simitis' record of macroeconomic stabilization relied on fiscal austerity, with a substantial increase in taxation which again dispersed the cost of adjustment across the general population. Chapter 7, however, notes that, unlike Papandreou's policies, Simitis followed a privatization policy that mostly involved the sale of minority shares in public-sector enterprises with the government retaining management control and the unionized employees preserving most of their employment privileges. Under strong structural and institutional pressures for reform, the economic policy of Simitis exhibited a pattern of *creative adjustment*, as the government designed and paced its policy in ways that safeguarded specific party commitments to client groups in the public sector. The policy record conformed to the politically optimal strategy according to which the government must launch the type of reforms that do not concentrate costs on its core client groups.

Of particular interest here is explaining the clientelist bias observed in the economic policies of the Simitis government, given his declared modernization agenda. Chapter 8 examines the strategic interactions over policy making that evolved inside PASOK and between the government and the labor unions under a PASOK-affiliated leadership. It shows that government policy making was heavily constrained by the party's informal commitments to these groups. Insofar as the government protected the core privileges of their client groups in the public sector, partial reform was facilitated thanks to the opportunistic behavior of key party cadres, who exhibited relative complacency with fiscal consolidation and new taxation. The chapter points to the central role of micropolitical considerations in shaping clientelist bias and refines earlier accounts that sought to explain Simitis' record of reform as the outcome of a clash between modernizers and recalcitrant actors. The observations bring center-stage the political party as the context in which policy preferences are not just negotiated and reconciled, but also formed and reshaped in view of preexisting mutual commitments and interdependences.

Chapter 9 examines specific developments affecting the supply of clientelism during the Simitis administration under tight fiscal constraints and new funding opportunities. After entry to EMU, Greece's newly found creditworthiness lowered the cost of debt servicing and allowed an increase in public borrowing. New resources such as European Union funds enabled the government to increase spending and fiscally sustain Greece's public sector, in which corruption flourished under the protection or tolerance of politically appointed managers. A qualitative shift, however, is observed regarding new appointments to the public sector, which mostly involved temporary contracts instead of permanent ones. In addition, the nature of new funds available shifted the predominant form of rent seeking to reported relations of 'collusion' between politicians and businessmen whose bargaining power was strengthened thanks to media ownership.[24]

Chapter 10 presents the effort of the New Democracy government under Costas Karamanlis to implement a 'mild adjustment policy' between 2004 and 2009 and tackle Greece's macroeconomic imbalances by incentivizing investment while avoiding deep austerity that could have caused a shock on the demand side of the economy. Although the emphasis shifted from taxation to a growth-oriented model of macroeconomic consolidation, this strategy failed because structural sources of fiscal profligacy were left unscathed, leading to the sudden soaring of public borrowing right after the 2008 global financial crisis. The chapter concludes with a general evaluation of the empirical findings from the whole period of economic adjustment prior to the crisis (1985–2004).

The Greek economic crisis that started in 2009 was a critical juncture for Greece's political and economic system. Chapter 11 summarizes the events following the country's resort to bailout programs run by the Eurozone countries, the European Central Bank and the International Monetary Fund. It traces the reasons behind the PASOK government's adoption of tough austerity measures and a structural reform program that eventually alienated the party from most of its support base. It also explores the motives of the main opposition party, New Democracy, first to vehemently oppose the first bailout program and later to sign up to the second package and join a coalition government with PASOK. The imminent collapse of Greece's financial and economic system led to the withering away of distributional resources, while the collapse of clientelist relations brought about dramatic political realignments, most notably, the shrinking of PASOK and the rise of SYRIZA (Coalition of the Radical Left), a radical left-wing party. Finally, in light of these empirical observations and the ensuing analysis, the conclusion in Chapter 12 revisits and refines the initial hypotheses on the impact of clientelism on economic policy.

24 The term 'rent seeking' is used in the book in the meaning defined by Gordon Tullock as cases in which individuals and organizations expend resources on lobbying government for special privileges that inflict costs on all others and have a negative social impact (Tullock 2005: x and 9–10).

2 The Greek political economy in historical perspective

This chapter revisits Greece's political economy in the post-war era (1945–1974) and the early post-junta period (1974–1985) to map out the political and economic developments that shaped clientelist politics in the following years. The Greek post-war economic model opted for policies of state intervention in the economy that generated elite-level rent seeking. It also allowed for discrimination on political grounds against left-wing supporters and the co-optation of center-right voters via clientelism. During the first post-war years, the Greek political system was characterized by loosely organized parties, fragile and shifting government coalitions and the strong presence of the military and paramilitary organizations inside and around the state apparatus. Despite Greece's early economic success and a short period of relative political stability in the late 1950s and early 1960s, the post-war system failed to prevent political turbulence, which culminated in a military coup in 1964.

After the fall of the military dictatorship in 1974, political reflection on this failure led to decisions that directed Greece's political economy towards broader social inclusion and further expansion of state intervention in the economy. Under the pressure of electoral competition, this shift was followed by extensive clientelist politics. New Democracy and PASOK established a stable bipartisan system and used patronage to engulf large and heterogeneous social groups. By the early 1980s, the two main parties came to occupy an unprecedented dominant position in politics, the economy and society, but the new political and economic environment they had established during that period planted the seeds for severe macroeconomic imbalances and hostility to economic reform in the years to come.

The state-sponsored economic model: patronage, corruption and structural weaknesses

After 9 years of Nazi occupation and the Greek Civil War, Greece embarked on a model of state-sponsored growth aided by US financial assistance. Right from the start, the allocation of foreign aid, initially as part of the American Mission in Greece (AMAG) and later as part of the Marshall Plan, created strong incentives for rent seeking. Foreign assistance became the target of a small circle of entrepreneurs who relied on personal connections with the political elite to gain access to finance (Thomadakis 2011: 432). Government distribution facilitated political patronage and corruption (Smith 1950: 227–28; Markoglou 1963). Politicians were building personal spheres of influence with the commercial and industrial class and were accumulating wealth.[1] Not surprisingly, Greek governments developed a preference for, and a dependency on, the continuation of foreign aid. Politicians were heavily invoking the fear of communist insurgency to keep receiving US assistance (Kofas 1989: 55; Thomadakis 2011: 432–433), and clashes among politicians over economic influence became a common occurrence (Thomadakis 2011: 419–420).

Throughout the 1950s, state-assisted development created a highly protected industrial sector. Because the rules of the game could be easily distorted by political intervention, business was, in large part, operating under a model of 'economic statism' that favored rent seeking (Gatsios 1993; Kazakos 1993). A great part of the economy was governed by the dense nexus between political and economic elites (Thomadakis 2011: 42 and 354). The economic elite remained dependent on loans from state-owned banks and, consequently, on political favoritism. Entrepreneurs with links to political power were given fiscal and credit benefits such as licenses, exemptions and direct and indirect subsidies (cf. Tsoukalas 1993: 62; Diamandouros 1994: 11; Alogoskoufis 1995: 152; Pagoulatos 2003: 34 and 41). Not surprisingly, there were recurrent grievances amidst the excluded. In a society still suffering from high levels of poverty, many Greeks viewed with suspicion the rise and antagonisms of a new economic elite that emerged thanks to political favoritism. The entrepreneurial activity that was oriented toward claiming rents was tainted in public discourse with neologisms such as 'gift contracts' (*kharistikes*) and 'sea loans' (*thalassodaneia*), which still survive in the Greek public discourse today.

Economic growth, although spectacular throughout the late 1950s and early 1960s, relied on the development of a productive base highly dependent on extensive regulatory intervention in capital, labor and commodities markets (Thomadakis 1997: 51). At a time when the state was creating large monopolies in the public utility sector and was building the basic infrastructure in electricity, telecommunications and railways, the Greek industry benefitted from abundant and cheap labor and developed labor-intensive activities producing low–added-value goods (Gatsios 1993: 194). The Greek industry later took advantage of Greece's membership in the European Customs Union since 1962, which generated favorable trade diversion effects as a result of relatively high duties imposed on products coming from countries outside the European Customs Union. Other entrepreneurs became involved in activities such as banking, commerce and shipping. Although the state-controlled banks consistently privileged large companies at the expense of small and medium enterprises (cf. Gatsios

1 The report of the head of the American Mission in Greece made an extensive reference to the ties connecting politicians and favored entrepreneurs.

1993: 194), numerous small and medium enterprises prospered by serving the rising domestic demand, which by the mid-1960s was boosted by transfers from commercial shipping, tourism and migrants' remittances. These mostly family-run companies were also profiting from petty patronage, flexibility in working arrangements and untaxed family contributions that allowed them to reduce their costs.

Political exclusion and instability

In Greek politics, the Civil War generated an iron division between those on the winning political center-right and those on the defeated political left under the leadership of the Communist Party (KKE). Broad segments of Greece's society loosely or allegedly associated with left-wing political activities were subjected to a strict system of surveillance and policing. An extensive network of secret informers in almost every neighborhood or workplace was commissioned to observe and report these activities to the police, which it filed in its records (*fakeloi*).[2] It was on the basis of this information that the authorities could issue the so-called 'certificates of social beliefs', which were requested as a condition for appointment in the civil sector or entry to university and for obtaining all sorts of licenses for a broad range of activities, such as becoming a sailor, a priest, an engineer or a bus driver; receiving a pension as a war invalid; or getting a driving license, until the mid-1960s. Many left-wing activists faced penal sanctions with an escalating degree of punishment – from a refusal to issue a passport or grant a loan, to loss of work, administrative harassment, imprisonment or exile in one of the 'concentration camps' set up in isolated islands.[3] By contrast, politically compliant citizens (the so-called nationally minded *ethnikofrones*) were allowed to claim access to resources such as loans, licenses and jobs mainly through patronage connections. Political favoritism rewarding a conservatively minded 'bourgeoisie' was seen as a way to buttress further political radicalization in Greece (Pagoulatos 2003: 46). Moreover, labor organizations were essentially under the control of the government which appointed their leaderships and was able to impose wage restraints and ban strike activity (cf. Gatsios 1993: 192; Alogoskoufis 1995: 169). This largely repressive and highly discriminatory system caused deep-rooted and

2 The decree 616/1948 allowed the opening of concentration camps for political detainees accused of being associated with the Communist Party. Other politically restrictive measures include the decree 516/1948 on 'control over the obedience to law by civil clerks and servants' and the decree 512/1948 'on security measures for public utility companies'.

3 'In the countryside, the gendarme [the police officer] was the king. Terrorism went hand in hand with corruption. Security services were turned into the praetorian guard of power . . . The extremely generous use of secret funds allowed, on the one hand, the elimination or co-optation of people who occupied key posts in several circles, local influential people, merchants, priests, trade unionists, journalists, politicians etc' (Eric Rouleau, 'The Greek Right' (in Greek), *Vima*, 14/9/1965).

long-lasting resentment among the excluded groups, which later became a central feature of the Socialist Party's (PASOK) discourse throughout the 1970s and 1980s.

By the mid-1960s, the political system was becoming less restrictive, and tensions arose between politicians who wanted further democratization and the hardliners who resisted the prospect of the Left being given a real opportunity to get in power. The King and his entourage (the Palace), part of the military and the political establishment, held different views about the desired degree and form of political liberalization. Two political leaders – Constantine Karamanlis, prime minister between 1955 and 1963, who attempted to make the executive branch stronger, and the centrist Georgios Papandreou, prime minister between 1963 and 1965, who propounded an agenda for political normalization and inclusion – had limited success in constraining the clout of informal power circles and para-state organizations – the so-called 'deep state' – which had infiltrated the bureaucracy, the secret services, the police and the army. These organizations were devising various plots aimed at undermining left-wing activities and moderate centrist political initiatives, and they were often involved in violent episodes. Political unrest culminated with the assassination of the left-wing member of parliament, Grigoris Lambrakis, at an open rally in Thessaloniki in 1963. The murder caused a public backlash and led to the resignation of Karamanlis as prime minister.[4] Among many centrists and left-wing voters, Karamanlis' legitimacy had been already tarnished by accusations of electoral fraud in the 1961 election which his opponent Georgios Papandreou consistently raised in his famous *anendotos* (unyielding) campaign.

Political instability escalated in 1965 when the Papandreou government was toppled down by members of his own party following his clash with the Palace over the allocation of Cabinet positions. At the same time, the gradual opening of the political system unleashed new rounds of social protest and youth movements, much to the fear of segments in the 'deep state', which reacted with escalating aggression. Rivalries among politicians competing for office, manifested in defections and opportunistic behavior regarding the formation of a new stable government after Papandreou's resignation, further contributed to political volatility. By the mid-1960s, it had become obvious that the political class with its weak and fragmented party structures, deep divisions and the incapacity to incorporate hitherto excluded political and social groups had failed to secure political stability. The military coup of 1967 temporarily put an end to political unrest, but outright coercion did not secure social peace long enough. A violent student uprising at the Athens Polytechnic School in November 1973 led to a within-junta coup a few months later. The military junta was eventually brought down in the summer of 1974 following the fiasco of a staged coup in Cyprus and the ensuing Turkish invasion of the island.

4 In his secret and hasty departure to Paris, Karamanlis reportedly uttered the famous phrase 'Who really governs this country?'.

Transition to democracy: Greece's new political landscape since 1974

The years following the restoration of parliamentary democracy in 1974 shaped Greece's political and economic trajectory for the period that followed, which is known as 'the *metapolitefsi*'. New political parties were formed from the leftovers of the previous party system and positioned themselves along the traditional spectrum of the political left, center and right. The new political system lifted the formal exclusions to political participation of the post-war era and avoided the divisions and instability that had previously afflicted Greek politics. However, political competition was heated at the backdrop of an enduring right–left political cleavage and accumulated grievances between the previous 'insiders' of the pre-junta political system and its 'outsiders'.

Returning from self-exile, Karamanlis became prime minister in August 1974 and founded the center-right party New Democracy, selectively inviting politicians from his previous party, ERE (National Radical Union), and the political center while excluding those who had collaborated with the military junta. In November 1974 New Democracy won a landslide electoral victory with 54.4% of the popular vote. A referendum abolished the monarchy a year later. The New Democracy party soon confronted the rising socialist party, PASOK (Panhellenic Socialist Movement), founded by Andreas Papandreou, son of former Prime Minister Georgios Papandreou. PASOK eventually became the dominant party of the center-left. By 1977, the political scene had been crystallized into a bipartisan system. The Communist Party, outlawed since 1947, was recognized as a legal political party in 1974, but its popularity remained stable at approximately 10% of the vote.

The institutional foundations of the 'metapolitefsi' period came to define and entrench a new paradigm in state–society relations. The 1975 constitution – still valid today after a series of amendments in 1985, 2001 and 2008 – reflected Karamanlis' preference for a stable party system and a strong executive. 'Popular sovereignty' was placed as the foundational principle of government (Article 1.1), which lies 'at the top of the hierarchical pyramid of all constitutional provisions' (Tsatsos 1993: 58). Constitutional amendments introduced by the PASOK government in 1985 further centralized the power of the prime minister, removing almost all the actual powers of the President of the Hellenic Republic that were originally granted as a check on government authority. Quite importantly, for the first time in Greece's constitutional history, an article explicitly allowed nationalizations (Article 106.3). The protection of individual rights by courts was guaranteed by a system of dispersed, ex ante and ad hoc control of the constitutionality of laws and administrative actions. At a time when government intervention in the economy was growing, constitutional provisions protecting individual rights allowed the government to invoke 'public interest' as the justification basis for the regulation of the private sphere. In addition, the protection of individual rights has been largely dependent on constitutional interpretations by individual judges of all ranks. Effective judicial checks on executive power were placed by the Council of the State, which in many occasions rescinded government decisions on state activities in areas such as property rights and environmental law. However, the efficacy of judicial checks on government power remained largely dependent on the real autonomy of the justice system from political interference. Greek judges have been part of a hierarchical structure in which decisions to sanction law as unconstitutional are regularly scrutinized by senior judges. Although formal provisions in the Constitution guarantee their independence, the government has considerable input in the appointment of judges to senior positions, including promotions in the three supreme courts. At times, several cases of promotions sparked political controversy,[5] and the workings of the justice system were tainted by numerous allegations of political intervention.[6] The independence of the judiciary was also vulnerable to informal clientelistic ties infiltrating almost all social circles in Greece.

Economic policy and ideology in the New Democracy years (1974–1981)

In economic policy, both New Democracy and PASOK adopted a 'patriotic' rhetoric that portrayed the state as the encapsulation of national, political and economic sovereignty and the legitimate recipient of people's demands. Although this rhetoric created expectations for social change, the two parties had different views of where the upper limits to government intervention should be. PASOK proclaimed as its target the nationalization of Greece's financial and credit system and its basic industrial units (Papandreou 1977: 70). Described as 'populist' and perceived by many as antisystemic, PASOK's economic rhetoric drew on the North-South debate and dependency theory, which had inspired many of the 'third world' socialist movements, and adopted a *sui generis* mixture of socialist rhetoric and nationalism, which was highly critical of social democracy, 'Eurocommunism' and the Eastern bloc (Clogg 1987: 134). New Democracy's economic agenda, on the other side, was bordering on a social democratic narrative propagating a mixed economy under tight state supervision,[7] as articulated in its Founding Declaration written by Karamanlis:

> [New Democracy] promises that the free economy which New Democracy believes in *cannot preclude the expansion of the economic sector controlled by the state;* and that private initiative cannot be vindicated without *the*

5 For instance, Constantinos Mitsotakis, the leader of New Democracy, accused the PASOK government of bypassing the seniority list of judges to change the composition of the Areios Pagos, one of the country's three supreme courts (*Proti*, 03/9/1986).

6 A well-documented record is offered by Nikos Themelis (1998), former president of the Court of Audit, one of the country's three supreme courts, who describes numerous cases of government intervention in the workings of this court (in Chapters 11 and 12).

7 *Vradyni*, a conservative newspaper, claimed that New Democracy's 'basic aim' was 'social and economic democracy' (Katsoudas 1987: 95).

> *parallel participation of the popular classes in the distribution of the national product*. Every citizen of this country should become both a worker for, and a participant in, the fruits of economic prosperity and should feel assured about his future and the future of his children.
>
> (emphasis added)[8]

At the party's first conference, Karamanlis named the party's ideology as 'radical liberalism'. This idiosyncratic term epitomized the statist, 'dirigiste' orientation of New Democracy in its early economic policy and ideology. Karamanlis himself was highly skeptical of unrestricted economic freedom:

> [. . .] our party believes in the creative zeal of the individual, in free competition . . . But just as anarchy destroys real freedom, so is unbound free competition shaking the roots of not only the economic but also the social life of a country.
>
> (Karamanlis speech at the 1977 ND preliminary conference, cited by Katsoudas 1987: 96)

The party's ideology was articulated at a time when left-wing ideology and a protest culture in songs, films and theatrical plays were increasingly popular with younger and urban population groups. In this climate, New Democracy's top politicians publicly rejected the authoritarian legacy of post-war politics, and most of them were careful enough not to make references to politically divisive issues in Greece's modern history. At the same time, most controls over the labor movement were removed, and the labor union movement became active in organizing strikes and rallies demanding higher wages and employment protection.

During the same period, the oil crises of the 1970s exposed Greece's structural weaknesses. The Greek industry had built a competitive advantage in labor-intensive production, benefiting from trade diversion and preferential treatment for its exports granted by the European Economic Community (EEC), but the picture was changing in the 1970s with the entrance of new international competitors and the emergence of structural rigidities in the Greek economy from recent regulations. There was widespread anxiety that Greece was entering a period of deindustrialization, due to rising costs, rising interest rates and the gradual reduction in tariff protection after Greece's entry into the European Community (Xanthakis 1989). The Hellenic Federation of Enterprises (SEV) attributed the problems of Greek industry to the combination of weak productivity, reduced investment and the increase of nominal wages exceeding the rate of productivity growth.[9] Much of the structural weaknesses can be associated

8 See New Democracy's *Founding Declaration of 1974*.

9 Reported by *Economicos Tahydromos*, hereinafter referred to as *Economicos* (16–17/4/1980: 26–27). In the industrial sector, returns to equity fell from 13.3% in 1974 to 3.8% in 1978 (*Economicos*, 25.9.1980: 32).

with the new regulatory framework that the government introduced, which reversed much of the pre-1974 favorable tax regime for business and increased taxes on profit (Alogoskoufis 1995: 170).

Faced with this economic and political climate, New Democracy intensified state intervention in the economy by introducing new regulation and protectionist measures and by considerably increasing the size of the public sector through a round of nationalization of banks and industrial units, which included Olympic Airways, the Aspropyrgos Oil Refineries, Athens public transport and, most notably, the forced nationalization of the Andreades Group, one of the largest business and banking groups in the country. Nationalizations were presented as a way to promote the modernization of enterprises in which the private sector was either unwilling or unable to invest (Kazakos 1993: 134). State intervention increased the volume of preferential loans from state banks to a number of ailing companies in the private sector that were running deficits (the so-called *problematikes*). Financial assistance in the form of relatively cheap loans created an overly indebted industrial base.[10] The owners and employees of these companies relied on their political connections and publicly invoked the risk of large-scale redundancies to continue receiving unsustainable loans which they could hardly repay.

State loans to indebted companies and later their nationalization brought significant changes to the relationship between economic and political power. The balance of power shifted to the side of political power.[11] By the mid-1970s, extensive nationalizations were causing anxiety among business circles. The vice-president of the Hellenic Federation of Enterprises openly stated that New Democracy's economic policy was governed by '*socialmania*'.[12] In 1977, New Democracy reassured there would be no more nationalizations (Katsoudas 1987: 95). This economic direction, however, was portrayed as part of the strategy to mitigate the effects of the economic downturn on unemployment. Besides this economic reasoning, the Greek government feared the political consequences of rising unemployment. State intervention was motivated by the desire of the government to appeal to voters' anxieties and expectations by using tools that resonated with the post-war tradition of state-sponsored growth (Kazakos 1993: 134).

10 For many export-oriented companies, devaluation and inflation were supposed to facilitate the repayment of the loans. However, declining competitiveness and soaring debts led many company owners to continuously exert pressure on the government to instruct the state-owned banks to grant them cheap loans. As debts accumulated, these banks eventually took over majority shares in these companies.

11 Eleni Vlachou, the editor of the center-right newspaper *Kathimerini*, once portrayed the asymmetrical power between the political class and the business class: 'What hides behind the industrialists' discontent? Perhaps, Karamanlis gave orders to the Director of the National Bank to cut them off the loans?', as reported in *Kathimerini* (29/3/2008).

12 Reported by N. Nikolaou in *Kathimerini*, 15/12/2007, and 29/3/2008 and by A. Ravanos in the centrist newspaper *Vima* (14/11/2008).

At the same time, there was polarized debate between New Democracy and PASOK over the desirability of Greece's forthcoming accession to the EEC in 1981. Greece's entry to the EEC was expected to reconfigure Greece's economic policy in the years to come. The European Community required a number of necessary policy adjustments away from its statist direction, most notably abandoning the protectionist barriers to exports and state assistance to industry. At that time, New Democracy's favorable stance to Greece's entry into the EEC was contradicted by its policies of state intervention in the economy. New Democracy's endorsement of Greece's adhesion to the EEC was said to serve as a substitute for its obscure political ideology (Katsoudas 1987: 94–95). It was also driven by security concerns that were fuelled by Turkey's aggression in Cyprus and the Aegean Sea. This political orientation towards Europe was epitomized in Karamanlis' famous phrase 'we belong to the West'. On the other side, Papandreou's skepticism towards the European Economic Community and economic nationalist rhetoric were expressed by his famous proclamation that 'Greece belongs to the Greeks'. PASOK strongly objected to Greece's participation in the EEC on the grounds that it would expose Greek industry and agriculture to competitive pressures and would severely limit the tools available for the government to direct economic growth. Most of PASOK's discourse presented the project of European integration as a trick of 'capitalist imperialism' (Botsiou 2002: 19). In response, New Democracy presented PASOK as an extreme leftist party and a threat to liberal democracy (Lyrintzis 1982: 311).

PASOK's march to power (1974–1981)

PASOK's ideology and public profile started as a Marxist party and moved significantly towards the political center as the party's organization improved and its popularity increased. In the first years since its establishment as a minor opposition party PASOK adopted a radical mixture of patriotic and Marxist rhetoric with the proclaimed vision to build a socialist society and a state structure that would express 'the hegemony of workers, peasants and salary-earners' (PASOK 1977).[13] The rhetoric of PASOK activated the right–left historical cleavage with sentimentally charged pleas to the long-lasting grievances of left-wing voters (Mouzelis 1986; Diamandouros 1997: 25–26). The discourse continuously raised 'a Manichean dichotomy between progress and reaction, between the forces of light and of darkness' (Pappas 1999: 157). PASOK vociferously attacked the right-wing dominance in the government apparatus and did not hesitate to portray the state as serving the interests of a few domestic and foreign interests (Clogg 1987: 218). The rhetoric was also largely anti-American (Moschonas 2001: 13), capitalizing on bitter sentiments over the history of US intervention in post-war Greece.

13 In PASOK's 1977 declaration cited by Clogg (1987: 134).

Between the elections of 1974 and 1977 PASOK doubled its share of votes. Papandreou's unique rhetorical skills, astute organizational capabilities and perceptive recruitment of both politically experienced politicians and young talent created a dynamic political organization. The party's organizations established a strong presence in labor unions, professional organizations, universities and even secondary schools. Members and cadres reproduced fierce polemics against the government and its 'capitalist foes', tailoring their discourse to the special groups they were addressing. Although membership in the party was open to everyone, PASOK's organizational structure became centralized, highly hierarchical and hostile to all the autonomous intermediaries between the leader and his 'people' (cf. Mavrogordatos 1984; Mouzelis 1993: 301). Local and sectoral committees were reduced to mechanisms for grassroots mobilization and campaign organization under the tight grip of Papandreou (Pappas 1999: 110). Party members had virtually no influence in shaping the party's political agenda. Open membership diluted and neutralized any discordant elements (Elefantis 1981: 10). Papandreou himself carefully chose the inner circle of his confidants. Dissenters were ousted from the party in dramatic purges, with Papandreou often sending open letters to the press, accusing them of being 'social democrats', 'elitists' 'Trotskyists', or 'old-fashioned' (*'palaiokommatikoi'*). Some of the expelled politicians later returned to the party after accepting Papandreou's undisputed authority. Through astute leadership, Papandreou succeeded in establishing the first noncommunist mass party in Greece whose ramifications reached the most isolated areas of the country (Mouzelis 1993: 301).

In the late 1970s, Papandreou adjusted his rhetoric to appeal to the political center. The idea of a future transition to socialism was dropped from the party's rhetoric (Elefantis 1981: 116; Pappas 1999: 60). Instead, the emphasis was on bringing political change in Greece that would end the right-wing power monopoly. At the same time, PASOK's message gave assurances that it would not threaten the private economy when in government, as long as the private sector was willing to cooperate and invest (Kotzias 1984: 428; Tsakalotos 1991: 142). PASOK pledged to be on the side of the 'average' Greek, 'with a house, a shop and a car' (Clogg 1987: 84). A vague ideological identity was now targeting a heterogeneous group that also included middle-class urban and agrarian strata, such as lawyers, technicians and public clerks (Pantazopoulos 1987; Pappas 1999). With a rather unclear and incongruous message for political and social change PASOK could entertain the political expectations of those who felt financially insecure. Change (*allagi*), the prominent slogan in the 1981 election, was a powerful message for the 'unprivileged' (*mi pronomiouhoi*) with whom almost the entire population could identify (Spourdalakis 1988b: 181). Quite importantly, PASOK embraced the demands of labor unions. PASOK's pre-electoral manifesto talked of nationalizations and government planning as 'the guiding and regulating instrument of economic and social policy' (PASOK 1981: 100).

In October 1981 PASOK won a landslide electoral victory with an outstanding 48.07% of the vote. Soon after the election, PASOK increased public spending for wages and announced the development of an all-encompassing welfare state. In 1982 PASOK introduced quasi-mandatory wage rises in almost all sectors, together with wage indexation (OECD 1993: 15). It also enacted highly protective labor laws (OECD 1993: 15). PASOK followed an expansive fiscal policy, which it presented as an application of Keynesian economic policy that also served towards the fulfillment of its promises for social justice (Tsakalotos 1991: 179). However, the fiscal stimulus to a small economy such as Greece unavoidably caused an increase in imports and rising public deficits (Tsakalotos 1991: 155). Quite importantly, income rises were not symmetrically distributed and were soon eroded by soaring inflation and currency devaluation, particularly the depreciation of the drachma by 15.5% on 10 January 1983.[14]

Moreover, PASOK further increased employment in the broader public sector, when in 1983 it officially nationalized the private companies that were indebted to state-owned banks.[15] Thirty-four ailing corporations with approximately 25,000 employees in manufacturing, textiles, defense and shipyards passed to government control under the Industrial Reconstruction Organization (OAE). Because nationalizations were popular in the public opinion,[16] PASOK's rhetoric during its first term in office (1981–1985) continued to favor state intervention and protectionism and remained hostile to the idea of privatization and market liberalization, to which it juxtaposed its desire to modernize the state-owned companies. The government announced that only shares from the companies that were not included in the nationalization program might be sold back to new private owners at some point in the future.

Another early PASOK initiative was to increase the participation rights of workers in the management of the nationalized companies and agricultural cooperatives.[17] Under the banner of 'democratization', the new rules offered labor organizations a strong say in the management of these companies. In similar fashion, a law introduced by Minister of Agriculture Costas Simitis 'on the restoration of the democratic operation of farmers' cooperatives' bestowed each member equal voting rights, regardless of the shares each member owned.[18] Because the law detached voting rights from one's stake in the cooperative, a huge number of farmers rushed to register in the cooperatives. The law was criticized by PASOK's opponents for acting as a vehicle for party control over

14 A second devaluation of the drachma by 15% took place on 10 October 1985. As a result, the average annual real wage increase during PASOK's 8 years in power was reported to amount to a mere 0.9%, quite behind the EEC average increase of 2.3% (Vergopoulos 1992, citing OECD, *Historical Statistics*, 1990: 94; EEC Commission, 1989, *Economic Convergence in the Community*, DOC COM(89) 333, 5 July 1989: 60).

15 Law 1386/1983.

16 In 1980, 61% of respondents to an opinion poll conducted by MRB wanted further nationalizations (*Kyriakatiki Eleftherotypia*, 15/9/1998).

17 Law 1365/1983 on the participation of employees in the management of public enterprises, and Law 1385/1983 establishing state control over mines.

18 Law 1257/1982.

the management of these corporations. Alarmed by PASOK's increasing influence in the public sector, the Communist Party accused PASOK of engaging in clientelism and blocking genuine popular control over the state sector of the economy:

> The right-wing says that the public sector is bankrupt and its leading figures demand a sell-out to private owners. But what was the kind of public sector that went bankrupt? It was the public sector of *rousfeti* (favoritism), of nepotism, of scandals, of red tape that went bankrupt. The public sector with the 'appointments from the back door' and paid inertia and large salaries for the few. . . In our country, the public sector has never been public.[19]

By politicizing wide areas of economic and social activity, the policies of nationalization and 'democratization' enlarged the scope for patronage politics. During its first tenure, PASOK introduced sectoral party organizations in each trade union and professional association, which consisted of many employees who had been appointed or promoted thanks to their party affiliations. Membership in these labor and professional organizations allowed PASOK's clients to gain collective benefits, such as privileged terms of employment, better wages and generous pension schemes. At the same time, to keep a tight grip on the labor movement, PASOK preserved the prerogative of the minister of labor to allocate funds from the compulsory contributions of wage earners to labor organizations of his own choosing (Kouzis 1996: 155). 'Democratization' was also invoked to justify legislative changes in higher education and schools. Student representatives were given a vote in boards and councils of university administration.[20] Student committees were introduced in secondary education too. The declared aim of this legislation was to promote social control over these institutions and make academics accountable to students' needs. In reality, it was youth party organizations that gained significant leverage over university administration.

PASOK intensified the politicization of public administration. Promotions and placements in key posts were largely determined based on party loyalty and personal connections. The new government removed New Democracy supporters from key administrative posts, claiming that senior civil servants were boycotting its policy agenda for social change (Sotiropoulos 1996: 106). Parallel agencies of political advisors assisting ministers were created, but they were mostly circles of political clients and friends (Tsakalotos 1991: 276). Several office holders appointed by PASOK carried on the 'tradition' of bribes that permeated the Greek state. Similar developments took place in the management of public enterprises. The new managers owed their position to ties with the governing party and were consequently susceptible to pressures by ministers to hire and promote party

19 Labor unionist and member of the Communist Party of Greece, Dimitris Gontikas, in *Rizospastis* (14/04/1984).

20 Law 1268/1982.

sympathizers. Given that their decisions were ultimately monitored by other party cadres and the party leadership, they most often conformed to political commands that reflected party-specific priorities rather than market signals.

Conclusion: Greece's political economy by the mid-1980s

This chapter has set the backdrop for the analysis of clientelism and its impact on political reform in the following chapters. By the mid-1980s, the Greek economy was defined by extensive state control over the economy, the politicization of state intervention and widespread patronage politics. The practice of clientelism enabled the two parties to establish a strong bipartisan system, while deteriorating economic performance exposed the structural weaknesses of the Greek economy and signaled the exhaustion of Greece's model of state-assisted economic growth. These developments would later evolve into two systemic features: *economic crisis* and *clientelist politics*, which became two contrasting developments, as Greece would come under increasing pressure to revise core elements of its economic model from the mid-1980s onwards.

Economic crisis

The post-war–era model of state-sponsored economic growth relied on a mixture of protectionism and favoritism, which essentially created greenhouse conditions for Greece's 'economic miracle' of the 1950s and 1960s. This policy direction reflected the dominant ideology in which state intervention was seen as the main vehicle to economic growth. In reality, the model of state-sponsored development degenerated into the particularistic allocation of benefits to selected recipients with access to political power. This discriminatory and protectionist economic model hindered competition, weakened any incentive to modernize production and created an oligopolistic market structure.

The impact of structural weaknesses on the economy became evident in the late 1970s with a decrease in Greece's international competitiveness, anemic growth rates and high public deficits.[21] Consistent with the tradition of state intervention and protectionism, the government sought to offset the rise in unemployment with a substantial increase in state employment. The alternative option would have been to allow unemployment to rise in the short run in anticipation of new and sustainable employment created by structural adjustment later on. That option was deemed politically unsustainable, particularly in the face of clientelist expectations and the prominence of ideas sympathetic to state intervention. Between 1974 and 1990, the state sector significantly grew in size and so did its funding needs. State enterprises were granted virtually unlimited

21 The budget surpluses of the early 1970s (0.7% of GDP in 1970 and 0.1% in 1971) gave way to deficits (3.0% in 1975, 4.4% in 1978 and 9.1% in 1981).The primary deficit reached 5.3% in 1981.

access to borrowing from state-owned banks. Indirect subsidies in the form of loans given by state-owned banks to private businesses prolonged the period of declining competitiveness and postponed the necessary restructuring of Greece's productive base. Financing an ailing public and private sector generated moral hazard, coupled with a rent-seeking mentality that led to rising operational costs and, eventually, deficits. The last round of nationalizations signaled the exhaustion of the model of finance by state-owned banks to entrepreneurs with political connections, a trend that had fostered an industrial base increasingly unable to withstand competition in domestic and foreign markets. As the then minister of economy acknowledged:

> . . . the banking system would not have taken such a direction had it not been subjected to the supervision of the government of the time. The industrialist of the 1970s spent [most of] his time at the antechambers of commercial bank managers and economic ministries for cheap credit and subsidies from the state budget. The government should have created incentives for him to go back to his factory to take care of the infrastructure and design a development plan which the banking system could have financed under conditions of transparency.[22]

By the early 1980s, Greece was entering a period of macroeconomic instability: inflation rose from 13.4% in 1975 to 24.5% in 1981, and interest rates soared from 10.0% in 1975 to 20.5% in 1981.[23] Fiscal deterioration will now pose serious limitations on the practice of clientelism. The recommended measures to deregulate or privatize may simultaneously limit the permissible scope for clientelism. By the mid-1980s, Greece's economic model felt the first pressures for a fundamental revision of its economic model.

Clientelism

The instability of the post-war regime under a fragmented political class, with its systematic exclusion and harassment of the political left, paved the way to the military dictatorship of 1967 and prompted the political forces of the post-junta period to proceed with deeper democratization. The failure of coercive tactics to secure political stability in the post-war era highlighted the prominence of distributional politics as the pathway towards party cohesion and political stability. State intervention was reconfigured by the two parties into a highly clientelist system which required the politicization of the economy. As a result, clientelist ties infiltrated all spheres of state authority, including those normally

22 Minister of Economy Gerasimos Arsenis speaking at a public event in the *Intercontinental Hotel* on 22.11.1984, retrieved from www.garsenis.gr/content/03/03c/04/22_11_1984.htm, on 12.5.2011.

23 All figures by Bank of Greece, *Economic Outlook*, December 1999, and European Commission 1999.

expected to remain relatively autonomous from political influence, such as the bureaucracy, the police force, the justice system, universities, trade unions, agricultural cooperatives and other professional associations. The combination of centralized party organization and extensive patronage allowed the two main parties to obtain a dominant position in politics and society.

3 Clientelism as a policy equilibrium

By the mid-1980s, clientelism had helped the two main parties recruit active members and secure party loyalty. Vast clientelist networks emerged inside the party networks, and cliques of rent-extracting clients with close ties to senior patrons were formed inside and around the broader public sector. Party clients also colonized labor unions and other professional organizations, a trend which eroded the autonomy of these associations from political power, but also endowed client groups with the organizational capacity and resources for collective action. As a result, a distinct system of interest intermediation emerged, in which 'organized' clients continued to extract individual benefits in a typical patron–client exchange, but as members of unions and associations they could access 'club goods', that is privileges offered to them by virtue of their membership in politically friendly unions. This clientelist-collective system gave organized client groups a considerable degree of bargaining power versus their patrons and a sense of entitlement to selective benefits.

These parameters formed the structure of incentives that shaped the design of economic policy in Greece in the following years. The relative capacity of parties for political mobilization was largely dependent on the strength and loyalty of their clientelist networks and, subsequently, on available resources for clientelism. Competition over the supply patronage locked the clientelist parties in a political equilibrium that dictated fiscal expansion to cover the increasing demands of current and prospective clients. This committed policy makers to the continuous expansion and preservation of patronage supply. Any unilateral move by the governing party to curb public spending and reduce the scope of patronage would have weakened the cohesion of the party's support basis and would have given its main rival party an advantage in political mobilization. This *clientelist game* dictated further expansion of clientelism, and the accumulated cost of clientelist supply was passed on to state finances.

Clientelism as the prevalent mode of interest accommodation

After the restoration of parliamentary politics in 1974, Greek political parties and individual politicians resumed the practice of clientelism promising or delivering favors (the notorious *rousfetia*) as the traditional tool to win voters and active supporters (Lyrintzis 1984 and 2005; Mouzelis 1993; Sotiropoulos 2001). Because the government distribution was taking a greater role in the allocation of economic resources, a distorted political 'market' in which government resources were exchanged for political support was fuelled by two parallel competitive processes. For economic actors, the terms of their competition were largely dependent on access to political power. Long-lasting privileged access to political power could offer them generous returns – as contractors, sellers, recipients of credit, employees, etc. – and protection from open market competition (cf. Kazakos 1993: 139). For political actors, engagement in clientelist politics was often vital for their political survival.[1] As Mouzelis noted:

> . . . The moment the parties get political power, their first target is to use the state mechanisms to entrench their position by rewarding their followers.
>
> (Mouzelis 1993: 301)

Given these incentives, clientelist exchange permeated all government functions,[2] such as the granting of licenses for business, the provision of credit by state-controlled banks,[3] tax controls, public-sector procurement, state contracts, appointments of managers in public companies, placements and promotions in public-sector positions, the terms of military service, information on incoming legislation and administrative acts or even erasing traffic police fines.[4] Complex administrative regulations and excessive red tape pushed citizens to the informal brokerage services of politicians who promoted claims that could have otherwise been blocked by time-consuming bureaucratic processes (Andreou and Koutsiaras 2002: 162), such as finding a bed at a hospital, transferring between universities,

1 Cf. Katsanevas in *Economicos* (19/06/1989: 15). Andreas Andrianopoulos, a deputy minister in the New Democracy government, confessed that he had to issue a written statement announcing that he would not deliver any special favors, regardless of any pressure from clients and local party bosses (*Nea*, 19/09/1979: 5). See also Sotiropoulos (1996: 61): 'Many PASOK deputies and ministers had counted for their successful election on their own personal clienteles or on the voluntary work of local PASOK organizations'.

2 Requests for favors included both lawful and unlawful actions, as Pavlos Bakoyannis noted in *Vima* in his article titled 'The State of Nepotism and Favoritism' (05/07/1977: 5). Thodoros Kassimis, the director of New Democracy's press office, once estimated that 8 out of 10 favors were lawful (*Economikos*, 20/04/1990: 34).

3 For instance, in Agricultural Bank (*Economikos*, 14/03/1991: 77).

4 Cases cited at *Vima* (26/09/1976: 9; 17/04/1977: 13; 5/07/1977: 5), *Nea* (09/03/1979: 7 and 24/04/1979: 7). The following excerpts give a picture of the scale of clientelism at that time: 'not a single concierge or even a cleaner can be appointed unless there is a prior "recommendation" by someone in the governing party' (*Vima*, 5/07/1977: 5); and ' [. . .] "I have a lawyer's license in Agrinio but I don't want to work there. I prefer to be a legal consultant at an Athens company. The minister can help me with this' (*Nea*, 9/03/1979: 7).

speeding up the payment of a pension after retirement and getting a loan from a state-owned bank.[5]

State employment was the most sought-after type of clientelist favor. Throughout the 1970s, rising unemployment fuelled demand for state jobs. Between September and December 1976, there were 2100 new appointments at a pace of 520 per month, on average (*Vima*, 17/04/1977: 13).[6] In 1975, New Democracy abolished the organization responsible for conducting examinations for entry to the public sector (ASDY) and replaced it with committees appointed by government ministers, who often exerted influence on all stages of the recruitment process, allegedly trying to accommodate their own political clientele (Sotiropoulos 1996: 165 note 21). Another way to bypass entry examinations was the hiring of temporary, seasonal or 'auxiliary' employees, who were later given tenure (*Vima*, 02/04/1977: 9).[7]

PASOK, first in opposition and later in government, followed the trend of patronage politics. Andreas Papandreou conscripted old politicians who brought their local patronage networks to the party (Pappas 2009: 3 17).[8] When PASOK came to power in 1981, it embarked on massive appointments of its supporters in the broader public sector (Sotiropoulos 1996: 62 and 99; Spourdalakis 1988a), particularly in the public utility companies (the so-called DEKO [Public Sector Utility Company]).[9] Key posts in the broader public sector were occupied by party cadres, and new legislation allowed the political leadership to ignore meritocratic criteria in promotions in the public administration (Sotiropoulos 1996: 106–107, and 13; Spourdalakis 1988a). Many party clients entered the public sector thanks to their connections to the party's 'Solidarity Bureaus', and formed its 'core' clientele (Sotiropoulos 1996: 62 and 99).[10] In public discourse, this move was justified with the rhetoric of social justice and solidarity. In reality, clientelist favors helped PASOK consolidate a loyal support base in public-sector companies and farmers' associations (Pappas 2009) at a time when it was reneging on its promises to nationalize strategic industries, withdraw Greece from the European

5 Cases cited in *Vima*, 26/09/1976: 9; 11/02/1977: 2; 17/04/1977: 13; 05/07/1977: 5; *Nea*, 09/03/1979: 7 and 24/04/1979: 7. In an interview in *Vima* (03/1/1980: 6), the former leader of the main opposition, Georgios Mavros, said that the practice of clientelism was widespread. See also journalist Giorgos Koumantos in the politically centrist newspaper *Vima* (28/11/1976: 12) and the left-wing *Kyriakatiki Eleftherotypia* (03/10/1993).

6 In a parliamentary question, New Democracy Member of Parliament Virginia Tsouderou deplored the fact that 8000 new employees had been appointed to two public-sector companies, OTE in telecommunications and Olympic Airways, without an exam process (*Vima*, 13/01/1977: 2).

7 PASOK gave tenure to fixed-term public employees (Law 1476/1984).

8 Papandreou showed a clear preference for the recruitment of office-seeking politicians over party partisans (Pappas 2009: 322).

9 As PASOK's former Minister of Economy Arsenis admitted (Arsenis 1987: 103–109, cited by Tsakalotos 1991: 220).

10 Also *Nea*, 04/03/1989: 19; *Vima*, 09/11/1990.

Community and NATO and remove the US military bases from the Greek territory (Lyrintzis 1987: 671; Moschonas 2001).[11]

PASOK's party networks permeated almost all spheres of economic and social life. The pool of would-be clients mostly consisted of middle-class strata (Pappas 1999: 199). They included entrepreneurs seeking access to loans from state-controlled banks and those involved in contracts with the public sector (*Nea*, 4.3.1989: 19). PASOK's sectoral party organizations (*kladikes*) soon became dominant in the labor unions of the broader public sector, which included the state monopolies in electricity, telecommunications, transport, water and sewage, ports and radio and television, as well as other commercial industries in petrol, defense, shipyards and cement. The extensive application of clientelism allowed PASOK to obtain a dominant position among public-sector employees and break the monopoly of New Democracy as 'the party of government'.[12] By the mid-1980s, PASOK had infiltrated the public sector to an extent that New Democracy had not previously achieved. Such was the fusion of the party and state that in 1984, 66% of the 140 members of the Central Committee of PASOK elected at the party's first congress (in May 1984) had occupied or were occupying public offices other than parliamentary seats (Sotiropoulos 1996: 62). According to the same source, 89% of the total of the card-carrying party members were somehow associated with the state (Sotiropoulos 1996: 62). As a former member of PASOK noted:

> A praetorian army was created in the service of Andreas Papandreou whose only concern was to climb up in the Movement and secure more privileges from a position of power at the expense of society.
>
> (Vassiliadis 2002: 47)

Membership in party branches, local committees, affiliated labor unions and student associations enabled the development of *horizontal relations* of mutual assistance, which helped clients overcome the hurdles of legalism and red tape and speed up administrative processes. Once appointed to key positions in the state sector, some party clients developed rent-extracting activities.[13] They formed

11 Antonis Karkayiannis, political commentator in the center-right newspaper *Kathimerini*, noted that PASOK had been a party offering its center-left supporters 'protection, moral recovery and a few rents' (05/09/2004).

12 See Sotiropoulos 1996: 57, 60 and 116; Pappas 1999: 202; Lavdas 2005.

13 Georgios Mavros, former leader of the opposition, stated that 'corruption plagues the state machinery' (*Vima*, 04/06/1981: 10). Ioannis Zigdis, leader of EDIK (Union of the Democratic Center), a centrist party, noted that 'five years after the fall of the junta, corruption has corroded the foundations of political and social life' (*Vima*, 22/07/1979: 4). A few years later, the mayor of Athens and future leader of New Democracy, Miltiades Evert, talked of 'a crisis of institutions, which are permeable to corruption' (*Vima*, 31/07/1989: 11):

cliques – subnetworks of clients appointed by virtue of their connections and loyalty to party patrons in particular offices, where they were able to extract rents or even take bribes.[14] Rent extraction inside the client groups flourished thanks to the high degree of administrative discretion and weak controls, which allowed cliques to offer informal brokerage services.[15] Cliques often operated under the protection of senior or middle-ranking party cadres.[16]

The widespread practice of clientelism offered the two main parties an unprecedented hegemonic position in society and the economy. With their vast clientelist networks, the two main parties engulfed the wider social strata and permeated almost all areas of economic activity, such as labor unions, agricultural cooperatives, universities, the army, the judiciary, public administration and local councils.[17] Many academics, judges, journalists and trade unionists also developed close ties with politicians for the benefit of themselves and their family members.[18] A similar pattern was observed in spheres of state authority typically expected to retain relative autonomy from politics, such as the army, the police and the justice system.[19]

Not surprisingly, the number of party members tended to rise when a party came to power. In 1982, a few months after its electoral triumph, PASOK had 140,000 card-carrying members. By July 1983 PASOK had reached 200,000 members (figures by Sotiropoulos 1996: 65 and 69) and in 1984 220,000 (Pappas 1999: 177). What is distinctive is that PASOK members increased significantly in the midterm period of 1983–1984, whereas the votes it received in the 1985 election slightly fell from the 1981 results (45.8% from 48.07%). It appears that the numbers do not consistently follow the popularity of the party, but they increase as the party gets further established in power. Similarly, in 1994,

---

> Some people take advantage of their relations and connections – often in the name of ideas and ideals, which they have turned into a lucrative merchandise – to climb up and enrich themselves by elbowing others who may be possibly better than them.
>
> (*Vima*, 31/07/1989: 11)

14 For instance, a PASOK minister of parliament (MP) accused government officials of engaging in favoritism such as distributing forest land to selected beneficiaries in the prefecture of Drama, which was later sold to a large paper company at very low prices (*Vima*, 04/09/1979: 1).

15 Ioannis Pesmazoglou from the small centrist EDIK party noted that strengthening the discretionary power of the tax inspector in determining taxable income had fostered arbitrariness and corruption (*Vima*, 19/12/1976).

16 An article in *Vima* noted that a tax collector accused of receiving bribes would go to this office the following day because nothing had happened (*Vima*, 18/09/1993: A2).

17 See, among many others: Mouzelis (1978); Mavrogordatos (1988); Spourdalakis (1988b); Tsoukalas (1993); Kouzis (1996); Sotiropoulos (1996); Spourdalakis (1998); Pappas (1999); Lavdas (2005); Sotiropoulos (2001); Lyrintzis (2002).

18 For instance, it was usual for academics to be appointed to one or more government posts. *Vima* presented a list of 5000 academics with government and party affiliations (*Vima*, 08/05/1994: 40).

19 Cf. *Vima*, 25 March 1990: 36; *Economikos*, 10/09/1981: 15

months after PASOK returned to power, party membership doubled from 1992, reaching 195,000 in 1994, a year after PASOK's electoral victory (all figures cited by Pappas 1999: 177).

Clientelism as a tool for party organization and political mobilization

Clientelist exchange served the main political parties as a powerful tool to recruit active supporters. Compared with general public policy, clientelism delivered individual benefits, improving the personal status of clients considerably enough to incentivize them to dedicate time and energy to the electoral campaigns of their patrons. The incentivizing effect of clientelism secured party loyalty and prevented defections and splits. Party members were aware that regular access to special benefits depended on their loyalty and active engagement in political campaigns and that they could lose these benefits if they chose to defect or failed to reciprocate as expected. In that way, clientelism served the two main political parties as a solution to a collective-action problem in terms of party organization and the problem of within-party fragmentation: becoming active contributors requires a great degree of political engagement, but party supporters now had a strong incentive to disseminate the party's messages in their own locality or sphere of professional activity. It was only the Communist Party that managed to preserve a loyal party base and a sizeable electoral appeal of approximately 10% of the popular vote in the 1977, 1981 and 1985 elections.

The expansion of the party's clientele meant that a mechanism was required to monitor reciprocity from its clients. The way the political parties solved the problem of monitoring reciprocity was to restructure the supply into hierarchically controlled party grassroots branches, where behavior could be easily spotted by peers, and 'free-riding' and defection could be reported to the leadership. As a result, the practice of clientelism became more bureaucratized (Lyrintzis 1984; Spourdalakis 1998) and the clients' loyalty was primarily directed to the central party.[20] Since the late 1970s patronage was delivered less by individual politicians and more increasingly via centrally coordinated party machines.[21]

This change became more pronounced with the arrival of PASOK in power in 1981. PASOK's sectoral party organizations (*kladikes*) were also the building blocks of its patronage network (Sotiropoulos 1996: 61). The party leadership

20 'Voters are recorded in special small-sized cards . . . together with all the demands they have asked and the favors they have received ('*rousfetia*'). In the end, there is an archive with tens of thousands of names who could assist the politician in the next election' (Andreas Deligiannis, *Vima*, 02/10/1975).

21 Pappas (1999: 72–73); Sotiropoulos (1996: 35 and 2001); Clogg (1987: 144); Kazakos (1993: 138); Mavrogordatos (1997); Lyrintzis (2005: 248). Allegedly, clientelist appointments in the public sector were governed by an allocation principle as follows: 40% by the central party, 40% by its MPs and 20% by the minister and the undersecretary in charge of the specific sector (*Eleftherotypia*, 14/02/1987 and *Economikos*, 19/03/1987).

sought to eliminate rival centers of intraparty power that had been built upon the old 'feudal-type' connections in local patronage networks (Sotiropoulos 1996: 63; Pappas 1999: 176). Local bosses remained powerful in smaller countryside towns.[22] The attractiveness of clientelist benefits, the prospect of high losses from defection and the leader's tight surveillance of political behavior strengthened the cohesion of the party during its first years in power. Party members were expected to be actively involved in the party's campaign and the activities of the party-affiliated labor organizations (PASKE, or Panhellenic Workers Movement). Loyalty to the leadership was requested and was rewarded with offices, privileged terms of employment in the public sector, access to a vast network of acquaintances and other personal benefits.[23]

Clientelism helped PASOK minimize its internal fragmentation. Hierarchy and centralized control in the broader party network further limited the scope for individual clients to express discontent (Loulis 1981: 78). Individual members had virtually little or no say in shaping party policy. When conflicts of interest between party members and groups broke up, the leadership was in a better position to demand compromise from its clients. The anticipation of further rewards also mitigated the reaction of individuals or groups who had considered themselves neglected in a particular instance. The party's electoral defeat or expulsion from the party for dissident behavior meant for a client loss of access to future personal rewards. At the same time, joining the opposition party was largely constrained by the right–left political divide, and a defecting client could not easily join an antagonistic party network, because defection could have been interpreted as a sign of disloyalty. With this incentive structure, animosities and within-party clashes were largely contained inside the party. Near election time, clashes and disputes had to be sidestepped to protect the party from frictions that could lead to the loss of political power and the subsequent loss of access to resources for clientelist distribution.

On the other side, patrons undertook the commitment to client groups that they would secure an ample scope for clientelist practice in return for their support and loyalty. Clientelism became the glue that bound office-seeking politicians and supporters from different social, economic and ideological backgrounds

22 'Local party bosses play the role of intermediaries in the chain that connects the politician with the voter . . . In provincial towns and villages their power exceeds that of official local authorities [who] closely "collaborate" with the party bosses and often get orders from them', Vasilis Paikos in the centrist newspaper *Vima*, 30/11/1980. Many of the local bosses were paid by the state to work in local MPs' offices, *Vima*, 03/08/1980: 15.

23 Damianos Vassiliadis, a former member of PAK (Panhellenic Liberation Movement – an anti-dictatorship movement founded by Andreas Papandreou) and PASOK, wrote in 2002, 'These are the people to whom Andreas Papandreou gave posts and material rewards, and turned them into pawns of his own objectives. This is a known method, familiar with Andreas Papandreou, when you want to buy off one's conscience and turn people into spineless instruments . . . He secured his election thanks to the large army that he had appointed to the state apparatus and [thanks to] the concessions [he had offered] to voters from the "progressive political camp", with money borrowed from abroad' (Vassiliadis 2002: 48).

within large parties, deterring serious splits and factionalism. Through patronage politics, both parties consolidated the characteristics of a catch-all party.

Clients in trade unions: the emergence of clientelist-collective rent seeking

By 1983, almost all trade union organizations eventually came under the control of PASOK (Mavrogordatos 1988). Their union leaders were quite often prominent political figures in the party. Their legitimacy depended on the endorsement of the party leadership. Those union leaders aspiring to a political career had a clear incentive to be complacent with the decisions of the leadership. As a result, the unions' autonomy vis à vis PASOK was weakened (Lanza and Lavdas 2000; Lyrintzis 2002: 92; Lavdas 2005). PASOK's hegemonic position in the trade unions served as an additional tool for exerting influence over social and economic life. When in government, PASOK could ask for the co-optation of trade unions; when in opposition, PASOK could mobilize trade unions into strike actions and rallies against the government:

> In essence, a 'common body' was created between PASOK and social organizations, trade unions, farmers' associations and co-operatives, student movements, cultural organizations, and the small and middle classes etc.[24]

Nonetheless, by infiltrating formal structures such as unions, party clients obtained the infrastructure to take up collective action to claim collective benefits. Unlike isolated clients in a one-off exchange with the patron, party clients in the public sector had a lasting association that secured benefits on a regular basis, both *collectively* as unionized employees and *individually* as clients associated with the party. Through union membership, party clients gained significant bargaining power towards their affiliated party, primarily PASOK, which they could use to restore some balance in their relationships with politicians. The unionists could exert pressure on the party leadership to accommodate their demands for 'club goods', such as wages that were higher than the private sector, generous pension schemes, early retirement, extra allowances and holidays. Club benefits were extended to all public-sector employees, including those who were not attached to political parties as clients. Outside patronage supply, there were those with little or no access to patronage networks who had to bear the fiscal cost stemming from extensive patronage supply.

Unionized clients, however, were still competing for personal favors such as promotions, additional fiscal compensation by participating in administrative committees and protection from disciplinary measures. The informal ties between clients in the unions and the party network allowed the party leadership to erode the autonomy of the unions and other social associations. The complex

24 Antonis Karkayiannis, *Kathimerini* 05/09/2004.

relationship between clients and patrons inside the public sector, with the overlapping roles of union members and party clients, created an overarching *interdependence of preferences*: union members had a stake in the electoral success of their patron party, whereas the party and many of its politicians depended on support by unionized clients which they could secure both with policy concessions towards the unions and with individual favors towards their members. PASOK developed a symbiotic relationship with these unions. Insofar as their collective interests were satisfied and clientelist benefits were available to their members, these groups would remain loyal to PASOK. To preserve its close ties with the labor movement, PASOK was sensitive to the collective demands of the unions in the broader public sector, offered extensive patronage to their members and allowed them to develop horizontal relations for mutual help and rent extraction.

The coexistence of two structural characteristics – *formal autonomy* of the unions and *informal interdependence* of their clients and patrons – gave rise to a *clientelist-collective* structure of interest intermediation. In that system, the optimal course of behavior for both the party and the clients in the unions was to prioritize their mutual commitments to the exchange of special benefits. The pattern of accountability reflected this intricate web of collective ties and personal relationships. PASOK's strong presence in the unions allowed the party to deploy a policy of co-optation of the labor movement, which included personal rewards to complacent unionists. This was manifested in an unusually low number of strikes during PASOK's first term. Papandreou's tight grip on the unions contradicted his declared agenda of democratizing the labor movement and giving it a strong say in the management of state-owned companies. Animosities were frequently expressed but largely contained within the party ranks. Interpersonal dependencies favored a moderate stance of union members against their patron party. Co-optation did not eliminate all tensions between unions and the party during its first term, particularly when the government attempted to place limits on the right of public-sector employees to go on strike in 1983.

The clientelist game

Party cadres and politicians regularly pledged to modernize the state and fight against patronage politics.[25] Prime Minister Karamanlis talked of 'the curse of favoritism' (*Vima*, 5/7/1977). In an interview, Prime Minister Georgios Rallis confessed that fighting clientelism was 'not in his hands' and urged the Greeks to respect the law: 'you, the citizens, should be convinced that favors [*rousfeti*] should

25 See PASOK's Declaration of the Third of September 1974: 'The People has (*sic*) a bitter experience with the party structures in the past, which had relied on a feudal relationship between leaders and deputies, between deputies and party cadres and between party cadres and voters . . . with party machines that had replaced principles, programs and democratic procedures with favors [*rousfeti*] and intrigue'.

disappear without any exception for yourself', he noted (*Vima*, 11/05/1980: 7). Papandreou described clientelism as 'the scourge that tortures Greek people' and promised that

> PASOK regards favoritism [*rousfeti*] as one of the basic causes of this country's evils as well as a hindrance to smooth democratic progress. This is why [PASOK] is the only party that has addressed in its program the fight against favoritism with its programmatic declaration of the 3rd of September.
>
> (*Nea*, 16/09/1976: 3)

The gap between rhetoric and practice was obvious. Although PASOK systematically employed clientelism, Prime Minister Papandreou proclaimed the separation of the party from the state in a speech to thousands of party functionaries in January 1982. In a symbolic gesture, he expelled a party member in charge of a party organization who had stated openly that the separation of the party from the government would isolate the party from power (Sotiropoulos 1996: 63). PASOK often couched many of its patronage provisions in the language of restorative and compensatory justice towards hitherto marginalized and excluded social strata (Diamandouros 1997: 28). As George Papandreou, politician and son of Andreas Papandreou, later confessed:

> I would agree with you that favoritism [*rousfeti*] is a great problem . . . ever since we came to power in 1981 there was a tremendous pressure on all of us to restore – within quotation marks – those who had been helped by previous governments and those who had been hit by them.
>
> (*Nea*, 15/11/1985: 12)

PASOK's resort to clientelism can be explained as its best strategy in response to New Democracy's prior practice of patronage. When New Democracy came to power in 1974, PASOK was a relatively small party in the opposition. New Democracy developed its patronage networks among traditional right-wing supporters. The historical right–left political divide, although quite porous for centrist voters, left vast segments of the population outside its clientelist network. Still, New Democracy's monopoly over the supply of clientelism gave the governing party an electoral advantage. PASOK managed to offset this by developing a patronage reputation among center-left voters. After 1981, patronage supply was distributed along the right–left political spectrum by PASOK and New Democracy, respectively. By making clientelist promises when in opposition and engaging in mass patronage immediately after winning power, PASOK defined the nature of clientelist politics as *bipartisan* and highly *competitive*.

Under the competitive political conditions of the post-junta period, PASOK's choice to engage in clientelism can be interpreted as a strategic response to the pre-existing structure of interest intermediation, in which clientelism had become the predominant form of interest accommodation and a strong tool for party organization. Had PASOK abstained from providing patronage to current and prospective supporters, it would have lost a strong tool for political mobilization at a time when Papandreou sought to strengthen the coherence of his newly formed party and contain grievances and disagreements among its ranks.

An analytic outlook

The development of clientelist politics by New Democracy and PASOK can be explained in the language of game theory as a strategic choice in a sequential-move game in which clientelist politics by both parties can be seen as the political equilibrium.

The first entry is New Democracy, the governing party between 1974 and 1981. The game's payoffs follow an ordinal scale that indicates only a preference ranking over possible outcomes (state of affairs) from best to worst. The preference schedule is shaped by prior knowledge about the political advantages which clientelism offers to parties in terms of internal cohesion and mobilization capacity. This game approximates a context of *complete information*, as historical experience with patronage politics in Greece had allowed each player to get a clear understanding of the payoffs and the strategies available to all players in a highly clientelist party system (Cf. Scharpf 1990). A party will prefer to engage in clientelism while its opponent abstains so that it can exclusively reap the benefits of patronage politics (Tables 3.1 and 3.2).

Backward induction in this decision tree (Figure 3.1) predicts that each party will choose to engage in clientelism and that the outcome will be a bipartisan and competitive clientelist system. When the first party (New Democracy) makes its choice, it expects that the opposition party (PASOK since 1977) will subsequently engage in clientelism. PASOK's leadership will similarly deduce that

Table 3.1 Preference schedule for New Democracy

Order	*Options for New Democracy*	*Options for PASOK*	*Payoffs*	*State of affairs*
1	Engage in clientelism	Abstain from clientelism	4	Monopoly over clientelism by New Democracy
2	Engage in clientelism	Engage in clientelism	3	Competitive clientelism
3	Abstain from clientelism	Abstain from clientelism	2	Competition without clientelism
4	Abstain from clientelism	Engage in clientelism	1	Monopoly over clientelism by PASOK

Table 3.2 Preference schedule for PASOK

Order	*Options for PASOK*	*Options for New Democracy*	*Payoffs*	*State of affairs*
1	Engage in clientelism	Abstain from clientelism	4	Monopoly over clientelism by PASOK
2	Engage in clientelism	Engage in clientelism	3	Competitive clientelism
3	Abstain from clientelism	Abstain from clientelism	2	Competition without clientelism
4	Abstain from clientelism	Engage in clientelism	1	Monopoly over clientelism by New Democracy

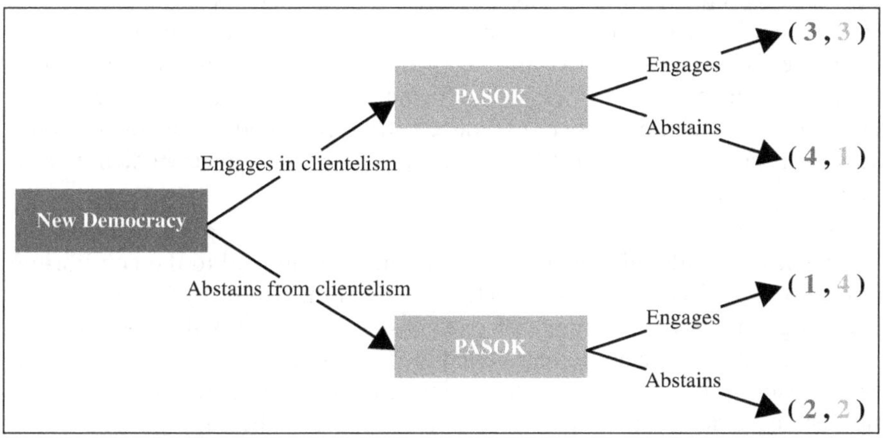

Figure 3.1 Clientelism as the 'best strategy'

engaging in clientelism will be its best choice in light of this prediction.[26] The state of affairs in which both parties engage in clientelism is the subgame perfect equilibrium.

In real terms, each party does not have to estimate the end of the game to experience the political benefits or costs stemming from its strategic move. After the first player moves, payoffs do accrue to each player: New Democracy engaged in clientelism since 1974 and first experienced gains in party cohesion and political mobilization. Hence, in real 'political time', each prior stage produces an outcome known to both players. While an opposition party, PASOK felt New

26 Actually, engaging in clientelism is the best choice for New Democracy no matter what PASOK subsequently ends up doing (the payoff from engaging in clientelism is always higher), and engaging in clientelism is therefore a strictly dominating strategy for New Democracy.

Democracy's advantage from patronage and subsequently chose to engage in clientelism in order to counterbalance this advantage. When it came to power, PASOK fulfilled these expectations and supplied patronage.

After the two parties are engaged in clientelism, there are systemic incentives for both of them to preserve and increase clientelist supply when in government. Increasing patronage supply allows the party to tackle grievances among its clients and recruit new ones. A larger range and intensity of clientelist benefits send signals to prospective supporters that they will enjoy similar benefits. It can be said that clientelism operates as a simultaneous game in two cases: when the party in government constantly confronts demands from its own party base to increase patronage supply (engage by increasing patronage), or when it confronts the dilemma to launch reforms that could reduce the supply of clientelism (disengage by reducing patronage), while still facing competition by the opposition. In the first case, both actors move simultaneously, concurrently developing their separate clientelist networks in view of the higher payoffs of patronage. For the same reasons in the second case, even if the government publicly announces measures to curb patronage, the other player cannot deduce how credible the governing party is, and will continue to promise patronage. A unilateral move by the government to reduce patronage will allow the opposition – which still promises clientelist benefits to its supporters – to strengthen its own mobilization capacity.

Table 3.3 presents the bipartisan game over the supply of patronage once the two parties have already engaged in patronage and moved to the equilibrium strategy (3, 3).[27] The dominant strategy dictates that no party in government should opt to reduce the supply of clientelism. This move will undermine the governing party's capacity to recruit and mobilize its members and will weaken the cohesion of its support base, triggering reactions from both their clients (on the demand side of clientelism) and the patrons (on the supply side) whose political success largely depends on granting clientelist favors. These two developments could lead to a change in relative organizational capacity at the expense of the governing party. For these reasons, a rational party leader should opt to supply patronage to supporters despite the fact that clientelism is a highly discredited practice in public discourse and politicians publicly pledge that they will take measures to curb it.

Table 3.3 Clientelist supply in a simultaneous game

		Party in opposition	
		Engage	*Disengage*
Party in government	Engage	3, 3	4, 1
	Disengage	1, 4	2, 2

27 Once the sequential-move game has already been played.

It is now quite obvious why both the pay-offs and the strategies in this two-party game differ from what Geddes predicts in her game of majority and minority legislators (Geddes 1994: 95). The key differentiation is that if the governing party unilaterally reduces clientelism, the opposition party can still promise to its supporters that it would resume clientelist supply when in power. This case is very likely, because, as the chapter shows, clientelism is not solely a tool used by parties to gain voters directly, but it is primarily employed as a method of party organization and political mobilization. Moreover, individual politicians and local or sectoral clientelist networks will not wish to support any attempt of the party leadership to limit clientelist supply, even when the party might expect considerable gains in popularity, as this motion could come at the expense of their own personal career prospects as prominent party cadres in a patronage party structure. Finally, the supply of patronage by the established parties raises barriers to other political entries which would find it more difficult to become serious political contestants without the credible promise of patronage. In that way clientelism reduces the volatility of the party system and the exposure of the clientelist parties to competition from new competitors. For these reasons, it is highly unlikely that any anticipated popularity gain from reforms reducing patronage will offset the expected cost for the party leadership in terms of party cohesion and mobilization capacity.

The economic impact of clientelist politics

The clientelist game indicates the structure of embedded systemic incentives that push political parties to preserve and intensify the practice of clientelism. However, because clientelist benefits are limited resources, selection in view of scarcity is likely to cause intense competition and clashes among party clients over their allocation. This could seriously undermine the cohesion of the party. To reduce the opportunity cost involved in the selection of clients, the governing party must increase the resources available for clientelist allocation and expand the scope for interest accommodation via patronage. Increasing the availability of clientelist benefits can prevent or accommodate any rivalry among clients competing for jobs, promotions, subsidies, loans and other brokerage services that concern benefits that are excludable and rivalrous. Other types of favoritism, such as a planning permission, licenses or the terms of military service, may cause less rivalry, but they also entail a selection process that may still exclude some. Disputes over the allocation of rivalrous resources can also be tackled with the promise of future benefits. Expecting future gains may prevent defections in the short run, but these promises had to be met within a reasonable amount of time.

In Greece, the expansion of clientelist supply by the two main political parties reflected these political calculations as the party system frequently had to tackle distributional conflicts, rivalries and animosities (cf. *Vima*, 30/11/1980: 8). As a solution to this problem, the two main parties expanded clientelism by increasing the involvement of the state in the economy and the scope for informal brokerage services *horizontally* inside the party network. This move also created a vested interest in preserving the complex system of administrative rules and procedures, which gave public-sector officials a high degree of discretion in the decision-making process and the opportunity to ask for bribes.

To finance the increasing needs of patronage supply, the Greek governments followed a loose incomes policy and an expansionary fiscal policy. The expansion of state control over the economy and the growth of distributional politics had adverse economic consequences. Greece abandoned the 'golden rule' of disciplined fiscal policies, which until 1975 had only allowed deficits to accumulate in public investment schemes. Since 1979, Greek governments relied on expansionary monetary policy too. The policy of drachma devaluation aimed to improve the country's competitiveness, fix the country's balance of payments and finance its public debt denominated in drachmas. The results, however, were negative. Fiscal profligacy and loose currency policies led to rising inflation. Throughout the 1980s there was a fall in private investment (Bank of Greece 1991: 28), partly associated with bureaucratic obstacles, lack of transparency, frequent changes in the legal framework and political uncertainty, which increased under the first PASOK government (OECD 1993: 15–20). At the same time, the gradual reduction of protectionism exposed the competitive weaknesses of the Greek production basis.[28] Productivity growth was hampered by the deteriorating state of the basic transport infrastructure – as a large part of public money was spent on consumption – and due to falling standards in the services provided by public utility companies (OECD 1993: 19), whose operation was largely governed by partisan politics.

Conclusion: the clientelist-collective system and its policy bias

This chapter has outlined the political and social structure that had emerged by the mid-1980s with the growth of clientelist politics in Greece. It noted the centrality of clientelism as a tool for political mobilization, the evolution of clientelism as a prominent mode of interest accommodation and the infiltration of patronage in labor and professional organizations. Thanks to its high mobilization capacity, clientelist exchange was employed by the two parties as a solution to a collective-action problem concerning the recruitment and mobilization of campaign resources. Clientelism gave strength to a strong bipartisan system which relied on active and loyal party bases and enjoyed low electoral volatility

28 Tsoukalis (1993: 28); Gatsios (1993: 194); Kazakos (2003: 133–134); Vergopoulos (1992). Between 1974 and 1985, the general productivity of factors of production fell by 0.4% as opposed to a 1.1% average increase during the same period in the 15 countries forming the EU in 1995 (Pantazidis 2002: 35).

and intraparty fragmentation.[29] The clientelist system of interest intermediation was defined by the following developments:

1 the colonization of trade unions by party clients and the erosion of their autonomy;
2 the empowerment of some client groups through unionization and party membership;
3 party commitments to clients as the result of their symbiotic relationship, which included the preservation of club goods to organized clients and a scope for rent extraction and horizontal collusion by cliques of party supporters;
4 a tendency for fiscal profligacy and state expansion to increase new patronage supply and a tendency for bureaucratization and lack of transparency to increase the turf for horizontal collusion.

The infiltration of civil society via patronage allowed PASOK and New Democracy to occupy a hegemonic position in Greek politics, society and economy. Clientelist networks undermined the autonomy of labor unions from the party. PASOK, in particular, became the dominant political force in labor unions and the public sector. The predominant form of interest accommodation included both the formal structure of interactions between the unions and the government and the more complex and informal linkages between client groups and the party leadership. Party clients organized in unions found a ready infrastructure for collective action. The pattern of patron–client relations embedded in labor unions' collective action reversed the direction of accountability from typical patron–client relations, where individual clients are held accountable for their actions to parties and politicians (cf. Stokes 2005; Lyne 2008; Kitschelt et al. 2010), to a pattern of mutual accountability and codependency between the patron parties and client groups. In that context, party members saw their membership as 'entitlement' to individual and collective rewards.

Given the social heterogeneity of party members of both New Democracy and PASOK, party cohesion was largely dependent on the availability of resources offered to organized clients collectively and individually. Resources for patronage were secured not only by expanding the role of the state and its resources for distribution, but also by 'outsourcing' patronage supply through membership in party cliques that were allowed to engage in bribe seeking that was targeting private economic actors.

As shown in the following chapters, the political party remained the main context in which preference formation took place over policy making. This placed limitations on the scale of collective action by discontented clients and the nature of decision making by government officials. Grievances and occasional clashes could be tackled with a 'carrots and sticks' strategy to secure the loyalty of the

29 Opposite view by Kitschelt et al. (2010).

party network and deter serious centrifugal tendencies. Ultimately, both political leadership and their clients had a vested interest in preserving their symbiotic relationship.

Clientelist bias in policy making

As the case of Greece indicates, the interdependence between clients and the party leadership may have distinctive implications for the design of economic policy. Political success in a clientelist system is largely dependent on accommodating the increasing demands of the party's clients. The party must offer its clients ample opportunities for rent seeking, both individually and collectively, in return for their loyalty. Reducing or removing the supply of clientelist benefits would cause serious dissatisfaction and protests by clients. In both cases, the cost of moving away from the clientelist equilibrium would include serious losses in terms of internal party cohesion and electoral mobilization capacity. The clientelist parties are, therefore, locked in a Nash equilibrium that dictates the preservation and expansion of clientelist supply, individually and collectively. However, profligate fiscal policies following the clientelist equilibrium can sooner or later lead to an economically suboptimal outcome.

It is the main theoretical argument of this book that party commitments to client groups are a major systemic hindrance to reform. Under these conditions, political actors have little or no incentive to consider the future cost of an expanding state sector or the cost of discriminatory and overly bureaucratic regulations, but they would rather seek to preserve these features as channels for patronage supply to clients even under dire economic conditions. Thanks to its position in the party system, the clientelist network is likely to be consistently and structurally the 'winning coalition' in the design of economic policy. In the remaining chapters, this claim is supported with further evidence of the policy bias that protected the existing channels of clientelist supply despite strong structural and institutional pressures for reform.

4 Muddling through reform

Crisis and policy response between 1985 and 1989

By the mid-1980s, fiscal profligacy, partly associated with the practice of clientelism, had caused serious macroeconomic imbalances in Greece's stagnant economy. In 1985 the PASOK government under Andreas Papandreou was forced to take action to tackle a crisis in the balance of payments. The range of possible policy responses included options that, if adopted, could seriously disturb patron–client relations. Given the nature of the exogenous pressure for reform, the crisis could have been a 'critical juncture' in Greece's political economy, signaling a significant shift away from the distributional policies that had contributed to the crisis but had also helped PASOK obtain a strong position in Greek politics and society. Throughout its second tenure (1985–1989), PASOK faced the agonizing dilemma of how to prevent fiscal collapse and a deeper economic crisis while, at the same time, preserve its clientelist commitments.

This chapter examines how these considerations defined the nature, pace and fate of the stabilization program which the second PASOK government implemented between 1985 and 1987. The government sought to raise its revenue by increasing taxation and boost competitiveness through wage restraint. Both options diffused the cost of adjustment among the general population – the taxpayers and wage earners. PASOK chose not to implement measures, such as structural reforms and privatization, that would have seriously harmed its core clientelist groups. In essence, macroeconomic stabilization was designed to protect PASOK's key support groups in public-sector companies and exhibited a clientelist bias. Although the austerity measures triggered an initial split among PASOK unionists, informal party ties between the party and its unionists helped the government contain the scale of reactions. PASOK was successful in isolating the defectors, but, faced with increasing political pressure, resumed public spending and patronage in the run-up to the 1989 election.

Economic crisis

Between 1980 and 1985, low rates of economic growth, falling investment, high inflation and large trade deficits increased the gap between Greece and the rest of the European Community economies. The Greek economy entered a vicious circle of growth stagnation and rising public debt levels. Large public deficits and excessive state intervention in financial, labor and product markets exacerbated Greece's structural weaknesses and public finance imbalances (OECD 1993: 36–42). Greece's rate of productivity growth slipped from the second position amongst the Organization for Economic Cooperation and Development (OECD) countries in the period between 1962 and 1973 to the twentieth in 1986 (Papaspiliopoulos 1996: 215). Profits in the manufacturing industry declined. Stagnant productivity was also the result of a shortage in technological investment, currency instability and the volatility of prices of oil, all of which generated an uncertain climate for business and contributed to industrial decline (Oikonomou 1992: 152–153). Lack of technological investment was associated with government subsidies to entrepreneurs. The use of currency devaluation to boost competitiveness temporarily lessened the need for the industry to invest in raising productivity and modernize its infrastructure to meet international competition. The sharp drop in private investment was also partly attributed to PASOK's wage policy until 1985 that had increased labor costs and had also fuelled inflation (OECD 1983 and 1986).

Furthermore, the inefficiencies of the public-sector companies had a negative impact on the economy (Kazakos 1993: 132).[1] The mismanagement of public-sector companies (DEKO) led to higher deficits and the rise of their total debt from 2% of gross national product (GNP) in 1979 to 5.5% in 1985, from which debt equal to 2.8% of GNP was covered by government transfers (Tsakalotos 1991: 170, 212. Also OECD 1987: 47).[2] Public spending, mostly channeled to consumption and the deficits of the public-sector companies, soared and was largely funded by government borrowing (Tsoukalis 1993: 21).[3] Public-sector consumption also crowded out private investment (OECD 1993: 17).[4] High levels of public spending and higher nominal wages in the first PASOK years led to a surge in imports which exacerbated the trade deficit (Kazakos 1993).[5] Soaring public deficits and high inflation led to an increase in interest rates that further undermined public investment. In its turn, the low growth rate led to a considerable increase in the ratio of public deficit as a percentage of GDP (Vergopoulos 1992).

1 Namely, bureaucratic concentration, the diffusion of accountability, inadequate cost controls, lack of business planning, confusion between management and supervision at the top of the hierarchy, a tendency to hire new employees, the shortage of highly specialized personnel, rising costs and very low productivity (Kanellopoulos 1984).

2 In just 2 years, 1984 and 1985, the total expenditure of the public enterprises rose by 21% and 42%, respectively (*Vima*, 24/12/1986: 18).

3 Law 1266/1982 allowed for the first time the issuing of bonds to cover public consumption and abolished the previous legislation of 1957 that only allowed public borrowing for state investment. Public spending rose from 33% of GDP in 1981 to 48% of GDP in 1989, whereas revenue increased from 24% of GDP in 1981 to 27% in 1989.

4 Gross private capital investment in the 1981–1985 period declined by almost a third compared with 1979–1980, and 60% of that decrease was recorded in housing investment (Spraos 1993: 84).

5 Between 1980 and 1989 the balance of payment deficit was around 5.2% of GDP, mostly financed by heavy borrowing from abroad (Spraos 1993: 59).

The stabilization program of 1985–1987

In January 1985, the governor of the Bank of Greece warned Prime Minister Papandreou that the bank's reserves had fallen considerably and would not be enough to meet the country's international payments (*Economikos*, 08/01/1998). Despite this warning, PASOK organized its electoral campaign in the 1985 election with the clear message that economic policy would continue to be generous towards the groups it had previously benefited, under the slogan 'There will be even better days ahead'. During this election year public-sector employment increased by 6.5% (Tsakalotos 1991: 179).

Right after the election in June 1985, Greece found itself on the brink of a current account crisis and default (Bank of Greece 1991). Net interest payments abroad had reached 3% of GDP in 1985, from 0.5% in 1979 (OECD 1987: 26). Facing a deteriorating current account, the government found it difficult to borrow from private markets and turned to its foreign exchange reserves to cover its transaction needs. With an imminent crisis, it was very likely that the country would have to resort to the International Monetary Fund (IMF) for financial aid.[6] In response, the government turned to the European Community and secured a medium-term loan of 1.75 billion European currency units (ECUs) to be delivered in two installments in 1985 and 1986 in return for a stabilization program that would restore the country's balance of payment, curb inflation and boost competitiveness. The second installment of the loan was made conditional on the country's progress in macroeconomic stabilization. The program was under the supervision of the Minister of Economy Costas Simitis and included the following:

- A tight incomes policy with wage increases determined on the basis of domestic inflation (minus the imported rate of inflation) and a modification of the wage-price indexation scheme (ATA, or Automatic Wage Indexation) to exclude the impact of import prices and adjust wages on the basis of projected – instead of past – rates of inflation. The wage determination system became compulsory for both public- and private-sector employees with significant reductions in real pay.
- A tight monetary policy with the reduction of the growth of domestic credit expansion, an increase in subsidized interest rates to selected borrowers and the gradual establishment of positive real interest rates.
- The devaluation of the drachma by 15%.
- Curtailing expenditure, raising taxes and increasing administered prices to reduce the public-sector borrowing requirement (PSBR) by about 4% of GNP in both 1986 and 1987.
- A reduction in new appointments to the public sector (Bank of Greece 1986; OECD 1987).

6 As Minister of Economy Arsenis admitted in the center-left newspaper *Nea*, 10/11/1985: 5.

Although the Community loan repaired the imbalance in the current account, the government had to create conditions for growth; otherwise, the crisis could still threaten the vitality of the Greek economy and the government's distributional policies, as Papandreou put it eloquently:

> Without growth, it is impossible to promote our social objectives. The socialist transformation we aim for, which goes hand in hand with our social policy, our welfare state, will degenerate under a stagnant and declining economy.
>
> (Papandreou's public statement on 12/10/1985, Papandreou 1989: 45–46)

The program was designed to reinvigorate the private economy, particularly the export industry. Export firms benefited from wage restraint and could offset previous increases in nominal wages in the manufacturing industry thanks to the depreciation of the drachma (OECD 1993: 26).[7] Thanks to falling production costs, the rate of return on equity in the private sector exhibited an increase of more than 20% on average between 1986 and 1992 (OECD 1993: 33).

Quite importantly, the design of policies reflected political considerations. PASOK's stabilization program rejected the emerging economic orthodoxy of the time that called for deregulation, privatization, the closure of ailing companies and the reduction of state-sector employment.[8] There were no layoffs to reduce the cost of running the public enterprises and no market deregulation which would have hurt the protected insiders of the public sector.[9] The government designed a policy mix that protected its clientelist groups in the public sector from suffering important losses in their income and employment status. The government took advantage of the long transition period granted by the Community (up to 1991) and continued to subsidize ailing companies and exports (OECD 1993: 17). Instead of privatizations, the government announced a plan to restructure and modernize public companies whose operational costs were covered by funds from the Community loan.[10] The modernization program was poorly implemented (Tsakalotos 1998: 117; Simitis 1989: 18) and was undermined by actions from managers and the labor unions (*Dimosios Tomeas* 101, September 1994: 9).

Fiscal policy was also inconsistent. The predicted increase of direct taxes revenue was unrealistic (OECD 1987: 9–10; Stergiou 2002: 73). There were disappointing results in curbing public spending by individual ministries and agencies,

7 Relative wage levels in the business sector declined between 1979 and 1990 (OECD 1993: 29).

8 See the IMF Report published in the center-right daily *Kathimerini*, 20/8/1987. Quite interestingly, the socialist government in Spain launched a privatization program in 1986.

9 The industrialists' association, SEV(Hellenic Federation of Enterprises), did not welcome the deregulation of imports in commodities (*Vima*, 10/11/1987: 22).

10 In 1991, the 10 biggest manufacturing loss-making companies were state controlled and registered losses that amounted to over 1% of GDP (OECD 1993: 35).

despite the noticeable increase in state revenue, particularly through indirect taxation, and there were also poor results in combating tax evasion (OECD 1987: 10–11). Notwithstanding the considerable rise in taxation, the 1986 budget predicted a rise in public expenditure from 1618 to 1899 billion drachmas, but expenditure eventually reached 2022 billion drachmas in 1986 (OECD 1987: 10). The 1987 budget actually increased expenditure by 19.2% and predicted a rise of 5.2% in the deficit for the same year. The mere result was that public deficits returned to the already high 1984 level at 11.7% of GDP. There was also a remarkable deviation from the target that had been set for the public deficit: instead of a rate of 9.7% of GDP of public deficit, it reached 13.4% of GDP, which Minister of Economy Costas Simitis later ascribed to the failure to curb public spending and raise more revenue (Simitis 1989: 18). Simitis confessed that wasting public money was still rooted in government spending:

> Waste is structural, because there is no serious mechanism for the financial and social assessment and ordering of expenditure in terms of effectiveness. (Simitis 1989b: 79)

Despite the implementation of the austerity program, the government hired new personnel in the broader public sector. Forty days before the announcement of the austerity package, the government nationalized the country's largest shipyard. Compared with 1985, state funding to public enterprises and public organizations and spending in social welfare funds rose in both 1986 and 1987 (OECD 1987: 10). Public-sector employees, who were already receiving extra benefits, experienced a relatively mild fall in their basic salaries that were still considerably higher compared with the average salary in the private sector. Most of their extra income benefits were left intact. Instead, there were substantial pay rises for a few public service categories (OECD 1987: 11; *Vima*, 03/08/1986: 1).

Structural reforms were limited and the stabilization program failed to tackle the basic structural problems of the Greek economy (OECD 1987: 20).[11] Despite the fall of inflation and the rise in private investment and business profitability, the increase in productivity was low, inflation remained high, support to ailing industries continued, tax distortions and disincentives were not lifted, social security deficits were growing and public corporations and enterprises were still making losses (OECD 1987). The program was short lived and inadequate (Bank of Greece 1992: 16). Soon government officials felt that the program's emphasis on austerity measures (particularly taxation) had also unintended and adverse effects on the already troubled domestic economic activity. Currency devaluation

11 Structural reforms included lowering the highest income tax rate, the abolition of export restrictions, the partial liberalization of interest rates (meaning that the government could no longer borrow under privileged terms) and the partial liberalization of capital movement. These measures were congruent with the country's commitments under the Single Market program launched by the European Commission during that time.

and the introduction of value-added tax (VAT) led to a temporary rise in inflation whose implications were not fully anticipated when the stabilization program was designed (Simitis 1989: 17). Inflation was later contained to 13.5% thanks to wage restraint, falling labor unit costs and tight monetary policy.

The stabilization program offered the ailing Greek economy a temporary breathing space. Wage restraint and currency depreciation gave a short-lived boost to the export sector (Oikonomou 1992: 157). It was stated that the net improvement in competitiveness thanks to this program partially offset the negative impact of the full abolition of import tariffs and export subsidies in the trade between Greece and the Community during that period (Spraos 1993: 76). Unemployment levels remained at the 1985 rate, and GDP growth was modest.

Reactions to the stabilization program and PASOK's U-turn

On the political front, the stabilization program caused serious disagreements inside PASOK and amidst its affiliated unionists. Many PASOK politicians raised their objections on economic grounds, claiming that the austerity program was reducing domestic demand and was fuelling unemployment (Simitis 1989: 22).[12] Most objections, however, reflected political calculations in the face of reactions coming from the governing party, the labor unions and the Communist Party. Right from the start, a number of PASOK's unionists voiced their opposition to the strict incomes policy and the currency depreciation that led to a sudden rise in the cost of living under already high inflation rates. Their complaints reflected the sudden discontent many union members felt since PASOK had reneged on its pre-electoral pledges to enact more generous economic policies. In October 1985, a serious rift occurred inside PASOK's labor organization (PASKE) in the country's general confederation of unions, GSEE (General Confederation of Greek Workers). The group of PASOK unionists who voted in favor of industrial action was expelled from PASOK and, a few days later, formed an alliance with the opposition parties and elected a new president of GSEE. The government responded by setting in motion a judicial process that decided that the election of a new leadership in GSEE was unlawful and deposed its elected leadership. The defecting unionists reacted by claiming that this process had several legal irregularities.

Eventually, GSEE under a new leadership that was friendly to the government moderated its reaction to the stabilization program. Many of the unionists who were expelled from PASOK formed a political organization but failed to forge strong social alliances and ultimately faced political isolation. Some of

12 The most prominent case was the resignation of Gerasimos Arsenis, former minister of economy during PASOK's first term, in protest against the emphasis which the program placed on austerity. Arsenis later founded a party, which scored poorly in the 1989 elections. He returned to PASOK in 1991.

them later returned to PASOK. For actors inside PASOK and the unions, this development served as a lesson about the optimal strategy towards economic reforms, the mutual gains from showing complacency with government policy and the value of co-optation as a strategy to achieve this behavior. Inside the party, the leadership also used the threat of expulsion to contain grievances (*Vima*, 25/01/1987: 3). For party politicians and unionists expulsion from PASOK meant loss of access to party patronage and political isolation. To avoid this, many PASOK cadres carefully framed their objections as concerns and worries driven by their desire to protect the party and its leader from those who advocated tough measures 'at any political cost' (*Vima*, 29/11/1987). As they could not launch a direct attack on Papandreou himself, they often targeted the Minister of Economy Simitis. (Simitis 1989: 26–27)

Game theory analysis

We can understand this episode of confrontation and its outcome through game theory analysis. The preferences of the government and the union leaders – both the recalcitrant and the co-opted ones – are traced from the setting of interactions, roles and incentives described earlier. This allows us to build preference schedules as an ordinal scale of expected payoffs.

The status quo before the beginning of the crisis was 'non-reform' from the side of the government and 'political alignment' of the majorities in the unions comprising Greece's main umbrella (tertiary) organization in the labor movement GSEE (G1, L1). Under pressing economic conditions, the government could not uphold the status quo that put at risk the sustainability of the distributional system, including its future commitments to client groups. To prevent the crisis from escalating, the governing party had to choose between two other options as part of a necessitated stabilization effort: either to implement comprehensive reforms that reduce or cut collective benefits and clientelist supply (G2), or create a package of reforms that protects its clients from serious losses (reform with clientelist bias, G3). The union leaders have two options: either to accept the policy (compliance) or react vocally against it (conflict).

In this game, the government knows that if it launches reforms that reduce or cut clientelist supply to its support groups, such as privatization and structural reforms, it could risk its cohesion and mobilization capacity. Yet only substantive reform can restore a sustainable path to recovery. The alternative option is to spare the supply of clientelist benefits from reform while taking other measures that diffuse the costs across the population – namely new taxes, wage restraint and fiscal constraint – and revamp the economy, at least temporarily, until the next election.

The governing party moves first in anticipation of reactions from the labor unions. But before launching its policy, the government may not know which party unionists are more likely to react strongly against this policy package and which ones are more prone to co-optation, given that clientelist benefits are

Table 4.1 Preference schedule for the governing party (PASOK)

Order	*Options*	*Payoffs*	*Explanation*
1	Reform with clientelist bias and acceptance by unionists (G2, L1)	5	• Secures the sustainability of the distributional system • Preserves ties with client groups • Prevents episodes of confrontation with labor unions
2	Reform with clientelist bias and conflict with unionists (G2, L2)	4	• Secures the sustainability of the distributional system • Preserves ties with client groups • Triggers confrontation with labor unions
3	Reform without clientelist bias and acceptance by unionists (G3, L1)	3	• Secures the sustainability of the distributional system • Undermines ties with client groups with a cost to party cohesion and mobilization • Prevents confrontation with labor unions
4	Reform without clientelist bias and conflict with unionists (G3, L2)	2	• Secures the sustainability of the distributional system • Undermines ties with client groups with a cost in party cohesion and mobilization • Triggers confrontation with labor unions
5	Non-reform and acceptance by unionists (G1, L1) – the status quo ante	1	• Risks the sustainability of the distributional system • Risks the sustainability of its ties with client groups • Prevents confrontation with labor unions
6	Non-reform and conflict with unionists (G1, L2)	0	• Risks the sustainability of the distributional system • Risks the sustainability of its ties with client groups • Triggers confrontation with labor unions

protected. In other words, there is incomplete information on the prevailing preferences inside the unions.[13] Eventually, there are two games: 1) one against the recalcitrant unionists, who value their role as labor unionists and their collective benefits higher than their party ties and, even if the government holds

13 This prevents the government from using backwards induction to predict its best strategy.

Table 4.2 Preference schedule for the recalcitrant PASOK-affiliated union leaders

Order	*Options*	*Payoffs*	*Explanation*
1	Non-reform and compliance (G1, L1) the status quo ante	5	• Secures both collective and individual (client) benefits • Welcomes that the government seeks alternative ways to consolidate the economy outside austerity • Does not raise questions about their autonomy as labor unionists • Preserves ties with PASOK
2	Non-reform and conflict (G1, L2)	4	• Secures both collective and individual (client) benefits and articulates demands for new ones • Welcomes that government seeks alternative ways to consolidate the economy outside austerity • Allows to reinstate their autonomy as labor unionists by claiming what PASOK had promised before the election • Risks their ties with PASOK
3	Reform with clientelist bias and conflict (G2, L2)	3	• Secures clientelist benefits but undermines collective ones • Pushes the government to seek alternative ways to consolidate the economy outside austerity • Allows to reinstate their autonomy as labor unionists • Risks their ties with PASOK
4	Reform without clientelist bias and conflict (G3, L2)	2	• Undermines both clientelist and collective benefits • Pushes the government to seek alternative ways to consolidate the economy outside austerity • Allows to reconfirm their autonomy as labor unionists • Risks their ties with PASOK
5	Reform with clientelist bias and compliance (G2, L1)	1	• Secures clientelist benefits but undermines collective ones • Yields to the government for not seeking alternative ways to consolidate the economy outside austerity • Demonstrates lack of autonomy as labor unionists • Preserves their ties with PASOK
6	Reform without clientelist bias and compliance (G3, L1)	0	• Undermines both clientelist and collective benefits • Yields to the government for not seeking alternative ways to consolidate the economy outside austerity • Demonstrates lack of autonomy as labor unionists • Preserves their ties with PASOK

Table 4.3 Preference schedule for the complacent PASOK-affiliated union leaders

Order	*Options*	*Payoffs*	*Explanation*
1	Reform with clientelist bias and compliance (G3, L1)	5	• Preserves personal ties with the party • Preserves supply to client groups • Secures the sustainability of the distributional system
2	Reform without clientelist bias and compliance (G2, L1)	4	• Preserves personal ties with the party • Cuts supply to client groups** • Secures the sustainability of the distributional system
3	Non-reform and compliance (G1, L1) – the status quo ante	3	• Preserves personal ties with the party • Preserves supply to client groups now, but seriously risks it in the immediate future • Risks the sustainability of the distributional system***
4	Reform with clientelist bias and conflict (G3, L2)	2	• Risks personal ties with the party* • Preserves supply to client groups • Secures the sustainability of the distributional system
5	Reform without clientelist bias and conflict (G2, L2)	1	• Risks personal ties with the party* • Cuts supply to client groups** • Secures the sustainability of the distributional system
6	Non-reform and conflict (G1, L2)	0	• Risks personal ties with the party* • Preserves supply to client groups now, but seriously risks it in the immediate future • Undermines the sustainability of the distributional system***

* With the last three options, the unionists risk expulsion from PASOK, which they want to avoid at any cost.

** This option cuts clientelist supply, but clientelism may later resume once the economy is stabilized, whereas the unionists could hope to retain personal access to clientelist supply thanks to their positions as top unionists and party cadres.

*** A crisis of sustainability makes future supply scarcer, but the labor unionists could hope to retain personal access to clientelist supply thanks to their individual status as both unionists and party cadres. However, if expelled (G1, L2), re-entry might be less feasible, given the damage to their reputation and the fact that the government would rather choose to reward its more trusted clients.

that reforms are necessary, they are willing to assert their autonomy by reacting against adverse government measures; and 2) one against the complacent labor unionists who do not wish to undermine their ties with the party and understand the need for reforms to secure the vitality of the distributional system as a whole. Each group has distinct preference orderings.

As the sequence of events showed, some of PASOK's leading unionists chose to confront the government over the announced austerity, and clientelist bias or any personal ties were not enough to make them change their stance. These unionists had been complacent over the previous status of club and personal goods – although they occasionally demanded more government concessions – but they were now willing to assert their autonomy as unionists representing employees in both the private and the public sectors and put their party ties to the test. Their reactions to the announcement of the stabilization program with defection led to open confrontation with the government and their expulsion from PASOK (G2, L2, Table 4.4).

The game explains why the PASOK government launched reforms with clientelist bias, anticipating tolerance by most unionists thanks to their strong personal ties with the party. Given how vital the clientelist ties are for its cohesion and mobilization capacity, the government prefers this order: G2 (with payoffs of either 5 or 4, depending on the union's subsequent move) > G3 (3 or 2) > G1 (1 or 0). The government is better off choosing G2, no matter how the unionists would respond, which makes G2 its dominant strategy. Because the PASOK government could not move to G3 without undermining its ties with its core clientelist base or to G1 without risking systemic collapse, it appointed a complacent union leader in GSEE to work with unionists who valued their political affiliation with PASOK and had no desire to react vocally against PASOK's stabilization policy. These two players' best strategies converged on enacting reform with a clientelist bias in return for the unions' compliant response (G2,L1 as Nash equilibrium, Table 4.5).

Table 4.4 Strategic interaction between the governing party and the recalcitrant GSEE union leaders in 1985

	Union leaders (GSEE) nonco-opted, 1985		
		Compliance L1	*Conflict L2*
Governing party (PASOK)	Non-reform G1	1, 5	0, 4
	Reform with clientelist bias G2	5, 1	4, 3
	Reform without clientelist bias G3	3, 0	2, 2

Table 4.5 Strategic interaction between the governing party and the appointed GSEE leadership

	Labor union (GSEE) appointed and co-opted, 1985		
		Compliance L1	*Conflict L2*
Governing party (PASOK)	Non-reform G1	1, 3	0, 0
	Reform with clientelist bias G2	5, 5	4, 2
	Reform without clientelist bias G3	3, 4	2, 1

The role of the opposition

New Democracy grasped the opportunity to attack the government for breaking its pre-electoral promises, but its policy stance was contradictory and confusing. New Democracy politicians criticized the government for its strict austerity measures and speculated that more adverse measures would be taken because the country was on the brink of economic collapse.[14] At the same time, the leader of New Democracy, Constantine Mitsotakis, and other senior spokesmen acknowledged the necessity for fiscal restraint and reforms in the public sector, but they vocally attributed the difficult economic conditions to PASOK's policy failures. Mitsotakis advocated further structural reforms and cuts in spending in the broader public sector (*Economikos*, 20/12/1987: 25; *Vima*, 22/11/1987):

> This is why I criticized the austerity measures of 1985; I did not denounce them as unnecessary . . . I said that – from a political and moral point of view – I could not accept sacrifices that lead nowhere; sacrifices that are eventually wiped out by a wasteful, devouring and corrupt State, which raises deficits so exorbitantly that we are heading for another disaster, even if we had endured [an] austerity [program].
>
> (*Vima*, 16/08/1987: 3)[15]

As the leader of the opposition, Mitsotakis promoted an economically liberal agenda that publicly denounced the tradition of favoritism, clientelism and corruption. Under Mitsotakis, the party's ideology shifted away from Karamanlis' statist economic policy towards a political agenda that espoused economic freedom and individual choice (Katsoudas 1987: 101). 'Liberal New Democracy' was chosen as the party's slogan for the 1985 election, much to the disdain of many party cadres, who held different ideological views.[16] A considerable number of party cadres later attributed the 1985 electoral defeat to the party's overly economically liberal agenda (Katsoudas 1987: 102). In response, Mitsotakis watered down his rhetoric after the election and openly endorsed the 1979 Karamanlis speech that had positioned 'radical liberalism' as the party's ideology.[17] Most of his later campaign against PASOK pointed to the alarming state of the economy and focused on cases of corruption and clientelism. Mitsotakis, however, remained clear that structural reforms were inevitable and that the size of the public sector had to be reduced considerably:

> [. . .] our program is bold enough to announce openly, at a time when the 'Green State' [the PASOK's nomenclature] occupies everything, that one

14 *Vima*, 07/08/1985 and 27/10/1985; *Mesimvrini*, 04/12/1985; *Eleftheros Typos*, 04/12/1985.

15 Simitis criticized the opposition for creating uncertainty over the prospects of the program without proposing anything specific as an alternative (Simitis' interview in *Nea*, 23/03/1987: 18).

16 Cited by Andrianopoulos in *Economikos*, 11/06/1992: 7.

17 See Mitsotakis' speech in the Second Congress of the New Democracy Party in Thessaloniki in February 1986 (Katsoudas 1987: 102).

> appointment will take place for any two public employees who retire. Nobody will get appointed simply because he belongs to New Democracy; [even if] we come under tremendous pressure from our [party] base.
>
> (Mitsotakis' interview in *Economikos*, 20/08/1987: 26)

The deteriorating state of the economy offered Mitsotakis the opportunity to advocate the need for a major redirection of economic policy (Kazakos 1993: 143). This message resonated with segments of Greek society that had been less favored or excluded from PASOK's patronage network – mostly owners of small and medium enterprises and private-sector employees. In 1986, New Democracy won the local administration elections against a physically ailing Papandreou, who, at the time, was accused of involvement in a number of corruption scandals. As the party was getting closer to the prospect of winning the next election, membership in New Democracy soared from 220,000 in 1983 to 400,000 in 1987 (official numbers, cited by Pappas 1999: 177). By 1987, it had become obvious to the leadership of PASOK that further implementation of austerity measures would exacerbate tensions inside PASOK and could cause serious political damage to the party (Tsakalotos 1998: 132). During that time the governing party was still under pressure from its ranks to hire new personnel.[18]

Faced with these concerns, Prime Minister Andreas Papandreou decided to end the stabilization program on 25 November 1987, a few months earlier than officially scheduled. The announcement of the return of the automatic wage indexation contradicted what Minister of Economy Simitis had announced a day before.[19] Immediately after, Simitis resigned with a letter, warning that the return to a relaxed incomes policy could undermine everything that the stabilization program had achieved (*Nea*, 27/12/1987: 3). In a similar tone, Mitsotakis claimed that the government's policy U-turn would lead to public deficits spinning out of control, which would destabilize the very foundations of the economy in the years to come (*Nea*, 26/11/1987).

However, the end of the stabilization program was welcomed by the PASOK unionists (*Nea*, 28/12/1987: 3). The return to distributional politics was celebrated and epitomized by the notorious phrase by Papandreou in a PASOK's rally in Peristeri, Athens, in April 1989, calling his minister of finance, Tsovolas, to give 'all the money to the people' ('*Tsovola, dosta ola*!').[20] A few months before the 1989 election, PASOK resumed patronage appointments.[21] The hike in

18 For instance, in OTE (Hellenic Telecommunications Organization) and ELTA (Hellenic Post), as a former minister of transport admitted in *Economikos*, 29/01/1987: 47.

19 There was previously an agreement in the government that the stabilization program would not end until the initially scheduled end date (*Nea*, 24/06/1987: 19).

20 This phrase was later repeatedly invoked by New Democracy as emblematic of PASOK's fiscal profligacy (for instance, in New Democracy's electoral leaflets "5 + 5 facts you cannot dispute" and 'Remember, think, consider and make up your mind').

21 Cf. *Nea*, 9.1.1989: 4. See also economist Louka Katseli in *Nea*, 12/01/1988. p. 4. Approximately 96,000 new employees were allegedly hired by PASOK before the 1989 election and reportedly cost approximately 250 billion drachmas (Stergiou 2002: 80).

public-sector appointments in 1988 and 1989 followed a 'clientelist' electoral cycle that was also observed in the elections of 1981 and 1985.[22] Although the austerity measures had previously caused a fracture in PASOK's cohesion, its return to patronage and distribution policies allowed the party to re-energize its loyal support base before the 1989 election.

By 1989, any macroeconomic gains of the stabilization program had been lost. Fiscal expansion led to further deterioration of the macroeconomic imbalances. Between 1980 and 1989 public deficits ran at 9.1% on average.[23] In 1989 the public-sector deficit reached 21.5% and public debt was approaching 100% of GDP (OECD 1990: 10–11). A rise in public deficits, debt and inflation, coupled with expectations for a devaluation of the drachma, led the country to the brink of a currency crisis in 1989 (Bank of Greece 1991: 31). Net borrowing needs increased by 80% between 1988 and 1989 (*Economikos*, 12/12/1991: 13).

Throughout the 1980s, the growth of the state sector and the ensuing fiscal profligacy primarily served the needs of PASOK's clientelist network. This is clearly manifested in the structure of government spending in which the share of welfare state, public health and education remained relatively low compared with the EC average. Most of the increase in public expenditure was directed to particular groups favored by government policy.[24] Between 1981 and 1989, the government relied on inflation and currency depreciation to suppress real wages and boost competitiveness because these two measures dispersed the costs among consumers (Vergopoulos 1992). Any income losses from the high rates of inflation were only offset for public-sector workers thanks to spectacular wage increases during PASOK's first term. Outside the public sector, however, real wages remained stagnant between 1980 and 1989 (Pantazidis 2002: 35).[25] This policy record contradicts the popular rhetoric that rising debt and the stagnant economy was a necessary price that Greece had to pay in order to establish a much-need welfare state on a par with the rest of the EC countries. Instead, favoritism towards clients in the public sector exacerbated the economic divide between insiders and outsiders. Conditions were particularly tough for small and medium enterprises that sought to bypass the cost of restrictive labor laws, taxes, red tape and inflation through informal employment and tax evasion.

22 Cf. Tsakalotos (1991: 179); Thomadakis (1997: 51).

23 European Commission (1999); Pantazidis (2002: 16–17).

24 A prominent case was the infamous 'national resistance' pensions established by the Papandreou government in 1982 for those who took part in the Greek resistance movement against the German, Italian and Bulgarian occupation of Greece during World War II. A candidate had to submit a signed petition and appear before a committee, together with two witnesses who would certify his or her involvement in the resistance movement (Law 1285/1982). This process lacked transparency and reportedly allowed party members to secure pensions thanks to the testimony of peers from their local party organization (*Vima*, 30/11/2003: 31).

25 Average wages fell from 55% of the average OECD wage in 1979 to 40% in 1990 (Vergopoulos 1992).

The second economic crisis in the protracted electoral period of 1989–1990

In a heated political climate and amidst rumors that Greece might be forced to resort to the IMF for financial assistance, New Democracy won 44% of the votes in the election of June 1989 but did not secure the absolute majority in the parliament due to the proportional allocation of seats by the electoral law, which PASOK had voted for a few months before.[26] New Democracy formed a coalition government with the left-wing coalition, Synaspismos, of which the Communist Party was the major partner, with the sole purpose of allowing the criminal prosecution of former Prime Minister Andreas Papandreou and his Cabinet ministers, as requested by the criminal prosecution authorities for their alleged involvement in several corruption scandals.[27] In terms of economic policy, however, this purpose-specific and ideologically heterogeneous government did not reach an agreement on fiscal consolidation measures at a time when international organizations were raising the alarm about the critical condition of the Greek economy.[28]

The next election of November 1989 also produced a hung parliament. The three major parties – New Democracy, PASOK and Synaspismos – formed an all-party coalition government and chose Xenophon Zolotas, a prominent post-war economist, as prime minister. Under deteriorating fiscal conditions the new government faced the prospect of not being able to afford to pay public-sector salaries and pensions in the coming months (*Economikos*, 09/11/1989: 15). Political uncertainty was generating business anxiety (*Nea*, 28/11/1989). The ideological heterogeneity of its government and political opportunism in face of the imminent parliamentary election prevented the Zolotas government from taking drastic measures for fiscal consolidation despite the urgency of Greece's economic situation. Zolotas later claimed that the crisis could have been tackled if he had been allowed to follow the recommendations by the IMF, the OECD and the report by prominent economists that the government had elicited (*Economikos*, 29/03/1990: 14). He also criticized the politics of that time for their extensive use of patronage:

> You know what happened in that first semester [of 1989]. Thousands of new employees were appointed and no measures were taken to deal with the situation.
>
> (*Economikos*, 26/07/1990: 26)

26 Mitsotakis claimed that it was PASOK's plan to prevent New Democracy from obtaining parliamentary majority because the next parliament was the one to decide whether Papandreou would be prosecuted for his alleged involvement in a number of scandals. The law on the criminal liability of ministers stipulates that unless the parliament that is formed after a general election votes to allow the prosecution of members of the Cabinet, their criminal liability is erased.

27 In accordance with the strict statute of limitations prescribed by the Constitution.

28 See the EEC report released on 19 October 1989 and the OECD report published on 8 February 1990.

By the beginning of 1990, the state of public finances was at a critical point. Government debt soared to 80.7% of GDP, and the public deficit amounted to an impressive 16.1% of GDP. Greece's borrowing needs rose to 19% of GDP (Bank of Greece 1991: 17). Whereas servicing the debt covered 11.8% of the government budget in 1980, the number rose to 31.8% in 1990.[29] More than half of the 1990 budget revenue (53.58%) was covered by borrowing (Hellenic Statistical Authority 1991: 35). The governor of the Bank of Greece warned that fiscal policy had been overly expansionary for far too long and that the situation was irreversible for that year (*Nea*, 21/12/1989: 17). On 19 March 1990, the president of the European Commission, Jacques Delors, sent a letter to Prime Minister Zolotas warning in an unusually dramatic tone that Greece's place in the Single Market, EMU and European integration in general was at stake and urging the government to take immediate and drastic economic measures (*Kathimerini*, 27/03/1990). At the same time, the international press dubbed Greece 'the sick man of Europe' (*The Times*, 21/02/1991) and 'the black sheep' of the European Community (*International Herald Tribune*, 09/04/1991).

Conclusion

A look at the stabilization program of 1985–1987 indicates that it was designed to disperse the cost of macroeconomic stabilization among taxpayers and consumers and spare the protected core of public-sector employees from structural reforms that could have undermined their employment status and privileges. The program, though triggered by economic urgency and the desire to secure extraordinary financial aid by the European Community, had a bias towards protecting the status of PASOK's core support groups. This policy mix amounted to a form of 'reverse' redistribution of the adjustment costs on the shoulders of the system's outsiders, taxpayers, wage earners in the private sector and consumers. Just as the cost of clientelism had previously burdened these economic actors through taxation and borrowing, the cost of reform to reinvigorate the ailing clientelist economy was again passed on them.

Both the nature of the stabilization program and the return to fiscal expansion in 1987 confirms the theoretical expectations postulated in Chapter 3 that clientelist bias is the optimal political response to pressures for reform. Change is unlikely in an environment of strong path dependency when key actors in positions of power still enjoy 'increasing returns' from clientelism. Rather than a critical juncture for Greece's clientelist system, the stabilization program of 1985–1987 allowed for a pattern of 'reproduction by adaptation', in which the temporary tightening of fiscal policy secured the system's sustainability for a few years, postponing the need to take more drastic measures for the near future. The chapter highlights some important trends in the

29 Annual Budgetary Report and *Economikos*, 12/12/1991: 13.

unfolding cycle of the clientelist system along the stages of expansion, crisis and reform:

- *The suboptimality of clientelism*

Clientelism remains the equilibrium strategy for the two main parties and creates a 'positive feedback loop', in which its practice creates new social demands that had to be accommodated by new supply. This tendency increases the fiscal costs on the system over time and takes its toll on public finances and the private economy. This could then trigger a crisis serious enough to threaten the sustainability of the clientelist system itself. If the government fails to engage in macroeconomic stabilization, it may not be able to borrow or raise income through taxes to finance the current and future demands of the clientelist system. A sharp drop in the available resources for clientelism will then trigger tensions and unrest within the party and may also lead to defections that would further weaken its mobilization capacity. Given these pressing conditions, the government comes under increasing pressure to implement some reforms to prevent systemic collapse while preserving its clientelist commitments to safeguard its own cohesion.

- *Clientelist bias as a response to the dilemma of how to stabilize the economy and preserve the clientelist supply*

The strategic course dictated by the payoffs of the clientelist game is that the design of reforms must preserve its ties with its client groups, who constitute the main campaign resources of the patron party. Preference will be given to the horizontal diffusion of adjustment costs amidst the general population with unpopular measures such as a strict incomes policy, rising taxation, currency devaluation and fiscal austerity. The clientelist party must avoid any deep-cutting structural reforms that would limit or abolish channels of clientelist supply. Path dependency is obviously at play, as the stability and resilience of the status quo is secured by strong endogenous dynamics, given the prevalence of actors with an embedded interest in systemic continuity. As a result, there is no radical change. The same incentive structure that pushed a party in government to intensify patronage during its first term in government defines the design of its reform program in conditions of crisis.

- *Clientelist ties constraining unions' reactions*

Reaction to government policy from the unions in a clientelist system will reflect an intricate set of considerations. Party-affiliated unionists have overlapping roles as both representatives of formal professional associations and leading actors of party client groups. Similarly, although union members are united by common occupational or social affiliation, many of them are linked to the party through personal political engagement. This means that union leaders can take action to protect collective interests and secure the ‘club goods’ their members enjoy, but their capacity to protest against their patron party in government at the collective level is circumscribed by the strong ties that connect them and most of the union members to the patron party. This gives the party leadership some capacity to discipline its clients. In that moment, coordination problems become manifested, and the strategies by which this problem can be mitigated are put to the test and include the options of co-optation and expulsion (a ‘carrots and sticks’ approach). In Greece, union leaders who reacted strongly against PASOK’s policies and defected from the party’s labor organization were ‘punished’ with expulsion, faced political isolation and were replaced by complacent unionists. Relations between unionists and the central party were again normalized once the government ended its austerity policy and resumed public spending.

- *A return to fiscal profligacy (‘clientelist electoral cycle’)*

Pressure from the opposition, as well as grievances inside the party and its affiliated labor organizations, exert pressure on the government to resume public spending and patronage supply. Because the government views economic policy in the short term, looking ahead to the next election, it will launch and implement reforms to the degree that they will temporarily revitalize the economy, prevent the outbreak of a systemic crisis during its term and defer the prospect of deeper reforms in the future.

5 Departure from the clientelist equilibrium

The economic agenda of the Mitsotakis government (1990–1993)

We have seen that the supply of patronage is the equilibrium strategy for two parties in a clientelist system. However, economic policy may still depart from this equilibrium for a number of reasons: the strong input of ideological or personal beliefs, insufficient information regarding other actors' benefit-and-cost calculations and behavior or political miscalculations about the anticipated political returns from reform. These factors may drive certain policy leaders to enact radical reform and try to break with the system's path-dependent model, particularly if they believe they could benefit from the revision of the status quo. This chapter revisits such a case and explores the implications for the cohesion of the party in government and the terms of interparty competition.

Faced with a fiscal crisis, the center-right Mitsotakis government (1990–1993) openly embraced privatization and market liberalization. This was Greece's first encounter with policies aiming at reducing both the role and the share of the state in the economy. This reform program, particularly the prospect of comprehensive privatization, threatened to abolish key channels of clientelist supply and triggered reactions from the opposition and inside the governing party. It offered PASOK the opportunity to sponsor protests against privatization and market liberalization and renew its ties with its client groups in the public-sector unions. At the same time, reactions inside the governing party of New Democracy undermined its cohesion and eventually contributed to the fall of the government in October 1993, when PASOK and its leader, Andreas Papandreou, won the election and returned to power.[1]

A new government facing a fiscal crisis

New Democracy obtained a small parliamentary majority in the third consecutive election in April 1990. Right from the start, Mitsotakis declared his intention to change the country's economic direction by reducing public deficits, selling or closing down ailing companies owned by the state, allowing private entrepreneurship in services that were at that time dominated by state-owned companies,

1 For a similar outlook on this period see Trantidis (2014).

liberalizing markets and improving the efficiency of the public administration. The proposed package of measures included cutting down subsidies to public enterprises, reducing and controlling their financing through state guarantees, reforming the regime of subsidies given to agricultural cooperatives, making state-owned banks conform to private banking standards in granting loans and guaranteeing managerial independence in the companies of the public sector.[2] Mitsotakis denounced 'the inconsiderate and unproductive expansion of the public sector' and openly expressed his economically liberal ideology.[3] Unlike Papandreou's program in 1985, New Democracy's stabilization program included both fiscal consolidation and structural reforms. It aimed to reduce the size of the state with extensive privatizations, real reductions of salaries in the public sector, a cut in subsidies to ailing companies and a decrease in subsidies to pension funds. These announcements signaled a major shift in Greece's economic paradigm.

During the first 2 years in power, the Mitsotakis government prioritized fiscal consolidation. Fiscal policy aimed at reducing the government's borrowing needs within a period of 3 years, from 13.0% in 1990 to 3.0% in 1993. The plan mostly relied on increases in taxation and less on cuts in public spending (Bank of Greece 1991: 22). The government followed a strict incomes policy with pay rises below the rate of inflation in order to reduce public deficits and control inflation. Nominal wage increases in the public sector were curbed. The strict incomes policy in the public sector also sent a signal to social partners in the private sector to reach an agreement on moderate wage increases below the inflation rate (Bank of Greece 1991: 24). Besides its effect on inflation, wage moderation was thought to offset the gradual abandonment of currency devaluation as the traditional tool to boost competitiveness. The incomes policy was, however, milder compared with contemporary programs in Portugal, Ireland and Italy during the same period (Detragiache-Hamann 1997). The foreign exchange policy was focused on the target of reducing inflation with a strong drachma policy.[4] Inflation eventually fell in 1991 by 5 percentage points, aided by the tight incomes policy, but rising indirect taxes and prices of the public utility companies undermined this trend (Bank of Greece 1992: 19–20). The policy mix was quite contradictory, as the shift in monetary policy away from aggressive devaluation and towards a stronger currency and slower credit expansion negatively affected competitiveness, requiring stricter wage restraint. Despite the new measures, the Greek government's borrowing needs were more than three times that of the EEC average (Bank of Greece 1991: 35).

2 Programmatic Declaration of the Prime Minister in the Greek Parliament on 24/4/1990, *Praktika Voulis*, Δ Session, pp.18–19).

3 Ibid.

4 The drachma was devalued at a rate lower than the difference in inflation rates between Greece and its main trading partners (Bank of Greece 1992: 26).

The need to raise new revenue led the government to take urgent fiscal measures in 1990, which included a considerable rise in fuel tax and the price of public utility services and a charge on property that was imposed twice, in May 1990 and in January 1992.[5] The government also announced new taxes in August 1992 despite its previous pledge not to do so during that year. There was a substantial increase in indirect taxes, particularly on fuel, cars, alcoholic drinks and tobacco, and the tax on interest paid to bank deposits. New taxation instead of expenditure cuts covered the shortfall in annual tax revenues. Rising taxes fueled inflation from 13.1% at the end of July to 15.9% at the end of

Table 5.1 The Mitsotakis economic program

Policy area	*Measures*
Fiscal policy	Direct and indirect tax increases
	Wage restraint in the public sector
	Inadequate measures to fight tax evasion
	Controls on public-sector appointments
	Wages in public enterprises increased considerably less than inflation
	Small fall in public-sector employment due to retirement, limited hiring and privatizations
Monetary policy	Tight credit expansion, limited depreciation of the exchange rate; liberalization of capital movements with EC countries
Structural reforms	Partial liberalization and deregulation of markets in products and services (particularly the banking system and the property rent market), abolition of price controls
	Labor market reforms increasing flexibility and imposing stricter limits on wildcat strikes
	Abolition of state monopoly in the post office and air transport
Pensions	Two reforms increasing the retirement age for those recruited after 1982 and creating a two-tier system phased between 1992 and 2007 for new employees without hurting those about to retire in the following years
Privatization	Nearly all enterprises under the jurisdiction of the Industrial Reconstruction Organization (OAE) were liquidated or sold by spring 1993
	Large privatizations included Athens Bus Transport and Heracles Cement Company
	Government planned to sell shares of OTE to the wider public and to a strategic partner, who was to take over the management of the company

5 The minister of economy justified this decision as 'a measure for the equal distribution of the burden [of economic adjustment], so that pensioners and salaried workers would not be the only ones to pay for the crisis' (*Kathimerini*, 29/01/1992).

October (Bank of Greece 1991). This rise was only partially offset by a decrease in the rate of currency devaluation, when the Bank of Greece increased its interest rate.

Fiscal policy in the first year was inconsistent with its declared targets. Some restrictions were imposed on spending for public-sector wages, pensions and the welfare state. Overall public spending, however, increased beyond what was predicted in the budget and higher than the inflation rate, which was between 18% and 22% around that time. Between 1990 and 1991, there was a 40.8% nominal increase in payments for public relations, a 34.0% increase in home travel expenditures for the members of the armed and security forces and a 21.1% increase in special benefits and additional payments of permanent employees despite the general pay freeze (Hellenic Statistical Authority 1991: 25). Expenditures for nonpersonal services rose by 42.8% (Hellenic Statistical Authority 1991: 24). Income support and other transfers to physical persons also increased considerably between 1988 and 1991 (Hellenic Statistical Authority 1991: 99). There was also a substantial increase in the budgets of all the ministries.[6]

In the end, the first stabilization program brought poor results in terms of curbing expenditure, raising revenue and combating tax evasion. The government policy just managed to curb the rate of increase of public debt.[7] In 1991 servicing the public debt amounted to an outstanding 54.6% of ordinary budget expenditures (Hellenic Statistical Authority 1991: 29). Rising borrowing costs continued to fuel public debt, which reached 98.3% of GDP at the end of 1991. Despite some progress with raising tax revenue,[8] tax legislation continued to offer the tax authorities a high degree of discretion in estimating tax without establishing any effective control over their decisions. Not surprisingly, the opposition criticized the government for its failure to reduce tax evasion.[9] Lack of

6 Hellenic Statistical Authority (1991).

7 In 1991, debt service absorbed 42.6% of the tax revenue (Bank of Greece 1992: 16). Primary deficits fell from 6.1% of GDP in 1990 to 2.8% in 1991, thanks to lower primary expenditure and rising government revenue (Bank of Greece 1992: 28).

8 Government action allegedly contributed to an increase in revenue from income tax, from 130 billion drachmas in 1989 to 800 billion drachmas in 1992 (at a 16% inflation rate). But despite the progress in raising revenue, tax evasion remained rampant. Minister of Economy Manos later admitted to a letter to the ECOFIN in September 1992 that

> It is disappointing that the decision to tax social groups such as farmers, self-employed professionals and many others who evade paying tax has not yet produced important results
>
> (*Economikos*, 12/11/1992: 62)

9 Talking about the deep causes of the government's inability to fight tax evasion, the president of the union of tax collectors noted:

> The government is vacillating between the pressures from strong groups asking for greater tax immunity and the harsh reality . . . Governments are particularly attentive to the population segments that evade paying tax, because they [are the ones to] decide the [electoral] result.
>
> (*Dimosios Tomeas*, November 1992, p. 13).

transparency inside the tax authorities was attributed to the presence of corrupt party cliques:

> Bribing has to do with the extent to which the public sector is independent or whether it becomes 'plunder' for the party that wins the election. Today we have a unique phenomenon in public organizations: the overwhelming majority of the heads of tax bureaus in the country are members of the governing party . . . On many occasions, the press revealed that there were notes . . . from the office of the Minister of Finance that were asking for the favorable tax treatment of 'their guys'.
>
> (*Dimosios Tomeas*, November 1992, p. 15)

Moreover, by 1990 Greece's pension system, whose spending needs had exceeded 15% of GDP, which was double the OECD average, was regarded as unsustainable in the medium term. Spending for pensions was growing at about 0.3% of GDP annually, whereas the ratio of contributors to pensioners remained very low (OECD 1993: 45). Prime Minister Mitsotakis talked of an unsustainable level of debt in pension funds stemming from a huge degree of evasion in the payment of social security contributions (Stergiou 2002: 100). In response, the government launched two rounds of reform of the pension system despite reactions from the opposition, the unions and politicians inside New Democracy. The first package of government reforms introduced relatively mild adjustments (Law 1902/1990). A more comprehensive reform was postponed until 1991, but the government followed a piecemeal reform strategy to sequence a set of moderate reforms (Law 1796/1991). An experts' committee was established with the participation of social partners to propose the reform measures. Quite soon, the representatives of the two main trade unions (GSEE and PASEGES) withdrew from the committee on the grounds that the government's initiative had ignored its workings.[10] A second package of pension reforms in 1992 introduced wider and deeper changes (Law 2084/1992). This package also triggered fierce reactions from the trade unions and the opposition parties.

The government also launched the first round of structural reforms, which included the full privatization or closure of relatively small deficit-running enterprises, a reduction in public enterprise employment and small-scale market deregulation. Structural reforms and fiscal austerity in the early 1990s prevented the spiraling of public debt that was fuelled by the deficits of the central government and the public utility companies, DEKO (OECD 1998: 104). Despite Mitsotakis' declared commitment to market liberalization, the government did not privatize any of the large state-owned companies. By 1991, all public-sector

10 What is particularly telling, however, is that PASOK's proposal for reforming the pension system included a number of measures that appeared to be tougher in relation to the proposals of the committee, yet these proposals triggered mild reactions inside the PASOK party and had little public exposure (Stergiou 2002: 102).

companies remained under full state ownership. A plan proposed by Minister of Commerce Andreas Andrianopoulos in September 1991 to privatize the majority of shares in the big state-owned companies was rejected by the new minister of economy, Efthymios Christodoulou, who insisted that the majority would stay in the hands of the state. This policy inertia regarding privatization and deep-cutting structural reforms reflected the ongoing division within New Democracy and the Cabinet over the economic ideology of the party.[11] Several center-right politicians were skeptical of market deregulation and privatization. For proponents of deep-cutting reforms, this was disappointing. In the words of Andrianopoulos, the government's record was inconsistent with its proclaimed liberal economic ideology:

> Neoliberalism means two things: reduction of the public sector on the one hand and reduction of taxation on the other. Here, we have had neither the one nor the other.
>
> (Andrianopoulos in *Nea*, 25/08/1990: 19)[12]

At the same time, New Democracy members and grassroots organizations were exerting strong pressure on government officials to accommodate the demands of their clients, who were mostly asking for appointments and promotions in the public sector (*Vima*, 26/09/1991: 26; *Economikos*, 15/03/1990: 13).[13] The Sunday newspaper *Vima* published a number of notes by local New Democracy branches and party bosses and MPs asking Cabinet ministers and managers of public enterprises to accommodate their patronage claims (all quotes from *Vima*, 09/05/1991: 40):

> Police officer D. M. to be placed as the head of the police station in Kalamata . . . The above-mentioned officers are active members of our party and a great service to our organization.
>
> A local branch asked for the appointment of one of its members: 'From 1983 to 1991 he was a member of ONNED [New Democracy's youth organization] and since 1991 until today an active member of the Local Organization'.
>
> A local party branch in [the prefecture of] Argolis expresses its dissatisfaction with the fact that the head of the archaeological service in the region was appointing PASOK members while 'our kids are waiting for eight years now for a chance'.

11 Minister of Economy Souflias stated his belief that 'the market should operate freely but there must be [government] control over cases of excessive profits' (*Nea*, 25/08/1990: 19).

12 Andrianopoulos described the first stabilization program as 'an imitation' of the Simitis program with a slant to privatization (*Economikos*, 11/06/1992: 5).

13 'Everyone knows that spending goes up considerably because of the clientelistic (*rousfetologiki*) politics of the government, and due to the increase in the payments received by the government's affiliates (*ton imeteron*) appointed in a number of committees (Ioannis Grivas, president of the labor union of tax collectors in *Dimosios Tomeas*, November 1992, p. 13).

Vima also published a letter allegedly sent by a New Democracy supporter to the prime minister, who was his daughter's godfather (*Vima*, 30/06/1991: 26–27):

> Our young members, who had been the vanguard of our party bosses but had been elbowed by PASOK, [had] their hopes let down completely, as they cannot be appointed to public or private jobs and, instead, they see others getting appointed . . . PASOK's people find a way to get [government jobs] because – let's be honest – they are still running almost all the public services today in camouflage . . . Although there are new managers, they still accommodate their demands . . . while they are shunning the people of our own party.[14]

The small fiscal room for new clientelist appointments in the public sector caused grievances and frictions among New Democracy MPs (*Vima*, 20/09/1992: 8). Minister Militiades Evert became the target of criticism by fellow ministers for his insistence on putting forward a set of objective criteria to govern new hiring in the public sector (*Vima*, 28/11/1990). Given the dire financial situation, the government could easier deliver favors ('*rousfetia*') that were not (too) costly for the budget – for instance, promotions – and favorable placements in the public sector (*Vima* 30/06/1991: 27; *Nea*, 18/03/1993: 19) or the military (*Kyriakatiki Eleftherotypia*, 3/10/1993).

Collective action against the first wave of reforms

As the main opposition party, PASOK vehemently criticized the government's economic policy.[15] The 1991 budget was dubbed 'the harshest and most class-biased budget of the last decades'.[16] The rhetoric helped the party reconnect with its affiliated labor unions and distance itself from the bitter memories of its own strict program a few years earlier. The labor unions organized sizeable demonstrations on the streets of Athens throughout 1990. They raised claims for pay rises substantially above inflation. PASOK's union leaders who controlled the country's two largest unions (GSEE and ADEDY) were adamant in advocating

14 It was customary for politicians to become godfathers of the sons and daughters of loyal political friends. The sender of the letter reportedly attached the birth and baptism certificates to prove that Mitsotakis was indeed her daughter's godfather. The existence of this letter was not disputed by the government.

15 PASOK reacted to the announcement of the first round of measures by predicting that they would lead to stagflation; its unionists accused the government of launching an attack on workers' income (*Nea*, 5/9/1990). PASOK's parliamentary spokesman stated that the 1992 budget was undermining Greece's growth prospect and was destabilizing the economy (*Nea*, 18/12/1991: 24). Vaso Papandreou, the Greek European Commissioner and a prominent PASOK politician, stated that the idea that competitiveness could be improved by lower wages was outmoded (*Nea*, 17.2.1992: 15).

16 PASOK's former Minister of Economy Arsenis in the discussion of the budget (*Nea*, 04/12/1990: 12).

for continuous strike actions, as opposed to many New Democracy and left-wing colleagues who showed signs of moderation. Strikes and rallies created a climate of social and political unrest.[17] This helped PASOK present New Democracy as a socially intransigent government.

Social unrest also undermined the efforts of the government to reform the education system. The initiative was blocked by the vocal reaction of part of the student community that organized sit-ins at schools and universities, often sponsored by PASOK's grassroots organizations. These student protests lasted for months and culminated in riots and clashes with fatalities in central Athens in the winter of 1991, most notably, the murder of a school teacher and unionist, Nikos Temboneras, by a member of New Democracy's youth organization during a clash at a school occupied by students in the city of Patra.

Political reactions delayed the announcement of other reform packages.[18] Despite its declared intention, the government made little progress towards market liberalization and, instead, implemented timid reforms in the labor market (Bitros 1992: 54). Only small, mostly deficit-running companies were sold or liquidated.[19] The program was compromised in view of harsh reactions from within the governing party, the opposition and its friendly unions. In reality, the government talked too much and did very little. New Democracy was experiencing a loss in popularity without actually delivering any of the ambitious reforms it had announced. By November 1991, it was lagging behind PASOK in opinion polls (*Nea*, 19/11/1991: 12).

Opposition to the second wave of austerity

The government's policies in the first 2 years brought mixed results. On the positive side, wage restraint and mild labor market reforms helped improve business profitability. Competitiveness was improved as real wage costs fell significantly (Bank of Greece 1992: 20). The most significant improvement occurred in the balance of payments: the current account deficit fell from 5.4% in 1990 to 2.2% in 1991, the second lowest during the last 15 years, partly with the help of Community funds (Bank of Greece 1992: 24). On the negative side, the balance of trade deficit remained high, reflecting the weakness of the Greek economy to increase exports (Bank of Greece 1992: 26). Returns to capital remained low, domestic demand was anemic, unemployment increased at 1 percentage point, reaching 8.1%, and growth resumed at a moderate 1.2% (Bank of Greece 1992: 21–23).

17 When GSEE agreed on a collective agreement with the industrialists' organization (SEV) on wage increases of 12.5% and 10.6% in the following 2 years (5 March 1991), Lambros Kanellopoulos, the head of GSEE, received a public reprimand from PASOK's executive bureau.

18 Lack of political courage and inexperience were the two reasons for the delay in reforms according to Minister of Commerce and Industry Andreas Andrianopoulos (*Nea*, 5/11/1991: 22).

19 *Economikos*, 14/03/1991: 76–77.

Greece's unstable economy and public finances led the government to prepare a second 'Convergence Program' (1993–1998) which included strict monetary and fiscal policies and a tight incomes policy with a wage freeze in the public sector for 1992.[20] It also announced further measures of market liberalization, privatization and an increase in public investment for infrastructure. The implementation of the stabilization program was supervised by the European Community.[21] To speed up reforms, Mitsotakis appointed as minister of economy an advocate of market liberalization, Stefanos Manos. Manos admitted that there had been serious divergence from the initial economic targets and that the government had to start from a worse position. He also implied that his predecessors had heavily relied on increases in taxation instead of cutting public spending, such as subsidies to ailing corporations and pension funds.

In a more critical tone, the former Prime Minister Xenophon Zolotas accused New Democracy of losing 2 years while the economy was plunging into recession. He described the government measures as inadequate and called for the two main parties to reach consensus in the design of economic policy (*Vima*, 17/02/1992 and 15/02/1992). Following two grim reports by the OECD and the IMF, Xenophon Zolotas and Angelos Angelopoulos, a prominent economist, openly criticized the government for its failure to cut down expenditures and warned that the country was heading to bankruptcy.[22]

The government also confronted international criticism for its poor progress with reforms. In February 1992, Henning Christophersen, vice-president of the EC Commission in charge of supervising Greece's stabilization program, announced that, despite the reduction in trade deficit, inflation and interest rates, Greece was late in implementing its privatization program, the reform of the social security system, public deficit reduction and the fight against tax evasion (interview in *Nea*, 24/02/1992: 12). He also reminded that the granting of Community funds was conditional on the implementation of the Convergence Program. In a similar tone, in May 1992 Jacques Delors talked of Greece's failure to follow a European trajectory in reforms despite its support from Community funds. In its reports, the Commission made note of erroneous government decisions between 1991 and 1992 and pointed out a number of policy inconsistencies in the tax reforms, as well as slow progress with privatization. During the same week, the EEC Monetary Committee issued a report that was highly critical of the Greek government's policy, in particular with regard to taxation and privatization. The text reported an increase in new appointments to the public sector of 1.2% and recommended more taxes and further cuts in spending (*Nea*, 17/04/1992: 16). In addition, the IMF urged

20 In the private sector, a 2-year collective agreement introduced wage increases at 5.4% in January and 4% in July, far below the rate of inflation (Bank of Greece 1992: 21).

21 The government received an emergency loan by the European Community to cover its borrowing needs for 1991 and accepted its terms and conditions that included a 10% reduction in the number of public-sector employees by 1993 (*Nea*, 12/12/1990: 25).

22 *Nea*, 25/07/1992: 16. See also Angelopoulos' interview in *Nea*, 23/09/1993: 10.

the government to reduce public-sector employment, reform the pensions system, curb the subsidies to deficit-running public enterprises, raise new public revenue mainly through indirect taxes and fight tax evasion (Ibid).

The new program was heavily criticized by PASOK on the grounds that it was both inefficient and socially unjust. PASOK supported the unions' protests with a new round of strikes in the public sector in March 1992.[23] As these protests were escalating, the popularity of the governing party fell dramatically.[24] In the Athens by-election at the country's largest constituency in April 1992, PASOK increased its votes by 30%, around 100,000 votes. A triumphant Papandreou called the government 'nonexistent' and the country 'ungoverned'. The victory of PASOK reflected the party's reinforced mobilization capacity. Throughout August and September 1992 strikes were organized in public transport, universities, the electricity monopoly, banks, gas stations, the post office and secondary education. The government's tax reform also caused protests from the professional bodies of doctors and lawyers, which were among the traditional support groups of New Democracy. Lawyers went on a prolonged strike that lasted for 9 months with few intervals in between. In 1993, the Athens Bar Association, which had previously elected a candidate supported by New Democracy (in May 1990 with 67.5% of the vote), this time voted for the candidate supported by PASOK.

The escalating reactions to protracted austerity pushed the cohesion of New Democracy to its limits. Right after the electoral results of April 1992, former Conservative Prime Minister Rallis asked the two large parties, New Democracy and PASOK, to form a coalition government, but both parties rejected his proposal. Inside New Democracy, Mitsotakis faced opposition from two aspiring leaders of the party. On the one side, Miltiades Evert, former Cabinet minister and the former mayor of Athens, formed a team with former Deputy Prime Minister Kanellopoulos and former Minister of Industry Dimas and issued an announcement calling for the postponement of the proposed economic measures which, in their view, were leading to recession and were socially unjust. In a public interview, Deputy Prime Minister Athanasios Kanellopoulos expressed his disapproval of the government's economic policy and said that the government measures were 'unjust and lacking imagination' (*Vima*, 09/01/1992). Kanellopoulos resigned from the government a few days later, saying that the prime minister refused to discuss economic policy with his Cabinet ministers. Former minister Miltiades Evert also accused Mitsotakis of short-termism in his approach to problems and characterized the government's economic policy as 'defensive' (*Vima*, 11/02/1992). In a parliamentary speech, Evert blamed the government for following a policy that shrank the economy and generated stagflation

23 In transport, telecommunication and electricity monopolies, the post office, Athens' water company, the port authority, the railways, the state-owned banks and the petrol company.

24 Government officials were booed by crowds at the celebration in honor of the Greek Olympic medalists at the Panathinaicon Stadium on 11 August 1992.

(*Nea*, 18/03/1992: 14). On the other side, Antonis Samaras, former minister of foreign affairs, whom Mitsotakis had dismissed after their disagreement over the handling of the 'Macedonian name' question, formed his own group of dissenters.[25] Mitsotakis also confronted intense criticism from other New Democracy MPs and faced notable resignations from his Cabinet and administration. In response to mounting unrest, Mitsotakis called for a vote of confidence in April 1992, which he won. Talking in the Parliament, he defended his economic policy and pledged to stick to the Convergence Program for another 2 years. Any deviation, he argued, would jeopardize the country's position in the EEC.

Reactions to privatization

The strongest reaction against the Mitsotakis government targeted its privatization agenda, especially after it was announced that shares of state monopoly enterprises in telecommunication, electricity and railways were to be sold with the government retaining control over their management and price policy (*Nea*, 24/12/1991). Privatization was a divisive issue in public opinion too.[26] The government had to rebrand privatizations as 'de-etatizations' (*apokratikopoiiseis*), a neologism invented to avoid the allusion that it was selling out to private business. But the ideological advocacy of privatizations was limited and defensive. The government made the case for privatization primarily as a way to cut subsidies and raise revenue and did not clearly communicate to the public any arguments about the economic gains from open competition and market liberalization.[27]

Each announcement of privatization plans triggered the reaction of labor unions, whose members in public-sector companies were fearful that their working status would be harmed.[28] Once again, PASOK politicians openly supported their cause.[29] Union leaders also viewed privatization as a threat to their influence in the companies. The unions' reactions escalated with rallies and accusations of corruption involving government officials.[30] A wave of strikes in public utility

25 Antonis Samaras resigned as a member of parliament on 21 October 1992.

26 In an opinion poll, 46.9% of respondents were against privatization, whereas 42.2% were in favor (*Nea*, 19/11/1991: 12). In another public survey, 50.3% of respondents held the view that privatizations 'serve the interest of particular big business rather than serving the general interest of the economy' (MRB Opinion poll, *Kathimerini*, 17/7/1993).

27 Cf. *Nea*, 23.3.1990: 2. The minister of economy suggested that raising the telephone bill charges would help the government raise the revenue it could achieve from the sale of shares in OTE (*Economikos*, 3/12/1992: 4). See also *Economikos*, 15/10/1992: 43, and Kazakos, *Economikos*, 26/12/1991: 33.

28 On several occasions: *Nea*, 25/05/1990: 14; 08/11/1990: 11; 23/02/1991: 16; 14/03/1991: 12; 20/03/1991: 11; 21/03/1991: 10' 18/10/1993: 12.

29 *Nea*, 28/05/1990: 22; 31/08/1990: 16; 28/11/1990: 10–11; 21/02/1991: 36; 15/03/1991: 26; 07/07/1993: 16.

30 See, for instance, *Nea*, 07/04/1993: 10; 06/04/1993: 10; 07/07/1993: 16; 17/07/1993: 14; 26/07/1993: 10; 12/08/1993: 12. Also *Vima*, 01/03/1992: 12.

companies sent a clear message to the government not to proceed with its privatization plans in telecommunications, electricity, railways, Olympic airways, the post office and the state-controlled banks. The unions blamed the government for not offering a comprehensive and effective modernization plan that would go beyond austerity and privatization.[31] The protests were enthusiastically endorsed by prominent PASOK politicians.[32] Andreas Papandreou repeatedly referred to the privatizations as sell-offs of national wealth to unlawful economic interests:

> The targets are crystal clear: privatization is a synonym of the sell-off of public property and national wealth to specific interests . . . Privatization is inextricably linked to economic scandals . . . it looks like 'the great feast'. In the meantime, the effort to thwart these sell-offs should be strengthened and extended to all places and peripheries of the country; it will have our unconditional support.
>
> (Talk to PASOK's Central Committee, *Nea*, 30/07/1993: 10)

PASOK publicly advocated the view that the state had to keep a strong presence and role in many areas of economic activity.[33] This involved government control of 'natural monopolies' and oligopolies such as electricity and telecommunications, the production of goods and services that have 'a predominantly social character' such as public transport, sectors of 'national-strategic importance' such as shipyards, large industrial companies that can be used as tools for government industrial policy, such as the Greek cement industry (AGET) and the large textile company of Piraiki-Patraiki, and the banking system that could channel funds to particular investment projects (Arsenis 1992; Also *Nea*, 6.4.1993: 11). These sectors were employment settings in which PASOK-affiliated unions were dominant. PASOK mobilized the reaction of employees, who were increasingly fearful of losing their jobs or their special terms of employment. The reactions to privatizations offered PASOK a chance to reinstate its dominant position in the trade unions there. At the same time, the measures proposed by PASOK for the reduction

31 For instance, OSE, the railway company, was running a deficit of 50.4 billion drachmas and received 21 billion in state subsidies; OSE's revenue only covered one third of its total expenditure: *Dimosios Tomeas*, November 1992, pp. 62–63.

32 Former Minister of Finance Tsovolas said that the privatization of the Skaramangas Shipyards was a 'sell-off' (*Nea*, 21/12/1991: 18); former Minister Mangakis called the proposed sale of shares in OTE a 'fire sale' (*Nea*, 17.7.1993: 9). See also the joint initiative by PASOK, SYN and KKE against privatization (*Nea*, 6.4.1993: 11), PASOK's statement on the privatization plan for OTE (*Nea*, 16.6.1993: 9) PASOK's former Minister of Interior Tsohatzopoulos' presence in a rally against the government's privatization program (*Nea*, 7.7.1993: 17) and his address to union members at the Aspropyrgos Refinery against the scheduled sale of the company (*Nea*, 17.7.1993: 8).

33 In a similar tone, the two left-wing parties (KKE and Synaspismos) opposed privatization and propagated the idea that public companies could operate efficiently if they were placed under meritocratic management that would involve their employees and labor unions.

of public deficits invoked the need to curb tax evasion and place emphasis on growth and the dialogue with social partners as a balanced way to achieve wage restraint.[34] There was, however, lack of clarity about how fiscal consolidation could be achieved without reforming the broader public sector.[35]

Objections to privatization were also raised by New Democracy politicians, who were part of what was known as the popular right (*laiki dexia*), as well as party-affiliated unionists who represented the interests of employees in state-owned enterprises and state-subsidized agricultural cooperatives.[36] They were alarmed by New Democracy's dramatic fall in popularity, especially among public-sector workers.[37] The New Democracy's labor organizations soon became vocal and outspoken opponents of the privatization program. Here's a characteristic announcement:

> We hope that the rumors about the privatization and [the granting of] the management [to a private investor] are just a crude mistake of the Minister [of Economy] and as such it should be turned down by the government right now. Otherwise, Thessaloniki's PET-OTE will be on the frontline of an unprecedented fight against the privatization plan.
>
> (*Nea*, 11/12/1992: 18)

Several managers of public-sector companies were also worried about their positions and expressed their concerns with privatization.[38] In a similar vein, a number of government ministers were unhappy with Mitsotakis' request to submit lists of public enterprises for privatization or closure (*Economikos*, 27/02/1992: 3). Soon a clash erupted inside the Cabinet between economically 'liberal' Andreas Andrianopoulos and Miltiades Evert (*Nea*, 24/09/1991: 2).[39] Andrianopoulos later sent a letter to the prime minister stating that he had been the target of 'entrenched interests' that were hurt by privatization, consisting of party unionists and

34 For instance, Papandreou placed emphasis on the absorption of Community funds (*Nea*, 11,11,1991: 12).

35 For instance, Vaso Papandreou, PASOK's prominent politician, defended the view that deficits for public investments were not always undesirable (*Nea*, 17/02/1992: 15).

36 As noted by *Economikos*, 22/07/1993: 15; 1/05.1997: 32. See also *Nea*, 22/05/1990: 24; 05/04/1991: 20. Miranda Xafa, economic advisor to Mitsotakis, admitted that, although there were favorable economic conditions for the implementation of a radical program in the beginning of New Democracy's term in power – for example, many foreign telecommunication companies such as the American AT&T and the Japanese NTT showed interest in the privatization of OTE – there were multiple political reactions, and some of the strongest were coming from New Democracy's politicians, *Economikos*, 01/05/1997: 32.

37 For instance, in 1993, there was a sizeable fall of 16.56 percentage points in the votes cast for New Democracy's organization in a major union of the banking sector, and a rise of 11.6 percentage points in the votes cast for PASOK's union organization (*Nea*, 26/05/1993: 17).

38 *Economikos*, 06/09/1990: 78–79; 27/02/1992: 4; 11/12/1992: 18.

39 Evert previously stated that there were no plans to privatize Olympic Airways or the state monopolies in electricity, telecommunication and railways, as well as any other company 'of national interest' (*Nea*, 24/05/1990: 17).

appointed managers of the ailing state-owned enterprises (*Vima*, 28/06/1992: 10; *Economikos* 15/08/1991: 79). Previously, the head of OAE, the organization in charge of the ailing enterprises lined up to be privatized, had resigned in protest of the fact that certain government ministers were causing delays to the implementation of the program:

> After working for more than a year I am certain that the ministers supervising the privatization policy are genuine children of statism, which is what brought them to prominence in the past, and that they cannot distance themselves from their old philosophy.
>
> (*Economikos*, 27/06/1991: 16)[40]

At the same time, the majority of the press presented the government as intransigent and callous. The mainstream press portrayed Prime Minister Mitsotakis and his shrinking circle of supporters as 'neoliberal zealots' who preferred privatization over any other effort to modernize public companies and – at the very least – turned a blind eye to issues of transparency.[41] This image was reinforced by the government's uncompromising stance in the privatization of Athens Bus Company (EAS) and the dismissal of 8000 employees in August 1992. The employees were offered the chance to buy individual buses at preferential prices, but the trade union, backed by GSEE and PASOK, rejected the scheme and staged public protests that led to clashes in the streets of Athens for several days.[42]

The privatization program was soon discredited by allegations of corruption.[43] PASOK's rhetoric was constantly talking of 'dirty sell-offs', 'the looting of national property' and 'services paid to friends and sympathizers'.[44] The selling of the AGET Cement Company, New Democracy's largest privatization, was shadowed by accusations of corruption raised by Andreas Papandreou himself. Papandreou warned the buyers that his government would scrutinize the terms of the sale in search of irregularities (*Nea*, 13/03/1992: 15). Allegations of corruption were also launched regarding the management of public-sector corporations.[45] A number of former Cabinet ministers publicly talked of 'dark' cases of possible corruption:

40 The head of the ETVA Bank, Eftyhia Pylarinou-Pipergia, sketched out the types of actors inside the public administration who raised objections to the privatization program: 1) managers and consultants who were afraid of losing their posts after the privatization, 2) government and opposition politicians who did not want to lose control over the appointment of their voters, 3) procurement contractors who did not want to lose their preferential treatment and 4) bankers and bank clerks who were fearful of penal sanctions for their involvement in the settlement of debt of the deficit-running enterprises on sale (*Economikos*, 19/12/1991: 115).

41 *Nea*, 19/11/1992: 13; *Economikos*, 22/07/1993: 15.

42 On 9 September 1992, around 100 former employees dragged some of the new owners out of their buses and stripped them of their clothes on the streets of central Athens.

43 Cf. *Nea*, 01/06/1990: 11; 03/11/1990: 8.

44 *Nea*, 05/05/1993: 5; 26/6/1993: 11. Also: *Nea*, 11/07/1990: 3; 31/10/1990: 23; 22/11/1991: 14; 28/12/1991: 16; *Vima*, 29/11/1992: 14.

45 *Economikos*, 15/08/1991: 79, referring to auditing reports and ensuing criminal persecutions.

in November 1992, Minister of Agriculture Hatzigakis resigned in protest over the government's decision to hire a private company to protect forests. A few days later he stated in an interview that 'he would have been an accomplice to a crime, had he signed the decision' (*Vima*, 29/11/1992: 1992). Former Minister of Health Sourlas also accused organized interests in pharmaceuticals of orchestrating his dismissal from the government (*Nea*, 04/12/1992: 14).

New Democracy's fall from power

The protests and reactions from the unions, the opposition and New Democracy politicians escalated when the government announced its plan to sell the management and minority shares of OTE, Greece's telecommunications monopoly. This was to be the largest and most significant privatization by New Democracy. It was seen by the trade unions affiliated with PASOK as a harbinger of a new round of privatizations involving other public utility companies (in electricity, railways, airlines, water, oil refineries, post office and state-owned banks). The union of the electricity corporation, GENOP-DEI, made an announcement talking of the prime minister's 'robbery plans' that were 'paving the way for a raid by foreign capital and the Prime Minister's company [of friends] at the expense of national wealth' (*Nea*, 24/07/1993: 7). Vaso Papandreou, PASOK MP and former European Commissioner, accused New Democracy of replacing a state monopoly with a private monopoly in telecommunications (*Economikos*, 22/07/1993). The strikes and rallies organized by the unions were already laying the ground for the incoming electoral period. Cheered by unionists and employees, Papandreou himself visited the headquarters of OTE and openly pledged to repeal the privatization agreement once back in power (*Nea*, 05/05/1993: 5). To avoid further confrontation, Minister of Economy Stefanos Manos promised that the electricity company would remain under exclusive state ownership (*Economikos*, 05/08/1993: 4).

The privatization of OTE caused a serious rift inside the governing party.[46] In a letter to the government and the party, New Democracy's unionists of OTE warned the government that they were on the point of a final break with the party (*Nea*, 15/07/1993: 8). Former Cabinet ministers Samaras and Evert openly expressed their objections to the plan (*Nea*,16/07/1993: 8 and 28.7.1993: 11). Because New Democracy had a parliamentary majority of just two seats, it was impossible for Mitsotakis to punish dissenters with expulsion from the party. The clash inside the party escalated in August 1993. In October 1993, Samaras and other MPs who had left New Democracy and founded a new party, Political Spring, withdrew their confidence in their government in protest of the handling of the 'Macedonian name' dispute. Mitsotakis resigned as prime minister, and a

46 Reportedly, the minister of defense and the minister of education were opposed to a private shareholder managing OTE (*Nea*, 08/07/1993: 6); see also *Nea*, 08/04/1993: 6; 12/07/1993: 8; 24/07/1993: 7.

fierce electoral period began.[47] Mitsotakis claimed that it was business circles dissatisfied with his privatization policies that plotted his fall from government.[48]

During the electoral campaign, PASOK criticized New Democracy for having an authoritarian and socially unjust policy record. New Democracy was dubbed 'the party of bankruptcy' that had failed to revamp the economy despite the harsh measures it had imposed on the population.[49] PASOK called the privatization program a 'fire sale' of national property and expressed its preference for state protection and subsidies.[50] PASOK's campaign created expectations amidst various social groups that fiscal policy after the election would loosen and that structural reforms in labor markets and pensions would stop:

> At last this is the end; the neoliberal parenthesis is being shut down for good. We are putting an end to the austerity policy, the high prices, the unemployment, the selling-off of national wealth, inequalities and authoritarianism. The right to hope (*sic*) is rising again.
>
> ('Greece is the vision, PASOK's campaign leaflet')[51]

PASOK's vague economic policy claimed that productivity growth for Greek industry was a viable alternative to austerity. It embraced the need for social dialogue and expressed its commitment to 'new forms of social solidarity, the completion of a new modern welfare state, a national plan for the creation of jobs, constant vocational training and job security'.[52] It was backed by most private media, which a few years ago had openly attacked Papandreou for alleged involvement in corruption.

47 It was estimated that a record-level amount of 1.5 billion drachmas was spent on political campaigning within 15 days of the announcement of the election date (*Eleftherotypia* 30/09/1993).

48 The right-wing press noted that entrepreneurs who controlled the media and had vested interests in the electricity and telecommunications state monopolies openly supported PASOK's campaign (cf. *Typos tis Kyriakis*, 03/10/1993).

49 Cf. PASOK's leaflet 'Enough is enough: there is another solution', in which PASOK criticized New Democracy for its policies that had produced 'unemployment, business closures, a dramatic reduction of income and an increase in social inequalities', and that they entailed the threat of 'commercializing the health system and selling out national property' (with direct references to the risk of privatization for the public enterprises in telecommunications, electricity, manufacturing, shipyards and public transport).

50 'We were appalled by the sell-off of our national property . . . We are demanding subsidies for new job posts, educational seminars for the young, incentives and support for new professionals and scientists, housing subsidies to new couples, support and protection for the newly employed, a stable meritocratic system of appointments in the public sector, priority in job appointments for people with special needs . . . We demand the permanent closure of the private para-universities' (PASOK's leaflet for the youth: 'Today, we turn the page: 1990–1993').

51 Cf. the article by Professor Kazakos in *Eleftherotypia*, 30/09/1993, about the high expectations PASOK's pledges had raised among its supporters.

52 'Greece is the vision', PASOK's campaign leaflet.

From a defensive position, New Democracy criticized PASOK's stance as outmoded and perilous for the economy.[53] Its campaign presented voters with a clear dilemma: a choice between reforms and 'fiscal responsibility' and PASOK's 'profligate and statist politics':

> What is that PASOK desires: power; without caring about Greece; a big public sector, because big public sector means a large scope for favors. It wants to surrender the organizations to its party members and its trade unionists. It wants to cancel the privatization process (*apokratikopoiisi*), because some will lose control over procurements . . . There was the easy way: endless promises, vote-buying, concessions, favors, appointments. This is the road PASOK knows very well. We have not followed it. We chose to stay consistent and irreconcilable with our positions, our values, our ideas. We have no fear of political cost.
>
> (New Democracy's leaflet 'Greece is not turning back')[54]

During the electoral campaign, New Democracy promised to relax its fiscal policy in the event it was re-elected to power.[55] Its electoral campaign was tainted with allegations that New Democracy's supporters had been hired to the public sector during the electoral period. This was later exposed with documents in a parliamentary discussion a few months after the party's electoral defeat in October 1993, when a New Democracy spokesman did not deny these accusations.[56]

Conclusion: the political implications of policies departing from the clientelist equilibrium

The Mitsotakis government was Greece's first encounter with an agenda of privatization and market liberalization. Its ambitious reform program came as a shock to many segments of Greek society, whose interests had been settled under

53 Minister of Interior Kouvelas stated in an interview:

> Whenever they [PASOK] exerted criticism, they asked us to implement their practices from the 80s. [PASOK] is against privatizations, they have always liked the giant-state . . . [Yet] we have not seen a new program. What its members propose is incoherent and contradictory . . . Their ideology is the same: third world socialism.
>
> (Eleftheros Typos, 05/10/1993)

54 A characteristic quote from New Democracy's electoral leaflet '5 + 5 facts you cannot dispute': 'We have to make a decision about the future of this land, the future of our children, between a strong Greece and an overly indebted Greece that is obliged to "beg" for borrowed money. We [New Democracy] have laid the foundations. At a time characterized by uncertainty and tensions, our country is safe, secure and peaceful. Now it takes strength and responsibility. Should we trust Mr. Papandreou with [governing] Greece? Will we risk it?'.

55 'We are in the position to say that the austerity is going to end', said Mitsotakis in an interview in *Eleftherotypia*, 03/10/1993. Minister of Interior Kouvelas promised 'generous increases for the public-sector employees' (*Apogevmatini* 01/10/1993 and *Makedonia*, 06/09/1993).

56 See Vyron Polydoras in Praktika Voulis, Synod A, Session ΝΓ, 02/02/1994.

the old model of political economy, and triggered a general rebellion by trade unions, the opposition and within-party factions. The stakes were high. The trade unions represented the interests of employees in public-sector companies, who were afraid that privatization would deprive them of job security, their special terms of employment and, for many of them, access to patronage benefits inside these companies. For PASOK, the privatization of the major public-sector enterprises, if it had succeeded, could have reduced PASOK's main turf for clientelism. Understandably, the privatization program became the prime target of PASOK's fierce campaign against the government. Structural reforms, privatizations and fiscal constraint marked a departure from the clientelist equilibrium, which moved New Democracy to a politically suboptimal position, triggering the dynamic reaction of organized groups in the public sector and the main opposition party. PASOK coordinated the reaction of organized unions and managed to reinvigorate its ties with its client groups there.

In addition, many aspiring New Democracy politicians distanced themselves from New Democracy's policies and built their personal leadership profile as dissenters. Government policies were further discredited by party cadres who openly expressed their objections to the efficiency of the measures and raised issues of transparency. Mitsotakis underestimated the collective-action implications of his ambitious agenda. Any fiscal gains from privatization were to be later enjoyed by the taxpayers who, at the time, were paying higher taxes under his fiscal stabilization program. But the party risked losing ground for partisan control for clientelist concessions and, possibly, corrupt dealings. Mitsotakis overlooked the fact that the majority in New Democracy had not changed its economic views in favor of state intervention and extensive distribution. For former government minister Andrianopoulos, New Democracy was far from being a 'neoliberal party'; it retained its 'old-fashioned right-wing mentality', with a few liberal views and ideas adopted (*Economikos*, 11/06/1992: 4). The editor of *Economikos* summarized the root cause of New Democracy's policy oscillations and inconsistencies:

> The party of New Democracy endorsed a smaller state . . . However, when it came to power, it realized with disdain that, in order to realize its pledge, it had to a) refrain from appointing its supporters, b) make redundant those who were not necessary, c) privatize deficit-running organizations and enterprises that should not be under state ownership anyway. All that presupposes the abolition of the clientelist system of party operation; naturally those in charge of [the party's] prospects posed a veto.
>
> (*Economikos*, 27/02/1992: 3)

In the end, most of Mitsotakis' plan of large privatizations and structural reforms was aborted, and his government failed to enact institutional changes that could have been an important redirection from Greece's economic model and a critical juncture for its clientelist system. Still, Mitsotakis' case illustrates that a program of radical reform can be initiated in an institutional environment in spite of strong path dependence, if a political leader feels that his or her own party has a lower degree of dependency on clientelist commitments embedded in the system and could make relative gains from the revision of the status quo. This is more likely in a situation of economic urgency, when the mismatch between the existing policy mix and the international context with its institutional prescriptions is felt and understood by the political leadership. Moreover, although exogenous pressure is seen as the prime force behind radical change in a path-dependent system, the Mitsotakis period highlights the importance of endogenous factors such as ideology and, possibly, strategic miscalculations when actors make decisions with imperfect information. Political choices may diverge from the 'best strategy' which a reasonably informed actor in a clientelist system would have chosen.

In that case, the governing party will clash with those who continue to expect 'increasing returns' from the established distributional channels. Any policy that threatens to limit patronage supply, either collectively to client groups or individually to its members, is likely to cause the reaction of actors situated in the opposition and the ruling party with a vivid interest in preserving the status quo. Reaction to this policy will come from both client groups that form part of the demand side of clientelism and politicians on the supply side, who will also expect significant losses. Any potential fiscal and economic gains from the reform package are dispersed and too uncertain to mobilize enough support that can counteract the strength of the social backlash. Whether dictated by the urgency of the economic condition, ideological conviction or political miscalculation, a departure from the clientelist equilibrium has negative implications for the party's unity.

Moreover, in the bipartisan political game, client groups organized in trade unions will rally around the main opposition party with whom they are affiliated. The opposition party will try to strengthen its ties with them in ways that improve its cohesion and political mobilization capacity. These two parallel developments change the relative strength of the two parties in their electoral competition. This negative outcome for the party launching this reform agenda offers useful 'feedback' to future policymakers about the perils of endorsing radical reform.

6 Clientelist bias in macroeconomic stabilization

Fiscal and monetary policy under PASOK (1993–2000)

When a major economic crisis is imminent and its outbreak is likely to occur within the government's life span, the government can no longer defer fiscal adjustment to future governments. However, the type of policies it will choose to achieve fiscal consolidation will again be defined by the terms of party competition. In a clientelist party system, the dilemma the government faces is how to implement deep-cutting reforms to avert a major fiscal and economic crisis in a way that is consistent with its commitments to client groups. In this decision-making process it can reflect on past experiences with politically successful or unsuccessful reform efforts.

The chapter reviews the stabilization program by the PASOK government between 1993 and 1999. During that period there were strong 'push' factors for reform: Greece was a candidate for entry into the European Monetary Union (EMU) which was conditional on its macroeconomic performance against the Maastricht Treaty criteria. Failure to meet these criteria could have led the country to severe macroeconomic instability and high premiums from the financial markets that could have jeopardized its public finances. On the political front, the Simitis government had proclaimed a 'modernization' agenda, and its electoral prospects were heavily dependent on securing Greece's entry into the EMU. This unique set of circumstances helps us draw some valuable lessons about what the politically optimal mix of fiscal and economic policies is when it is imperative to reform a highly clientelist economy.

The first part of this chapter presents the measures taken by the last Papandreou government. The following sections focus on macroeconomic policy implemented by Papandreou's successor, Costas Simitis. Prime Minister Simitis accelerated the pace of macroeconomic stabilization and succeeded in improving Greece's most crucial economic indices under conditions of relative social peace. However, the distribution of the costs of economic adjustment reflected political imperatives. PASOK implemented austerity measures which included wage restraint and increases in taxation, but it did not reduce the level of public spending, which could have subsequently reduced the funds available for distribution. Clientelist bias is again observed in the pattern of dispersed costs across the general population (through taxation and incomes policy) and the preservation of concentrated benefits for key client groups in the public sector. Moreover, macroeconomic stabilization heavily relied on the Bank of Greece's monetary policy and triggered a virtuous circle of disinflation and growth, aided by a not-so-inconsistent fiscal policy. Part of the program's success can also be attributed to the astute management of the expectations of social partners and investors about the prospects of the Greek economy at a time when the country was getting closer to Eurozone membership. This carefully designed policy mix enabled the government to succeed in its stabilization effort while sustaining high levels of government spending and consumption. This macroeconomic improvement made deep-cutting structural reforms less urgent to enact.

The urgent need for macroeconomic consolidation

The Greek economy in 1993 was trapped in a vicious circle of low growth and soaring public deficits.[1] After the capital market liberalization in the late 1980s and early 1990s, the government had to offer higher interest rates for its bonds to make them attractive to investors, given that Greece was suffering from a high rate of inflation and economic uncertainty.[2] High interest rates increased the cost of borrowing for both the government and the private sector. This was fuelling the level of public debt. High debt levels, in turn, kept real interest rates high, making debt servicing even more difficult and undermining private investment in productive activities.[3]

During that period, the Maastricht Treaty added a strong institutional impetus for fiscal discipline. Participation in the European Monetary Union was made conditional on the fulfillment of the Maastricht criteria for price stability, exchange rate stability, low levels of fiscal deficits and convergence on the levels of public debt among the candidate countries. Under this new regime, each candidate country was required to submit a Convergence Program for approval by the European Commission. Its implementation was annually monitored by the European Council. Stabilization was to be complemented by the implementation of structural reforms in labor, goods and capital markets, following recommendations communicated under the Broad Economic Policy Guidelines (BEPGs) and the Open Method of Coordination.

The stakes were high for Greece. Failure to stabilize its economy and exclusion from the monetary union (EMU) meant economic uncertainty about the prospects of the economy, leading to higher interest rates for government borrowing and, possibly, monetary and fiscal instability. This prospect was to have a negative impact on the careers of the political leaders who were responsible for economic policy at the time. Entry to the EMU was expected to trigger the

1 Ioannis Boutos, governor of the Bank of Greece, admitted that the Greek economy continued to face stagflation and severe fiscal imbalances (*Nea*, 17/01/1994: 10). In his annual report, the governor stated that large deviations from the 1993 budgetary targets had reversed the progress in deficit reduction achieved in 1992.

2 Monetary financing of public sector borrowing (PSBR) was prohibited in 1994.

3 In 1994, debt service amounted to 30.3% of total government expenditure (14.1% of GDP).

opposite effect – a virtuous circle of falling interest rates and inflation, with better terms of servicing public debt and an improved climate for private investment. Entry was thought to prevent, once and for all, speculative capital investment driven by fears of exchange-rate volatility. This prospect also enjoyed widespread interparty consensus as part of the political vision of Greece's integration into an ever-closing European Union.[4] Pure economic concerns, however, such as whether the Monetary Union was an optimum currency area, were not extensively discussed. Instead, the two main parties expected that the 'spill-over' dynamic of European integration would later lead to stronger transfer mechanisms within the EU.

PASOK's political dilemma

PASOK's electoral victory in 1993 with 47% of the votes gave the third government of Andreas Papandreou a strong parliamentary majority. PASOK's voters were now expecting the new government to honor the numerous promises the party had made while in opposition to restore much of what the Mitsotakis policies had previously undone – most of all, putting an end to austerity and securing government control over public-sector companies. At the same time, persisting high levels of inflation, a fall in private investment, fears of capital flight and rising unemployment made it increasingly difficult for the government to borrow cheap to refinance its debt obligations. Urgent fiscal policy measures were needed to prevent a macroeconomic crisis. High levels of debt and deficit meant that large primary surpluses were required to restore fiscal balance for a long period (at around 6% of GDP). Moreover, failure to act in accordance with the European Union's policy prescriptions could jeopardize the Greek government's bargaining position, above all, in its negotiations for a share of the EU funds for infrastructure works and investment in public enterprises.[5]

With contradictory political expectations and economic imperatives, macroeconomic stabilization understandably became a source of political anxiety for PASOK's leadership. Wide-sweeping reforms could alienate its support base and undermine the cohesion of the party that was highly attached to the unreformed broader public sector. To appease any reactions, PASOK could invoke the scale of the economic difficulties ahead and could put the blame for the current economic conditions on New Democracy's record in power. But it was now this government's responsibility to stabilize the state of public finances and put the Greek economy on a path to recovery. Moreover, since October 1993, New Democracy had a new leader, Miltiades Evert, who was distancing the party's ideology from the so-called 'neoliberal' philosophy of former Prime Minister

4 In the Greek Parliament, only the Communist Party opposed Greece's membership in the EU.

5 The European Union in its annual reform warned the Greek government that the flow of resources from the Cohesion Fund would be interrupted if the government failed to pursue policies to achieve the targets set up by the Stabilization Program (*Economikos*, 24/08/1995: 83).

Mitsotakis. Increasing speculation that a new election could take place in the spring of 1995, in the event that the Parliament would not be able to elect a new president of the republic, was making PASOK's dilemma even more pressing.

Spreading out the costs of adjustment: hard drachma policy and increased taxation

In 1994 the Papandreou government submitted a revised stabilization program in line with the policy requirements of the Maastricht Treaty. The program was adopted by the Council of Finance Ministers (ECOFIN) on 19 September 1994 and prioritized disinflation that was expected to lead to lower interest rates, which would then make borrowing and debt servicing easier. Anti-inflationary policy mostly relied on a '*hard drachma*' exchange-rate policy implemented by the Bank of Greece. This choice reflected the shift in the early 1990s away from the expansionary monetary policy that had used an inflationary money supply to help the government pay its public deficit liabilities toward a tight monetary policy that was thought to curb inflation and soon bring lower interest rates in open market transactions. At the same time, the program predicted high levels of GDP growth (partially driven by lower interest rates as the result of lower inflation) as the way to reduce the ratio of public debt as a percentage of GDP in the coming years. It was feared, however, that an exchange rate set to support a hard currency, which initially required the Bank of Greece to maintain high interest rates, would contradict the government's expectation of economic recovery because this policy could have a possibly negative short-term effect on investment (*Economikos*, 13/01/1994: 15). The government was willing to take that risk. It held the view that as long as inflation started falling, market confidence would bring interest rates down. Besides, the hard-currency policy was thought not to generate important political losses (*Economikos*, 07/03/1996: 17).

Next to the anti-inflationary monetary policy, Papandreou sought to increase state revenue instead of lowering the level of public spending. This option diffused the cost of adjustment across taxpayers and helped the government avoid implementing deep-cutting reductions in public spending which could harm its core support groups in the public sector. Other social and economic side effects from increasing taxation were largely dismissed (cf. Ioannis Stournaras, *Vima*, 31/12/1995: 12).

The government also made an effort to expand the tax base. A law in May 1994 established 'objective criteria' for the presumption of taxable income of entrepreneurs and independent professionals (lawyers, doctors). The measure was justified as a response to the failure of the 1992 reduction of tax brackets to curb tax evasion, when the New Democracy government claimed that it was introducing a more 'realistic' rate of taxation (*Vima*, 17/12/1995: 4).[6] Tax brackets were

6 The same law raised the income level for each tax bracket and the tax rate for the highest bracket from 40% to 45%.

not adjusted to internalize inflation-adjusted raises in taxable incomes (*Economikos*, 21/12/1995: 155). As a result, the tax burden was mostly spread across middle-income taxpayers. However, the inadequate organization of the tax authorities undermined the effort to collect more tax (*Economikos*, 21/12/1995: 155). By the end of 1995, the disappointing record of state revenue led the government to increase indirect taxes despite the anticipated negative effect on inflation (*Vima*, 21/01/1996: 2). Finally, the government implemented a relatively tight incomes policy in the public sector and reached an agreement with the unions for wage restraint in the private sector.[7]

Avoiding a clash with the party base: structural reforms and public spending

PASOK's reliance on taxation and monetary policy helped the party avoid the kind of political confrontation that had wrecked the Mitsotakis government. Papandreou halted structural reforms and the privatization process, keeping a clear distance from the policy prescriptions suggested by the IMF and the OECD (cf. *Economikos*, 21/10/1993: 17). Faced with criticism for the absence of structural reforms,[8] the government justified state intervention as part of a gradualist approach that was sensitive to social policy concerns.[9] For instance, Minister of Economy Yannos Papantoniou noted:

> My own estimate is that New Democracy had gone too fast with liberalization or, in any case, faster in relation to what the market could sustain and in relation to the policies by New Democracy for competition. You know, the same thing happened in England with Thatcher where speculation phenomena appeared when 'the lid was lifted' – If I may use that phrase.
>
> (*Economikos*, 19/01/1995: 17)

The government also argued that a sudden drop in public spending would stifle growth and would trigger a surge in unemployment. However, because the additional tax revenue was channeled to public spending, domestic demand was simply recycled through government taxation and redistribution. The high level of public spending was funded by increases in taxation. The cancellation of the Mitsotakis' privatization program put additional pressure on public finances. A great deal of the revenue from additional taxation was channeled to the broader public sector. The government further burdened its budget by assuming the cost

7 The government kept the increase in public-sector wages and pensions to levels slightly below the rate of inflation (*Economikos*, 25/06/1996: 15).

8 The European Commission repeatedly criticized the government for its failure to reduce appointments in the public sector and for delays and omissions in the privatization program. (Cf. reports by the IMF report and the Industrialists' Association, *Economikos*, 24/08/1995: 83.)

9 Cf. the Under-Secretary of Finance: 'everyone admits that the state must interfere so that the whole economic balance is not disrupted' (*Economikos*, 30/11/1995: 128).

of its 'modernization plans' for public companies such as the Olympic Airways and the ETVA Bank (the Industrial Development Bank), with 450 and 250 billion drachmas, respectively, in 1994, and by hiring new personnel that added approximately 100 billion drachmas (*Economikos*, 09/12/1995).

The Papandreou government had no plans to reduce the size of public employment and instead, increased spending for wages by hiring new public-sector employees.[10] The government failed to comply with its prior commitment to hire one new employee in place of two who retired (*Vima*, 30/04/1995: 3). Although PASOK could no longer engage in new massive public employment appointments or heavy extra spending, it appointed party cadres in senior public offices following a clientelist logic.[11] Moreover, government officials cultivated expectations of higher wage increases in the coming years (*Vima*, 30/04/1995: 3). Prime Minister Papandreou publicly denounced the term austerity as an accurate description for the 1996 budget (*Economikos*, 23/11/1995: 107). The Minister of National Economy declared that

> . . . there is neither a social nor an economic justification for extending the austerity for public employees . . . It is impossible to have shrinking incomes for salaried workers, at a time when there is an explosion of business profits especially for the big companies.
>
> (*Vima*, 30/04/1995: 3)

The Bank of Greece repeatedly warned against the idea that fiscal profligacy could boost domestic demand (*Vima*, 30/04/1995: 7). It reminded that sustainable economic growth depended on macroeconomic stability and structural reforms to increase competitiveness (Governor of Bank of Greece in *Economikos*, 25/05/1995: 14). The governor of the bank urged the government to curb public spending in order to build fiscal credibility and gain the trust of markets and called for more transparency and efficiency in the public sector to save resources (*Economikos*, 05/05/1994: 13).

At the end of 1995, there was an alarming increase in the level of spending in public corporations and social security funds (*Economikos*, 01/02/1996: 16). Subsidies to social security funds and public transport organizations continued to account for a large part of government expenditure. Public debt also increased, as the debt was transferred from the broader public sector to general government.[12] The government assumed the debts of the public radio and television corporation (ERT, 400 billion drachmas), the Skaramangas Shipyards (80 billion) and Athens Transport Company (OASA, 550 billion) and covered the special reduction of

10 By 256 billion drachmas in 1996, *Vima*, 03/12/1995: 19.

11 For instance, it was common practice that many politicians who had failed to get elected were appointed as heads of public enterprises (cf. *Nea*, 19/10/1993: 19).

12 In 1993 4,810 billion drachmas, in 1994 1,493 billion. This transfer was drastically limited in 1995 to 225 billion drachmas (*Vima*, 03/12/1995: 28).

oil prices offered to farmers (60 billion) and additional spending for healthcare (120 billion) (*Economikos*, 25/05/1995: 15).

In that environment, it is clear that political priorities defined the pattern of stabilization. The prospect of a new election ahead led a number of PASOK cadres to push the Ministry of the Economy to relax fiscal austerity (*Vima*, 30/04/1995: 3; *Economikos*, 28/09/1995: 20). In response, the budget for 1996 presented the familiar pattern of increased taxation with a rise in expenditure higher than the rate of inflation (9.5% against a predicted rate of inflation at 5%). It included new rises in income and indirect taxes (on automobiles, state bonds and foreign exchange deposits), the abolition of certain tax exemptions and the tightening of transfers and subsidies (*Economikos*, 30/11/1995: 131). The additional tax revenue was channeled to public spending. The cost of the 'modernization programs' for public-sector companies in 1996 was set to increase by 78%. There were also generous increases in research and development (R&D) spending, education and healthcare, part of which was channeled to public contracts for the construction of new schools and hospitals (*Vima*, 03/12/1995: 19). Six billion drachmas were to be spent on rehiring previously dismissed employees whose contracts were not renewed by the previous government (*Vima*, 03/12/1995: Δ20). In contrast, public investment funds were cut by 50 billion (*Economikos*, 23/11/1995: 107).

On the opposite side, New Democracy's economic policy proposals were ambiguous. Its criticism and pre-electoral proposals in 1995 called for increases in public investment, education, healthcare spending and agricultural pensions; a small relaxation of incomes policy; and a small budgetary reserve (*Vima*, 24/12/1995: 4). This extra spending was to be funded by the reduction of government's 'wasteful' activities and subsidies (*Vima*, 17/12/1995: 4).

Limited progress in macroeconomic stabilization

Under strong pressures for fiscal discipline, the Papandreou government halted major privatizations and did not launch structural reforms that could have harmed its clientelist party base.[13] Anti-inflationary measures mildly affected wages and pensions in the public sector, and lower inflation made it easier for the unions to tolerate a higher level of taxation (*Nea*, 19/10/1993: 19). Public enterprises, on the other hand, the main sources of public spending, remained unreformed in line with PASOK's pre-electoral commitments to its syndicated clientele. Employees in the broader public sector continued to enjoy better terms of employment and extra financial benefits. The operation of the broader public sector under these terms undermined the target of reducing government expenditure and improving the country's competitiveness.

13 Privatization included the sale of state-owned casinos, which gave the government 20 billion drachmas (*Economikos*, 25/05/1995: 15).

For all its policy inconsistencies, however, the Papandreou government succeeded in preventing further economic deterioration. It controlled the growth of primary spending and achieved a primary surplus, mainly through taxation. Between 1993 and 1996 there was considerable improvement in public finances; the deficit fell as a percentage of GDP from 14.2% in 1993 to 7.6% in 1996 (*Economikos*, 12/09/1996: 16), the inflation rate in 1996 fell to the lowest point in 24 years, and there was a sizeable rise in the level of investment, partly in response to the decline of inflation and interest rates (*Vima*, 31/12/1995: 11). Part of the economic recovery was attributed to public investment funded by the Community.

Lower inflation rates, the emergence of primary surpluses and the small reduction in debt improved the business climate. Consumption levels and export performance remained stable (*Vima*, 31/12/1995: 11). Industrial production slightly recovered after 8 consecutive years. Public finances withstood the full deregulation of capital movement in the EU and the loss of Greece's capacity to monetize its public debt (as noted by economist Stournaras in *Vima*, 22/01/1995: 8). The drachma survived the turbulences of the 1994 international currency crises. By the beginning of 1995, reports by international organizations and the Commission were acknowledging the progress achieved in fiscal consolidation in Greece. The 1994 OECD report endorsed the Bank of Greece's anti-inflationary policy, but it remained critical of the omission of consecutive Greek governments to implement structural reforms to address persisting macroeconomic imbalances.

Despite its relative success, the convergence program exhibited significant deviations from its initial targets. Inflation did not fall below the rate of 10%, and the budgetary target for public borrowing was not met. Central government debt reached 123.8% of GDP instead of the projected 120.8%.[14] The government failed to hold back deficit spending in several public organizations and corporations. Instead, it had to curtail the public investment budget and lose a share of EU funds that were attached to it. The government reportedly used creative accounting tactics by transferring certain government expenses to the public enterprises budget or transferring the extra spending directly to public debt figures without making them appear as part of the year's deficit (*Economikos*, 21/09/1995: 15; 19/11/1995: 41). Subsidies to public enterprises were recorded as extra public debt for the ensuing fiscal years.

Fiscal policy under Simitis

In January 1996 Andreas Papandreou resigned as prime minister while he was hospitalized in critical condition. PASOK's parliamentary team elected Costas Simitis as the new prime minister. Six months later, following Papandreou's death, Simitis was elected the leader of the party, with a narrow margin of votes over his main rival, Akis Tsohatzopoulos. His victory was interpreted as a fragile

14 Ministry of Economy, *Fiscal Management Bulletin*, 22/04/1996.

yet important realignment for the party away from its left-wing and populist segment and towards the self-proclaimed 'modernizing' faction. To reconfirm his position as prime minister with a fresh electoral mandate, Simitis called an early election in September 1996. PASOK's electoral victory showed that the party could remain united after its founder's death and that its popularity had not been harmed by the prolonged period of macroeconomic stabilization.

The political cost of failure to enter the EMU

Under the banner of 'modernization' PASOK took the mandate to lead Greece to the European Monetary Union (*Economikos*, 13/11/1997: 28). The prospect of Greece's entry into the EMU was popular with the public.[15] Simitis presented himself as the prime minister who could take Greece to an economically united Europe and hoped to win the next election once the target of EMU membership was accomplished (*Nea*, 14/03/1998).[16] The government referred to EMU membership as an issue of national importance for which the Greeks had to endure a last round of financial 'sacrifices'.

For the Simitis government, Greece's entry into the EMU became its main political priority. It was feared that Greece's failure to enter the EMU could bring about a 'punishment-from-the markets' event, which could have triggered a vicious circle of high interest rates, high inflation, high deficits and, possibly, currency depreciation, with higher risk premiums levied on Greek businesses to cover the foreign exchange fluctuations of the drachma. Greater prices for servicing the debt could then cause fiscal derailment and greater economic uncertainty. Long-term foreign investment would be channeled to countries with stable currencies and macroeconomic environment, and Greece would be able only to attract speculative short-term capital investment. In that event, the Bank of Greece, while retaining the liberty to determine interest rates, would be obliged to set interest rates higher than the EMU rates in order to placate fears of imminent currency depreciation, and this could harm the Greek economy. On the political front, it was thought that failure to enter the EMU would have a devastating impact on the political career of the prime minister and his close allies in government.[17]

These calculations indicated that despite the anticipated political cost of stabilization policies, the path to fiscal consolidation and economic reform was much preferable than policy inertia and the risk of a systemic collapse. In the

15 An opinion poll showed that an overwhelming majority of Greeks were in favor of the euro as a new currency for Greece – at 77% (among the five highest) compared with 72% in 11 candidate countries and 68% in the EU-15 (European Commission published in *Vima*, 15/11/1998).

16 'We are admitted to EMU on our own merits, thanks to the sacrifices of the Greek people; nobody has given it to us like a gift; we have made it happen', said Simitis (*Nea*, 15/02/1999).

17 *Kathimerini* illustrates Simitis' personal stake in securing Greece's entry into the Eurozone: 'Mr. Simitis prefers to fight for [the next] parliamentary election with the ticket of EMU at hand . . . The Prime Minister believes that, if he secures Greece's entry to Eurozone in the most official way, he will reverse the climate and will be able to successfully take part in the battle for power' (*Kathimerini*, 10/01/1999).

Table 6.1 Main characteristics of Simitis' macroeconomic policy

a) Emphasis on creating disinflationary expectations and building confidence in the economy, mostly through tight monetary policy that contributed to exchange-rate–based disinflation
b) Fiscal consolidation based on raising revenue through taxation and partial privatization
c) Modest and inconsistent incomes policy
d) Relative social stability with an agreement with social partners on wage restraint
e) Postponement of deeper structural reforms for the period after accession
f) Little progress in curbing the level of public spending
g) Limited reform of public enterprises and organizations

words of Minister of Finance Papadopoulos, the country would otherwise face 'a menace to its own survival' (*Economikos*, 30/11/1995: 128):

> Even if Maastricht hadn't existed, we should have adopted a Convergence Program regardless of which way European Integration is heading to. We live in a competitive society; therefore, fiscal adjustment is a matter of survival.
> (*Economikos*, 30/11/1995: 7)

Moreover, the government had to show some improvement in public finances during the stabilization period in order to be entitled to receive Community funds (the so-called Cohesion and Structural Funds).[18] Finally, a coherent effort for macroeconomic stabilization under a clear benchmark could serve as a signal to investors that the Greek government was now committed to sound economic policies (see Table 6.1).

Fiscal consolidation

By the mid-1990s, the leaderships of both PASOK and New Democracy had accepted that macroeconomic stabilization was the country's first policy priority.[19] The main target was to lower the rate of inflation, which would later bring down interest rates and could greatly help the government service the soaring public debt, which by the mid-1990s came to absorb around 35% of the government

18 Minister of Economy Papantoniou noted that unless there was considerable progress with fiscal consolidation and deficit reduction in accordance with the Convergence Program, there was the risk that Community funding would be discontinued (*Vima*, 17/11/1996: 10. See also *Economikos*, 01/08/1996: 15).

19 Under-Secretary of Finance Christodoulakis defended the strength of this policy mix:

> At this point, we should note that the recent de-escalation of interest rates in Greece is to a large extent attributable to the credibility of the economic policy and the gradual stabilization of basic macroeconomic figures. This fall lowers the cost of borrowing for consumers, businessmen and workers and has a direct positive impact on the whole of the economy.
> (*Economikos*, 26/12/1996: 37)

budget. For that purpose, the Simitis government had limited policy tools. The liberalization of capital movement had weakened government control over interest rates which, in turn, had made debt servicing difficult to manage. Monetizing deficits through expansionary monetary policies could backfire by fueling inflation. Moreover, among the most crucial issues was how the government would tackle the debt generated by public companies.

Like its predecessor, Simitis heavily relied on tight monetary policy, moderate fiscal austerity and tax increases. Tight monetary policy contributed to lowering inflation, leading to lower real borrowing costs. Fiscal policy succeeded in increasing tax revenue by 21% between 1995 and 1996 through higher tax rates, new taxes, the abolition of tax exemptions and improvements in the tax-collecting capacity. New taxes were also imposed on business, stock exchange sales and bond yields, whereas some tax deductions were cut. The tax policy mainly burdened salaried workers and pensioners who could not hide their income from the tax authorities. Not surprisingly, the government was regularly under attack for heavily targeting these social groups for tax purposes. In response, the government introduced a new electronic system of collecting and processing tax information, *taxis*, to facilitate the collection of taxes, but a great deal of extra revenue was still coming from one-off regulatory arrangements between tax-evading taxpayers and the tax authority over the final closure of their outstanding cases.

Just like Papandreou's early policies, the policy mix by the Simitis government during the first 2 years exhibited noticeable inconsistencies. There was considerable progress in terms of fiscal consolidation because public expenditure rose at a rate smaller than public revenue. Some savings were also made thanks to the drop in interest rates. But progress with reducing spending in the broader public sector was limited. Although the pace at which public spending was increasing was now lower than before, public spending remained stable as percentage of (a growing) GDP. The education and healthcare budgets were increased considerably. Expenditures on special social policy measures, such as the payment of low pensions and child benefits, also increased generously (*Vima*, 8/12/1996: 3). This policy mix failed to curb tax evasion, curtail public spending and stick to the declared target of incomes policy in the public sector. Just like the Papandreou government, the Simitis government was criticized for its emphasis on raising government revenue instead of reducing the level of public spending.[20] The governor of the Bank of Greece, Lucas Papademos, stated this clearly:

> Greater emphasis should be given to the reduction of primary spending with restraint in the operational costs of the public sector and [its] subsidies combined with a more effective control over public organizations.
>
> (*Economikos*, 24/10/1996: 22)

20 The Bank of Greece warned in its reports that the policy mix was ineffective without further restraint in public spending, wages and pensions. In addition, structural rigidities on the supply side were undermining the stabilization effort (see Bank of Greece Reports for between 1996 and 1999, and *Economikos*, 23/05/1996: 15; 01/05/1997: 25; *Vima*, 27/04/1997: 2; 21/02/1999: 7; 06/05/2000: 35; *Nea*, 06/04/1998: 46).

Although macroeconomic stabilization required the government to radically reform the broader public sector, the government did little to reform the companies it controlled and curb wasteful spending there. The average salary for public-sector workers rose slightly above the predicted rate of inflation. Deficits run by state-owned companies rose from 486 billion drachmas in 1995 to 961.8 billion at the end of 1996, putting an extra burden on public debt.[21] Most government ministries and agencies were unwilling to have their budgets cut. For instance, when ministers were asked to submit a budget before the preparation of the annual budget of 1996, most of them failed to submit one and refused to propose cuts as requested by the Ministry of Finance (*Economikos*, 10/08/1995: 13). There were rumors that certain Cabinet ministers were putting pressure on the minister of finance to exempt their portfolios from spending cuts (Ibid). Not surprisingly, it was questioned whether the government had the willingness 'to overcome the usual clash between rhetoric and action, between macroeconomic policy announcements and actual microeconomic policy (*Economikos*, 07/03/1996: 17).[22] As a political commentator, Nikos Nikolaou noted in the politically centrist newspaper *Vima* that it had to constrain 'the profligate and demanding nomenclature that forms the body of PASOK' (29/12/1996: 2).

The 1997 budget sought to partially change this fiscal policy trend. Primary public spending increased at lower pace compared with the previous year,[23] whereas the level of subsidies to local councils, pension funds and other state-funded entities was constrained. The number of new appointments in the public sector was also limited. Minister of Economy Papantoniou called the 1997 budget 'the first to try [to implement] a sharp cut in expenditure', but he expressed his fear that state officials would resist its implementation (*Vima*, 24/11/1996: 4).[24] In fact, the implementation of the 1997 budget was also derailed by wage increases higher than the predicted level (*Vima*, 26/10/1997: 24).[25] Public utility corporations continued to rely on heavy external borrowing, which remained a main source of macroeconomic imbalances. Once again, the government had to cut public investment to lower primary spending (*Economikos*, 23/04/1998: 22).[26]

21 However, part of the boost in Greece's growth rates was attributed to the investment program of these deficit-running companies (*Economikos*, 12/12/1996: 56).

22 'While Mr. Papadopoulos [the Under-Secretary of Finance] "is resisting" pressures to raise low pensions that would cost the budget 110 billion drachmas, he happily keeps the Eleusis Shipyards under state control at a cost of 148 billion drachmas . . . Similarly, we observe the selective "resistance" with regard to the cost of "modernizing" ETVA (more than 1.5 trillion drachmas in the last three years), Olympic Airways, the Skaramangas Shipyards, Piraiki Patraiki [textiles] company etc.' (Dimitris Stergiou in *Economikos*, 07/03/1996: 87).

23 This was 7.5% in 1997 compared with 14% in 1996, close to the rate of inflation.

24 'The crucial problem is [for the Prime Minister] to check and discipline the wasteful and spoilt nomenclature which, without any constraints, has led the state coffers to bankruptcy' (*Vima*, 24/11/1996: 4).

25 There were also unfavorable international fluctuations in the price of oil and food commodities during that time.

26 The 1998 budget substantially raised spending for defense and social policies higher than the rate of inflation. Public spending in 1999 increased at 4.3% of GDP (*Kathimerini*, 17/09/1999: 25).

The government's tax policy paid scant attention to the impact that higher taxes had on productive activity. Increased taxation in what was initially a stagnant economy put extra pressure on business activity – a tendency that worried the European Commission (*Vima*, 06/12/1998: 8). The 1998 report by the Bank of Greece governor warned that the government's increasing overreliance on direct and indirect taxation was undermining the country's international competitiveness. Taxes pushed the inflation rate upwards and might have contributed to the rise of unemployment throughout the stabilization period. Moreover, increased taxation loosened the incentives for fiscal constraint. Although rising taxation generated excessive state revenue beyond the initial expectations, most of the extra taxed revenue was used to cover the rising levels of public spending. Once again, the Bank of Greece called for structural reforms and further deficit reduction (*Economikos*, 07/05/1998: 26).

By the end of 1998, the scope for further taxation had been exhausted, following a significant rise of public revenue as a percentage of GDP far beyond the budgetary predictions for the years 1998 and 1999 (Bank of Greece 1999: 32). In response, the government lowered a number of indirect taxes in 1999 to offer some financial relief and reduce the impact they had on the level of inflation (*Kathimerini*, 17/09/1999: 25). In 2000, the government announced a package of tax breaks costing 270 billion drachmas, or 0.7% of GDP (*Athens News*, 11/10/2000). The revenue losses were expected to be covered by the new revenue generated thanks to higher annual growth rates.

Finally, the government's incomes policy was also inconsistent. The Bank of Greece noted a significant rise in gross wages and labor costs for 1996, with higher increases recorded in the public sector with a generous rise at 15.6%, whereas real wages in manufacturing fell (*Vima*, 27/04/1997: 2). In the following year, wage increases for public-sector employees were much lower (around 2.5%), causing the reaction of the public-sector trade union, ADEDY (Civil Servants' Confederation; *Vima*, 19/10/1997: 7). In 1998, the government had to further tighten its incomes policy to reach its inflation target and sponsored an agreement between employers and private-sector unions (the 'social partners') for wage restraint. To persuade the unions to accept low nominal wage increases, the government invoked its target to lower inflation as part of the country's effort to meet the Maastricht Treaty's benchmark for EMU membership. As a result, per-unit labor costs declined in 1998 and 1999. In addition, several state-controlled enterprises lowered their bills in tune with the government's anti-inflationary policy. There was also a considerable rise in investment by public-sector companies in telecommunications, electricity, oil, railways and air transport (*Economikos*, 23/04/1998: 23).[27]

Despite the inconsistencies of the policy mix, there were soon obvious signs of macroeconomic consolidation. The improved economic climate was manifested in a sharp drop in real interest rates in 1997 (*Vima*, 26/10/1997: 24), and the

27 The 1999 budget raised public investment by 22%.

economy withstood fears of capital flight in the aftermath of the Asian financial crisis (*Economikos*, 13/11/1997: 22). By the end of 1999 the vicious circle of macroeconomic instability and economic decline had turned into a virtuous circle of lower deficits, lower inflation and higher growth. This change was aided by the government's improved creditworthiness, thanks to its tight monetary policy and the country's better fiscal performance. A tight monetary policy helped lower inflation rates, which led to a further de-escalation of real interest rates for both the public and the private sectors. The fall of interest rates removed part of the burden of debt servicing. Lower interest payments saved the government billions of drachmas.[28] Despite the significant increase in taxation, lower interest rates, low inflation and the elimination of currency risk reduced economic uncertainty for investors, too, and gave a boost to economic activity. Greece saw healthy growth rates for the first time after 20 years and, thanks to higher growth rates, public-sector deficits declined as a percentage of GDP.[29]

On 16 March 1998 the drachma entered the European Rate Mechanism at 357 drachmas per European Currency Unit (ECU) and was later depreciated to 340.75 drachmas per euro in January 2000. Greece's entry into this mechanism protected the drachma against speculative pressures when, on 25 March 1998, the European Commission announced that Greece did not fulfill the Maastricht Criteria for entry into EMU on the first wave and deferred the case to a new assessment to take place in 2000. The June 1998 ECOFIN report recognized the 'remarkable' progress that Greece had made in tackling its macroeconomic imbalances. Two years later, in 2000, the European Commission and the European Central Bank (ECB) approved the country's entry into the EMU in 2001. Although Greece fell short of meeting the Maastricht Criteria, the decision reflected the political approval by the EU countries of the economic and institutional progress Greece had achieved.

This political decision overlooked the fact that the stabilization program was tainted with the extensive use of accounting tricks that had been employed to 'hide' debt, such as three revisions of GDP upwards, which resulted in a smaller recorded share of debt in GDP, the transferring of debt from the year's deficit accounts, a tendency to underrate expenses in the budget and overestimate revenue (with the exception of 1998 and 1999) and the capitalization of interest-rate payments, which were not properly calculated in the deficit account.[30] Debt from state guarantees for the unpaid loans of public corporations and ailing state-owned

28 The Commission's report noted that 30% of deficit reduction by 9.2 percentage points between 1993 and 1997 was attributed to the recorded drop in interest rates, whereas the rest of the reduction was equally attributed to new government revenue and cuts in public spending (*Economikos*, 23/04/1998: 22).

29 From 11.3% in 1994 to 6.5% in 1997.

30 'These accounting arrangements and omissions do not promote fiscal transparency and credibility, but they cast a shadow on the success recorded in other sections of fiscal management' (IOBE Report, *Economikos*, 23/05/1996: 15). See also *Economikos* 09/05/1996: 87; 23/05/1996: 15; 03/10/1996: 13 28/11/1996: 24; *Vima*, 20/04/1997: 4, 23/11/1997: 18.

companies remained 'hidden' from the budgetary record of annual deficits. The government set up a public enterprise (DEKA: Public Company for Mobile Assets) to buy stocks and bonds of these corporations in secondary markets in order to lower the amount of direct transfers and the recorded debt of the broader public sector by several billion drachmas. Instead of issuing government bonds to fund public organizations, the government allowed them to sell shares in the stock exchange, which DEKA bought. These indirect state subsidies were not recorded as public debt (*Economikos*, 11/11/1999: 30). Years later it was revealed that the Simitis government and the US-based investment bank Goldman Sachs had agreed on a swap of a 10-billion euro loan originally denominated in yen. Goldman Sachs' swap converted the original loan into euros based on lower rates, which reduced its nominal value by 2.8 billion euros, and issued a bond by which Goldman Sachs was to receive annual payments of 360 million euros until 2019 (*The Guardian*, 18.02.2010). Creative accounting helped the Greek government 'hide' the real level of public debt. This was known to PASOK's opponents. The former leader of New Democracy, Miltiades Evert, accused the government of becoming a 'master' in creative accounting compared with any previous government:

> Of course, there have always been alchemies to present a reduced deficit level. This vicious trend had now gone too far. Accounting tricks have assumed unprecedented proportions. The current government feels there's no need to keep up appearances.
>
> (*Vima*, 23/11/1997: 18)

Bias in the design and implementation of stabilization policies

Like the Papandreou government, macroeconomic policy under Simitis followed the familiar pattern of *concentrated benefits and dispersed costs*. This is clear in the extensive use of monetary policy and the preferred pattern of fiscal consolidation. The two initial 'pillars' of this virtuous circle of stabilization, monetary policy and taxation, diffused the costs of fiscal adjustment among the population. Lower inflation was achieved mostly through a tight monetary policy, whereas fiscal consolidation heavily relied on increased state revenue and the effect of lower inflation on interest rates. Macroeconomic consolidation later helped economic recovery, thanks to increasing private investment boosted by low inflation, low interest rates and the Community funds that revamped both public and private consumption. Between 1996 and 1999 the level of public deficit fell spectacularly (both as a percentage of GDP and in nominal value).[31] Much of the reduction was the result of the significant drop in interest rates (from 8% to

31 Public deficit as a percentage of GDP was reported to have been reduced from 15.9% in 1990 to 3.1% in 1998 and 1.6% in 1999, below the 3% threshold of the Maastricht Treaty.

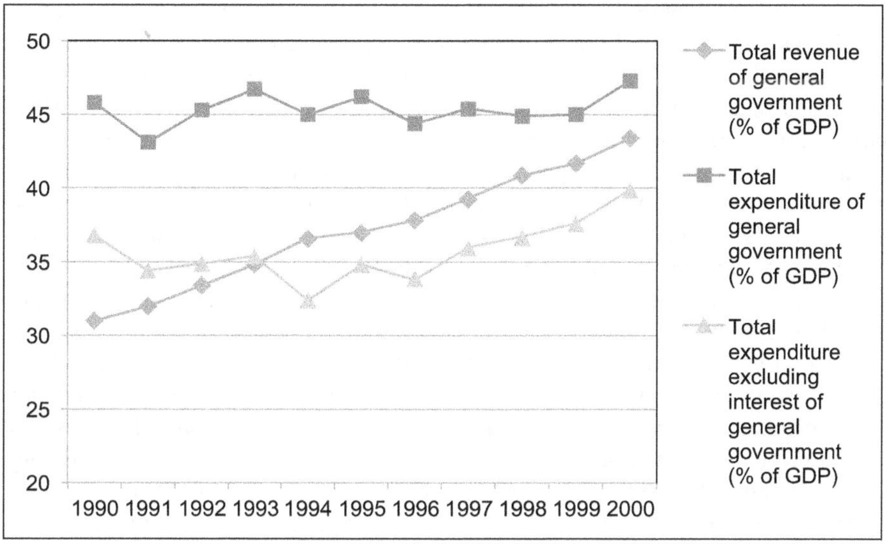

Figure 6.1 Revenue, expenditure and interest rates (1990–2000)
Source: Bank of Greece numbers (several years).

around 3.5%) following the fall of the inflation rate. Public debt was stabilized at around 100% of GDP by 1999 from 114% in 1993.[32] Government spending as a percentage of a growing GDP remained almost unaltered but increased in absolute numbers.[33] The moderation of the rate of increase in public spending was mostly the result of the falling cost of debt servicing thanks to lower interest rates and inflation (see Figure 6.1).

Results were less impressive on the side of government spending, mostly due to increased spending for government wages and subsidies to pension funds and public enterprises. The government did little to restructure deficit-running enterprises and restrain wages in the broader public sector below the inflation rate (*Vima*, 21/01/1996: 2). It continued to grant subsidies to Olympic Airways, DEI, ETVA Bank (Industrial Development Bank), public transport companies and the Skaramangas Shipyards. These were areas where most of PASOK's political supporters were concentrated. Indirect transfers took the form of recapitalization of deficit-running public enterprises such as ERT (state radio and television) and the ETVA Bank.[34] The government made little effort to move away from the long

32 See Annual Reports by the Bank of Greece for 1994 and 2000.

33 The reduction of central government spending was notably small, from 48.8% of GDP in 1993 to 46.4% in 2000. Moreover, primary spending as a percentage of GDP rose by 3.2 percentage points between 1994 and 2000 (Manessiotis and Reischauer 2001: 133).

34 The Bank of Greece repeatedly noted that new transfers were irreconcilable with the country's fiscal situation (*Vima*, 30/06/1995: 7; and 05/03/1996: 12; 27/04/1997: 18; 26/04/2000: 4).

tradition of governments covering the losses of public enterprises, either directly or through loan guarantees.[35] The assumption by the government of the debt of public companies since the mid-1990s led to a sizeable increase in public debt.[36]

In general, the main reason behind preserving high levels of public spending under heavy taxation was not to boost growth, but to keep the level of redistribution intact. Because monetary expansion was no longer available to fund (inflationary) spending, the government raised extra tax revenue to fund its expenditure. The level of taxation during the Simitis administration went up. Rising levels of taxation led to 2 years of state revenue exceeding budgetary targets (with a small surplus of 31 billion drachmas accumulated by the end of February 1999). Taxation meant that funds were withdrawn from the private market and were channeled back to demand through public consumption. The tax system became more regressive, burdening mostly middle-income taxpayers (a trend since the early 1980s; Manessiotis and Reischauer 2001: 134). Higher levels of taxation increased the fiscal burden on consumers, salaried employees and entrepreneurs in the private sector. The tax burden of employment (including security contribution costs) remained one of the highest in the EU (together with Germany, France and the Scandinavian EU members) and was seen by economic experts as one of the reasons why Greece was not an attractive destination for foreign investment (*Economikos*, 29/06/2002: 12).[37]

Moreover, the inflow of Community funds, in particular, lessened the need for the government to borrow to cover its spending (Christodoulakis and Kalyvitis 1998). The decline in state aid to public utility companies was also partly the result of an increase in Community funding and revenue from the sale of shares (*Economikos*, 05/10/1995: 51). EU financing had propped up growth rates the year before Greece's assessment for entry into the EMU, and the government tried to absorb as much as possible from the pool of Community funds (*Kathimerini*, 17/09/1999: 35). As a result, the percentage of the national budget allocated to subsidies to public companies fell considerably.

This reform path that PASOK engineered smoothened out the effect of macroeconomic consolidation for its party base. Although 'social justice' was invoked to justify the government's failure to cut public spending,[38] in reality, public spending failed to benefit the most vulnerable segments of the population, and most of the new funding was directed to the social benefits enjoyed by privileged employees in public enterprises (*Vima*, 06/12/1998: 8). The government kept protecting public companies, which formed the core of its clientelist base at a

35 Between 1993 and 2000, debt assumption was steadily reduced to 6814 billion drachmas, which amounted to 14.4% of public debt and 16.7% of GDP. A rise in state guarantees occurred in 1995 and 1996 and a sizeable drop in 1997 and 1998.

36 Total deficit-debt adjustment amounted to 14% of GDP in 1999.

37 See Eurostat, 'Structures of the Taxation Systems in the EU' (2006): 83–86.

38 As Minister of Economy Papantoniou admitted, the 'comparative' political advantage of PASOK was that it had 'the charisma to pass the message to wide strata of the Greek society that there is a government that embraces social justice' (*Economikos*, 19/01/1995: 18).

time when most of the burden of adjustment was placed on wages and pensions. The employees of the public sector were spared from real reductions in income and enjoyed additional financial benefits such as generous compensation for overtime work (sometimes for fictitious overtime work), participation in committees, long-distance traveling and 'special responsibility' benefits, as well as generous pension schemes. Party sympathizers enjoyed additional benefits as they were promoted in higher positions and received higher revenue, which further mitigated any negative impact higher taxes could have had on them (*Vima*, 12/10/1997: 14; *Economikos*, 09/03/1996: 86).

There were also other notable policy failures: the tight monetary policy through the appreciation of the drachma by 22% between 1985 and 2000 contributed to the decline of Greece's competitiveness and Greek exports.[39] The rise in production costs from the inconsistent incomes policy, market rigidities, red tape and high interest rates further burdened economic activity. Unemployment increased throughout the period of macroeconomic adjustment, from 6.1% in 1994 to 10.4% in 1999 (OECD, 'Main Economic Indicators', May 1999), partly due to various market rigidities and the burden of taxation (Manessiotis and Reischauer 2001: 117). When Greece joined the euro, the economy exhibited a persistent high level of public debt, stagnant competitiveness, a declining share of exports as percentage of GDP, low levels of foreign investment and high unemployment rates (Bosworth and Kollintzas 2001).

Finally, the government did little to fight corruption and tackle cases of what was said to be 'criminally wasteful fiscal management' (Table 6.2; *Economikos*,

Table 6.2 Systemic sources of fiscal profligacy

- Deficit-running enterprises (Athens public transport, railways, Olympic Airways)
- Assumption by the government of the debt of agricultural cooperatives and public corporations (mainly through state guarantees, which increased moral hazard)
- Direct subsidies to public enterprises and organizations, and new 'modernization' loans under state guarantee
- Hospital expenses and spending for pharmaceuticals and medical/paramedical examinations by the social security funds
- Generous retirement schemes associated with modernization plans for several state-owned enterprises
- New appointments in public enterprises and local councils
- Extra benefits to public-sector employees in the form of overtime payment, compensation for extracurricular activities, such as participation in various committees, and traveling expenses
- Subsidies to local councils, pension funds and social security organizations
- Rising operational expenses in public administration (e.g. energy bills, stationary, fuel, etc.)
- 'Dark' public procurement contracts and other cases of alleged corruption in public investment projects and public consumption contracts with the private sector

39 From 17% of GDP in 1980 to 9% by 1999 (Tsaveas 2001: 352).

25/04/1996: 15). There were sporadic attempts to reduce spending, when the Ministry of Finance sent directions to other Cabinet ministers to make further cuts in their expenses (*Vima*, 19/04/1998: 3), or when the prime minister announced a committee to record and monitor the level and sources of social spending (*Vima*, 06/12/1998: 8). But the government did not go as far as to implement the proposals by the Ministry of Economy and the Committee of Economic Experts to penalize deviations from the budgetary targets that had been set up for public corporations and organizations (*Economikos*, 01/08/1996: 15). Many other organizations and agencies subsidized by the state had no obligation to submit a budget to the supervising authority for the purpose of transparency and accountability (*Economikos*, 01/08/1996: 15). Not surprisingly, the Simitis government was heavily criticized for poorly tackling fiscal profligacy and corruption. In a letter to the prime minister and the head of the European Court of Audit, the president of the Council of Audit reported a number of omissions in controlling state expenses (*Vima*, 21/03/1999: 52). The letter told the prime minister that the court was understaffed and lacked the requisite technical infrastructure in order to fulfill its mission adequately and that, unless those issues were resolved, the government's effort to curb waste and unlawful spending would be seriously undermined. It was later noted that new rules introduced by the government actually prevented the court from putting the necessary preventive checks on unlawful fiscal spending.[40] Not surprisingly, there was talk that the government was unwilling

> . . . to cut the umbilical cord connecting the public enterprises and the party . . . Since a decade ago, the gospel of Mr. Costas Simitis' political platform has been to denounce the clientelist system. Yet, the management of public enterprises and organizations by the actual nomenclature is the basic source that feeds the clientelist system. Why are all those statements not implemented so far?
>
> (*Economikos*, 08/02/1996: 14)

Entry to the Eurozone

Greece's entry into the Eurozone created a climate of optimism regarding the long-term prospects of the Greek economy. Greece's shift to stability-oriented policies secured, to a considerable extent, a degree of nominal convergence with the European Union's macroeconomic performance. Starting from an anti-inflationary monetary policy, the government seemed to have triggered a virtuous circle in the economy. The relative improvement of the state of the Greek

40 'With the submitted bill, the waste of public money and the increase of the already immense public debt would be easier . . . Without these constitutionally derived guarantees of fiscal legality and discipline, certain adept fortune hunters will continue to get richer and provoke with their opulence, while others will suffer' (*Economikos*, 23/11/1996: 34 and 36).

economy had important political and economic implications for the period after entry to the European Monetary Union. In politics, the government's success in stabilizing the economy weakened New Democracy's political reputation among center-right voters as the party of sound economic policies. New Democracy adjusted its criticism of PASOK by focusing on developments in the 'real economy', namely rising unemployment levels, the deterioration of Greece's competitiveness, the stagnation of industrial production and poor results in tourism. It vociferously criticized the government for tolerating corruption and allowing the inefficient management of the public sector. It also pointed to the inconsistencies of the government's policy mix, such as the hiring of new public employees and its unwillingness to fully privatize public enterprises and cut public spending on a larger scale (*Vima*, 10/12/1995: 5 and *Economikos*, 29/05/1997: 23).

In the economy, there was the general feeling that EMU entry secured macroeconomic stability for Greece, which would enable greater and longer-term capital investment (*Kathimerini*, 10/01/1999). Exchange-rate fluctuations were eliminated, and interest rates, which in the past had derailed the public debt level, were significantly reduced. Following entry into the EMU, the country's credit rating was upgraded to A and A- status by international rating agencies. The government could now borrow with lower interest rates and issue bonds with prolonged maturity, which pushed the bill further away in the future.[41] Short-term debt declined, reducing debt sensitivity to short-term interest rates. Long-term interest rates for the Greek bonds converged around the EU average (a difference of 0.8 percentage points). Until 2002 the reduction of the cost of interest-rate payments was driving much of the improvement in Greece's fiscal performance. As a result of high levels of growth, the government was now able to borrow more at cheaper nominal rates and see the deficit fall as a percentage of a growing GDP.[42] This trend further lessened the immediate need to curb public spending significantly. A growing GDP and lower interest rates also widened the scope for distributional policies, including transfers to clientelist groups. In that way, the success of macroeconomic stabilization unleashed new resources for political distribution, part of which was channeled to the needs of the clientelist system. At the same time, Greece secured additional EU funding for public investment projects. The net transfers from the EU amounted, on average, to 4% of the country's GDP.[43] This was a significant source of government revenue and had a direct contribution in boosting domestic demand and propping up annual growth rates. It was estimated that about 24.9 billion euros in total were

41 The maturities of the Greek bonds were significantly longer, 6 years in 1999 from 1.6 years in 1994.

42 Despite the considerable rise of public debt in absolute numbers, public debt as a percentage of GDP fell.

43 European Commission (2000b: 199); Bryant, Garganas and Tavlas (2001: 25); Tsaveas (2001: 339); Pagoulatos (2003: 209).

Table 6.3 Winners and losers from macroeconomic adjustment by employment and income status

Winners	*Losers*
Public company employees	Small and medium enterprises entitled to special financing under the previous financial regime [1]
Central government employees (esp. party clients)	Exporters[2]
Government bond holders	Farmers[3]
Importers	Low-income taxpayers[4]
Medium-high–income taxpayers[4]	Private-sector workers (particularly in manufacturing)[5]
	Pensioners

Sources: *Economikos, Vima*, Pagoulatos 2003: 150–178 and Mavrogordatos 1988: 88.

1 The favorable regime was prolonged until the early 1990s due to their lobbying activities.

2 Exporters were divided over those exclusively exporting and those with mixed activities.

3 The gradual liberalization of loans by the Agricultural Bank made it more difficult for farmers to access credit, but they were still receiving Common Agricultural Policy funds,

4 Stable tax ratio brackets means that inflation tends to increase the overall tax burden. The government raised the tax burden on annual income under 6 million drachmas by 5.3% and reduced the burden for over 6 million by 3.7% (*Economikos*, 14/01/1999: 61; 12/02/1998: 131).

5 They had small real wage increases and were also burdened by new taxation and faced a higher risk of unemployment.

channeled to Greece by the third Community Support Framework (Papadimitriou 2005; Tinios 2005).[44]

Conclusion: sanctions, timing and clientelist bias

Macroeconomic stabilization in the 1990s was necessary to secure the stability of the party system and its capacity to distribute resources. It was also a personal stake for Prime Minister Simitis and his circle of supporters in government. Despite the observed inconsistencies, the Simitis government succeeded in securing Greece's entry into the EMU. The stabilization effort towards the benchmark of the EMU exhibited policy 'revision' (cf. Hacker 2004: 248) in two areas: the monetary policy was tightened to serve the goal of stabilization, and the fiscal policy became less expansionary compared with the 1980s. The most interesting observation from that period, however, is how the Greek government tackled the dilemma of achieving macroeconomic consolidation and avoiding the political cost of this effort. It generated a particular pattern of winners and losers where its party clients in the public sector were placed safely on the winning side (Table 6.3). The way the Simitis government addressed this critical dilemma

44 The Common Agricultural Policy also channeled funds to the Greek economy. Direct financial assistance to farmers, a large and politically important group in the countryside, accounted for about half of their income in the late 1980s and most of the 1990s (National Bank of Greece 2008).

offers useful lessons of how reform is likely to be configured in a clientelist party system.

A serious effort for macroeconomic consolidation becomes inevitable if failure to stabilize the economy could provoke a crisis expected to occur within the lifespan of the government. In that case, it can be said that the fiscal and economic sustainability of this system becomes a 'club good' for the political forces in charge. This means that they can no longer postpone reforming aspects of the system. This observation refines the hypothesis on a clientelist bias by putting forward a *crisis-in-tenure* prediction for reforms in a clientelist system. If it is anticipated that failure to stabilize the economy will bring about a 'punishment by markets' event that will fall within the political lifecycle of a government, the government can no longer avoid making a serious effort for macroeconomic consolidation. However, it can still design a policy response in ways that will diffuse the cost of macroeconomic stabilization among taxpayers and consumers and will preserve its commitments to its client groups. This pattern strengthens the hypothesis that *clientelist bias* continues to govern economic policy during the reform effort, even when a significant revision of economic policy takes place. It also indicates that any policy revision will actually aim at the regeneration of the distributional system. As the next chapter shows, EU transfers, lower borrowing costs, revenue from privatization and high growth rates mitigated the pressure for Greece to tackle the inefficiencies of the public sector, reduced the urgency of politically risky structural reforms and provided new resources for government spending.

7 Clientelist bias in structural reforms

The case of PASOK (1993–2004)

The book's initial hypothesis is that the dominant strategy in a clientelist system suggests that the government will opt for a mix of reforms that disperses costs among taxpayers and producers and preserves concentrated benefits for its client groups (clientelist bias). Equally, when economic conditions are pressing, policy reform is expected to secure the sustainability of the economy on which government distribution relies. At certain times, however, the room for maneuvering is further limited by the urgency of economic conditions and by specific institutional pressures that explicitly prescribe a set of structural reforms which, compared with other measures of economic reform, could seriously undermine existing channels of patronage. These measures may involve privatization, market deregulation and administrative reforms. In that case, government policy must be tailored to reduce the harm imposed on its core supporters as much as possible. The government can launch reforms in a gradual, almost experimental, step-by-step basis, driven by a careful observation of within-party reactions. It must offer its core support groups some reassurance that their key interests will be protected. The government should also search for new resources for distribution. This pattern of *creative adjustment* is further explored in this chapter.

In Greece, structural reforms were necessary for the country to return to sustained economic growth after decades of stagnation and create a stable and healthy environment for private investment (Bank of Greece report, *Vima*, 05/05/1996: 12; Mylonas and Papaconstantinou 2001: 504). The governor of the Bank of Greece had repeatedly called the government to move beyond its emphasis on monetary and foreign exchange policies – the main tools of macroeconomic stabilization since 1986 – and include reforms in production markets and privatizations (*Economikos*, 11/03/1995: 15). As Minister of Interior Alekos Papadopoulos put it, the country was in need of a shock therapy that would involve reform at all levels (*Nea*, 25/07/1997).

Moreover, the economic case for structural reforms was strengthened by Greece's institutional commitment to EU policies, its EMU candidacy and later membership in the Eurozone. The expectation was that, besides nominal convergence with the EU on fiscal performance indices, Greece had to exhibit real convergence in growth and competitiveness (*Kathimerini*, 10/01/1999). The Commission and the ECB assessed favorably Greece's convergence progress – stating with enthusiasm in May 2000 that Greece had achieved striking progress towards convergence. But they cautiously pointed to the economic risks associated with the country's persisting structural rigidities (European Commission 2000a: 98). Greece's restrictive regulatory environment continued to make Greece an unattractive location for private investment (Burtless 2001). Greece scored poorly in foreign direct investment (FDI), which can be used as an indication of the confidence of international investors in a national economy (Bosworth and Kollintzas 2001: 188 and 197). After Greece entered the Eurozone, private investment declined, inflation increased, foreign investment remained at low levels, public finances deteriorated and unemployment stayed high between 9% and 10%. The young and the long-termed unemployed (over 12 months) were the worst hit. Supply-side weaknesses associated with structural rigidities were also manifested in the generally poor performance of Greek exports and increasing imports at a pace higher than the rate of GDP growth.

These structural weaknesses, if left unaddressed, would keep undermining Greece's international competitiveness as a member of the Eurozone, particularly because the government could no longer make use of monetary policy, as it had done before. In addition, it was difficult to disentangle the primary target of fiscal consolidation from the need of structural adjustment in adjacent policy areas; for instance, meeting the requirement for low-deficit budgets (under 3%) as stipulated by the Stability Pact could be facilitated by reforms that improve efficiency and reduce government spending, such as administrative reforms cutting down wasteful government activities, reforms in the welfare system reducing the state's contribution to pensions and health insurance and privatizations from which the government could raise money to pay its bills and attract foreign investment.

Given the party's clientelist ties with employees in the public sector, the prospect of structural reforms became a major cause of concern for the PASOK governments throughout the period between 1993 and 2004. The fate of the Mitsotakis reform agenda had already revealed the political cost of radical reform that included privatization and market liberalization. These policies could undermine the privileges of groups of PASOK's core supporters in the public sector, who enjoyed generous payments and retirement schemes. Structural reforms could also reduce the range of activities susceptible to party clientelism and could hurt the intertwined interests of the party and the unions:

> . . . to achieve this difficult target, the government should literally make a revolution in the broader public sector, coming in direct confrontation with, and prevailing over the wasteful and demanding nomenclature that forms the body of PASOK.
>
> (Nikolaou in *Vima*, 29/12/1996: 2)

As this chapter shows in detail, Prime Minister Simitis embracing structural reforms was a step into unchartered waters given his weaker grasp over the party, compared with Andreas Papandreou. Following the Papandreou period of reform inertia (1993–1995), the Simitis government took a gradualist and piecemeal approach to designing and pacing structural reforms in ways that preserved the privileged status of public-sector employees, most of which were affiliated with PASOK through the trade unions. Privatization involved few full sales of state-owned companies and mostly the sale of minority shares in large public utility corporations (through 'flotation') with the government retaining control over their management. This secured the monopoly status of large public-sector enterprises, while it provided the government with much-needed revenue and offered an injection of capital to the public utility enterprises. State-dominated sectors such as telecommunications and energy were formally liberalized – although with significant delay – but these markets continued to be dominated by giant state-controlled companies. Further market liberalization was cancelled. There was also limited reform of the labor market and the pension system. Labor market reforms conformed to binding EU directives that introduced flexible working hours and wage flexibility in part-time and fixed-time employment, but other labor market rigidities remained in place and continued to contribute to high levels of unemployment and slow rates of labor productivity (Bryant, Garganas and Tavlas 2001: 26). As a result, reactions from the unions to privatization and structural reform were remarkably mild with few notable exceptions.

Economic and institutional pressures for structural reforms

The need for structural reforms gained worldwide momentum in the mid-1990s as a way to boost economic growth and help public finances. These reforms involved privatization and market liberalization, the reduction of state expenses, the merger or abolition of a number of public organizations, the modernization of public administration, the reform of the pension and social security system and supply-side measures to encourage investment and facilitate entrepreneurial activity. It was expected that structural reforms would increase productivity, improve the business environment and reduce the rate of structural unemployment (European Commission 2003b: 59–68).

Throughout the mid- and late 1990s, market liberalization, privatizations, the restructuring of the social security system and the lifting of bureaucratic obstacles to entrepreneurship were linked to the framework of the Maastricht Treaty, which consisted of a system of policy recommendations designed to act as a soft pressure for the member states to coordinate their economic policies around 'best practices' communicated through the Broad Economic Policy Guidelines, the Open Method of Coordination for social policy and the European Employment Strategy for labor markets. Following the creation of a monetary union, these processes were integrated into the 'Lisbon Agenda', a 10-year program aimed at market liberalization and labor market flexibility. In addition, throughout that period, Article 90 of the EC Treaty (now Art. 88) was a powerful instrument for the Commission to ban the granting of state aid to enterprises, including state-owned companies. This further pushed governments towards market liberalization and the break-up of government-controlled monopolies. With the notable exception of employment law in the 1990s, the guidelines promoted the deregulation of key sectors of the economy.[1]

In Greece during that time public deficits were fueled by the operation of deficit-running, state-owned monopoly companies (the DEKO) that had remained under full state ownership. Other public monopolies, although profitable, had high operational costs, relied on large and regular capital injections by the government and could make a profit primarily thanks to their monopoly status.[2] By the mid-1990s, there were around 50 large public enterprises, a number of banks and several important industrial firms which were taking financial assistance from the central government equivalent to nearly half of Greece's debt (OECD 1998: 94).[3] When Simitis came to power, there was great uncertainty over the actual level of their deficits (*Economikos*, 21/03/1996: 14).

In addition, Greece had to improve its public finances and fix long-standing structural distortions in labor and product markets, which were dominated by state companies. Part of the private sector was highly skeptical of government involvement in the management of public-sector enterprises, which had been identified as part of 'an avaricious clientelist political system' working at the expense of general taxpayers and economic actors (*Economikos*, 28/11/1996: 22). This concern was quite explicitly voiced by the president of Athens Commerce and Industry Council, Yannis Papathanasiou:

> The Government must decide at last that the [whole of the] economy should operate on the same terms, not with special criteria that privilege public corporations and hurt private ones.
>
> (*Economikos*, 07/03/1996: 17)

Structural rigidities on the supply side were undermining the stabilization effort and had a negative impact on the balance of payments and the level of unemployment, which, according to the Bank of Greece, was to become more obvious under the competitive conditions and the fiscal policy limits of the EMU.[4] Employment law created an inflexible labor market with relatively high labor costs and social security contributions. The Bank of Greece urged that, despite the recorded progress in public finances, the government had to restructure the state sector by lifting subsidies to public enterprises, banks, shipyards and farmers associations (*Vima*, 27/04/1997: 2). Its effort for macroeconomic stabilization

1 See the Helsinki European Council Conclusions of December 1999.

2 OTE in telecommunications made a profit of 300 billion drachmas; OPAP, the sports bookmaker, made a profit of 129 billion; and Hellenic Petroleum made a profit of 80 billion (Ministry of Nation Economy and *Vima*, 02/11/2000: B-IV).

3 By the end of 1997 equity injections and debt write-offs under state guarantees had cumulatively amounted to 7.5% of GDP (OECD 1998: 96).

4 The report had a quite dramatic tone for a technocratic document. Similar criticism was voiced by international organizations such as the OECD and the IMF.

could no longer rely solely on monetary and fiscal policy and could not avoid taking measures, such as privatization and market deregulation, to address the structural weaknesses of Greece's production base (Bank of Greece 1995: 65):

> Structural weaknesses in the productive process limit the country's growth potential on the supply side and, unless tackled in time, would have obvious consequences in the coming years, particularly for the balance of payments and unemployment figures.
>
> (Bank of Greece 1997; *Vima*, 27/04/1997: 8; and 27/04/1997: 2)

Given its structural rigidities, the Greek economy fell short in both labor productivity and multifactor productivity, with the sharpest divergence occurring between 1980 and 1994 (Bosworth and Kollintzas 2001: 156). As a result, Greece continued to be regarded as a less attractive location for foreign direct investment, lagging behind Ireland and Portugal.

The political challenge of structural reforms

PASOK's first experience with privatizations and early reactions

Right after the fall of the Mitsotakis government, the Papandreou government put a halt to the privatization program and fulfilled the promise which PASOK made as an opposition party that it would protect the employment status of the unionized employees in the broader public sector when back in government. This policy shift happened at a time when the state of public finances was deteriorating and was putting extra pressure on the government to cut spending and reform the companies of the broader public sector that were generating deficits.[5] Tackling the deficit-running companies and privatization was recommended as a quick way for the government to raise revenue and reduce the annual budget deficit. However, both liquidation and privatization were politically costly given PASOK's pre-electoral commitments to its support groups (Pagoulatos 2005: 360). The unions of the public sector were categorically opposed to any form of privatization, including the idea of selling minority shares in the stock market (*Nea*, 24/05/1994: 55). In a similar vein, politically appointed managers and unionists in the public sector were expressing their reservations over the deregulation of the markets dominated by state monopolies such as electricity.[6] Privatizations would signal a clear break from PASOK's electoral promises and past

5 To some extent, the government could rely on the fact that the monopoly status of most of these corporations lessened the need for the companies to increase efficiency, reduce production costs and increase productivity (*Economikos*, 05/10/1995: 56).

6 A member of the executive board of the electricity company DEI expressed the idea that the government should compensate the corporation for any damages produced by its liberalization policy (*Nea*, 07/09/1994: 53).

ideology. They would hurt the interests of party supporters in the companies under privatization and could possibly trigger reactions inside the party

Very soon, the issue of privatization – if and how the government would proceed with privatization – became a major source of anxiety inside the party ranks and its affiliated unions. The new government sought to entertain any criticism that it was about to renege on its pre-electoral pledges and proceed with privatizations (*Economikos*, 14/07/1994: 31). In that context, the government moved cautiously with a first exploratory step towards privatizations in September 1994, with the sale of a small shipyard in Syros, which had been shut down since 1992. With the exception of the shipyard's syndicate, the sale did not trigger the scale of reactions that New Democracy confronted a few years earlier when it had planned to sell the shipyard to private owners (*Economikos*, 12/05/1995). The sale, however, marked a U-turn regarding PASOK's stance on privatization, much to the disappointment of many party supporters, unionists and officials. Less than a year after, the government attempted to sell the much-larger Skaramangas Shipyard, following the decision of the European Commission (Decision EE C 138 6 February 1994) to enact the infringement process (under Art. 88 of the EEC Treaty) for Greece's omission to privatize this company by the end of 1993.

This attempted sale caused political confrontation over the government's stance on privatization. New Democracy supported the idea of privatization, but it criticized the government for its handling of the sale and raised issues of transparency (*Nea*, 31/08.1995: 60). More importantly, the plan drafted by Minister of Industry Simitis triggered complaints from several ministers and PASOK MPs, particularly because it would have given the new owner the right to dismiss employees (*Economikos*, 07/09/1995: 81). Simitis gave explicit assurances that any dismissed employees could choose between a special retraining program and a 24-month benefit that was 60% higher than the general unemployment benefit (*Nea*, 22/02/1995: 25). The chance of mass redundancies was low given that the contract would have offered the new owner a series of government defense contracts for the next 15 years (*Nea*, 15/03/1995: 13).

Mounting unrest inside PASOK pushed the government to eventually cancel the sale of the shipyard (*Economikos*, 15/06/1995: 30).[7] PASOK-affiliated groups in public enterprises managed to find strong supporters and allies among PASOK top politicians and union leaders. This episode would later offer a lesson for the Simitis government how (not) to proceed with forthcoming privatizations.[8] The government must take special care of the status of the employees in the broader

7 The Skaramangas Shipyard was sold a year later in 1996, but the new owner withdrew in 1998. The Simitis government sold it again in 2001, together with its contractual obligations for the construction of submarines for the Greek navy.

8 The Skaramangas Shipyards is another prominent case of state assistance to an ailing company. In 2008, the European Court of Justice ruled that the loans which the shipyard had received from the state-owned company, ETVA, and their guarantee by the state were both unlawful under Article 88 of the EEC Treaty on state aid (Decision T-391/08).

public sector (their so-called 'acquired rights') when designing its future reform plans.[9] During the last months of the Papandreou government, the issue of privatization and the direction of economic policy absorbed much of the energy of political discussions inside PASOK. Cabinet ministers were openly critical of the government's economic policy in order to appeal to discontented party members (*Nea*, 21/04/1994: 6).

The modality of privatization: the 'flotation' model

When Simitis became prime minister in January 1996, the previous policy inertia regarding structural reforms had contributed to the deterioration of public finances. State guarantees for public companies had already cost 1.8 trillion drachmas, and their deficits were mostly covered by the issuing of new loans (*Economikos*, 01/02/1996: 84). The so-called 'modernization plans' for the restructuring of several public-sector companies were far too expensive.[10] The pressure for more drastic measures to tackle this source of deficit spending was mounting, as noted by the governor of the Bank of Greece:

> The state should address the problem of deficit accumulation that is eventually covered by imposing taxes on citizens, primarily salaried workers . . . Unfortunately, it has been proven that, in reality, many public companies do not operate efficiently: they either generate deficits that put a burden on society or they offer services of high cost and low quality and, in some cases, they generate deficits and provide services of inadequate quality.
>
> (*Nea*, 06/04/1998: 46)

In that environment, the Simitis government had to find a way to promote structural reforms in view of the party's ideological and political commitments. Simitis' pledge to launch structural reforms increased the anxiety felt by public-sector employees. With the exception of a few Cabinet members, most of PASOK top politicians carefully abstained from publicly embracing the case for structural reforms (*Vima*, 25/10/1998: 4). Cabinet ministers and party cadres asked the government to give assurances to the labor unions over the scale and nature of privatizations, whereas party unionists were frequently criticizing the government for keeping them uninformed about its reform plans (*Economikos*, 07/05/1998: 33). In response to this criticism, the government established a special party–government committee to coordinate decisions on structural reforms presided by the minister of economy (*Economikos*, 07/05/1998: 33).

9 'PASOK ministers make decisions . . . in conformity with the commands of the party base which – when it is not governed by ideological dogmatism – acts as a vested interest [*syntehnia*]' (Nikolaou, *Nea*, 21/04/1994: 6).

10 Modernization programs until 1996 had cost 600 billion drachmas for the Olympic Airways, 400 billion for the ETBA Bank and 120 billion for the Bank of Crete (*Economikos*, 01/02/1996: 84).

Caught between structural pressures to privatize and the ongoing anxiety inside the party, the government chose to follow a model of partial privatization through *flotation*, namely the sale of shares in the stock exchange with the government keeping control over the management. This piecemeal approach aimed to minimize social reactions. The government sequenced phases of partial sales of shares and justified its decision to keep control of the management of the partially privatized corporations as a way to prevent the emergence of private monopolies and continue to serve public-interest objectives (Pagoulatos 2005: 365). Government officials presented partial privatization as the option that struck the right balance between the public and the private sphere in the economy.[11] Nikos Christodoulakis, who was at the time deputy minister of finance, said that flotation is 'privatization for the people' and promised to protect the pension schemes of the employees whose companies were selected for partial sale:

> Flotation can be the ideal opportunity to address the problem with the pensions' he explicitly said as their pension funds could be 'endowed with a package of shares'.
>
> (*Nea*, 08/07/1998: 12)

This form of privatization was seen by economic experts as inferior to full sales, especially in terms of gains in management efficiency (Bank of Greece 1997: 66). For the government, however, partial privatization was a significant source of revenue, which was its urgent priority. A great part of the revenue from flotation funded the expanding investment program of the public utility companies (DEKO) and lessened the need for the government to make direct capital transfers or loan guarantees, as was previously the norm (OECD Economic Survey 1998: 48). Revenue from flotation also funded the increasing needs of the pension and social security funds of the DEKO employees. Privatization proceeds were used to retire public debt and reduce the debt-to-GDP ratio (Manessiotis and Reischauer 2001: 124) and helped the government report a primary surplus.[12] In that way, flotation lessened the need for politically costly new tax rises or cuts in public spending. The number of privatizations and revenue from privatization rose significantly for 3 consecutive years between 1997 and 1999 during Greece's run-up to euro membership and fell significantly in 2000, the year of the general election, with a moderate rise in 2002 and 2003 (Rapanos 2009). In 1999, the year when Greece's entry to the EMU was to be decided on the basis of fiscal performance, revenue from privatization peaked at 4% of GDP (OECD 2001: 27).

11 'One cannot privatize everything and let the market operate as the unique mechanism for economic, social and political organization' (Simitis' advisor Giannitsis in *Economikos*, 24/07/1997: 21).

12 Between 2001 and 2003, privatization proceeds amounted to a cumulative 6% of GDP and helped pay for government debt (European Commission 2004b: 112).

The partial sale of shares through flotation was the preferred option mainly for political reasons. The government wanted to avoid a battle against the unionized employees of the public sector, who constituted its core political clients ('the party nomenclature', as top political commentator Nikolaou called it in the center-left newspaper, *Nea*, 21/04/1994: 6).[13] Moreover, the sale of minority shares did not undermine the position of politically appointed managers and party-affiliated unionists in control of the 'wasteful, unproductive and corrupt state sector' (*Economikos*, 22/01/1996: 7). The editor of *Economikos*, Yannis Marinos, noted that

> The entry of private shareholders to the ownership and management [of the public enterprises] would both reveal and, possibly, obstruct the uncontrolled use of the DEKO's revenue and capital, the unaccountable wage increases and allocation of benefits to employees, the sharing of ownership by the government and the trade unions, in which the latter have a veto power and can use it to appoint their children, friends and relatives . . . whose consent is needed for procurements and works of billions [of drachmas] to be carried out . . . Flotation will not lead to the loss of state ownership of the majority of shares and, as a result, the DEKO will continue to be as unproductive, wasteful and unaccountable as they are today.
>
> (Yannis Marinos, in *Economikos*, on 22/01/1996: 7)

In a similar vein, former Prime Minister Mitsotakis hinted that partial privatization protected specific corporate interests that had secured preferential access to public-sector contracts:

> The squalor of nationalizations and of the trade unions that squeeze the simple taxpayer has returned in all its glory . . . In OTE, the huge program of modernization stopped, because the government is not willing to give up the management. The only thing they are occupied with is to fulfill the obligations they had undertaken, by giving [contracting out the building of] the digital lines in a scandalous manner.
>
> (Interview by Vassilis Zissis, *Economikos*, 02/10/1994).

The Simitis government implemented few full privatizations. Significant structural reform took place in the banking sector through the full privatization of relatively small state-owned banks and the subsidiaries of the National Bank of Greece. Privatization in the banking sector was followed by subsequent mergers and acquisitions of domestic Greek banks and was coupled with financial

13 With full privatization 'the governing party and its people would have lost the privilege of reigning over these companies and, of course, the capital and money that they manage' and would have given up control over appointments and public procurement (noted by Yannis Kotofolos in the center-right newspaper, *Kathimerini*, 17/02/2002).

deregulation in compliance with EU law, which transformed Greece's banking system. By the end of 1998 the share of state-owned and state-controlled banks in the banking sector fell from 87.5% in 1993 to 61.7% (Eichengreen and Gibson 2001: 556). Four of Greece's major banks remained under the de facto control of the government.[14]

Preservation of the clientelist system: reassurances and compensation

Although the method of flotation was chosen as a way to retain government control over the companies on sale, there were still sensitive issues to be addressed. PASOK unionists were adamantly against the prospect that superfluous or underperforming employees could be dismissed. In response, the government reassured the unions and the party that the changes in the DEKO enterprises would not harm the current salary and pension rights of the employees. The minister of economy was clear: 'we shall not cut wages and we shall not make anyone redundant' (*Vima*, 12/03/1998). Employees in the broader public sector would continue to enjoy permanent status.[15] The sale of shares happened under arrangements concerning the management of these corporations and employment conditions that made sure that the status of the existing personnel remained almost intact. There were only a few changes in the terms governing promotions, performance monitoring and evaluation, effective disciplinary action and training. The employees preserved their employment privileges in relation to most private-sector workers, such as high salaries and benefits, generous working hours and holiday schemes, generous pension schemes, loose disciplinary control and most, of all, job protection (*Economikos*, 04/06/1998: 33). They continued to receive total compensation nearly twice as high as in the private sector, together with other nonwage advantages such as limitations on geographic and functional mobility, additional remuneration in periods of high demand, good compensation for overtime work and nightshifts, paid rest time and other payment benefits and benefits in kind (Table 7.1; OECD 1998: 106; Law 2579/1998). Public-sector employees continued to enjoy lower retirement ages, which for many of them was below the age of 55 (Mylonas and Papaconstantinou 2001: 508).[16]

In addition, part of the privatization proceeds was given to the social security funds of the employees in public-sector companies.[17] Public enterprises offered

14 The Commercial Bank of Greece, the Postal Bank, the Agricultural Bank and the National Bank of Greece, Greece's largest bank, remained under government control.

15 In 2005, a law by the New Democracy government abolished the permanent status of the employees in the companies in which the government had a minority share.

16 For instance, male employees of the National Bank of Greece were entitled to retire at the age of 55 (whereas for employees in private banks, the age of retirement was 65) at total replacement rates reaching up to 120%, and their pensions after their death were transferrable to their unmarried or divorced daughters (Börsch-Supan and Tinios 2001: 408).

17 Law 2773/1999, and Börsch-Supan and Tinios (2001: 404–405).

Table 7.1 Estimated average compensation per employee, year 2000

	Monthly compensation (thousand drachmas)	*Ratio to compensation in the whole economy*
Whole economy	434	100
Public enterprises	688	158
DEI (electricity)	654	150
Hellenic Petroleum (fuels)	1,098	253
OTE (telecommunications)	612	141
OASA (urban transport)	715	164
Olympic Airways Group	955	220
OSE (railways)	601	138
EYDAP (water and sewage)	689	158
ELTA (post)	629	154

Source: Mylonas and Papaconstantinou 2001: 509, citing Ministry of National Economy.

their employees generous pension plans, including a tax-free, lump-sum, end-of-service stipend equivalent to 2 or more years' salary (OECD 1998: 106). In the social security system, public enterprises remained 'islands of privilege in a sea of insufficient provision' (Börsch-Supan and Tinios 2001: 431). Higher employer contributions were in some cases financed by taxes on the product of the firm (Börsch-Supan and Tinios 2001: 402). Given the oligopoly or monopoly status of these companies in the product markets, the consumer was ultimately bearing much of the cost of their social security schemes. Higher wages, other financial benefits, better terms of employment and generous pension schemes were, in essence, a redistribution of the monopoly profits of public-sector enterprises to these privileged groups.

The government offered additional forms of 'compensation' to facilitate the sale of shares. On many occasions, the employees were given the chance to buy shares at lower prices. Older employees were offered generous financial incentives to retire. These incentives for retirement were the only way for state-controlled firms to renew their personnel, and later became a general trend in the broader public sector.[18] At the same time, to renew human capital, the managers were hiring private contractors to assign many of the tasks previously performed by permanent employees, such as security, cleaning and maintaining public buildings and infrastructure. The newly appointed employees were hired under different employment terms, often as temporary contract workers. For the remaining employees, average wages in public enterprises grew faster than wages

18 The early retirement scheme for 1280 Olympic Airways employees cost around 11 billion drachmas (*Economikos*, 25/04/1996: 15). These early retirement schemes allowed OTE and Olympic to reduce the numbers of employees (Mylonas and Papaconstantinou 2001: 508).

in the private sector (cf. OECD 1998: 105). As a result, a medley of employment terms emerged: on the one side, the old staff retained their preferential employment status and, on the other, newly hired employees were employed under more flexible terms.

New legislation strengthened the power of managers over decisions regarding labor relations and reduced the input of trade unions in the management (Law 2469/97). The government increased its power over the definition of the terms of employment in deficit-running public enterprises in the event that bargaining between the managers and the unions did not lead to an agreement within 6 months. It was now clear that the special employment status of the old staff was predominantly in the hands of the government and its appointed managers.

PASOK's base was ready to accept partial privatization as long as the management was appointed by the government and there were safeguards for the status of the old employees.[19] Thanks to safeguards and compensations, the sales of shares through flotation triggered mild reactions amidst trade unionists. Protests were mainly limited to firm-level unions (*Nea*, 22/04/1998: 54) and were supported by a few PASOK politicians and union leaders (for instance, in the case of the Petrol Oil Monopoly, DEP, *Nea*, 21/05/1994: 69). Occasional criticism inside the party mostly reflected anxiety over the uncertainty that the announcement of a new round of structural reforms generated (*Economikos*, 07/05/1998: 33). The unions had a 'wait-and-see' attitude, repeatedly asking the government to pledge that the state would maintain managerial control in the partially privatized companies.

This formula allowed the Simitis government to launch a wider program of partial privatizations of public enterprises with minimal reactions from the trade unions and its members.[20] However, the pace and nature of privatization remained a contentious issue within the Cabinet and the party, and occasionally caused tensions between the prime minister's allies and his rivals, who wished to capitalize on discontented PASOK supporters (*Nea*, 15/06/2002: 41; 17/10/2003: 67). Simitis' adversaries were invoking ideological objections to appeal to groups that were concerned with the future of their employment status. Minister of Development Tsohatzopoulos repeatedly stated that the privatization program 'should not end up as a sell-off' (*Nea*, 30/10/2002: 53). Tsohatzopoulos openly opposed the planned sale of shares in the electricity monopoly company, DEI (*Nea*, 15/06/2002: 41). Other Cabinet ministers who were skeptical towards privatization formed a 'buffer zone' between the minister of economy, who wanted further privatization at a faster pace, and the worried unionists of the public sector. This criticism helped let off the steam inside the party and offered

19 Minister of Economy Papantoniou stated: 'The successful experiment with OTE demonstrated that both society and the markets are braver than we thought. We need to proceed in that direction with determination, without prejudices and blinkers, but with the necessary safeguards for transparency and mutual gains for the economy and the employees' (*Economikos*, 08/05/1997: 33).

20 In 2001, public enterprises accounted for 6% of total employment (OECD 2001: 12).

the government the opportunity to defend its piecemeal approach to privatizations as 'the middle ground'. The government could also justify the delays in its privatization program as the outcome of its preference for 'a synthesis of conflicting interests' (cf. Giannitsis in *Economikos*, 24/07/1997: 21).

In the meantime, amidst concerns voiced about the anticipated reactions, the Cabinet rejected a package of structural measures proposed by Minister of Interior Alekos Papadopoulos similar to the ones implemented in Spain and Portugal, which would have included the privatization of shares in the public utility companies above the 49% threshold, as well as proposals for deeper reform in the social security system and further market liberalization (*Nea*, 16/03/1998). Minister of National Economy Papantoniou agreed on the essence of the package, but he reportedly said that further reforms had to wait until after the next election (*Nea*, 16/03/1998). After the 2000 election, the government announced its decision to lift the privatization law that banned private majority ownership in the public utility companies. The government's share of OTE and Hellenic Petroleum fell below 51% in 2001, but the government retained a blocking voting minority. The privatization program experienced further delays, often reflecting strong disagreements inside the Cabinet (*Nea*, 15/06/2002: 41). Sales of shares in DEPA, the petrol industry and the Postal Bank were aborted, while the government continued to own and subsidize the deficit-running Olympic Airways. The government ignored pressures from the European Commission to speed up its privatization program (*Vima*, 27–29.10.2000). Through partial or full ownership the government kept control of the key economic sectors of telecommunications, electricity, the petrol industry and natural gas and maintained a significant presence in the banking system.

On the opposite side, New Democracy had an ambivalent political stance on structural reforms. The party officially embraced the privatization of the banking system and the insurance companies, which the banks owned, and advocated the entry of the private sector into the energy sector (*Vima*, 10/12/1995: 5). The new leader of the party, Costas Karamanlis, openly proposed an economic policy that called for the reduction of public spending, the strengthening of competition, market liberalization and privatizations (Interview in *Eleftherotypia*, 31.03.1997). Still, the party was divided between a minority faction that had been favorable to the Mitsotakis' agenda and openly supported the redirection of government policy towards spending constraint and further privatizations, and the majority in the party that was criticizing the government for neglecting the social implications of its economic policy (*Economikos*, 03/10/1996: 13). This division within New Democracy culminated in a clash between former Minister of Economy Souflias and New Democracy's labor unionists (DAKE) over the party's position on the government's plan to reform the social security system. The unionists called for disciplinary action against Souflias for his favorable position on the government report (*Vima*, 19/10/1997: 7). Karamanlis sought to put an end to internal party divisions in 1998 and expelled from the party six prominent New Democracy politicians, including Souflias and the former Minister of Economy Manos on the grounds that they had defied the party line. In that way, Karamanlis strengthened his leadership position in the party and, at the same time, distanced himself from 'neoliberal' politicians who were associated with the Mitsotakis period.

Deficit-running companies: the nationalization of deficits

A large number of deficit-running companies, most notably Olympic Airways, the railways and public transport, were left outside the privatization program of the Simitis government. While economists argued that full privatization would offer greater gains (Koutsogeorgopoulou and Ziegelschmidt 2005: 30; OECD 2005), both their managers and the labor unions opposed the prospect of full privatization (OECD 2001: 42). The government chose to draft a series of 'modernization plans' to restructure these companies: 1) the government undertook the responsibility to pay their debt to banks, their electricity and telecommunication bills and their contributions to social security funds; 2) the tariffs and prices charged by the public utility companies increased (DEKO), which put an extra burden on consumers at a time of austerity; 3) the companies designed heavy investment programs, mostly funded by EU funds, which reduced the companies' borrowing needs; and 4) the government increased its participation in the companies' stock (in telecommunications, the post office and the petrol companies) instead of granting them direct subsidies (*Vima*, 01/12/1996: Δ17).[21]

Despite the government's efforts to introduce good management practices (OECD 2001: 28, 196, 276, 304–305), most of the broader public-sector companies continued to run deficits.[22] Public companies continued to be poorly managed and generate costly price distortions that reduced employment creation in the private economy and dragged down economic growth rates (OECD 2001: 10 and 12). The companies also kept using obscure accounting practices (Mylonas and Papaconstantinou 2001: 510). The effort to 'modernize' public-sector enterprises was further undermined by informal clientelist ties connecting Cabinet ministers, public-sector managers and union leaders. As a result, Greece remained at the bottom of the OECD list regarding productivity in the largest sectors of electricity, telecommunications, energy and transport, partly due to the dominant presence of state monopolies (Mylonas and Papaconstantinou 2001).

By 2004, when Simitis stepped down as prime minister, partial privatization and inconsistent market liberalization had not broken the state monopolies in landline telecommunications, electricity, natural gas, railways and water. A large number of companies remained under full government control, such as ports and

21 In 1998, the government launched a 'modernization' program for Olympic Airways that cost 300 billion drachmas and an investment program in OTE that cost around 1 trillion drachmas, the latter mostly funded by the EU. The implementation of OTE's investment program raised questions of transparency after the exposure of the Siemens bribery scandal in Greece by a German tribunal in 2008.

22 The railways company (OSE), the Athens transport system and Olympic Airways recorded the biggest deficits (Mylonas and Papaconstantinou 2001: 507).

airports, state real estate, the large Commercial Bank of Greece, DEPA (in natural gas), the Post Office Bank, Olympic Airways and the Greek Hippodromes, among many others.

Understanding incomplete market liberalization

The privatization of monopoly rents

The Greek government followed a dilatory approach with regard to the deregulation of service and product markets that were dominated by state monopolies. Greece's transposition rate of internal market directives remained the second lowest in the EU (European Commission 2003a: 73). The government had previously asked the EU for derogations from the general deadlines for the liberalization of the electricity, natural gas and telecommunications markets (OECD 2001: 16). This was widely interpreted as an indication that the government 'lacked commitment' to create competitive markets (OECD 2001: 95). When these derogations expired, the state-controlled monopolies (such as OTE and DEI) had already established a dominant position thanks to heavy investment. Numerous de facto barriers to entry and competition made it difficult for new entrants to compete with the incumbent companies (OECD 2001: 57, 89, 93 and 104; see Table 7.2). Licenses, permits and regulations required from private entries to enter these sectors were 'unnecessarily burdensome' (OECD 2001: 11).[23] Entrepreneurs complained about the multitude of administrative procedures, the many formalities they had to follow with government ministries and other public agencies and the discretion these agencies enjoyed in the interpretation of particular laws and regulations, (OECD 2001: Chapter 2). Delays and the selective implementation of the law acted as informal protectionism measures that circumvented the legal obligations that Greece had undertaken under EU binding

Table 7.2 Informal barriers to market entry, year 2001

- Long and dispersed pieces of legislation (red tape)
- Regulatory uncertainty
- Long and complex administrative procedures for licenses and transactions
- Dispersed legal competences
- Delays by public authorities in issuing certificates and documents
- Considerable discretion in the interpretation of rules
- Selective enforcement of rules
- High set-up and operation costs for the private sector compared with other OECD countries

Source: OECD 2001: 34–39 and Chapter 2 of the report.

23 In the electricity sector, the 'Greek authorities have made several policy choices, such as not creating immediate competition by splitting [electricity] generation, whose combined effect is to discourage entry and ensure that the sector remains a stable monopoly' (OECD 2001: 84).

directives. Discriminatory government measures protected the dominant position of the incumbent companies in what were only nominally liberalized markets in electricity, gas and telecommunications (OECD 2001: 82, 85 and 94).

The electricity sector is a characteristic case of indirect protectionism. Informal barriers to the entry of competitors to the electricity market protected the government-controlled DEI, which retained a de facto monopoly in the electricity market (OECD 2001: 30; European Commission 2003a: 73). Legislation in conformity with EU directives was introduced in 1999 and 2003, but a number of administrative hurdles remained in place, eventually leading the European Commission to launch an infringement procedure against Greece for failing to comply with its public service obligations (PSOs) and the conditions for granting supply licenses required by EU law (Directive 2003/54/EC). Another barrier to entry was the fact that the company's access to fuel (natural gas and lignite), as well as its electricity prices, were not reflecting the true cost of supply (OECD 2001: 85). In addition, tenders for a license to operate power plants were delayed and effectively blocked by bureaucratic procedures, and DEI's bidding practices were found to be 'predatory' by the Regulation Authority (Iliadou 2009). As a result, the only market in electricity was limited to the purchase of electricity by the dominant monopoly (Iliadou 2009). In the years following the formal liberalization of the electricity market, only two 'independent' power stations had been constructed, one of which was owned by DEI (Iliadou 2009). Until 2009, DEI controlled 95% of total power generation and had exclusivity over the transmission system. Throughout that decade, the company expanded its activities in mining and power generation and created subsidiaries in telecommunications, renewable energy, nickel production and the development of energy projects (Iliadou 2009).

Through their monopoly or quasi-monopoly status, the state-controlled companies in telecommunications (OTE), bookings and lottery (OPAP), duty-free shops, the petrol industry (EKO and ELDA) and electricity (DEI) remained profitable and dominant in their respective sectors despite their inefficiencies. Public enterprises accounted for over a quarter of total investment in the Greek economy (27% in 2001, OECD 2001: 12). Since 1996, dividends from these profit-making enterprises helped the government cover its spending needs. Moreover, indirect protectionism of the partially privatized firms made their shares attractive for sale in the stock market, which offered additional revenue to the government budget.

Indirect protectionism also safeguarded the interests of the private investors in these companies. The actual monopoly status of the partially privatized corporations in electricity, telecommunications, water, sewage and lotteries offered the opportunity for a low-risk investment with good returns. The state had previously assumed their debt to pension funds, banks, DEI, OTE, etc. Investors also benefited from Community funds and other capital transfers from the central government, which further helped these companies reduce their debt liabilities and mitigated the need to borrow money to finance their investment programs (OECD 1998: 96).[24] Finally, legislation to protect consumer interests in electricity, transport and communications remained insufficient in terms of design and implementation (OECD 2001: 16). Under these circumstances, flotation was an invitation to private investors to invest in a protected monopoly that could guarantee a rentier's return, in exchange for the fact that the government would keep a say in the management and retain control over its procurement programs, while the unionized employees would retain their privileged employment terms.

Formal and informal barriers to entry outside the state sector

Outside the broader public sector, administrative burdens, such as business licenses and permits, were important barriers to entrepreneurship (OECD 2001: 12). Excessive state controls, complex and unstable rules and red tape caused severe distortions in the operation of the private sector and were hindering private investment (OECD 2001: 42; Bank of Greece 2005: 89). Business surveys estimated that, on average, more than 10% of an entrepreneur's time was spent on administrative formalities, and the cost of complying with tax regulations covered around 2% to 5% of gross profits (OECD 2001: 38). OECD reported that substantial capital was normally invested by firms and entrepreneurs to acquire the status of the 'insider' in government procurement and investment plans; this partly explained why foreign investment in Greece was so low and why it had mainly taken the form of acquiring existing firms (OECD 2001: 44). Entrepreneurs had to obtain information to advance their interests through informal avenues. The de facto exclusion of 'outsiders' through administrative discretion and red tape created a turf for patronage settlements and corruption in which politically appointed managers and cliques in the public sector were reportedly involved. This was a 'game' most foreign firms did not know how to play (OECD 2001: 44, 56–57 and 76).

During Simitis' administration, modest progress was recorded in terms of improving the business environment. A few measures were taken to simplify regulations that restricted competition (OECD 2001: 104). There was some progress in reducing the administrative burden on business, but the cost associated with setting up a new company remained high by EU standards. (European Commission 2002: 69 and 2003a: 73). Moreover, although the Greek government had established a one-stop shop for foreign investors (the Hellenic Centre for Investment, or ELKE), the agency failed to perform its task (OECD 2001: 77–78). Investment plans were still halted by excessive bureaucratic procedures (Liargovas 2007: 150). In general, there was no systematic attempt towards the codification

24 The energy-sector companies – electricity (DEI), gas (DEPA) and petroleum – had the largest financial needs (Mylonas and Papaconstantinou 2001: 507). Financial support from the government and the European Union reached around 3% of the GDP on an annual basis (Mylonas and Papaconstantinou 2001: 507).

and simplification of legislation, and a number of laws remained inert.[25] There was no progress in deregulating the so-called 'closed' professions, which included taxi drivers, cross-city bus transport, engineers, real estate agents, trucking, notaries, the bread industry, pharmacies, sea transport and cruise ships, despite the economic gains estimated by economic analysts to reach between 0.8% and 1.6% of GDP in 2000 (*Kathimerini*, 18/05/2009).

Finally, the stability, effectiveness and transparency of the tax system remained a serious problem (*Economikos*, 01/06/2004). For the business community, the tax system was one of the most serious disincentives for investment (*Economikos*, 03/09/1999: 40, and 29/06/2002: 12 and 14). Tax laws allowed wide discretion for tax officers and a scope for intervention for politicians. Tax reforms during Simitis' administration involved a few steps towards reducing the complexities of the tax system. The operation of the online tax control system, *taxis*, brought some good results in the area of auditing, but its operation was incomplete. Some critical subsystems for revenue control and cross-checking were never put into operation 'for reasons not associated with the quality of the software'.[26]

Partial reform in the labor market and the pensions system

Greece's low level of productivity was associated with persisting rigidities in the labor and product markets, low investment in human capital and the late development of the 'knowledge-based society'. During that time, the Lisbon Process, launched in 2000, prioritized reforms in the labor market towards greater flexibility in terms of working hours and the cost of overtime work. Labor market flexibility on the firm level was recommended as a way for the country to offset asymmetrical shocks after entry into the EMU, when currency devaluation was no longer possible (cf. Bank of Greece Governor in *Economikos*, 06/05/2000: 35).

In conformity with binding EU directives, the Simitis government passed a number of labor market reforms (see Table 7.3). Outside the legally binding directives, however, the government achieved 'a partial degree of implementation' of the 2002 Best Practices Guidelines for reforms in the pension system and the labor market (European Commission 2003a: 70). A first round of measures in August 1998 towards working time flexibility and wage diversity were not adequately implemented (see the 1999 IMF Report and *Vima*, 04/07/1999: 16). Another round of reforms in December 2000 actually tightened employment protection for employees in large enterprises (European Commission 2002: 67). There was no progress in reducing nonwage costs as requested by the Broad

25 'While efforts are underway to improve the business administrative environment, this has still to be translated into a comprehensive process of regulatory quality improvement, and companies remain broadly dissatisfied with their country's regulation and the efficiency of the public administration' (European Commission 2002: 66; and Council of the European Union 2003: 30).

26 See the interview of Kaiti Frantzeskaki, former director of a tax inspection team, in *Neoi Fakeloi*, on *SKAI* on 23/01/2012 at www.skai.gr/player/TV/?MMID=223688, retrieved on 12/02/2012.

Table 7.3 Labor market reforms

1. Institution of part-time employment in the public sector
2. Incentives to employers to decrease overtime work
3. Incentives to hire new personnel by lowering social security contributions in the case of low-paid workers
4. Reducing the tax burden on labor
5. Lowering the taxation rate on corporate profits (from 40% to 35%)
6. Incentives to those seeking part-time employment by increasing compensation for part-time jobs
7. Widening the upper limit to collective dismissals

Source: OECD; various European Union reports; and Laws 2638/1998, 2974/2002 and 3174/2003.

Economic Policy Guidelines and no significant change in the wage bargaining process (European Commission 2004a: 61).

Despite these measures, employment protection in Greece remained among the strictest in the OECD countries. Greece had a relatively high minimum wage, insufficient wage differentiation and strict employment protection laws (European Commission 2003a: 68). Labor law protected the 'insiders' of the labor market, whereas the unemployed were facing high barriers to entry. On the other side, employers in smaller firms in the private sector continued to rely on informal flexibility (in the so-called 'black market' for labor) to avoid rigid employment rules (OECD 2001: 38). By the end of Simitis' administration, 'unduly restrictive labor-market regulations' (European Commission 2003b: 25) and rising labor costs continued to undermine the competitiveness of the Greek economy, accounting for relatively low levels of employment despite the sizeable rate of growth over the previous decade (Bank of Greece 2005: 27).

Finally, the government had to tackle the extremely segmented, complex and cost-inefficient pension system. By the mid-1990s, questions over the long-term viability of the pension system led the government to establish a technocratic committee in 1996 (the Spraos Committee) whose report proposed a number of wide-sweeping reforms. The report on the state of the pension system showed that social policy in Greece had been used as a pretext for the continuation of privileges and the preservation of clientelist relations (Commission for the Review of Macroeconomic Policy 1997). In response, a law was voted for in 1998 (Law 2676) that led to a degree of regulatory consolidation and the unification or abolition of more than 60 pension funds. But the Greek pension system remained fragmented (Burtless 2001: 465). Greece's ageing population continued to burden the pension and social security systems. Between 1993 and 2001, Greece and Portugal were the only EU countries that had increased transfer spending for social protection (European Commission 2001: 88). At the same time, social security contribution rates in Greece were among the highest in the EU, accounting in 2004 for more than 34% of total gross labor cost (OECD 2005: 104). The government postponed any decisions for further reform until the 2000 election. Following pressures from the EU (European Commission 2002: 65) the government put forward a policy agenda of far more comprehensive reforms in the labor market and the pension system in 2001. The proposal triggered strong protest by the trade unions and led the government to introduce a milder reform plan (Law 3029/2003).[27]

Public administration and the regulatory system

As part of its greater project for economic and political modernization, the Simitis government announced its decision to reform the Greek public administration and enhance transparency in state–society relations. Because there were no binding prescriptions by the EU in that policy area, the government enjoyed a wide degree of discretion in the design and pace of these reforms. Moreover, unlike austerity, the case of reforming Greece's administration was popular among voters. There was widespread consensus that the Greek public administration and justice system suffered from persisting deficiencies: complex and time-consuming procedures, a high level of discretion by public servants, inconsistent application of the law, insufficient accountability, legal formalism, slow and expensive delivery of justice and occasionally blatant political interference and corruption.

The most notable administrative reform by the Simitis government was the establishment of the Ombudsman and other 'Independent Authorities' following other European Union countries. The Ombudsman gave citizens the right to contest the legality of administrative decisions without necessarily resorting to courts. Furthermore, the Simitis government established 'Independent Authorities' to regulate key economic and social activities, including monitoring the formally deregulated markets in electricity and telecommunications. Their members were appointed by the Council of the Presidents of the Greek Parliament with a qualified majority. This process still allowed some scope for bargaining among political parties over the list of the appointees.

The creation of these agencies was seen with skepticism by ministries who were reluctant to cede power (OECD 2001: 59). The law placed certain crucial Independent Authorities under government control, such as the regulatory authority for the telecommunications and postal services market (EEET, Law 2867/2000 art 3) and the Competition Commission (EA, Law 703/1977), whose members were appointed by the Cabinet and were under its disciplinary control. The Independent Authorities, such as the Ombudsman, the Internal Audit Service of Public Administration and the Court of Audit, had no effective power to find and punish employees who broke the law, and their task was limited to reporting cases of corruption and maladministration in the public sector (Pavlos Eleftheriadis, law expert, in *Vima*, 15/10/2006). Quite importantly, it is not certain the

27 For a detailed coverage of pension reforms, see Featherstone, Kazamias and Papadimitriou (2001); Matsaganis (2002); Featherstone (2005b); and Tinios (2005). See Chapter 8 for the political context of the unions' protests against the proposed reforms of 2001.

degree to which the real independence of these agencies was compromised by the informal ties between members of the independent agencies (or their family members) and political parties and politicians.

In addition, PASOK agreed with New Democracy on a round of constitutional amendments in 2001, which involved low-key changes that were far from introducing a general modernization plan to strengthen the rule of law (Eleftheriadis 2005: 329). This modest record of constitutional reforms reflected a general aversion among the political class to the idea that there should be strong checks on majoritarian party-based political power (cf. Eleftheriadis 2005: 329).

Minor reforms included the creation of 'one-stop shops' (the 'Citizens Service Centers', or KEP) and telephone call centers, which brought a noticeable improvement in terms of people's access to administrative documents and the settlement of routine bureaucratic procedures. These small steps were not accompanied by a much-needed comprehensive reform of the regulatory framework, which would actually reduce the amount of red tape required by public administration processes. Broadly speaking, the profusion of reformist rhetoric exceeded the actual record of reform (Spanou 2012: 171).

Despite a favorable public opinion and the strong economic rationale for the reform of public administration, the actual reform record was poor, particularly with regard to the issues of transparency and corruption. Accountability remained weak: the disciplinary committees in the public sector operated under the influence of unionists and politicians (Eleftheriadis in *Vima*, 15/10/2006). Wages and promotions in the public sector continued to be disconnected from performance and productivity (Alpha Bank 2005: 4). Reforms were often stalled in the implementation phase because law provisions were not activated by ministerial decrees or there were frequent changes of legislation and contradictory jurisprudence (OECD 2001: Chapter 2; Spanou 2008: 163).

By the end of Simitis' term, Greece retained an administrative model characterized by extreme legalism and politicization (Sotiropoulos 2004a). These weaknesses were manifest in the mounting number of cases of alleged maladministration that were awaiting adjudication in the justice system. Administrative burdens, in particular, business licenses and permits, continued to place important barriers to entrepreneurship and entrenched unfair competition against new market entries (OECD 2001: 110). Together with Hungary, Greece had the highest estimated cost of public administration in the economy among EU members (Rapanos 2009: 54). Delays in the reform of the public administration took their toll on economic activity:

> Nowadays, the state has expanded to areas which does not belong to, or where it proves to be inefficient, squandering precious productive resources which could have been allocated in development. By contrast, the state appears to be at times completely absent or to have a rudimentary presence in crucial areas of its responsibility . . .
>
> (Yannis Provopoulos, professor of economics who was later appointed governor of the Bank of Greece, in *Economikos*, 29/06/2002: 11)

Conclusion: clientelist bias in structural reforms

Unlike the Papandreou government, the Simitis administration embarked on structural reforms driven by the necessity to reinvigorate the Greek economy and by strong pressures from the European Union to redirect Greece's economic structure away from state control and monopoly over key economic sectors towards a freer market environment. Partial reform coupled with fiscal consolidation helped the government create positive expectations about the prospects of the Greek economy. Between 1996 and 2004, Greece recorded growth rates above the EU average, which the Bank of Greece attributed to the improvement of macroeconomic indices, the drop of borrowing costs, credit liberalization that propped up private investment and consumption, the progress of structural reforms and the inflow of Community funds (Bank of Greece 2005: 70 and 86). The government seemed to have successfully set in motion a virtuous circle of economic growth and macroeconomic consolidation.

What is quite noteworthy is that Greece returned to considerable growth rates with little sacrifice of its distributive and clientelist politics. The government retained control over significant economic sectors and avoided or delayed deep-cutting structural reforms. The government mostly used partial privatizations as a funding opportunity to raise revenue. The sale of minority shares in public-sector monopolies through flotation allowed the government to:

1 Keep control over managerial decisions, including public-sector procurement;
2 Raise revenue and lessen the need for greater spending cuts or new taxes;
3 Reduce the fiscal burden of state subsidies to the investment program of these corporations; and
4 Protect the privileges of client groups in the public sector (clientelist bias).

To secure Greece's entry into the EMU, the Simitis government navigated itself between the desire to preserve its commitments to key support groups in the public sector and the need to secure the sustainability of the Greek economy upon which its redistributive politics relied. Partial and incomplete structural reforms were carefully selected to achieve stabilization in the medium term, whereas more radical structural reforms necessary for long-term sustainability were avoided. EU prescriptions for reform were filtered through domestic political priorities. The Simitis government was careful not to reduce government control over key organizations of the state sector in which the party and its client unions had developed close ties for 2 decades. Partial reform protected most of the privileges enjoyed by PASOK's client groups in the public sector and secured new resources that renewed Greece's highly distributional model. This allowed PASOK to preserve its political ties with its clients and the trade unions and avoid intense reactions of the type the Mitsotakis government had previously confronted. A political commentator noted:

> Indeed, the main reason for this situation is the contradiction underlying the governing party, which, on the one hand, has to reduce, reform and

> modernize the state sector and its harmful intervention in the economy while, on the other hand, it relies on a large state and the privileges and clientelist relations that had been built around it for support and reproduction in power.
> (Yannis Kotofolos in the center-right daily *Kathimerini*, 17/02/2002)

The slow pace of liberalization meant that the market position of the state-controlled companies remained strong. Finance to public enterprises was secured through European Union funds and revenue from privatization, which replaced to a significant degree direct capital transfers from government and preferential loans from state-owned banks. Through indirect protectionism, the government privatization program sold monopoly profits to investors who secured safe and greater returns. The high level of public spending (around 40% of GDP) and the inflow of EU funds kept a great part of the private sector dependent on public-sector procurement, subject to an intricate and nontransparent allocation system. According to OECD, Greece had the worst record of compliance with EU liberalization directives, and this amounted to 'self-handicapping in a footrace', given the country's urgent need for economic reform (OECD 2001: 101). The Greek government placed 'higher priority on protecting established interests than on meeting consumer needs and supporting economic vitality' (OECD 2001: 101).

The recurrent theme in Greek economic policy was that 'clientelism and capture of the policy process by interest groups' displaced policy making 'in the general public interest' (OECD 2001: 104). It was the symbiotic relationship between the party, managers of public-sector companies, private business and the unions that assured mutual gains and prevented further and more comprehensive reform (cf. Spanou 2001). The pattern of reforms reshaped and reinvigorated Greece's model of state-sponsored capitalism. Despite the relative improvement of the macroeconomic indices, structural rigidities in product and service markets persevered. Although growth increased, employment levels did not rise accordingly. Greece's legal and regulatory environment remained unfriendly to the creation of new jobs in the private sector. Lack of adequate structural reforms led to price increases in public utilities and jobless growth. In the end, both the cost of the largely unsuccessful modernization effort and the costs of the monopoly or quasi-monopoly status of these corporations were borne by taxpayers and consumers.

In light of these observations, the ex post assessment of the Simitis period disproved earlier expectations that Simitis could mark a modernizing turn in PASOK's actual politics (Featherstone and Kazamias 1997; Verney 1997; Moschonas 2001; Pagoulatos 2003), and later accounts in the literature became more critical of PASOK's omissions and failures, which they attributed to lack of capacity and unwillingness to implement deep-cutting reforms (Kassimeris 2004; Lyrintzis 2005: 250; Mitsopoulos and Pelagidis 2006; Moutos and Tsitsikas 2010; Polychroniou 2011; Fouskas 2013; Pappas 2013).

Clientelist bias: an analysis

The reform pattern under the Papandreou and Simitis administrations (Table 7.4) add empirical strength to the view that in a clientelist economy, client groups

Table 7.4 Economic reform under PASOK (1993–2004)

Policy area	*External institutional pressures*	*Party ideology (public discourse)*	*Key stakeholders*	*Public opinion*	*Policy output*
Fiscal austerity (expenditure)	Strong	Tolerant	Public-sector employees and contractors**	Negative	- Pre-EMU, 1993–2000: mildly restrictive - Post-EMU, 2000–2004: expansionary
Raising taxes	Strong	Tolerant	Taxpayers	Negative	Throughout the period with hikes between 1985 and 1987 and before entry into the EMU (1995–2000)
Strict incomes policy	Moderate	Tolerant	Salaried workers in the public and private sectors	Negative	- Pre-EMU, 1993–2000: mildly restrictive - Post-EMU, 2000–2004: expansionary
Privatization	Strong/moderate*	Changed to endorse partial privatization	Labor unions** Private contractors	Mostly negative, then divided	Mostly partial privatization with management under government control and informal monopoly status (1996–2004)
Market deregulation	Strong/moderate*	Changed to endorse some measures of market deregulation	Labor unions,** private contractors and professional associations	Negative in particular sectors	Partial liberalization following EU directives and indirect protectionism (1996–2004)
Banking sector liberalization	Strong	Endorsement	Labor unions** Bankers	Indifferent	Full liberalization following EU directives The government retained partial control over the banking sector
Labor market	Strong/moderate*	Timid endorsement	Salaried workers in the private sector	Mostly negative	Partial liberalization following EU directives
Pensions and social security	Moderate	Initially tolerant, later divided	Salaried workers in the private sector, and public-sector employees**	Negative	Partial liberalization mostly affecting younger employees, following EU pressures and sustainability issues
Corruption and transparency	Weak	Endorsement	Party cliques in the public sector** and private contractors	Favorable	Limited initiatives with poor results

*Strong pressure from binding EU directives (state aid, labor law) or fiscal rules, and moderate pressure from 'soft-law' recommendations (Open Method of Coordination guidelines and the Lisbon agenda)

**Client groups

are the most politically significant groups for the party in government. When there are strong structural and institutional pressures for economic reform, the governing party must seek ways to deliver reform in a way that protects its clientelist commitments to core groups. Reform must be tailored to prevent a general crisis of fiscal sustainability that could undermine established 'supply' mechanisms. The issue of reform becomes an exercise of sequencing and selecting policies in a manner that diffuses its costs among taxpayers and consumers.

The case of Greece shows that this clientelist bias in the design of structural reform can be manifested as partial privatizations, delays and omissions to modernize or close down the deficit-ailing companies, debt assumption by the government and indirect protectionism of the monopoly status of government-controlled companies. In addition, the government may also search for alternative pathways to compensate for the loss of old channels of clientelist supply (substituting resources). This modality of reform leads to a pattern of 'reproduction by adaptation' (in the language of historical institutionalism: Streeck and Thelen 2005: 4) regarding the key properties of the clientelist model. This process unravels gradually, without any dramatic disruptions, under the impact of the 'increasing returns' that clientelist politics still offer to parties and patrons. As the next chapter shows, this process is conditioned by intraparty commitments and interdependences and often evolves through coordination and negotiation between the main stakeholders: the party leadership, party politicians and the unions.

8 Within-party dynamics in clientelist politics

PASOK under Simitis

Stabilization and growth policies can threaten the status of actors with vested interests in the previous economic structure. For the public-sector unions, deregulation and privatization can change the privileged terms of employment their members enjoy. For individual politicians, economic reform may reduce the scope for the supply of clientelist benefits to their supporters. For party leaders, structural reforms can reduce state control over the economy and can undermine existing channels for exerting political influence over social groups. These changes could threaten the cohesion of the party itself. As outlined in the previous chapter, these considerations make the governing party adopt a dominant strategy and tailor its polices to safeguard the status of its client groups even under pressing conditions. The chapter shows how interactions among actors with a concern for party unity and their personal political success give rise to behavior that is conducive to a clientelist bias. In this environment, the government must find ways to anticipate possible reactions from its client groups to its reform initiatives in order to adjust and pace their content and prevent a major clash.

As the previous chapter has indicated, the reform record by the Simitis government exhibited a pattern of bias towards protecting core party commitments to client groups. For an observer, this is puzzling because the prime minister's agenda was widely seen as modernizing and unusually technocratic given Greece's prior record of politicization.[1] Observing the relationship and interactions between the government and recalcitrant political actors inside PASOK indicates how party roles, ties and mutual commitments shaped this approach to reforms. The Simitis government sought to avoid reactions inside its broader party network which could have undermined the party's unity. It repeatedly provided reassurances that its reform agenda would spare its political clientele in the public sector from direct losses. The government also took advantage of the informal ties

1 PASOK could benefit from a 'Nixon goes to China' effect, which describes the idea that a left-wing government is more likely to convince the public to accept reforms associated with a conservative political agenda than a right-wing government 'because it is more credible in conveying the message that it is solving an important social problem rather than acting according to a partisan logic' (Saint-Paul 1996: 281).

connecting the unions with the governing party and heavily relied on tactics of co-optation offering personal rewards to complacent party unionists, such as the opportunity to embark on a political career in central politics. It also took seriously into account the experience with previous rounds of reforms.

The types of interactions that took place between the government and its politically affiliated unions differs from the typical interest-group schema because, as this chapter shows, policy preferences were codependent; they were shaped and tested in the context of an ongoing synergy between the government and the unions that were both situated inside PASOK's broader client network. At times, episodes of confrontation, occurred, but conflict was kept at bay, as considerations of mutual interest prevailed on both sides, favoring political compromise in order to safeguard the unity of the party.

Safeguarding the cohesion of PASOK

Prime Minister Simitis openly endorsed an ideological profile influenced by 'Third Way' social democracy. Simitis also relied on a 'there-is-no-alternative' discourse with the message that Greece's failure to join the EMU would seriously undermine PASOK's electoral prospects in the forthcoming election in 2000. Although this agenda found a skeptical audience in the party and its affiliated labor organizations, it was attractive to centrist voters, which PASOK needed to win the election. Electoral victory in the next election meant that career-orientated PASOK officials could keep their offices. It was also expected that economic improvement and EMU membership would also restore PASOK's popularity among center-left voters. Moreover, access to EU funds, which financed a considerable part of government distribution, had been made conditional on Greece's progress in achieving macroeconomic consolidation. These high stakes were hinted at by Prime Minister Simitis when he defended his policy agenda in front of PASOK's Central Committee:

> The great dependence of both the State and the whole of the economy on borrowers leaves us no room for policy maneuvers. Don't have any illusions. Growth policy, social policy, defense policy, foreign policy that depend on loans are an impasse . . . This is why fiscal consolidation, macroeconomic balance and reduction of the state's dependence on borrowing constitute the prime requirements of our program. *This is the only way we can untie our hands*.
>
> (*Economikos*, 01/08/1996: 15, emphasis added)

Managing within-party opposition

Simitis' position as the party leader was dependent both on the success of his effort to secure Greece's entry into the EMU and on how he tackled preferences, claims and anxieties inside his party, including the aspirations of his opponents in the party. Compared to his predecessor, Simitis' control over party politicians and the party base was much weaker. The prime minister had to build and preserve a support coalition inside a heterogeneous and highly factionalized party. This included striking opportunistic alliances around his self-proclaimed 'modernization' agenda, not only on the basis of ideological convergence, but also through the use of co-optation tactics. A balanced allocation of offices could keep dissent at bay and prevent cracks in the unity of the party.

The allocation of posts in the Cabinet and the party was careful not to exclude influential PASOK cadres. Simitis took advantage of the office-seeking mentality of PASOK politicians to forge an ideologically vague and heterogeneous power bloc inside the party. Many of Simitis' previous opponents were also given important positions.[2] This was a rational strategy for a number of reasons. By including his opponents, the prime minister was sharing political accountability and the risk of political failure, including the responsibility to secure Greece's entry into the Eurozone (*Kathimerini*, 10/01/1999). Any act of open defiance, let alone defection from the party, would then deprive them of access to power.[3] Access to power acted as a check on opportunistic behavior. The prime minister allowed his opponents personal space for political influence with enough room to cultivate personal relations with other party cadres and unionists.[4]

For both Simitis' friends and foes, access to power depended on party unity. The downfall of the Mitsotakis government had shown them that internal wars of attrition tended to generate a collectively harmful outcome. Prominent politicians who had previously left their parties, such as Antonis Samaras from New Democracy and Dimitris Tsovolas from PASOK, faced political isolation. Their fate offered a useful lesson for dissenters or aspirant successors to remain loyal to their party and its leadership. Although they had conflicting personal aspirations, they toned down their divergent views or disagreements. No party faction was willing to organize a sizeable and vocal opposition bloc within PASOK. Any orchestrated attempt to topple down Simitis in such a politically sensitive phase could trigger a crisis inside the party, as well as political instability in the country, for which they would, most probably, take the blame.

Despite occasional complaints about the distribution of offices in the party and the government, unity was a common concern and the recurrent slogan in all PASOK's conferences (*Vima*, 23/6/1996; 21/07/1996). PASOK's rank and file believed that Simitis was the most qualified leader to secure the country's entry into the EMU and PASOK's electoral victory. They were aware that Simitis had

2 Both opponents of Costas Simitis in the 1996 PASOK leadership contest, Akis Tsohatzopoulos and Gerasimos Arsenis, served as Cabinet ministers under his administration.

3 Former Finance Minister Tsovolas was a prominent politician who left PASOK and founded a political party in 1995 (DIKKI) winning a respectable 4.43% of votes in the 1996 election. His party failed to enter the parliament in 2000.

4 For instance, Akis Tsohatzopoulos, the prime minister's main rival in the 1996 party leadership contest, accepted the post of minister of defense and did not challenge Simitis throughout the PASOK administration. Tsohatzopoulos adjusted his rhetoric so as not to provoke a clash with the prime minister and his supporters.

earned the respect of prominent politicians in the European Union and the trust of private markets (*Kathimerini*, 25/10/1998). Simitis' success guaranteed the political success of PASOK and the future of its leading politicians in the government. When Simitis stood as the candidate for the party leadership in two PASOK conferences in 1999 and 2001, he received 62% and 71% of the votes, respectively. As long as his appeal as prime minister was improving PASOK's chances of victory in the next election, his position as leader of PASOK was secure.

The prevalence of an office-seeking mentality was manifested in the way party cadres reacted to PASOK's monumental U-turns regarding privatization, fiscal restraint and foreign policy. There was little ideological discussion about the party's impressive and sudden transformation in both rhetoric and policy – most noticeable in 1993 and 1996. Complaints within PASOK were limited to policy details or procedural issues, for instance, whether party institutions operated with openness and inclusion. Dissenters broadly referred to the social cost of economic policy, voicing their concern that PASOK might lose the next election due to 'the mistaken handling of certain policy issues' (*Nea*, 29/03/1998; *Eleftherotypia*, 01/09/2001; 10/07/2001). They also repeatedly made reference to PASOK's commitment to a patriotic foreign policy and social justice.[5] Criticism often involved ambiguous, almost coded, messages and innuendos about how politically sensitive issues had been handled by the government, particularly the handling of specific privatization plans (*Vima*, 21/07/1996). Vague criticism was tolerated, or perhaps welcomed, as it was venting accumulated grievances inside the party while making it possible for some party officials to reconnect with disillusioned supporters. This rhetoric masked anxieties concerning the loss of traditional PASOK supporters, as well as personal clashes over the allocation of offices (*Vima*, 12/04/1998; *Eleftherotypia* 02/08/2001). Quite often, the expression of discontent and anxiety was designed to increase one's bargaining power in the party. Complaints and personal grievances were much more vociferous behind closed doors at party meetings.

An analytic outlook on within-party relations

The observed relations inside PASOK had the following pattern: the prime minister offered his within-party opponents access to state offices and resources in return for their moderate stance on reforms and their abstaining from openly undermining his leadership. In turn, his opponents adopted a complacent stance towards Simitis as long as they could access political power, mostly by occupying public offices or expecting to get one. This pattern – co-optation by the party leader and complacency by his opponents – was likely to emerge as interactions were repeated and the actors involved had information about the cost of open

5 Such as pleas to protect 'the social profile of PASOK', *Vima*, 21/07/1996.

confrontation. Previous cases allowed these 'players' to understand the gains from cooperation and adopt it as the mutually best strategy.

This setting helps us trace the order of preferences of the two sides and understand why cooperation among opposing factions inside the clientelist party is their best strategy. The party leadership primarily wants to stay in power and get re-elected, but it has to address its opponents inside the party. It also wants to promote a reform agenda, preferably without causing severe frictions that could undermine the party's cohesion. In tackling within-party opposition, the leader could either confront his or her opponents (isolate them and expel them from the party) or co-opt them with public offices. Yet, if confronting the opposition causes tensions that could undermine party unity, this could harm the party's chances for re-election. The party leader would rather employ a strategy of co-optation. The worst scenario for the party leader is the one in which internal frictions undermine party unity (Table 8.1).

The leadership's opponents inside the party have the options of either openly confronting the leadership or accepting its co-optation offer and sharing power. The most preferable situation is one in which they could openly confront and undermine the party leader's policies without risking retaliation from the party leadership in the form of expulsion and without causing a conflict that could undermine the party unity (confrontation, co-optation). This situation will allow them to undermine the leader and prepare the ground for career advancement

Table 8.1 Preference schedule for the party leadership

Order	*Leader's options*	*His/her opponent's options*	*Payoffs*	*Explanation*
1	Confrontation PL1	Complacency O2	4	• Does not involve sharing office with his/her opponents • Clears dissenters from the party • Does not trigger a response by them that could undermine party unity
2	Co-optation PL2	Complacency O2	3	• Involves sharing office with his/her opponents • Silences dissenters, as they accept the co-optation offer • Does not trigger a response by them that could undermine party unity
3	Confrontation PL1	Confrontation O1	2	• Does not involve sharing office with his/her opponents • Clears dissenters from the party • Triggers a fierce response by them that undermines party unity
4	Co-optation PL2	Confrontation O1	1	• Involves sharing office with his/her opponents • Fails to silence dissenters • Triggers a fierce response by them that undermines party unity

following a change in leadership in due time. As a second preference, the leader's opponents will be complacent with government policy to the extent that their behavior is rewarded with a share in offices in the party and the government (complacency, co-optation). This is their second preferred option because, unlike the leader's supporters, they cannot enthusiastically endorse the party's official policy in view of their commitments to the dissenting segment of the party, which they are supposed to represent, and because by endorsing these policies they will also find themselves accountable in case the party loses the next election. An open clash (confrontation, confrontation), however, may lead to their expulsion from the party or isolation inside the party, which are both undesirable outcomes. Although the party leadership may suffer damages from a confrontation with dissenters, within-party opponents will suffer a greater and immediate damage: loss of access to power and exit from a power mechanism into a political field that is hostile to outsiders. The least desirable situation is the one in which the leader pushes them to exit and they do not take any action that could return some damage to the leader (complacency, confrontation; Table 8.2).

Table 8.2 Preference schedule for within-party opponents

Order	*Within-party opponents – options*	*Leader's options*	*Payoffs*	*Explanation*
1	Confrontation O1	Co-optation PL2	4	• Allows them to share power • Undermines and possibly helps replace the party leadership • Keeps them in the party with access to its power mechanism • Secures party unity for the next election
2	Complacency O2	Co-optation PL2	3	• Allows them to share power • Fails to undermine the party leadership • Keeps them in the party with access to its power mechanism • Secures party unity for the next election
3	Confrontation O1	Confrontation PL1	2	• Excludes them from access to power • Undermines the party leadership • Risks their expulsion from the party and political isolation • Triggers a fierce response by the leadership that undermines party unity for the next election
4	Complacency O2	Confrontation PL1	1	• Excludes them from access to power • Fails to undermine the party leadership • Risks their expulsion from the party and political isolation • Triggers a fierce response by the leadership, which manages to get rid of opponents without causing great damage to the party

Table 8.3 Game between the party leadership and within-party opponents

		Opponents (Opp.)	
		Confrontation O1	*Complacency O2*
Leadership of the party in government (PL)	Confrontation PL1	2, 2	4, 1
	Co-optation PL2	1, 4	3, 3

Given this set of preferences, we can see why episodes of confrontation are likely to take place inside the party, when players move with no prior communication or cooperation. In the first scenario, the two players have to take a stance against one another with incomplete information and almost simultaneously after the announcement of a policy: both the leadership and its opponents do not know each other's payoffs, and each player does not know the 'type' of person her or his opponent is (risk-averse, risky, etc.), hence, the players are not able to deduce or predict what their opponents are going to do. In a climate of mutual mistrust and if players are risk-averse, given the high stakes involved here (loss of power), they may follow the 'maximin strategy'. In that case, they will look at the worst possible outcome at each option and select the highest one of these (the players will choose the option that maximizes the minimum gain they can get among two options). The party leadership will consider which of the worst-case scenarios for each of the two possible actions (co-opt or confront) offers the highest payoff. If the leadership chooses to co-opt its opponents, the worst payoff it could get is 1. If it decides to confront, the worst payoff would be 2. In that case, it will choose to confront. The leadership's opponents anticipate a higher payoff of 2 if they confront the leadership and the payoff of 1 if they get co-opted (see Table 8.3).

Under this strategy, it is rational for both players to choose confrontation over complacency because of incomplete information and risk aversion, but both the party leadership and the opposition will end up with PL1O1 (2, 2). Although this is a Nash equilibrium, it is a suboptimal outcome because there is a situation that offers both players a higher payoff (3, 3), but no actor has an incentive to unilaterally change strategy. This context – which resembles the 'Prisoner's Dilemma' – appears to describe the clashes that happened between Prime Minister Mitsotakis and a segment of his opponents in the party. These events, however, served as a useful lesson for PASOK politicians.[6]

The same suboptimal outcome may be reached if each player moves with incomplete information, this time in sequence. If the party leadership moves first

6 Note that because this payoff ranking is ordinal, these numbers do not indicate equal distance between expected gains (3 versus 2) and that, in reality, the suboptimal outcome will cause great harm to both parties.

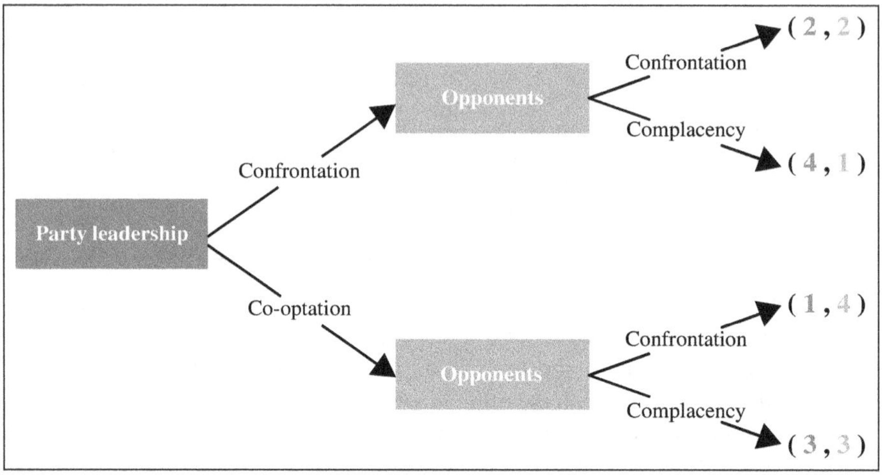

Figure 8.1 Decision tree with complete information

and chooses to be complacent towards the opposition in anticipation of complacency in return, the opposition may misread this signal as weakness and choose to confront the leadership. The leadership may then retaliate, leading the two players to the same suboptimal equilibrium (confront, confront), whereas higher payoffs could be gained by the option of complacency/co-optation.[7]

Nevertheless, by observing prior incidents of within-party confrontation, the players gain useful information that allows them to predict their opponents' payoff structure and understand the risk of both ending up in a suboptimal position. With complete information, the players could calculate their subsequent moves based on what may resemble a 'decision tree' (Figure 8.1). When players are aware that there will be a suboptimal outcome of the game thanks to previous episodes (knowing the payoffs and employing backward induction) and find a way to communicate and agree to avoid this result, they can avoid the subgame perfect equilibrium point that is a suboptimal outcome (2, 2). The players understand that although they have conflicting interests, they can both achieve mutual gains through cooperation, if the game becomes cooperative. When the two sides find it useful to communicate with each other, they can strike informal

7 In theory, if a noncooperative game is played many times, the players can adopt various other strategies. For example, they can adopt a 'tit-for-tat' strategy in which they start by playing PL2 and O2, and they both continue doing whatever the other player did in the last round (i.e. respond to cooperation in the previous round with cooperation and to defection in the previous round with defection). Adopting this strategy can make the optimal outcome PL2O2 a Nash equilibrium. Yet, in actual party politics, if players find themselves in the suboptimal equilibrium of mutual confrontation, the damage felt in their circumstances and in the party's cohesion and electoral mobilization may be so severe that the first players (the leader and his or her opponents) are replaced by new ones and, in that case, there will be no opportunity for repeated games.

agreements to avoid the shared losses in the event the party loses power. The opposition can inform the party leadership that it would choose complacency insofar as the party leadership chooses co-optation and, in the opposite case, it would choose confrontation if the party leadership chooses confrontation. The two players may reach an agreement for ongoing co-optation/complacency in order to secure the payoff distribution of 3, 3. Once this mutually advantageous outcome is achieved, informal agreements, compliant behavior and communication are likely to strengthen mutual trust.

Managing relations with the trade unions

The shared interest in protecting party unity, as well as cooptation tactics, also defined the relationship between the party leadership and PASOK's leading unionists. Following the electoral victory of 1993, PASOK made an impressive U-turn in its economic policy away from its pre-electoral rhetoric regarding privatizations and structural reforms and confronted remarkably mild reactions among the unions. This was unexpected. When Simitis became the prime minister, his economic agenda caused fears that there might be reactions, divisions and defections by PASOK's union leaders and unionized supporters. The first generation of union leaders had entered central politics,[8] and it was uncertain whether their successors would be equally complacent with government policy (*Vima*, 29/09/1996; 08/03/1998). Privatization became the most contentious issue, given the significant role of union leaders in the public-sector enterprises. Minister of National Economy Papantoniou openly admitted that trade unionists were actually running public enterprises and state banks together with their managers:

> Co-management means securing privileges and some of them are not willing to lose them and react for that reason.
>
> (*Nea*, 25/05/1998: 48)

The prime minister and his Cabinet ministers sought to placate the anxieties of the unionists by using tactics of co-optation that built upon the close ties between the party and the unions.[9] The majority of unionists, including two consecutive presidents of GSEE (General Confederation of Greek Labor), supported Simitis in his bid for party leadership in 1996 and made a strong

8 See also *Kathimerini*, 01/12/ 2004; *Vima*, 15/11/2009; 30/03/2010. Former president of GSEE, Polyzogopoulos, once admitted that many unionists saw their trade unions as a platform for a political career (*Vima*, 21/01/2001). Polyzogopoulos was one of the protagonists of the unions' revolt against the pension reform proposals in 2001. A few years later he stated that he had never hidden his party identity and that he had fought hard within PASOK to promote the unions' views. He later retired from the union movement 'in order to get a new role in his party' (*Vima*, 02/07/2006).

9 The 'unions' nomenclature', as they were called by Petros Efthymiou, a journalist in the politically centrist newspaper *Vima*, who would later become PASOK's Cabinet minister (01/02/1998).

contribution to Simitis' victory (*Vima*, 03/11/1996; 12/04/1998).[10] They were possibly driven by the belief that Simitis could secure electoral victory in the coming election:

> During the PASOK conference, many were wondering how it is possible that a segment of ideological and political hardliners such as the trade unions identified with modernizer Simitis and broke their long-standing 'blood' ties with Akis Tsohatzopoulos. One explanation (but not the only one) is the self-preservation instinct of trade unionists, which they get from their everyday interaction with society.
>
> (Panayiotis Lampsias in *Vima*, 03/11/1996)

The close ties of union leaders with the party favored moderation. It was known that these union leaders presided over trade unions whose membership was dominated by public-sector employees largely sympathetic to PASOK. It was estimated that more than 200,000 PASOK members served in the broader public sector and enjoyed several privileges attached to party membership such as promotions, favorable placements and special financial rewards (*Kathimerini*, 28/04/2002). In return for these privileged terms of employment, PASOK could rely on their political support and loyalty as party supporters and union members. In addition, the PASOK government capitalized on fears that if New Democracy came to power, it was likely to implement deep-cutting structural reforms that could radically change the ownership status and employment conditions of many public-sector companies. These ties of loyalty and co-dependency can be contrasted to the militancy of farmers, loosely aligned with New Democracy or the Communist Party, who frequently organized vocal protests and sit-ins on the country's national roads network.

Furthermore, the government's attitude towards reforms offered the unions the opportunity to take part in an informal process of co-decision, which mitigated the uncertainty surrounding the distribution of costs and benefits of reform. Policy initiatives followed three explorative steps: announcing a broad and ambitious reform agenda, tracing the initial reactions by the unions and adjusting the final policy proposals to address these reactions.

Stage 1: *Preparing the ground*: Economic circumstances and, quite often, direct EU pressures, pushed the government to consider initiating reform in a given policy area. At times, the government set up a technocratic committee to file a report with its policy proposals (e.g. the Spraos Committee for pensions and the Georgakopoulos Committee for tax reforms). The government officially endorsed 'the spirit' of the proposed reforms, but it left it open whether it would

10 In return, Simitis rewarded some of his supporters in the unions with offices in the party and the government. After becoming Cabinet members and PASOK MPs, these former unionists stood opposite the new generation of union leaders who, on several occasions, reacted against Simitis' economic plans.

follow all the recommendations, and invited the unions to take part in a social dialogue.

Stage 2: *Anticipating reactions*: The announcement of reform proposals tended to have a 'hit and run' effect on social actors. The government expected the stakeholders to react by demanding either the moderation or the cancellation of the reform agenda.

Stage 3: Adjustment to reactions: Depending on the scale of the initial reactions and the urgency of the reform in question, the government would choose one of the following options: watering down the reform (as happened with the 2001 pension reform) and adopting only 'the most necessary measures' in tune with the concerns raised (*Eleftherotypia* 02/04/2002; 16/04/2002), inaction (as in Olympic Airways) or the implementation of a full-scale reform (as in the case of the Ioniki Bank).

This sequence gave the government the necessary time and the valuable information to gauge reactions and consider a scope for compromise. With a 'piecemeal' and 'wait-and-see' attitude to reforms, the government could contain the escalation of protest against its reform initiatives. At the same time, the government made use of any opportunity to repeatedly explain the importance of reforms in securing Greece's EMU membership. This rhetoric was coupled with the government announcing that its fiscal policy would relax after Greece's entry into the EMU (*Kyriakatiki Eleftherotypia*, 29/07/2001). In that way, the governing party could avoid provoking a clash with its key support groups. Finally, by engaging in social dialogue, the government could demonstrate to the EU that reforms were under way.

In this context, the new union leadership could be explicit in their policy criticisms to the degree they could claim that their motivation was to protect PASOK from policies that could cost the party critical voters.[11] Their reactions to contentious issues, such as privatization, reflected their dual position inside PASOK and the labor movement, which pushed union leaders to strike a balance between their role as leaders who were expected to promote sectoral interests and as politicians representing their party in their workplace. As prominent party officials, they were aware that a general rebellion could undermine PASOK's cohesion and could precipitate the return of New Democracy to power. Given that employees in the broader public sector constituted the largest share of union membership (*Vima*, 08/03/1998) and most of them were PASOK's supporters, the union leaders knew that they could secure their position by being responsive to the specific demands of PASOK's clients in the public sector, which favored mutual-interest accommodation.[12] Moreover, elections for the leadership of the

11 'Mr. Polyzogopoulos [president of GSEE] stated that "I would not let the party lose because of Mr. Tsovolas [former PASOK minister of finance and leader of a minor opposition party, DIKKI) and KKE [the communists]".' (*Vima*, 03/11/1996).

12 In a 1995 survey, 55.8% of the respondents replied that GSEE was 'dependent on government policy' (*Vima*, 08/03/1998). In another poll, 32.1% of the respondents had a positive view of GSEE, 35.7% a negative view and 27.4% had no position (*Vima*, 08/03/1998).

party's union organizations were largely influenced by dynamics and antagonisms inside the party.[13] Trade unionists were aware that promotions within the party and appointments to government offices largely depended on the approval of the central party and were often offered as rewards for loyalty to the party. In addition, many union leaders had their own aspirations for a career in central politics. The prospect of a political career was also strengthening the linkage between unionists and PASOK's leadership and served as an incentive for complacency with government policy:

> Trade unionists learn quite early who the boss is; who punishes and who rewards. As a result, their choice is between submission to the party or retreat.
> (Theodoros Lianos in *Vima*, 07/09/1997)[14]

Engagement with the unions became 'an extremely lucrative profession' securing membership in committees and managerial boards in the public sector (*Kathimerini*, 02/02/2003). The partisan affiliation of top unionists and most of their members compromised the autonomy of the union movement. The overlapping roles of party unionists is epitomized in the statement by Andreas Kollias, the leader of the union that protested against the privatization of the Athens bus company in 1992:

> If they tell me to stand for MP, it would be a great honor. But let me be clear, I am not doing all this in order to be knighted as an MP.
> (*Vima*, 05/04/1998)

Co-optation tactics led the unionists to exhibit a generally mild response to government policies, manifested in the small scale and mild character of their rallies and protests (*Vima*, 03/11/1996; *Kathimerini*, 01/07/2001).[15] By carefully preserving its ties with the trade unions, PASOK secured conditions of relative social peace.[16] In 1997 the unions signed a Social Pact with the employers for wage moderation to help the country's run-up to membership in the EMU. This 'trust agreement' linked wage policy to the rate of inflation and the productivity rate. A number of significant concessions were attached in return. The decision of the leadership of the labor unions to agree on wage moderation stood in sharp contrast to decades of labor unrest and confrontation with austerity-implementing governments.[17] Minister of Economy Papantoniou later praised the unions for their 'responsible stance' and promised to strengthen social policy once Greece

13 *Vima*, 02/11/1997; 08/03/1998, 22/03/1998 and 12/04/1998.

14 See also comments in the centrist newspaper *Vima* by Georgios Bitros (14/06/1998).

15 According to the president of the Athens Workers House, the control that political parties had over the unions was the main reason for the demise of the labor movement (*Vima*, 08/03/1998).

16 The only notable exceptions were the labor organization controlled by the Communist Party (PAME) and farmers' organizations attached to either the Communist Party or New Democracy.

17 GSEE unionists who were affiliated with the opposition parties opposed the agreement (*Economikos*, 13/11/1997: 25).

entered the Eurozone and came to enjoy the 'benefits from a successful economic policy' (*Kyriakatiki Eleftherotypia*, 29/07/2001).

Occasional clashes between unions and government and their settlement within PASOK

Unions and union leaders were widely seen as PASOK's strategic partners. They were often portrayed by the press as agents employed 'by the party to manipulate the demands of the workers' when in government and to serve 'as the spearhead of its opposition tactics' when in opposition.[18] However, personal ties, the use of co-optation by the government and a clientelist bias in the design of reforms did not always prevent confrontation with the labor movement. The privatization of the middle-sized Ioniki Bank led to serious confrontations between the government and the unions during Simitis' first term.[19] The full sale of the bank was one of the few deviations from the model of partial privatizations and became a critical test for the relationship between the government and the unions. Government officials justified the privatization of Ioniki as part of the country's obligations to meet the Maastricht Criteria (*Vima*, 02/08/1998: 16). The government reassured the employees that they would keep their jobs because their fixed-term contracts were to be extended until their retirement age (*Nea*, 02/06/1998: 50). Despite these assurances, however, PASOK-affiliated unionists expressed their objection to the full sale of the bank. The unionists reminded the government that the planned privatization contradicted PASOK's program (*Nea,* 12/05/1998: 51). GSEE and ADEDY organized a series of strikes.[20] Outside the bank's union, the level of participation in the protest against the sale was low (*Vima*, 28/06/1998).

The government insisted on its decision to proceed with the sale. For the government, the sale was a test of its determination to stick to its privatization program. If the government had backed down in the face of sectoral reactions, it would have sent the wrong message about how serious it was about structural reforms in its stabilization effort (*Economikos*, 04/06/1998: 33). Criticism within the Cabinet focused less on the decision to privatize the bank and more on the way the Ministry of the Economy was handling the sale, particularly the fact that the government sent the riot police to end the occupation of Ioniki's headquarters (*Nea*, 01/06/1996: 8). But in the aftermath of these reactions, bolder

18 A comment by Stamos Zoulas in center-right newspaper *Kathimerini*, 01/12/2004. See also Mouzelis in *Vima*, 20/03/2005. New Democracy and other opposition parties had a similar attitude towards their labor organizations (*Vima*, 15/11/2009).

19 See also Trantidis (2015). The privatization of Ioniki had a small impact on the degree of state ownership and control of Greece's banking system; 70% of the banking-sector activity continued to be under state control (*Vima*, 31/05/1998).

20 Yannis Marinos, a veteran political commentator, wrote in the centrist newspaper *Vima* that the unionists who opposed full privatization were defending their power in Ioniki Bank over 'appointments, placements and disciplinary action' and were 'catering for their own interests and their future political career' (28/06/1998).

proposals for structural reforms by the minister of the interior and former Minister of Finance Papadopoulos were rejected by the Cabinet.[21] Fearing stronger reactions from the unions, the government watered down its plan for the reform of labor relations in 1997.

The most serious clash between the government and the unions broke up over government plans to reform the pension system in the spring of 2001. Proposals to reform the pension system found a skeptical audience among PASOK politicians and Cabinet ministers (*Eleftherotypia*, 3/11/2000; *Ethnos*, 20/11/2000). When the plan was announced, the government was surprised by the scale of reactions and the capacity of the unions to mobilize large numbers of people to protest.[22] Initially, the rallies held by the labor unions had little support of prominent PASOK politicians. However, in the summer of 2001, a poll showed that 72% of PASOK's voters were unhappy with the government's economic policy and wanted a change in its direction (*Kathimerini* 03/07/2001). Around a hundred PASOK-affiliated unionists issued a declaration urging the government 'to hear the voice of society' (*Eleftherotypia*, 03/08/2001). Soon, the relationship between the 'reformist' ministers Papantoniou and Giannitsis and PASOK's union leaders became tense (*Eleftherotypia*, 03/08/2001; 07/08/2001). This led to fierce and mass protests that eventually obliged the government to back down on its initial plans. Minister of Economy Papantoniou promised to start the dialogue on pension reform from scratch and 'without any commitment to the directions and principles of the previous approach':

> I would like to remind you that I have been the Minister of Economy and Finances for seven and half years and I have addressed many great economic and social problems. In all these cases, there were disagreements from the start. Eventually, we always found a consensual solution, at least one that confronted the least possible reactions, and that is to the credit of GSEE [the largest trade union].
>
> (*Kyriakatiki Eleftherotypia*, 29/07/2001)

The government later enacted a modest reform package. The unions' reactions served as a demonstration of their resilient mobilization capacity after years of relative complacency. The new generation of union leaders was reassuming some degree of autonomy versus the central party and reconfirmed its role as the intermediary between PASOK's support base in the unions and the party leadership. Following confrontation over pension reform, many PASOK-affiliated unionists became openly critical of the government's reform agenda. This stance

21 Such as the privatization of state-owned banks, including the National Bank of Greece – the largest bank in the country – the abolition of the 49% cap on the share of public enterprises that could be sold to private investors, the reform of the pension system and further market liberalization (*Nea*, 16/03/1998).

22 Minister of Social Security Giannitsis admitted that he had miscalculated the degree to which the party was willing to accept reforms (Giannitsis 2007: 21).

of the unions became a source of anxiety for Simitis (*Vima*, 12/04/1998; *Eleftherotypia*, 13/08/2001). As tensions were mounting, leading PASOK politicians were carefully distancing themselves from government policy (*Kathimerini*, 19/06/2001). In view of the strenuous relationship between the government and the unions, Simitis decided to cancel a number of scheduled reforms and called a PASOK conference in October 2001, earlier than initially scheduled (*Eleftherotypia*, 07/08/2001).

By calling a party conference, Simitis sought to reinstate the party's unity and strengthen his position as the party leader. Although the prime minister was the only candidate for the party leadership, the number of votes he would receive would indicate how popular he was in the party.[23] During preparations for the party conference Simitis sought to reconnect with the party's base. Cabinet ministers were instructed to meet party cadres and low-ranking government officials for 2 consecutive days at the party premises to discuss their demands and complaints. PASOK's special secretary for party–union relations held various meetings with several unionists in an attempt to establish a climate of trust, with a view to finding 'a new policy synthesis' (*Eleftherotypia*, 11/09/2001). Simitis also promised to establish a regular dialogue with the unions. Finally, in a highly symbolic move, the prime minister ordered a lavish celebration of the anniversary of Papandreou's death, reportedly to appeal emotionally to PASOK's members and traditional supporters (*Eleftherotypia*, 13/06/2001).

Talking to the press a few months in advance, Simitis asked for 'a strong and clear mandate' from the conference and reminded his party colleagues that they were all 'marching together' (*Eleftherotypia*, 01/09/2001). At the conference, the prime minister made it clear that he would not change his policies and warned against PASOK becoming a 'miserably introverted party' tarnished by 'a tug of war' between personal antagonisms, whereas New Democracy was their common opponent (*Eleftherotypia*, 12/10/2001). This message was reiterated by other supporters of the prime minister:

> . . . this conference should not allow political positions to act as a Trojan horse to challenge and weaken certain government choices.
>
> (Deputy Minister of Labor and former trade unionist Protopapas, *Eleftherotypia*, 01/09/2001)[24]

This message found a largely sympathetic audience. Conference members appeared united in their desire to keep PASOK in power. It was calculated that

23 It was thought that if Simitis were to win but with a low percentage of votes, he would be obliged either to call an early election or essentially share power with the party barons (*Kathimerini*, 19/06/2001; *Eleftherotypia*, 27/07/2001).

24 In his dramatic plea for party unity PASOK's veteran politician, Evangelos Yannopoulos, told his party colleagues: 'PASOK is not our enemy. The [political] right is our opponent. We are alone, comrades . . . Are we heading for the conference united or divided in two camps? Our opponents are ruthless, and they are fighting against us with all available means' (*Eleftherotypia*, 01/09/2001).

out of 5200 conference members, around 3500 held government positions (*Kathimerini*, 28/04/2002).[25] Moreover, PASOK politicians with aspirations to party leadership were far from willing to challenge Simitis, knowing that their career aspirations relied on the prime minister's support and that they could make their move after Simitis' voluntary retirement as party leader in the near future (*Kathimerini*, 14/07/2001; *Eleftherotypia*, 30/08/2001). In that context, Simitis' opponents could only hope that the number of votes cast for Simitis would be less than the prime minister expected so that Simitis' position in the party and the government would be weakened.

The conference also served as a social opportunity for party cadres to revamp their connections with other party officials and build new ones (*Eleftherotypia*, 29/07/2001).[26] Many members spent a lot of energy cultivating personal relations rather than discussing actual policies (*Eleftherotypia*, 11/10/2001). For PASOK's senior politicians, the so-called 'party barons', the conference was a chance to have their political influence measured in terms of the votes they or their supported candidates would receive as candidates for the party's central committee. If they gathered strong support within the party, they could better bargain for a government position (*Eleftherotypia*, 29/07/2001; 19/08/2001; 11/10/2001). As expected, the conference became an arena for antagonisms among various political groupings (*Vima*, 07/10/2001). PASOK's secretary had the role of arbitrating amidst competing demands by party factions, disputes and personal clashes (*Eleftherotypia*, 05/09/2001).

The conference workings revealed that the dissenters constituted a politically and ideologically heterogeneous group. The party unionists also appeared divided in different party factions (*Vima*, 07/10/2001). Some of them filed a 'manifesto' that vaguely expressed dissatisfaction with government policy, particularly privatization and pension reforms. The text served to air the grievances discontented party supporters had accumulated over a long period (*Eleftherotypia*, 27/07/2001). During the conference there were general and rather vague pleas for the government to change its policy direction. Left-wing rhetoric was widely employed to appeal to the party audience and often covered actual rows over the allocation of party positions.[27]

25 'It is obvious that this crowd of privileged PASOK supporters has little interest in the ideological and political choices of the party. They are mostly concerned with PASOK staying in power as the guarantor and protector of their privileged "rights", which will eclipse, of course, if the "opponents" win the election. This anxiety is widespread in local PASOK branches, and it is transmitted, of course, to the MPs and government officials' (*Kathimerini*, 28/04/2002).

26 *Eleftherotypia* called the conference 'two days of [celebrating] statism' (*Eleftherotypia*, 17/05/2002).

27 As noted by Minister of Public Health Alekos Papadopoulos (*Eleftherotypia* 23/07/2001). Giorgos Karelias in the center-left newspaper *Eleftherotypia* (27/07/2001) also noted: 'this is not the first time when PASOK as a party appears to be more on the left side of politics than the government it supports. Who remembers the pre-election pledge by PASOK politicians (under Simitis) that 51% of large public sector enterprises would remain under state control, whereas a few months later the government broke that promise with no reactions at all?'.

Talking to the plenary session, Simitis' former rival Tsohatzopoulos openly expressed his support for the prime minister who was, in his view, the person to lead the party 'towards a new great victory'. He called for 'a new synthesis' that would break the boundaries between Simitis' loyalists and his within-party opposition (*Eleftherotypia* 13/10/2001).[28] Tsohatzopoulos urged the government to strengthen its distributional policies and insisted that the EU funds, amounting to 1.5 trillion drachmas, 'could lead PASOK back to the [political] forefront' (*Eleftherotypia*, 14/04/2002).

Simitis won a landslide victory at the PASOK conference, which strengthened his position as party leader (*Kathimerini*, 21/10/2001). For the first time it was felt that the prime minister was free to allocate government posts at his own will without the need to consult with other top party politicians (*Eleftherotypia*, 11/09/2001). Appointments in other managerial posts in public administration were also defined on the basis of party loyalty (*Kathimerini*, 23/06/2002). Still, to avoid new grievances, Simitis had to offer Cabinet posts to some of the discontented MPs.[29]

An analytic outlook

The strategic interactions between the government and the party-affiliated union leaders in the period between 1996 and 2004 can be described as a game in which the government made the decision to implement a reform agenda but also wanted to avoid strong reactions by the unions, whereas the unions wanted to preserve and increase the collective benefits their members enjoyed, and the union leaders wanted to reconcile their party affiliation with their official responsibility to represent the collective demands of their members.

When proposing a reform package, the government can either ignore the unions or seek to strike a compromise with them. The unions have the options of confronting the government openly or showing complacency. For both parties, confrontation could undermine the party's cohesion and mobilization capacity and possibly risk the party's re-election, which is their shared objective. For the party leadership, policy compromise makes sense, provided that the unions will reciprocate with a mild reaction to its reform initiative (Table 8.4). For the union leaders, a complacent stance towards the party leadership in government makes sense, if the government is sensitive to their demands and compromise on its policy proposal. Moreover, leading unionists do not want to risk their place in the party, but they also want to reassert their role as union leaders who are

28 Conference members at the plenary session voiced the rhyming slogan: 'Simitis, Don't Leave, Carry On and Lead' (*Eleftherotypia* 15/10/2001). In his comment on PASOK's conference, *Eleftherotypia's* Victor Netas noted: 'When a party is in power, there is no room for a conference based on dialogue and confrontation that could jeopardize its cohesion and could lead to a change in leadership. Political power brings unity, and does not allow for clashes' (*Eleftherotypia*, 15/10/2001).

29 As noted by Stratis Liarelis, a political commentator in *Eleftherotypia* (19/11/2001).

Table 8.4 Preference schedule for the party leadership

Order	*Party leadership*	*Union leaders*	*Payoffs*	*Explanation*
1	Ignore	Complacency	4	• Implements its policy plans • Triggers a mild response by the unions that does not undermine party unity for the next election
2	Compromise	Complacency	3	• Implements part of its policy plans • Triggers a mild response by the unions that does not undermine party unity for the next election
3	Ignore	Confrontation	2	• Implements its policy plans • Triggers a fierce response by the unions that can undermine party unity for the next election
4	Compromise	Confrontation	1	• Implements part of its policy plans • Triggers a fierce response by the unions that can undermine party unity for the next election

expected to defend the 'club' goods their members enjoy. If these benefits are at stake, they have good grounds to react, and for this reason, they are willing to stretch and strain their relationship with the party leadership, but not to the extent that they will entirely sever their personal ties to the party (Table 8.5).

When the game can be portrayed as simultaneous and noncooperative with incomplete information (the players do not know each other's payoffs), the government is likely to choose to 'ignore' the unions, if it chooses a 'maximin strategy' due to risk aversion. The same outcome will be reached if the government assumes that the unions would choose complacency, on the basis of past behavior (this is a prior expectation about the 'type' of the 'opponent') or on the assumption that the party-affiliated unions will also choose a 'maximin strategy' due to risk aversion (see Table 8.6).

In each case, payoffs accrue accordingly (PL1U2: 4, 2). The unions will demonstrate complacency, and the government may think it can ignore them. However, this is not a Nash equilibrium. Once the government announces a reform package which union members strongly disagree with (government chooses to ignore their reservations), the unions are better off confronting the government – something that the government did not initially anticipate due to incomplete information. The unionists can now get a higher payoff (3) if they move to confront the government. This leads to a suboptimal outcome (PL1U1: 2, 3).

In reality, both players can achieve mutual gains by tackling the problem of incomplete information and communicating with each other with a view to reaching an agreement (cooperation). They can use backwards induction to anticipate the results (Figure 8.2) and, on that basis, agree to adjust their strategy

Table 8.5 Preference schedule for the unions' leadership

Order	*Union leaders*	*Party leadership*	*Payoffs*	*Explanation*
1	Complacency	Compromise	4	• Protects the collective benefits of its members • Helps them keep their credentials as union leaders • Allows them to preserve their personal ties with the party leadership • Secures party cohesion and does not undermine the party's electoral prospects
2	Confrontation	Ignore	3	• Pushes the government to reconsider its policy, possibly helps pre-empt further negative policy changes • Allows them to reassert their autonomy from the party and (re)gain their credentials among union members • Undermines their personal ties with the party leadership • Undermines party cohesion and the party's electoral prospects
3	Complacency	Ignore	2	• Allows the government and future governments to take further negative policies • Demonstrates lack of autonomy from the party and undermines their credentials as union leaders • Helps them preserve their personal ties with the party leadership • Secures party cohesion, but the policy measures may alienate some union and party members
4	Confrontation	Compromise	1	• Protects the collective benefits of its members • Helps them reassert their autonomy from the party, possibly asking for more policy concessions, and helps them (re) gain credentials among union members • Undermines their personal ties with the party leadership • Undermines party cohesion and the party's electoral prospects

Table 8.6 Interactions between party leadership and unions' leadership in a simultaneous game

		Union leadership	
		Confrontation U1	*Complacency U2*
Leadership of the party in government (PL)	Ignore PL1	2, 3	4, 2
	Compromise PL2	1, 1	3, 4

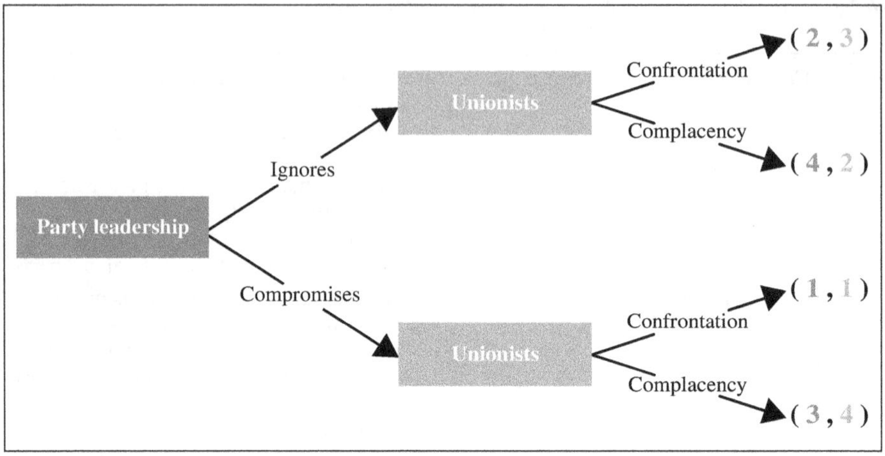

Figure 8.2 Decision tree with complete information

towards policy compromise and complacency to get the highest payoff (PL2U2: 3, 4). This situation captures the final output from the initial reaction of the unions following years of relative complacency to the announcement of social security reforms and their subsequent interactions with the party leadership when communication was established before and during PASOK's conference in 2002 and the gains from cooperation were understood by both players. Once room for negotiation opened up, the two sides gained knowledge of their 'opponents' preferences and strategic options, and shared that knowledge as depicted in the decision tree in Figure 8.2. Most importantly, they reached an informal policy settlement that moved the state of affairs to that of 'policy compromise' by the government and 'complacency' by the unions.

Relaxation of fiscal discipline and clientelist bias

Throughout the implementation of its fiscal stabilization program, PASOK was under constant pressure from its cadres, members and union leaders to relax fiscal austerity. Many PASOK members and politicians interpreted the poor results for PASOK in the 1999 local election as the outcome of the prolonged period of fiscal consolidation. This caused great anxiety among the party's cadres because the following year was an election year. In a similar tone, New Democracy's economic program promised voters that it would introduce tax reliefs for lower and middle incomes and would reduce business tax on profits, while still pursuing fiscal consolidation through cuts in public spending.[30] The

30 George Alogoskoufis, economic policy spokesman for New Democracy, talking to *Ethnos*, 23/05/1999.

opposition leader, Costas Karamanlis, also promised higher welfare policy transfers in the event that his party won the next election (*Vima*, 28/09/1999: 4; 13/02/2000: 29). The government rejected these commitments as unrealistic.[31] Greece's prospective entry into the EMU left no space for a relaxation of budgetary discipline. However, the government cultivated expectations that it would loosen its fiscal policy after the general election, following the success of its stabilization effort. When asked about the prospect of an increase in public spending after the 2000 election, Under-Secretary of Finance Christodoulakis promised that the government would be able to give targeted social transfers to the most vulnerable social groups: the low-income pensioners, low-income farmers, new couples, new farmers and the unemployed (*Economikos*, 04/11/1999: 19). The government also promised that its forthcoming annual budgets would offer real wage increases.

PASOK won a narrow electoral victory in 2000. Right after the election, the second Simitis government was under increasing pressure to relax its fiscal policy, given the economy's improved macroeconomic outlook.[32] Following entry into the EMU, there was talk inside PASOK of an 'adjustment fatigue' and the need to strengthen social policy and redistribution, which was thought to be feasible now thanks to the reportedly better state of public finances.[33] Political imperatives also dictated the relaxation of fiscal policy. PASOK politicians were anxious about PASOK's falling popularity, as manifested in low popularity scores, and were asking for a generous increase in social spending (*Eleftherotypia*, 20/08/2001: 45–47; *Kathimerini*, 27/10/2002). In response, the prime minister repeatedly stressed that his policies had a strong 'welfare' dimension which involved actions such as subsidized employment placements, a minimum guaranteed income and benefits to socially vulnerable groups (*Kathimerini*, 02/09/2001; *Eleftherotypia*, 08/09/2001). The promise to diffuse the benefits of EMU entry through social policies for low-income employees and pensioners became a recurrent theme in the government's rhetoric (*Kyriakatiki Eleftherotypia*, 29/07/2001).

Once EMU membership was secured, Greece implemented a new and less strict mechanism for monitoring fiscal performance compared with the high

31 Under-Secretary of Finance Christodoulakis expressed the view that if proposals of Mr. Karamanlis on the economy had been implemented, the cost would have reached 1 trillion drachmas, leading the Greek economy 'to fiscal collapse with incalculable negative consequences for the country's position in EMU, its competitiveness and employment'(*Vima*, 28/09/1999: 4).

32 In the first half of 2000, average annual inflation fell to 2%. General government deficit fell to 1.6% of GDP in 1999, from an average of 4.5% between 1995 and 2000 (data reported at that time). Public debt was stabilized at the reported rate of 104.4% of GDP at the end of 1999 (Ministry of the Economy figures). Between 1995 and 2000 annual growth of GDP averaged 3.2% compared with 0.8% between 1980 and 1994. The annual growth of fixed investment between 1995 and 2000 averaged 7.3%, as opposed to the annual average decline of 2.2% as between 1980 and 1994 (figures from OECD and National Statistical Service of Greece).

33 Minister of Economy Papantoniou refused to relax fiscal policy despite pressures from PASOK's politicians and base (*Eleftherotypia*, 07/10/2001).

stakes of the Maastricht Treaty benchmark.[34] It was now easier for the Greek government to relax fiscal policy during its second term and yield to pressures from PASOK politicians and public-sector unions for increases in wages and pensions above the rate of inflation. For the first time in decades, taxes as a share of GDP fell marginally. Moreover, the government's improved creditworthiness enabled it to increase its external borrowing (Tsaveas 2001: 352). This was good news for investors too: because the fall of inflation outweighed the fall of nominal interest rates, government bonds offered them higher yields.

The return to primary deficits – recorded between 2000 and 2004 gave the government a double gain in the short-run: first the injection of foreign capital into the domestic economy through government borrowing temporarily boosted economic activity; second, the government was able to sustain a high level of consumption and investment (including part of its clientelist commitments) without the need to heavily tax the domestic economy. Hence, the pressure for more government spending and distribution was temporarily tackled thanks to the *opportunistic time lag* which external borrowing offered. Tax liabilities were transferred to the future, making public spending an issue of *intergenerational* distribution instead of *intergroup distribution* at the present time.

However, following entry into the Eurozone, fiscal profligacy was riskier because Greece had no control over its currency. Borrowing was denominated in the euro, a hard currency, and debt monetization was not possible. Hence, although the nominal cost of borrowing became lighter, the actual burden of debt was higher in real terms.

It is important to note, however, that only part of the new spending was directed to social policy spending and low-income population groups. The structure of public spending in Greece differed substantially from the EU average. Greece remained in the penultimate position among OECD countries in terms of spending in education as a percentage of GDP (3.0% in 1995 and 4.1% in 2002). Although public-sector spending as a percentage of GDP was approximating EU levels and public expenditure on social protection as a share of (a growing) GDP increased steadily,[35] the composition of expenditure indicated a bias towards targeted allocations to beneficiaries inside the public sector (Sotiropoulos 2004a: 18 and 33). Because the next election was getting closer, the government's priority was to meet the demands of its support groups. The government increased real wages, benefits and allowances in the public sector at a rate above inflation (*Eleftherotypia*, 30/07/2001).[36]

34 The Stability and Growth Pact required the Eurozone countries to run an annual budget deficit below 3% of GDP and make an effort to keep or reduce their national debt below 60% of GDP. If a country was found to deviate from the annual deficit threshold, it was subjected to financial supervision by the European Commission after a decision by the European Council. Understandably so, this sanction was not as severe as exclusion from the EMU under the Maastricht process.

35 Reaching 22.1% in 2003 from 18.5% in 1993.

36 Higher wages for public-sector workers led the unions of the private sector to demand higher wage increases of 7% (*Ependytis*, 07/12/2003).

In 2003, a year before the scheduled election, Prime Minister Simitis launched a 'Convergence Charter', a 3-year program of welfare transfers and redistribution policies aimed at raising incomes to EU-average levels, which was to be implemented by PASOK if re-elected. The charter increased public-sector wages and pensions and offered social security grants and subsidies to farmers and people with low incomes. It committed the government to an increase of social transfers by 2.36 billion euros, or 1.4% of GDP in 2004 (European Commission 2004b: 231). In a similar vein, New Democracy's economic program promised to increase social spending which was to be paid thanks to anticipated savings from its policies against corruption and wasteful spending in the public sector (*Kathimerini*, 23/12/2003).

Despite the increase in public spending, PASOK's popularity was falling in the opinion polls, and so was the appeal of Prime Minister Simitis inside his party (*Eleftherotypia*, 30/07/2001). By the beginning of 2002, Simitis was increasingly seen as a liability for PASOK (*Kathimerini*, 28/04/2002). Simitis could no longer rely on his reputation as the leader most likely to secure PASOK's next electoral victory (*Kathimerini*, 28/04/2002). The prospect of a defeat in the next election led Cabinet ministers and PASOK MPs to think closer about their career prospects the day after.[37] Many younger PASOK politicians wanted to lead the party in the post-Simitis era (*Vima*, 12/04/1998).[38] Inside the party, rumors circulated that Simitis would resign from the party leadership before the 2004 election, following pressures from leading PASOK politicians driven by a discerning 'survival instinct' (*Eleftherotypia*, 03/07/2002).[39] Simitis eventually stepped down as leader of PASOK in February 2004 and was replaced by George Papandreou, minister of foreign affairs and son of Andreas Papandreou.

Conclusion: client groups and the design of economic policy

The empirical findings of this chapter highlight the way dynamic interactions between key actors inside the broader clientelist network generate a pattern of clientelist bias in the design of economic reform. First, in a clientelist system, the patron party must primarily accommodate the preferences of its client groups. This suggests that, when assessing the relative strength of different interest groups, the clientelist party emerges as the *privileged* group itself, whose demands must be given priority. In Greece, policy making under Simitis was a balancing act

37 'Several Cabinet ministers with the ambition to succeed Mr. Simitis do only what's absolutely necessary in their area of responsibility, and avoid to show any sign of solidarity with other ministers in tackling problems . . . whereas simple MPs of the governing party abstain from parliamentary discussions and any other political activities that could give them a share of responsibility in government choices' (Dora Dailiana in *Eleftherotypia*, 01/03/2002).

38 As noted by political commentator Stamos Zoulas in the center-right newspaper *Kathimerini* (10/06/01).

39 'Many party politicians are hoping that [the tactic of] "changing the Captain while the boat is still afloat" could prevent the imminent electoral disaster or, at least, contain it into a decent defeat' (Antonis Karakousis, *Kathimerini*, 15/07/2001).

between two potentially contrasting goals: on the one hand, preserving the privileges of PASOK's client groups, which secured the party's access to power and his position as party leader, and on the other hand, securing the sustainability of a highly redistributive and clientelist political economy, which involved accommodating the policy prescriptions of the European Union and reassuring international markets about the state and prospects of the Greek economy.

Second, this effort takes place under conditions of uncertainty and informational asymmetries. The party leadership must be able to find out how different reform options are likely to affect its relations with its client groups. Early signs of protest by unions can serve as warning signals that the proposed policy mix goes too far and seriously hurts the interests of its core support groups. With incomplete information, the design of policy making is not a straightforward exercise, but it becomes an exploratory task that leads to piecemeal reform in view of feedback that tracks the level of tolerance from the party's client groups. As long as the government is sensitive to these signals, either proactively or retrospectively, the escalation of confrontation can be avoided. When the government crosses the threshold of tolerance, it has to back down on its policy proposals in order to reinstate a dialogue with the policy stakeholders and safeguard party unity.

In Greece, we observe how interactions endogenous to the party shaped Simitis' choice of gradual policy change that was anchored to the commitments and interdependences connecting critical stakeholders inside the party. The design of economic policy involved careful reflection on the possible implications that the reform agenda might have on PASOK's cohesion. To achieve this dual objective, it was politically imperative for the party leadership to track information about possible reactions from inside the party and the unions. Working under uncertainty and with incomplete information, the government occasionally proposed reforms that triggered confrontation within the governing party and was, in most occasions, forced to back down and revise them. In the end, both unionists and politicians with ties to PASOK's client base understood that it was important to communicate and avoid triggering an open clash that could seriously threaten the unity of the party.

Third, a strategy of co-optation can also mitigate reactions from leading union leaders and party politicians. Union leaders associated with broader party networks in a clientelist system have overlapping roles in the labor movement and the party: they represent their union members – many of whom are clients linked to the central party – they occupy important posts in the party and they may use their position in the unions as a stepping stone for a political career in central politics. Although the typical image in government–union relations is that of unionists bargaining for club goods on behalf of their members, unions permeated by patronage relationships consist of leaders and members whose clientelist ties to the central party might be equally or more important than the 'club good' at stake. Top unionists may have their own political aspirations, which enables the government to co-opt them by offering posts in the government in return for their complacent behavior. This further weakens the autonomy of union leaders versus the party leadership. The capacity of the government to allocate offices and resources strengthens its bargaining power over its within-party opponents too. In that context, party politicians and unionists cannot openly undermine party cohesion without risking their personal career because they are accountable to the party base, which mostly consists of clients interested in preserving the party's access to power. Dissenters within the broader party network are allowed to express their discontent to the degree that it does not seriously damage the party's unity and electoral prospects.

In Greece, PASOK's leadership combined policies driven by a clientelist bias with a strategy of co-optation towards the union leaders and its political adversaries inside the party. To preserve party unity, Simitis and his loyal Cabinet ministers kept invoking the shared desire to keep PASOK in power. By accommodating the aspirations of career-oriented politicians, Simitis anticipated relative complacency from the unions and his personal opponents.

However, blatant complacency with government policy may discredit the union leaders in the eyes of their members when their core interests are at stake. Union leaders rely on their reputation as representatives of party-affiliated unionized employees and, over time, may have to assert a degree of relative autonomy when they and their members find that a set of proposed reforms is harmful to their interests. In that context, they will push the government to withdraw its plans. Top unionists can also use these episodes of confrontation to strengthen their personal positions inside the party. In response, the government must be responsive to their demands and adjust its policy agenda accordingly. In return, the unions must show signs of complacency once a more modest reform package replaces the previous policy proposal.

9 Beyond clientelist bias

The impact of economic restructuring on the nature of distributional politics

Adverse economic conditions and the introduction of economic reforms such as privatization and market deregulation may limit the available resources for government distribution. This may subsequently diminish the scope for patronage politics. At the same time, if economic reforms succeed in preventing the breakup of a systemic crisis, new economic resources can be found for the government to sustain its level of distribution. Depending on the nature of the new resources, new distribution may involve patronage exchange or typical 'rent seeking' by actors with a higher degree of autonomy from the government. If the latter type becomes more pronounced, the balance between political and economic power could be disturbed.

This chapter identifies this shift during the Simitis administration. Since the early 1990s, fiscal limitations restricted the range and type of clientelist favors which the government could offer to its clients. Although it was possible to deliver benefits that were not (particularly) costly, such as promotions and favorable placements inside the public sector, it was fiscally unsustainable for the government to make mass appointments and increase considerably the size of public-sector employment, as had happened in the 1980s. Faced with increasing patronage demands but with a limited scope for supply, the government chose to offer less costly forms of clientelism, such as temporary positions with fixed-term contracts and traineeships and introduced legislation that limited the input of patronage in fully tenured appointments. This marked the beginning of a period of 'diminished clientelism' under institutional limitations and fiscal constraints.

Although economic constraints in the late 1990s and early 2000s reduced the scale of top-down clientelism, new funding from the European Union fueled rent seeking by private economic actors who were involved in public procurement and construction. This brought to prominence typical forms of rent seeking involving relatively autonomous business actors. Media ownership gave some of these businesspeople more autonomy and stronger bargaining power versus the government. An attempt by the government to pass legislation that would restore some symmetry in the relationship between political power and the media was aborted due to incompatibility with EU law. Moreover, for the old clients in the public sector, the improvement in public finances and economic growth offered a greater scope for the extraction of rents by cliques under the protection of senior party politicians and party-appointed managers. The public sentiment was that corruption was endemic and the regulatory framework was insufficient to fight corruption, which allegedly implicated prominent politicians, state officials and businesspeople. During the early 2000s, corruption and 'collusion' (*diaploki*) became the recurrent slogans in political debates.

Legislation limiting patronage appointments in the public sector and its loopholes

In the mid-1990s, structural pressures and Greece's commitment to fiscal consolidation under the Maastricht Treaty made it difficult for the government to increase the numbers of employees in the public sector with mass new appointments of permanent personnel. There was little room to meet the increasing demand for state jobs at a time when employment growth in the private sector was low (*Kathimerini*, 19/05/2002 *Vima*, 27/10/2002). To thwart the mounting pressure for patronage appointments, in 1994 the government established an independent agency, ASEP (Supreme Council for Civil Personnel Selection), to conduct general exams for entry into the public sector (Law 2190/94). The establishment of this agency lifted the pressure from party politicians to accommodate the increasing claims of their supporters for appointment to the public sector, which they were unable to meet at the time. PASOK politicians could use this law as a reason not to promote favors in recruitments in the public sector (*Vima*, 26/05/1999: 3). The law was generally hailed as an important step towards transparency and meritocracy and was seen as a measure of 'self-limitation' regarding patronage.

The establishment of a nonclientelist process to govern new appointments could be seen as a departure from the dominant political strategy. This was a unilateral move to limit the clientelist supply that could favor the party of the opposition if it promises a return to patronage. Not surprisingly, the enactment and implementation of the ASEP law was opposed by a number of party politicians, office holders and unionists in the broader public sector – mainly those 'who used to have a strong say in appointments' (*Vima*, 26/05/1999: 3). The opposition's stance on the establishment of ASEP was ambiguous. New Democracy publicly welcomed the initiative and criticized the law for its loopholes that kept some room open for favoritism (*Vima*, 02/11/1998: 8). But it was also rumored that New Democracy politicians promised their local clientele that a New Democracy government would abolish the law and would accommodate their demands for jobs in the public sector (*Vima*, 26/05/1999: 3).

However, the high visibility and formality of the exams conducted by ASEP and its popularity as a new institution made it politically risky for New Democracy to openly pledge to abolish it. The ASEP process soon gained public legitimacy and created expectations among prospective candidates that meritocratic criteria would govern future recruitment in the public sector. Moreover, in 2001, a constitutional amendment was passed to protect its status from future revisions.

No party could credibly tell its supporters that it would abolish the ASEP process and resume mass appointments to the public sector. The constitutional amendment of 2001 made it unlawful to abolish the ASEP process. The constitutional guarantee further changed the terms of the clientelist game so that the opposition could no longer promise massive patronage to its supporters. This locked the two parties in a 'constrained' situation, in which promising mass patronage appointments by abolishing the ASEP process was no longer seen by the public as realistic, given the new institutional limits.

Loopholes and diminished forms of patronage

The ASEP law initially excluded from its scope the enterprises of the public sector. This allowed some room for favoritism in hiring new personnel there. Other opportunities for favoritism were reported in the 'special treatment' clauses for people with special needs who were allowed to go through an appointment process outside the ASEP system. There were rumors that to obtain a 'special needs' status and get appointed, healthy people were furnished with fake documents, allegedly thanks to 'the interference of ministers, MPs and prefects' (*Nea*, 27/03/1996: 6). At the same time, local councils were also exempt from the control of ASEP and became the main turf for new patronage appointments (Greek Ombudsman 2004). Because the opportunities for favoritism in central politics were limited, some aspiring politicians found the prospect of a career in local administration more appealing than central politics (*Vima*, 22/11/1998: 16).[1] Although the ASEP law was extended in 1997 to cover permanent appointments to local councils and public-sector enterprises, there were still many exceptions that allowed patronage appointments.[2] The main type of exception involved the possibility of hiring fixed-term employees (article 25 of the Law 2190). Clients were offered temporary contracts (Pappas and Assimakopoulou 2012: 148–149). The recruitment of temporary workers under fixed-term contracts became a 'cheaper' alternative to hiring permanent personnel. This practice confirmed the resilience of clientelist incentives in defiance of a major institutional reform that was designed to keep patronage at bay:

> The law [introducing ASEP] was passed . . . to absolve Members of Parliament from the intense pressure of their voters. But as the Romans say, 'the law is found; now we shall find its twists'. One way [to circumvent the law]

1 The Ombudsman confirmed that the rules of transparency and legality had been broken in several cases. It observed several cases of failure to select candidates on the basis of merit – for instance, in appointments by local mayors to the so-called Citizens Service Centers, a newly established service whose task was to cut down on red tape (Sinigoros 2004: 2). Prime Minister Simitis later acknowledged that 'patronage mentality was particularly strong' in local authorities (Simitis 2005: 249–360).

2 In legislation, Laws 2266/1994, 2247/1994, 2349/1995, 2525/1997, 2190/1994, 2738/1999, 2839/2000 and 3051/2002.

> is through [the signing of] the 'contract to provide services' . . . the second is the 'fixed-term employment contract'. The law [later] prohibited these practices, but these provisions were not respected 'as if they never existed at all'.
>
> (*Vima*, 06/01/2000: 3)

Persistent favoritism, although in diminished form, was associated with the desire of the governing party to accommodate its clients' demands (*Kathimerini*, 19/05/2002). Contract employees (*symvasiouhoi*) lacked employment protection and were even more susceptible to clientelist pressures after appointment. They could lose their job if the next election led to a change in government. In the meantime, politicians could still deliver fiscally costless favors, such as promotions, better placements and the settlement of administrative issues.

The tens of thousands of employees who had been recruited on fixed-term contracts soon became a fiscal and political liability. Upgrading to permanent employment status became the type of favor most temporary workers were persistently asking for (*Vima*, 06/01/2000: 3). Job tenure was given to temporary workers in several rounds in 1994 and 1997. A law in summer 1998 granted permanent status to 30,000 temporary employees who had been hired in the public sector under private law contracts. PASOK MPs reportedly asked for amendments to the bill to tackle their own clients, whereas the bill was criticized by the New Democracy spokesman as 'ridden with favoritism' (*Vima*, 01/08/1999: 9). The government also helped 2500 temporary workers in local councils gain temporary employment status through a point system which gave extra credit for previous work experience (*moriodotisi*; *Vima*, 13/06/1999: 51). By 2002, the government had broken its commitment to hire one new employee in place of five retiring employees (*Vima*, 16/06/2002: 8; 27/10/2002).

This trend soon created pressures for further institutional change. Facing public criticism, the government agreed to revise Article 103 of the Constitution to forbid the automatic granting of permanent employment status to fixed-term contract employees in the public sector. The constitutional ban was again circumvented by a law which gave temporary employers additional 'points' for job experience when applying for permanent employment posts (Law 3051/2002, and Spanou 2008: 158/164).

During Simitis' second tenure, Greece improved its public finances, and the influx of Community funds made it easier for the government to appoint more contract employees in the public sector.[3] New agencies and organizations were

3 The minister of economy told the press that he was sympathetic with the idea of new appointments in sectors that were funded by EU subsidies (*Kathimerini*, 19/05/2002). Two labor unionists and former members of PASOK reported that PASOK's union organization (PASKE) was hiring personnel in state-controlled banks as temporary workers and was using them as strikebreakers (Tsakiris 2003: 13).

Table 9.1 Options regarding patronage appointments to the public sector as reconfigured by fiscal constraints and institutional changes

		Government		
		Promise mass appointments	*Promise temporary contract appointments*	*Do not promise contract appointments*
Opposition	Promise mass appointments	A. Not possible since 1994	B. Not possible since 1994	C. Not possible since 1994
	Promise temporary contract appointments	D. Not possible since 1994	E. Both parties gain	F. The opposition gains
	Do not promise contract appointments	G. Not possible since 1994	H. The government gains	I. Both parties lose

created, making room for fixed-term appointments.[4] Some of the new agencies were operationally inert.[5] At the same time, politicians could reportedly promise their clients entry into the programs run by the government employment agency, OAED – also partially funded by the EU (*Kathimerini*, 13/07/2001). It appeared at that time that the strict rules of the ASEP law were 'a thing of the past' (*Kathimerini*, 19/05/2002).

Loopholes in the ASEP law and fixed-term appointments changed the terms of the clientelist game (Table 9.1). Fiscal constraints and the ASEP process made it impossible for the government to promise fully tenured patronage appointments in the public sector (the gray boxes in A, B, C, D and G); this prospect was ruled out by law and, later, by a constitutional provision. But the government was allowed to hire temporary employees under contracts and bypass the ASEP process (box B). Faced with increasing demands from its own clients for government jobs, the opposition party could not abstain from promising similar forms of patronage too. The dominant strategy moved to box E, a situation in which politicians in both parties promised the appointment of their clients as temporary employees: a conditional gateway to permanent tenure.

4 Around 40 joint-stock companies were established since the mid-1990s in what was described as the trend of 'agencification' (Spanou 2008: 158–160).

5 A number of experts who had been hired under the ASEP process to work in agencies responsible for the management of Community-funded investment programs remained inert for about 2 years, and some of them were given 2-year unpaid leave of absence (*Eleftherotypia*, 08/10/2001). Among these inert organizations were the National Research Institute of Theodoros Kolokotronis (*O Geros tou Moria*; founded in 2003), the International Freedom Academy (2003), the Museum of Science and Technology (2001), the High Technology Business Participation Fund (2001) and the Organization of Libraries for Children and Adolescents (1993), all abolished in 2014 (*Vima*, 15/01/2014).

An analytic outlook

The establishment of the ASEP process allows us to theorize on self-limitation in a clientelist system as follows. Under pressing economic conditions, the governing party wants to prevent a systemic crisis and can no longer afford to make certain types of fiscally costly patronage favors. The government resorts to measures of self-limitation regarding the scope and type of clientelist supply available. Ideally, the government prefers a situation in which the opposition will equally limit its clientelist promises too. However, the opposition will prefer the government to bear the cost of self-limitation while it can still gain from promising patronage to its supporters. In that specific situation the opposition does not want fiscal profligacy – especially if it results from the governing party appointing its own clients – because this could cause a systemic crisis, and it is uncertain whether the crisis will break up after the opposition comes to power. However, in case the government chooses not to self-limit in patronage supply, the opposition is better off promising clientelism than unilaterally withdrawing from patronage politics by limiting its promises to its client groups (Table 9.2 and Table 9.3).

This order of preferences is known to the players, and backward induction in this sequential-move game suggests that the best strategy for the government is to reduce clientelism even if the opposition still promises patronage to its supporters under the new institutional constraints (payoff of 3 for the government and 4 for the opposition, which is the subgame perfect equilibrium; Figure 9.1).

Table 9.2 Preferences and payoffs for the government

Order	*Strategic moves by governing party*	*Reply by opposition*	*Payoffs*	*State of affairs*
1	Reduce clientelism	Curb expectations	4	Bilateral self-limitation
2	Reduce clientelism	Promise clientelism	3	Unilateral self-limitation
3	Sustain clientelism	Curb expectations	2	Crisis and systemic breakup
4	Sustain clientelism	Promise clientelism	1	Crisis and systemic breakup

Table 9.3 Preferences and payoffs for the opposition

Order	*Reply by opposition*	*Strategic moves by government*	*Payoffs*	*State of affairs*
1	Promise clientelism	Reduce clientelism	4	Unilateral self-limitation
2	Curb expectations	Reduce clientelism	3	Bilateral self-limitation
3	Promise clientelism	Sustain clientelism	2	Crisis and systemic breakup
4	Curb expectations	Sustain clientelism	1	Crisis and systemic breakup

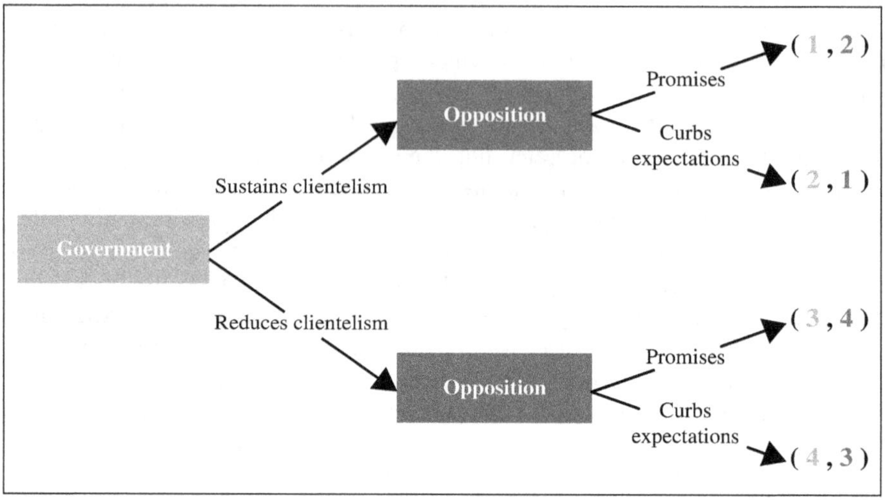

Figure 9.1 Decision tree regarding self-limitation in patronage supply

Given this outcome, the government may want to make the opposition a 'constraint maximizer' under a conditional strategy that will reduce the overall clientelist expectations in the party system. Although the government cannot expect the opposition to hold back from promising patronage, it can change the rules of the game through constitutional reform to take some forms of clientelist supply off the menu of clientelist benefits which a political party could credibly promise (tying the hands of future governments). This will give the government a payoff of 4 and the opposition a payoff of 3. At the same time, the government can still offer 'diminished' forms of patronage and allow its clientelist networks and cliques access to rents, as we will see in the following section.

Patronage supply in the existing clientelist networks

Although the ASEP law introduced a policy of self-limitation with regard to the hiring of clients, party clients in the public sector were still able to claim individual benefits as clients and continued to enjoy privileged terms of employment (*Vima*, 08/06/1997: 16; Pappas and Assimakopoulou 2012).[6] In return for these

6 A reader's letter sent to Yannis Marinos, a leading political commentator in the politically centrist *Vima*, described the employment situation in DEI, the electricity monopoly, in the region of Kozani: 'a few who got a job [in DEI] thanks to favoritism are [now] "milking the cow" while, outside DEI, qualified workers are jobless or, at best, get a wage of 5,000 drachmas working for contractors who exploit all profits in cooperation with the managers and the unionists' (*Vima*, 08/06/1997).

favors, party members and sympathizers had to overtly demonstrate their loyalty to the party in various social and political settings:[7]

> Wherever you go . . . you will see party representatives who take decisions following the party line 'top-down'. There are party branches even in the justice system, the police forces and the army.
>
> (Antonis Karkayannis, political commentator in the center-right daily, *Kathimerini*, 28/06/2003)[8]

In a report circulating at PASOK's conference, the party secretary admitted that large numbers in new member registrations reflected the desire of most new members to secure special benefits through access to power (*Eleftherotypia*, 06/10/2001). Loyalty was secured through the promotions and placements that continued to be largely determined by favoritism and personal connections with government ministers and party officials.[9] Political opponents and defectors were punished with employment downgrading or office stripping, a punishment known inside the public sector as 'putting them to the fridge'. In a TV interview on SKAI, a former director of a local tax authority office talked about his experience in the 'fridge':

> I never understood what that agency was doing – it never did anything. It was like a gulag, they were sending either New Democracy followers or PASOK supporters, whoever they wanted to stay inert. Honestly, I was doing nothing at all . . . I used to go in the morning, sit down, sign in, drink a coffee, make a stroll around, close down my office and leave. What else could I do?[10]

Clientelism continued to be a practice prevalent in many spheres of social activity: in municipalities, local communities, prefectures, trade unions, universities,

7 Pantelis Boukalas from *Kathimerini* derided the behavior of ministers, MPs, local party leaders and sympathizers in public events every time the party leader made an appearance: 'They run and make way for the "hegemon", they squeeze themselves [to get] next to him and be recorded on camera while he is making some hefty announcement, they nod their head in every word he says to show that they agree with him (can't they do otherwise?) and find his commonplace rhetoric very wise and path-breaking. Even Moses descending from the top of the mountain would have experienced less adoration' (*Kathimerini*, 01/03/2003).

8 *Kathimerini* observed 'an army of journalists' working for hundreds of government or quasi-government agencies in which they secured a 'luxurious way of shirking work' with 'a price tagged to their independence' (*Kathimerini*, 02/02/2003).

9 A survey of public-sector employees revealed that 88% of the respondents believed that their colleagues had been placed in their posts without having the appropriate qualification. Fifty-four percent thought that the majority of their colleagues had been not been hired on the basis for merit. Seventy-seven percent of the respondents reported that political interference had played a crucial role in promotions. Sixty-three percent reported substantial political interference in their work. Sixty-nine percent replied that public administration was not free from political interference (*Vima*, 30/03/1997).

10 See interview by Neoi Fakeloi, on *SKAI*, on 23/01/2012 on www.skai.gr/player/TV/?MMID=223688, retrieved on 12/02/2012.

hospitals and other social organizations. Clientelist exchange determined the terms of one's military service,[11] access to vocational training programs for the unemployed, finding a bed in a hospital, speeding up administrative processes such as the issuing of a pension, getting a business license for entrepreneurs or receiving subsidies or debt relief for professional and other nongovernmental associations such as sports clubs.[12]

Moreover, both PASOK and New Democracy had active student organizations at higher education institutions, which offered many of its members networking opportunities and a springboard for a future political career in higher party posts.[13] Student members could also expect personal favors such as easy access to postgraduate programs or even unlawful bribes by private companies that were bidding for student events (*Kathimerini*, 24/01/2007):

> Youth activists act as 'party agents . . . who start their political career in the university. When they graduate (God knows how they take the diploma) they enter the trade unions for a career as union leaders, and with a bit of luck and a lot of party support they will become MPs and – God save us – ministers, and will continue to destroy this hopeless country.
>
> (Theodoros Lianos in *Vima*, 30/05/2008)

Party student organizations established a strong position in universities thanks to a law that granted student representatives 80% of the voting weight in elections for university administration boards (Law 1268/1982). As the press reported, student leaders often had control over who had access to student houses, restaurants and cafes, and often distributed exam questions to their members, 'which appeared to be the same questions for the end-of-term exams' (*Kathimerini*, 24/01/2007). Student organizations could also influence the election of university principals, deans and academic senates by exerting pressure on the electors to favor their preferred academics. This system opened the door for alleged cases of corruption involving academics and youth leaders.[14] According to a professor at Athens University of Economics:

> We know that student leaders give lists of student names to pass the course; students who have left a blank exam paper get an excellent mark. We see

11 Mostly concerning the placement and living conditions of the conscripts (*Vima*, 08/02/1998: 13).

12 *Nea*, 16/09/1994: 6; *Vima*, 31/12/2000: 56; *Kathimerini*, 01/12/2002; *Kathimerini*, 28/09/2003; *Eleftherotypia*, 07/06/2010. For instance, the vice-president of the Council of State, one of Greece's supreme courts, claimed that clientelist exchange drove decisions to turn forest land into development land (*Kathimerini*, 26/06/2003).

13 The political parties had a strong presence in universities. PASOK's youth organization alone had an estimated membership of around 50,000 members in 2001 (*Eleftherotypia*, 26/09/2001). Theodoros Pangalos, PASOK's top politician, called these youth organizations 'anti-chambers of clientelist careers' (*Vima*, 23/11/1997).

14 See *Vima*, 13/11/2005.

> doctorates where it is evident that our colleagues have written it. Whoever reacts to this [trend] gets attacked. In the end, everybody gives up.
>
> (*Vima*, 13/11/2005)

In that environment, legislative measures introduced to fight patronage were inadequate, superficial and often dotted with blatant loopholes and exceptions. No substantial reforms were implemented to reduce the degree of politicization in public administration, the universities, the justice system, the police force, the employment agency (OAED) and the public utility enterprises. A neologism, 'partitocracy', was widely used in public discourse to indicate the degree to which party politics had infiltrated most social settings.[15] It was reported that widespread clientelism also undermined the independence of civil society organizations (OECD 2001: 53). Civil society groups were too weak to push the government to take measures to increase transparency and accountability (OECD 2001: 53). Allegations of favoritism in the public sector dominated public discourse. Months before the 2000 election, the government passed a law delivering favors to key support groups.[16] Patronage was alive and well, despite the negative effect on PASOK's self-proclaimed image of a 'modernizing' political force. PASOK was accused of operating a clientelist machinery 'funded primarily by EU packages and government activities in general directing huge economic resources' (*Economikos*, 01/07/1999: 24).

Party cliques and low-level corruption

In addition to the typical top-down supply of clientelist favors by party patrons, cliques in the public sector and local administration could extract rents (*Kathimerini*, 30/05/10), often under the protection of their political patrons.[17] Corruption flourished thanks to rules that offered public servants a large scope for discretion in decision making. This enabled some employees to ask for bribes in order to permit or speed up lengthy and complex administrative petitions and procedures – a practice which became ironically known as a 'facilitation tax' (*grigorosimo*) (*Vima*, 27/11/2000; *Kathimerini*, 22/10/2002 and 30/08/2002; Lambropoulou et al. 2008: 29). Corruption cases were reported most notably in healthcare, urban planning, public work construction and defense procurements. Corruption also affected the workings of the tax authorities, with a negative effect on tax

15 Nikos Mouzelis, LSE Professor of Sociology, in *Vima* (29/06/2003).

16 *Vima*, 107/12/2001: 13; 01/04/2003: 17; *Nea*, 04/12/2003; *Kathimerini*, 23/01/2004.

17 For instance, a former mayor of Thessaloniki, Greece's second largest city, was convicted in 2013 of the embezzlement of 17.9 million euros between 1999 and 2008. The three-member Court of Appeal for Felonies sentenced the former mayor to life imprisonment. The judge talked of 'a machinery of embezzlement' that was 'engaged in corruption activities the moment they got to office' (*Kathimerini*, 27/02/2013).

collection.[18] The Court of Audit, one of the three supreme courts in Greece, in charge of checking the legality of public spending, reported recurrent law infringements in the fiscal management of public agencies and other state-controlled legal entities. The court found that several public-sector procurements and service contracts were allocated without open competition in breach of the law. The court also identified numerous cases of unlawful favoritism inside and around the public sector.[19] Despite the repeated exposure of breaches of law in previous years, the 2004 report of the Court of Audit stated that publicity 'did not prevent their re-emergence'.

Equally condemning of Greece's record of corruption was Transparency International in its Corruption Perception Index reports between 1997 and 2004. In 2004 Greece had the worst ranking among all 15 EU member states. Furthermore, a public poll showed that 52.6% of respondents believed that corruption had worsened in the previous years and that it was prevalent in the police force (51.8%), the tax authorities (51.6%), the planning authorities (47.8%), the justice system (47%) and the technical control of vehicles (46.4%). In the poll 33.8% of the respondents admitted they had 'first-hand' knowledge of a corruption case during the last semester, and 22.7% admitted that they had made use of political favors (opinion poll by *Kappa Research* in *Vima*, 29/03/2000: 7). Low and middle-ranked corruption had a negative effect on private economic activity by increasing business costs and deterring investment (see Table 9.4). By 2003 Greece continued to rank poorly in the Global Competitiveness Index filed by the World Economic Forum, with the lowest scores recorded in the Public Institutions Index.

In response, the government took a number of measures to limit middle-level and petty corruption. Inspecting bodies were established, the most prominent of which was the General Inspector of Public Administration in 2002, with the authority to check and discipline public employees, as well as the Financial and Economic Crime Unit (SDOE). However, SDOE soon became dominated by PASOK sympathizers and its operation was tainted with allegations of corruption. It was abolished in 2004 by the New Democracy government.

Legislative measures to limit low-level corruption met the resistance of cliques in the public sector. Among many such cases was the plan to reform the public health sector by introducing an evaluation program for Greece's doctors (National Health System or ESY) and improve transparency by centralizing and strengthening control over spending through the Organization for the Management of Health Resources. The law also stipulated that public health managers were to be appointed on the basis of meritocratic criteria (Law 2889/2001). PASOK MPs

18 As Alekos Papadopoulos, minister of finance, acknowledged in a letter to *Vima's* editor (18/09/1994: 4).

19 The court's investigation disclosed the undue payment of benefits, subsidies and payments inside the public sector, as well as to third parties such as private foundations (Court of Audit 2003: 35–40 and 2004: 49–58).

Table 9.4 Types of middle- and low-ranked corruption and clientelism as reported in the public discourse between 1993 and 2004

Party-level corruption and clientelism	Public procurement and contracts: social security and the health sector (pharmaceuticals, private health outsourcing, hospital materials)
	Public procurement and contracts: public works
	Public procurement and contracts: local administration (contracts and appointments)
	Appointment of contract employees in the public sector (*symvasiouhoi*)
	Placements and promotions in the military for professional staff and conscripts
	Bribes to state officials for granting 'development' subsidies from Community funds to business projects
	Mismanagement of funds in state-owned companies
	Subsidies to private organizations, farmers' cooperatives and NGOs on the basis of party affiliation
	Favoritism in the treatment of criminal law convicts in prisons as a result of political interference
	Politicization (on the basis of partisan affiliation) of promotions in the public sector and human resources management in public administration
	Increase in politically appointed advisors to Cabinet ministers
	Politicization of administrative and disciplinary councils
	Patronage arbitration through red tape
	Clientelism in the police force (for placements and promotions)
	Patronage promotions, hiring and student selection at postgraduate level in universities
Low-level cross-party or nonpartisan corruption	Hospitals (*fakelaki*)
	Driving licenses and Ministry of Transport (MOT) tests
	Speeding up administrative processes such as business licenses and access to Community funds programs (*grigorosimo*)
	Urban planning permissions
	Tax controls (through bribery of tax collectors)
	Customs controls

Sources: *Vima*, *Kathimerini* and *Nea* (several press releases), Court of Audit 2003, Transparency International (several years).

and Cabinet ministers with links to civil servants' associations were dissatisfied with the shift of power away from the chairs of the hospital boards (Mossialos and Allin 2005). Critical stakeholders in the health sector who expected personal or political losses from the reform effectively blocked the plan (Mossialos and Allin 2005).[20] While struggling to defend his reform amidst reactions, Minister

20 The minister of public health at that time described these stakeholders as 'termites' eating the flesh of the health sector (*Vima*, 28/01/2001).

of Public Health Papadopoulos did not have the support of Prime Minister Simitis and eventually resigned from his position in June 2002.[21] Papadopoulos later announced his decision to abandon central politics. Following his resignation, an amendment to the law was passed that significantly increased the power of the PASOK-controlled public sector union ADEDY in the management of the health system (Mossialos and Allin 2005).

Lack of transparency and failure to combat corruption by party cliques is associated with the prominence of patronage relations inside the public sector. Cliques could get involved in corruption thanks to the protection or tolerance of politically appointed managers, who they were themselves promoted to these posts thanks to their ties with senior politicians and government ministers. This 'nomenclature' of party cadres occupied multiple posts in the broader public sector and constituted 'the real power of this land and the expression of the party-clientelist state'.[22] Given the prevalence of party cliques inside the administration, it was widely felt that it was almost impossible for a central authority to monitor public spending and fight middle-level and petty corruption.[23]

> Political power – regardless of political affiliation – does not dare to take drastic measures. The central administration of public agencies (ministries, regions, prefectures) and organizations 'controls' the system and promotes 'yes men' in the hierarchy.
>
> (*Kathimerini*, 26/06/2003)

Government failure to combat rampant corruption and political impunity from criminal prosecution led many political commentators to raise doubts about the government's actual willingness to address drastically this phenomenon:

> This is happening not just in cases in which politicians are personally involved in bribing. In most cases, corruption is tolerated because it is associated with clientelist relations developed inside the party by various politicians.
>
> (*Kathimerini*, 22/10/2002)

Both petty corruption and elite-level corruption were connected in a feedback loop: as former minister Stefanos Manos put it, tolerance of petty corruption across society was cultivating people's tolerance of corruption in high politics. Manos presented the distinction between high-level predation and mass

21 The former minister of health said in an interview that he had defied the political cost and had chosen to clash with organized interests in the healthcare system – the pharmaceutical companies and medical procurement contractors (*Nea*, 31/07/2000).

22 As Nikos Nikolaou noted in the political centrist newspaper *Vima* (09/11/1997).

23 A government report acknowledged that the extensive practice of bribing in the public sector was facilitated by excessive red tape and was covered by 'a law of silence' (Fotini Kalliri in *Kathimerini*, 27/01/2002).

corruption across client groups, like the distinction between 'soft' and 'hard' drugs (*Kathimerini*, 24/09/2006), whereby mass clientelism was preparing politicians and public servants psychologically to turn a blind eye to the abuses of the politically powerful.

High-level corruption and 'collusion': the rise of autonomous rent-seeking actors

The Simitis government received generous financial assistance from the European Union. These new resources were less susceptible to allocation through the typical channels of clientelist supply, but they opened new opportunities for rent seeking by private actors bidding for public-sector procurement and construction projects. Access to rents largely depended on their ties to political power. These rent-seeking actors differed from typical client groups in terms of autonomy and source of bargaining power versus political power. Entrepreneurs lacked the numerical strength of traditional client groups, but they were not affected by the idiosyncratic collective action problems which, as noted in the previous chapter, constrained the capacity of these groups to stand against political patrons. Many of them invested in mass media in an effort to strengthen their bargaining position versus government officials (Papathanassopoulos 1999; Hallin and Papathanassopoulos 2002: 178). They were keen to pay the high cost of operating media outlets in a relatively small media market in order to maintain a powerful source of political influence (Papathanassopoulos 2001: 519). This marked a shift in the relative power between politics and established economic actors. Thanks to media power, these 'press barons' could create circles of friendly politicians whose electoral success was largely dependent on press coverage.[24] These businessmen were dubbed 'national contractors', a term which graphically describes the dominant position they established in particular areas of the public sector. They were poised every time a public contract or work project was announced by the government, seeking to profit from confidential information over scheduled public-sector projects and imminent decisions by public enterprises (and DEKA) in the stock exchange. During those processes, the press barons were sending implicit 'messages' to the government, registering their satisfaction or dissatisfaction with the way they were treated in their business deals (*Eleftherotypia*, 28/01/2002). Those who felt neglected by government decisions could use their journalists to launch attacks against their competitors or against Cabinet ministers (*Kathimerini*, 28/05/03). The media could also pick a favorite politician and increase his or her visibility, or they could focus on a public issue related to the type of public procurement the owner was interested in and expose several irregularities.[25]

24 See Lambropoulou et al. (2008).

25 'The ignorant citizen is being bombarded by arguments in favor of the procurement of a defense system and against another [purchase], without knowing that behind these press releases lie the interests of arms dealers, which, on several occasions, trigger clashes in the Parliament' (Massavetas 1996: 299).

Throughout his administration, Prime Minister Simitis enjoyed the support of the majority of the mainstream media. The center-left media and, at times, the centrist media portrayed him as a mild and technocratic modernizer who was laboriously working to secure Greece's place in European integration. Simitis' media image was one of the main factors behind PASOK's enduring electoral success, as New Democracy politicians well understood:

> . . . PASOK's strong weapon is undoubtedly the mass media, money and the state. These ones are, at the same time, PASOK's weaknesses; being identified as the establishment and a corruption regime, associated with mismanagement, bribes and predation.[26]

Faced with EU pressures to increase transparency, the government passed legislation establishing a mathematical formula to govern decisions awarding public construction contracts. The law also strengthened the powers of the Court of Audit in reviewing the legality of the contracts. The mathematical formula for the allocation of contracts for public works was criticized by the opposition, among others, for placing specifications that systematically favored a cartel of construction companies (*Kathimerini*, 19/07/2003). The technically complicated formula facilitated collusion among these construction companies to prearrange their bids in order to gain contracts.[27] The government was also criticized for not adopting the opposition's proposal to establish an independent agency to monitor public procurements (*Vima*, 28/09/1997).

In a similar effort to increase transparency, the government passed a law governing the financing of political parties and politicians, but both parties and politicians were able to circumvent its restrictions and receive money from entrepreneurs through various means such as unregistered cash, the purchase of anonymous coupons, support in kind such as free campaign material and working space, promotion in the press or valuable information about incoming stock exchange investments (*Vima*, 13/02/2000). The law turned out to be inadequate to prevent corruption, particularly given the infamous Siemens bribery scandal, which was exposed in 2009, as the next section presents in more detail.

Clashes among the press barons and between them and politicians were a recurrent theme. The competition among businessmen over the allocation of the Community funds soon evolved into a major source of anxiety for the Simitis government (*Kathimerini*, 24/02/2002). The Simitis government promoted legislation and constitutional amendments to prohibit owners of private mass media above a threshold of registered share ownership from participating in public procurements (the so-called *Vasikos Metohos* Law). The law was an attempt to curb the increasing power of the media, as well as a clear indication of the scale

26 New Democracy spokesman, Sioufas, in *Kathimerini*, 20/07/2003.

27 According to a report by the Technical Chamber of Greece (TEE) on 19/01/2010, retrieved from http://portal.tee.gr/portal/page/portal/TEE_HOME/dimosiaerga.pdf, on April 2013.

of rent seeking affecting the granting of public contracts. Talking about this legislative initiative in April 2001, Simitis stressed the need to 'secure a clear distinction between political and economic power, since economic power had the capacity to shape public opinion and, at times, it can even shape crucial decisions. (Simitis' personal website, visited on 21/10/2012).

The two large parties, ND and PASOK, agreed to this provision in principle. However, few politicians openly defended the law, and many others remained silent or expressed vague reservations regarding its legal status. The rules were also known to be incompatible with EC law, and the law was subsequently repealed when the European Commission threatened to reduce Community funds for Greece (Lambropoulou et al. 2008). In the end, this effort failed to weaken the bargaining power of public-sector contractors who had grown strong thanks to media ownership and had made powerful allies inside the political elite.

Because government decisions often upset the delicate balance among antagonistic business interests and PASOK's popularity was falling, some of the press barons who had previously supported Simitis adopted a less favorable stance on the government (*Kathimerini*, 24/02/2002). During his second term, Simitis was increasingly portrayed as a liability for PASOK (*Kathimerini*, 15/07/01):

> The moment they saw the government taking a downturn, they [the press barons] changed their own position . . . They like Simitis, but they think he is finished and they will not let him take them down too. This is why they have already approached Costas [Karamanlis, the opposition leader] and they are dusting out their ties to New Democracy's cadres. At the same time, they are poised to direct the succession at PASOK. They have picked up the horse on which to bet: George (Papandreou) suits them perfectly.
>
> (Antonis Karakousis, *Kathimerini*, 15/07/2001)[28]

In May 2003, Prime Minister Simitis publicly referred to 'vested interests' in the private sector that were conspiring to undermine his position and topple his government (*Kathimerini*, 24/02/2002). He later attributed their stance to their competition over who was getting access to Community funds and licenses for their radio and TV stations (*Kathimerini*, 28/05/2003).

Political confrontation over the issue of corruption

Throughout the Simitis years, questions of transparency regarding public procurement and the management of Community funds, as well as allegations of

28 In the same article on the shifting alliances of the press barons and public-sector contractors:

> In reality, the relation of the Prime Minister with PASOK's barons is that of a competitive alignment which has an end date: the electoral defeat; unless October's [political] climate is so negative that there will be a leadership issue by then.

corruption, were recurrent themes in the press and in the political discourse.[29] A system of exchange and 'collusion' between government officials and state-sponsored entrepreneurs was said to govern corporate competition for public infrastructure contracts (*Vima*, 12/10/1997: 14; *Economikos*, 09/03/1996: 86; 26/06/2003).[30]

The most outstanding corruption scandal was the involvement of Siemens in a number of public-sector procurement schemes. The participation of Siemens in digital telephony contracts started in the late 1980s with a contract for 47,000 telephone lines, which was awarded by OTE directly to a joint venture by Siemens and a local Greek firm. The incestuous relationship between political power and Siemens was a hugely confrontational issue in Greek politics throughout the 1990s and 2000s.[31] Former Prime Minister Mitsotakis claimed that the fall of his government was primarily attributed to his decision to privatize OTE's management because several business interests in Greece would have lost their privileged access to the company's procurements. In the following years, there were allegations that informal 'power centers' within the organization largely controlled the OTE management and strongly wished to preserve the established routines in the procurement record through 'intrigues, plots, dirty blows and unholy alliances' (*Eleftherotypia*, 21/01/2002). Throughout that period, investigations into corruption-related offences did not lead to criminal charges, and the scandal was ultimately revealed by a German court in 2008. In 2010 Siemens representatives admitted that they had given 'donations' to PASOK and New Democracy, as well as state officials in the state monopolies of telecommunications and railways, and even the army, in the late 1990s and early 2000s.[32] It was disclosed that financial 'transfers' by Siemens to PASOK and New Democracy was around 2% of the cost of the procurement contract 'in

29 See *Kathimerini* 03/03/2002; 26/06/2003. Prominent cases involved the crimes of fraud, money laundering, bribery and espionage (*Kathimerini*, 23/12/2001; 24/02/2002).

30 In a similar vein Antonis Karkayannis, a top political commentator, made a distinction between the notion of collusion between political and economic interests and typical clientelism:

> When we talk about 'collusion' we mean the political promotion of large private interests through the ownership of press, radio and television. Collusion [*diaploki*] differs from party clientelist relations, from the '*rousfeti*', that meets demands in return for votes.
>
> (*Kathimerini*, 31/08/2003)

31 Since the second PASOK government (1985–1989), Siemens established a leading presence in procurement contracts by OTE, DEI, railways, metro, state radio and television and other ministries. A second contract between OTE and Siemens was signed under the short-lived Zolotas government under the agreement of the leaders of all the coalition government parties. Yannis Kefaloyannis, who was then the deputy minister of transport and communications, later wrote to the newspaper *Kyriakatiki Eleftherotypia* (20/06/2010):

> Unfortunately, at that moment the great collusion of the political system began, which still takes place today.

32 See *Eleftherotypia*, 28/01/2010; 27/05/2010; 07/06/2010; 11/06/2010; *Kyriakatiki Eleftherotypia*, 20/06/2010; *Kathimerini*, 28/05/10; 24/06.10.

order to secure the strongest linkage with Greek politicians similar to other big Greek companies'.[33]

During Simitis' second term, the center-right press repeatedly referred to collusion and corruption by 'industrialists, developers, importers, suppliers, and foreign companies, who pay bribes to politicians, state officials, employees and party agents'.[34] Simitis' image was now being tarnished on moral grounds (*Kathimerini*, 19/10/03).

> Corruption literally went out of control during the second Simitis term, since impunity convinced the big contractors and suppliers that the state was theirs, and that they could rob it without being exposed or punished.
>
> (Nikolaou in *Kathimerini*, 13/09/2006)

A prominent political commentator and editor of the center-right daily *Kathimerini*, Alexis Papahelas, noted:

> The Simitis administration coincided with a 'party' of unbridled corruption and complicity that involved even the very trusted personal staff of Mr. Simitis.
>
> (*Kathimerini*, 30/05/10)

Not surprisingly, New Democracy made the themes of corruption and patronage its political flagship. In July 2000, New Democracy leader Costas Karamanlis sent a letter to the prime minister asking for the establishment of an independent administrative authority that would review contracts for state projects and procurements, just as PASOK had promised before the election. The government rejected this proposal (*Athens News*, 12/06/2000). In that letter, Karamanlis accused the governments of blocking New Democracy's initiatives on 'the immensely significant problem of the [improper] intertwining of political and economic interests and certain mass media' (*Athens Voice*, 12/06/2000).

Political confrontation over issues of transparency was so heated that the opposition leader publicly dubbed Simitis 'the High Priest of collusion' (*'diaploki': Kathimerini*, 01/09/01).[35] Karamanlis talked of the government creating 'a greenhouse of opacity' (*Kathimerini*, 10/07/03) and 'a state plunging in corruption, waste and mismanagement', by 'the greed of the establishment' that had 'exceeded all limits' (*Kathimerini*, 23/12/2003). New Democracy filed evidence from Greek and European reports (including OECD and Transparency International) of cases of mismanagement and lack of transparency in public administration in a booklet called 'the Dark Bible' (*Kathimerini*, 18/10/2003).

33 The full ruling of the Munich Magistrate was published in *Vima* on 13/08/2008. For a well-documented report on the Siemens scandal, see the book by Tassos Telloglou (2009) *The Network: The Siemens File* (in Greek, *To Diktyo: O Fakelos Siemens*), Athens: SKAI.

34 As noted by Nikos Nikolaou in *Kathimerini*, 13/09/2006. See also: *Kathimerini*, 30/08/2002.

35 Simitis replied that New Democracy remained the main spokesman of big corporate interests (*Kathimerini*, 01/09/01).

On the eve of the 2004 general election, Karamanlis attacked the government for the last-minute passing of legislation that allegedly delivered 'favors and protection' to its inner circle of cadres, for instance, regarding possible criminal liabilities of state officials for the handling of public-sector investment in the Stock Exchange around 2000.[36] At the same time, the leader of the opposition pledged to 'reinvent' the state and establish institutions ensuring greater efficiency and transparency (*Kathimerini*, 05/10/2003). Inside PASOK, leading party cadres also frequently aired their anxiety over 'suspicious' ties between PASOK politicians and businessmen (*Kathimerini*, 10/05/03; 19/10/03). As allegations of corruption and mismanagement continued to mount, Simitis replied that whoever had evidence about corruption 'must pay a visit to the prosecutor' (*Kathimerini*, 11/05/03).

Although allegations of corruption were frequently raised, the investigation of actual cases in which politicians and other state officials were allegedly involved was often delayed and, in many cases, not permitted by the statute of limitations of the Law on the Criminal Liability of Ministers (*Eleftherotypia*, 29/05/2010).[37] The constitutional protection enjoyed by current and former Cabinet ministers and members of parliament from criminal prosecution for alleged involvement in corruption cases cast a heavy shadow on the Simitis administration. In a similar vein, criminal charges of defalcation in the project of building a land registry in Greece were dropped 8 years later by the court of cassation, which ruled that the initial charges had been pressed on the basis of the wrong article of the penal code. By that time no further prosecution was allowed. The decision raised serious questions over the independence of the justice system in Greece. In 2006 criminal prosecution resumed for 26 people allegedly involved in the management of the land registry company (*Ktimatologio*), but the criminal liability of the involved government ministers had been already erased by the special statute of limitations.[38] Two other corruption cases regarding the alleged bribery of ministers and officials for the purchase of the faulty German submarines and the Tor M1 missile system were never examined by the justice system due to the same law. When the opportunity to change the constitutional protection of this law came up in the 2001 constitutional amendment process, PASOK voted against New Democracy's proposal to revise the articles

36 Karamanlis asked rhetorically, 'Who are the ones who had confidential information and made use of it? Who are those people who were involved in manipulating the Stock Exchange?' (*Kathimerini*, 23/01/2004).

37 The most notable case involved a former advisor to Prime Minister Simitis and PASOK's 'cashier', who publicly admitted that he had received a payment by Siemens which he forwarded to the party's coffers. Another former Cabinet minister under Simitis confessed to a parliamentary committee that he had also received money from Siemens. Both cases could have led to criminal prosecution, but the criminal liability of the two politicians had already been erased at the time of their public confession (*Eleftherotypia*, 29/05/2010).

38 The Law for the Criminal Liability of the Ministers as prescribed by the Constitution.

granting immunity to Cabinet ministers and members of parliament. The former leader of New Democracy, Miltiades Evert, heavily criticized PASOK's stance:

> This [motion] reveals the intention to reproduce the same practices; it undermines the standing of parliamentarism; it tends to eliminate any trace of credibility for the political establishment.
>
> (Evert in *Vima*, 23/10/1998)[39]

In addition to the law protecting Cabinet ministers and MPs from criminal prosecutions, there were allegations of unlawful political interventions in the justice system aiming to affect the choice of the judges entrusted with the investigation of several corruption cases (*Eleftherotypia*, 29/06/2002; 12/07/2002). The case was raised by public prosecutor Zorbas, who launched an investigation on bribes allegedly paid to officials, but he had the case taken from him, and he was sent to serve in the provincial town of Ioannina in 1998 (*Vima*, 06/07/2010). On many other occasions, promotions of judges to senior positions were criticized by the opposition as reflecting partisan criteria. For instance, on the event of the appointment of a chief justice of the supreme court (Areios Pagos), New Democracy accused the government of bypassing the established list of seniority (*Eleftherotypia*, 12/07/2002).

Conclusion: diminished forms of clientelism and the growth of autonomous rent seeking

Macroeconomic consolidation and economic reforms can alter the nature of rent seeking in directions that are unforeseen and, often, undesirable for the party in government, and can disturb established social and political relations. Fiscal constraints may make it impossible for the government to accommodate the mass demands for forms of patronage that are fiscally costly, such as appointments in the public sector. To avoid bitter grievances from its clientele, which could undermine the cohesion of the party and favor the opposition, the government must tie both its hands and the hands of other parties and future governments so as to achieve a more limited scope for patronage. This can be done by popular institutional reform that establishes a transparent and highly reputable system of appointments. To stop the opposition from promising to rescind this reform, the government can grant the new institutional framework constitutional protection from revision. The popularity of the reform can further prevent the opposition from credibly promising a return to the previous status quo.

However, ongoing pressures for patronage will push the government to find alternative ways to supply favors to the party clients. In Greece, patronage took

39 Evert denounced the fact that politicians were protected from penal prosecutions: 'Parliamentary immunity protects even an MP engaged in defamation, forgery, fraud, [or] accomplice to murder' (*Vima*, 23/10/1998).

less costly forms such as fixed-term employment and internships instead of full employment. This supply channel was a return to the clientelist game between the two larger parties. PASOK and New Democracy were still locked in a political equilibrium dictating the provision of patronage, although in 'diminished' forms.

Second, economic restructuring may leave intact the scope for corruption inside the public sector by cliques of public officials and employees with patronage linkages to senior party politicians and state officials. Excessive red tape and administrative discretion allow public officials and clerks to ask for bribes in return for the settlement of administrative disputes and the delivery of public services. Corruption flourishes in an environment of loose law enforcement, political protection and favoritism. Inside the broader party network, clients with links to senior party cadres can engage in middle-level or petty corruption under a general climate of immunity, which is primarily designed to protect high-ranking officials. Most importantly, tolerance and protection of petty corruption inside the broader clientelist network is another form of clientelist favor, which this time places the fiscal burden on the consumers of public services rather than directly on the government budget.

Third, other resources for government distribution may foster forms of rent seeking outside the typical top-down patronage. In Greece, EU funding strengthened the model of state-sponsored growth and fueled rent seeking by entrepreneurs engaged in business with construction projects and other government procurement. Unlike typical clients, private entrepreneurs were interacting with the government in the typical framework of lobbying. Media ownership gave some of them a considerable degree of bargaining power versus the political elite. This unsettled the balance between political and economic power. Politicians were more interested in securing and preserving privileged relationships with the press barons, and, to some extent, this took the focus away from typical clientelist commitments. It also created tensions in the political system. The strong bargaining power of the press barons versus political power, as well as the intense competition between entrepreneurs, led the leaders of the two main political parties to express their desire to redefine the power relations between politics and the media. But the government's initiative to constrain media power was resisted by the press barons and was ultimately annulled as a violation of European Community law. Few politicians openly defended it, and many others opposed it in an attempt to gain the favor of powerful media owners.

The case of Greece demonstrates that clientelism is resilient under changing conditions, but its range and types are reconfigured by the nature of the available resources. Although new patronage supply may diminish in nature and scope, previous patronage networks will breed corruption inside the public administration. Patronage mostly takes the form of protection or arms-length tolerance of their activities by senior party politicians. The *symbiotic relationship* between the party leadership and the party network explains the flourishing of a system that combines high-level corruption with mass patronage and petty corruption (cf. Grzymala Busse 2008). Corruption continues to be a prominent form of making private gains for politically appointed state officials. This is facilitated by a legal framework designed to give impunity to politicians facing criminal accusations. As the case of Greece demonstrates, efforts to limit corruption are likely to be patchy and inadequate because patronage and corruption are well embedded in the public administration and in party networks. New institutions may be established alongside the existing institutions, but the introduction of new formal rules does not automatically prevail in a given environment where there is a built-in bias for the status quo, which is strongly fostered by powerful interests well entrenched in the old institutional setting.

10 The slippery slope to the Greek crisis (2004–2009)

As the previous chapters have shown, the way consecutive Greek governments addressed economic and institutional pressures for reform and fiscal consolidation can be summed up as five distinctive patterns of creative adjustment:

1 *Necessitated reform*, which diffused costs among taxpayers, consumers and producers and protected the status of the party's clients under urgent economic and fiscal conditions.
2 *Nonequilibrium reform*, which caused reactions from the opposition, the labor unions and politicians inside the governing party.
3 *Partial reform*, when the economic case was less pressing, which also exhibited a clientelist bias and involved the co-optation of stakeholders
4 *Reform avoidance*, especially in the absence of external pressures and economic urgency.
5 *Exploitation of new resources* for government distribution, mainly the fiscal resources and borrowing creditworthiness offered by EU membership and other domestic resources thanks to the relative success of prior reforms to temporarily offset the crisis and boost investment or consumption (see Table 10.1).

This reform record was not sufficient to secure the vitality of the Greek economy in the following years. Public debt was fueled by the accumulated deficits of public-sector companies through the state guarantees for their loans and the recapitalization of their equity. For years, little was done to eliminate or reduce the sources of deficits in public enterprises such as the railways monopoly, public transport and Olympic Airways. By the end of Simitis' administration, Greece continued to have one of the largest shares of public-sector companies in the economy among the EU states (Rapanos 2009: 30, 32). Public debt was also burdened by pension and social security spending, which was relatively generous towards pensioners of the broader public sector. The large increase in social security spending for an ageing population added new liabilities to future budgets (European Commission 2004b: 50). Failure to tackle the systemic sources of government spending and deficits risked macroeconomic stability. Once in a monetary union, the government could no longer monetize public debt and instead

Table 10.1 Observed patterns of reform and other pertinent variables

	Observed pattern	*Pertinent variables*			
Chapters		Imminent crisis	Strong ideological advocacy by the government*	Institutional pressures for reforms**	Popularity of government policy***
Ch. 4	Necessitated reform in fiscal policy with clientelist bias – reform avoidance in all other policies (1985–1989)	Yes	No	Moderate for fiscal constraint Weak for structural reforms	Very unpopular
Ch. 5	Necessitated reform in fiscal policy – nonequilibrium reform in structural policies (1990–1993)	Yes	Yes	Moderate for fiscal constraint Weak for structural reforms	Very unpopular
Ch. 6	Necessitated reform in fiscal policy with clientelist bias – partial reform of structural policies	Yes	Yes	Strong	Tolerated
Ch. 7		Yes	Moderate	Moderate	Tolerated
Ch. 9	Exploitation of new resources and reform avoidance regarding the transparency and efficiency of public administration	Yes	Opposite rhetoric	Not significant	Unpopular

* Regarding its actual policy record, including its omissions to act in accordance with external reform prescriptions.

** By European Union institutions under binding commitments and sanctions.

*** Manifested in opinion polls, social reactions (strikes and protests) and press commentary

had to service its debt entirely by government revenue, either through taxation or through new government borrowing. As long as the cost of servicing its public debt remained substantially high, Greece's fiscal situation was precariously sensitive to the level of borrowing rates offered by foreign investors. In the years following Greece's entry to the Eurozone, persisting structural weaknesses will lead to further decline in exports relative to the growth of imports (European Commission 2003a: 67). The large migration of small and medium enterprises to nearby Balkan countries in search of cheaper operation costs was another testimony to structural rigidities in the Greek product and labor markets (Alpha Bank 2005: 30).

New Democracy in power (2004–2009)

In March 2004 New Democracy won the parliamentary election with 45.36% of the popular vote. The new government led by Costas Karamanlis presented a program of structural reforms aiming at creating a business-friendly regulatory environment that would increase Greece's competitiveness, create new jobs and further improve the rate of economic growth. To restore Greece's public finances without disrupting economic activity, New Democracy announced a fiscal policy of 'mild adjustment' ('*ipia prosarmogi*') which involved moderate spending increases at a rate lower than Greece's GDP growth. Fiscal consolidation was expected to rely on privatizations, the reduction of wasteful government spending and a revamped rate of economic growth. This would allow for targeted wage increases above inflation, no new taxes and new tax credits for businesses and several financially vulnerable groups, as well as fiscal benefits to small and medium enterprises and the unemployed. The strategy of 'mild adjustment' appeared to be the opposite of the Simitis government's dependence on rising taxation levels. Fiscal consolidation would no longer rely on heavier taxes, but the government would curb spending as the economy was growing. Without dramatic wage adjustments or an overall increase in taxes but with spending savings, the success of this strategy depended on continuous healthy growth rates for the Greek economy and the government taking an uncompromised stance on fiscal discipline. This target was ambitious, given Greece's real state of public finances.

One of the government's first decisions was to order a fiscal inventory ('*apografi*') at a time when the European Commission was raising doubts about the reliability of Greek fiscal data. Costas Karamanlis had previously accused the Simitis government of 'fiddling the books' and creating a 'transvestite' economy whose real level of debt was disguised (*Vima*, 07/08/2008). The inventory found that the Simitis government had submitted falsified fiscal data to the European Union in order to secure Greece's entry into the EMU. In 2004 Greece recorded a deficit of over 5% of GDP, and its deficits from 1997 to 2003 were found to have exceeded the 3% Maastricht Treaty threshold. Eurostat, the European Commission and the Council of Ministers confirmed that the financial data that the previous government had provided were inaccurate, despite the objections raised by the two former PASOK ministers of finance. In view of these findings, Greece was submitted to the strictest terms of the Excessive Deficit Procedure, which involved tight financial surveillance of Greece's effort to reduce its budget deficit below the threshold of 3% of GDP. The Greek government was requested to send regular reports on its fiscal consolidation efforts and performance for approval by the Commission and the Council of Ministers under the threat of fines and cuts in Community subsidies. The European Commission exerted pressure on the government to take further fiscal measures and, in particular, to freeze government grants to social security funds and public-sector companies at the 2004 level as a percentage of GDP, minimize the guarantees given by the government for the borrowing needs of public enterprises and organizations and raise revenue from a new round of privatizations.

The Karamanlis government insisted that it would be able meet the agreed-upon fiscal targets by cutting government spending rather than raising new taxes. The government had already set public-sector wages to increase above the inflation rate and had approved a small reduction in income tax (*Vima*, 23/1/2005). For Minister of Economy and Finance George Alogoskoufis, 'mild adjustment' was the government's key economic strategy by which lowering corporate tax and protecting economic actors from extraordinary and sharp austerity could spur growth without causing social unrest or disrupting consumption levels (*Vima*, 30/01/2005). He acknowledged, however, that this target was not easy to achieve given the structural sources of deficit-spending, since

> . . . the budgetary problems arise not only from central government expenditure and revenue alone, but also from the activation of guarantees in the broader public sector, which is 'hidden' debt.
>
> (*Vima*, 32/01/2005)

Throughout 2005 and 2006 the government relied on the recorded growth rate to ease the need for fiscal constraint. Despite the tight fiscal situation, most statistical figures showed that by mid-2000s the economy was performing well and exhibited some improvement in competitiveness. However, previous borrowing had taken its toll on public finances. Public debt exceeded the country's GDP, and Greece had to pay 10 billion euros to loan maturities – a sum comparable to the money allocated to both government wages and pensions (*Kathimerini*, 01/07/2005). Government revenue stagnated, and the government had to cut the budget for public investment (*Kathimerini*, 24/12/2005). The growing level of government deficit and increasing pressures from the European Commission led the government in March 2005 to increase the value-added tax (VAT) from 18% to 19% (*Vima*, 20/03/2005).

At the same time, the government made little progress regarding market liberalization and structural reforms. The Karamanlis government took steps to privatize several state-controlled banks and the deficit-running state-owned airline, Olympic Airways. It introduced a number of piecemeal reforms in the labor market, the electricity market and the pension system (the banks' social security funds). The government also sought to modify some of the employment terms governing the state-sector companies and incentivize older employees to take an early retirement (*Vima*, 17/07/2005). Having a smaller support base among employees in these enterprises, New Democracy was in a better political position to enact bolder reforms in the broader public sector. Still, a number of ministers and government MPs expressed concerns about the 'social implications' of these policies, and some of them reportedly asked the government to make new 'policy concessions' that could entice voters in view of the upcoming local elections (*Vima*, 27/09/2010).

During the same period, there were rumors implicating New Democracy politicians in corruption scandals and patronage practices, which ran counter to the government's anticorruption rhetoric that had been previously targeting the Simitis government (*Vima*, 22/10/2006). It was reported that party members and cadres were exerting pressure on government officials to replace PASOK-appointed public-sector managers with New Democracy supporters (*Vima*, 28/03/2004, *Kathimerini*, 01/12/2004; 12/01/2005; 14/01/2005; 02/06/2007). In addition, a new bill governing the terms of hiring in the public sector gave Cabinet ministers the right to appoint three out of the five members of the selection committees and, therefore, the opportunity to interfere in the selection process.[1] This raised suspicions that the process could be susceptible to favoritism towards New Democracy's clients (*Vima*, 27/05/2007). However, given the fiscal constraints at the time, there could only be a limited 'supply' to the increasing clientelist 'demand':

> It is certain that partisan appointments, regardless of their extent, remain the main vehicle through which clientelist power is being reproduced. But . . . demand for jobs in the public or broader public sector is so high that [it] exceeds the most ambitious capacity. If the government decides to hire, say, ten party loyalists, it will upset a hundred friends and foes.
>
> (*Kathimerini*, 02/06/2007)

In addition, there was no significant progress in curbing government spending. The European Central Bank estimated that the cost of red tape, clientelist practices, unnecessary commissions and maladministration in Greece was around 39% of the government budget at that time (*Kathimerini*, 17/09/2006).[2] Among the supporters of economic liberalization in New Democracy, there was a sense of disillusionment with the government's inconsistency between its pro-reform rhetoric and its actual policy record.[3]

Following a turbulent summer when fierce and widespread forest fires tested the government's organizational capacity, New Democracy called an early election and was reelected with 41.84% of the votes in September 2007. Right after the election, the government decided to speed up the reform of the pensions system,[4] streamline the sale of shares in OTE (to Deutsche Telecom) and Olympic Airways and strike a lease agreement with a large Chinese company for the use of the Piraeus Port in Athens. There was less progress, however, in terms of

1 Professor of sociology Nikos Mouzelis noted: '[I]t may be the case that the Prime Minister and the Minister of Interior honestly want to limit partisanship. But they cannot achieve this [target] when, on the one hand, a bill allows discriminatory selection and, on the other, there are huge pressures by New Democracy's base on the government "to take good care of their children [supporters]" ' (*Vima*, 19.04/2004).

2 One of the main sources of wasteful spending was hospital and medicine expenditure (*Kathimerini*, 10/06/2007).

3 Karamanlis later admitted that there had been serious delays in substantive reforms (*Vima*, 14/09/2008).

4 This partial reform involved reducing early retirement schemes, aligning the retirement age for men and women, bringing new pensions below the level of the pensioners' last salary and lowering pensions for those who chose early retirement (*Vima*, 17/10/2007; 25/12/2008).

improving the environment for business investment. The start-up process for a new business venture continued to be lengthy, commercial law remained complex and several production and service markets were kept highly regulated, such as the professions of lawyers, civil engineers, advertisement and tourist agencies, taxis and commercial vehicles, pharmacies and architects (*Eleftherotypia*, 20/12/2009). Moreover, the government did not fulfill its promise to abolish hundreds of 'redundant' state agencies, committees, organizations and councils, or limit their personnel. Many public-sector companies continued to run deficits, whereas the special status that public-sector employees enjoyed was mostly left intact (*Kathimerini*, 27/07/2008).

This mixed record left the Greek economy vulnerable to exogenous shocks. Until 2007, the ratio of public debt to GDP was kept stable despite the debt's nominal increase thanks to the hitherto considerable annual rate of GDP growth. However, in the aftermath of the global financial crisis in 2008, Greece entered a period of low growth and, later, a recession, which the government sought to tackle by increasing its borrowing and spending. The government's response to the unanticipated crisis overlooked the broader economic and fiscal repercussions of this exogenous shock to a structurally problematic economy. Public spending soared when the government allocated 28 billion euros to recapitalize and fund the banking sector. Finance Minister Alogoskoufis insisted on the viability of its 'mild adjustment' strategy, claiming that Greece had already committed to fiscal adjustment at 0.5% of its GDP every year in order to bring the deficit down to zero (*Vima*, 31/08/2008). Later government action to offset this hike in public deficit involved new taxes and new controls against tax evasion with disappointing results. The degree of deficit spending led the European Commission to warn the Karamanlis government that Greece was heading towards a fiscal crisis.[5] The scale of fiscal derailment would be later exposed in 2009, when Greece was found to have recorded a deficit of 12.7% of GDP.[6] Following these findings, international private lenders revalued their risks regarding the creditworthiness of the Greek government. Greece found itself in danger of being cut off from private markets for its government bonds (*Economist*, 22/01/2009).

During the same period Greece was shaken by street protests and violent riots following the murder by two policemen of a 16-year-old student in a protest event in Athens in December 2008. New Democracy's popularity was falling amidst social unrest and accusations of corruption involving Cabinet ministers.[7] Publicly acknowledging the sharply deteriorating state of public finances and

5 EU Commissioner Joaquin Almunia claimed that the Greek government ignored this warming (TVXS, 16/06/2013).

6 This figure was revised upwards to 15.4% in 2010.

7 In May 2009, Karamanlis made the decision to formally conclude the parliamentary period and open a new one; this gesture was interpreted by his political rivals as a move that activated the strict limitations of the Law for the Criminal Liability of Ministers and absolved Cabinet ministers from penal liability for any offenses committed before the previous election (*Eleftherotypia*, 08/05/2009).

the need for austerity, Karamanlis called a snap election in September 2009. Under George Papandreou, PASOK campaigned with the promise of a fairer distribution of state resources that largely understated the scale of the ongoing fiscal derailment and the urgent need for tight fiscal policies.[8] PASOK won the election and returned to power.

'Mild adjustment': an assessment

New Democracy's 'mild adjustment' was an ambitious strategy that was poorly implemented. Whereas fiscal consolidation by the Simitis administration largely relied on higher taxes and partial privatization, New Democracy designed a policy strategy that was supposed to avoid the economic cost and the political damage from either a sharp rise in taxes or a sharp cut in public expenditure. Mild adjustment, however, relied too much on projected high annual growth rates and failed to curb tax evasion and tackle systemic sources of wasteful government spending in a consistent way. The New Democracy government did little to open markets and improve administrative inefficiency, which could have addressed Greece's persistent structural rigidities. The privatization of several profit-making enterprises gave the government new revenue, but several deficit-running companies remained unreformed. The government also failed to reduce red tape and combat rampant corruption in other sectors of public administration.[9] Ultimately, this strategy failed to generate sustainable public finances and a dynamic economic structure, which meant that the government had to remain dependent on cheap borrowing from private markets to continue to boost domestic

8 Epitomized in George Papandreou's phrase in his electoral campaign in September 2009 'There is enough money' ('Lefta yparhoun'). Papandreou refined this statement by claiming that additional resources could be secured thanks to a fairer tax system, the prudent organization of government spending and new investment in Greece (*Kathimerini*, 16/09/2014).

9 See a survey by PriceWatershouseCooopers (*Eleftherotypia*, 19/11/2009). As former Finance Minister George Alogoskoufis later admitted:

> We should have tried harder to make public administration more effective, to reduce red tape and effectively control the level of spending in local administration and the health sector (*Vima*, 06/10/2009).

Dr George Anastasopoulos, former secretary general of the Ministry of Development claimed that corruption was forcing business out of the country:

The authorities fail to understand the market's agony; while designing the imposition of new taxes and new control mechanisms, they either nod 'yes' or, at best, turn the blind eye to corruption (*Kathimerini*, 25/12/2009).

In an interview Orestis Papadopoulos, owner of a chocolate factory in Greece, expressed his view about red tape in Greece: '[F]or 30 years there has been systematic waste of social and human resources in Greece. It may be the case that economic indices were improved but as a society we are on a downward spiral. Corruption and maladministration are on the rise . . . Let me tell you that only the administrative burden on business in Greece amounts to 6.8% of GDP or 16.7 euros billion, whereas the EU average is 3.5% . . . When you fight against this type of administration, you cannot expect industrial growth' (*Eleftherotypia*, 10/05/2009).

demand, which was possible as long as Greece was considered a credible borrower.

These reform omissions by New Democracy are, at first glance, perplexing, given the party's ideological attachment to the ideas of market liberalization and free entrepreneurship. Bolder reforms could have been introduced with less friction compared with PASOK's earlier shift in attitude towards privatization and structural reforms. The actual pattern of reform, however, can be associated with New Democracy's links to professional groups that benefited from protective regulation, such as pharmacists, lawyers, notaries and civil engineers that politically leaned towards New Democracy and had important ties to the party's top-ranking politicians. What's more, tackling the source of waste in government expenditure would have reduced the turf for corruption and patronage for party cliques extracting benefits and bribes from decision-making positions in the public sector.[10] Finally, the government's desire to avoid social confrontation made it hesitant to take measures that could significantly alter the employment status in deficit-running companies. This preference led to a piecemeal approach to their restructuring and privatization.

It can be argued that the Karamanlis governments operated under the same type of incentives that push a government to keep the level of public spending stable or rising, if possible, and protect the regulatory framework that provides for the distributional demands of its main support groups. What was different now is that professional groups outside the public-sector enterprises were closer to its party structures (Table 10.2).

Greece before the crisis (1985–2009): a general assessment

At the onset of the global financial crisis, Greece was trapped in a vicious circle: high levels of government deficit were boosting consumption and growth rates, but they were fueling Greece's government debt and deepened its dependence on external borrowing, while structural rigidities worsened its competitiveness problem. Consecutive Greek governments took advantage of the country's entry into the Eurozone, which lowered its costs of public borrowing and gave a new bloodline to their distributional policies. The debt-fueled boom allowed both PASOK and New Democracy to increase nominal borrowing while keeping the debt/GDP ratio stable and avoid fixing structural rigidities in labor markets or curb public spending and excessive red tape. At the same time, both public borrowing and Community funding fueled the demand-led boom, mainly in the

10 A leading commentator in *Kathimerini* talked about the complicity of the clientelist parties: '[A]s the two main parties converged ideologically and politically, Greek citizens were expecting some consensus on how to tackle the country's big problems (structural reforms, labor markets, pensions etc.) . . . Instead, there is sharp and hypocritical animosity surrounding these issues, which is even more unacceptable, when the two parties are converging on actions of vicious partisanship, aiming at buying votes and preserving clientelist relationships' (Stamos Zoulas in *Kathimerini*, 16/09/2006).

Table 10.2 Party allegiance and behavior of key stakeholders

Group	*Degree of clientelist incorporation*	*Degree of autonomy from party politics*	*Dominant party*	*Support for the second party*	*Clashes with the dominant party*
Organized labor (private sector)	High	Weak	PASOK	Small for New Democracy Autonomous and vocal organization under the Communist Party	Moderate
Civil sector	High	Weak	PASOK	Moderate (ND)	Moderate to mild
Public enterprises	High	Weak	PASOK	Small-moderate (ND)	Moderate to mild
Farmers	Medium-high	Medium	No dominant party, Factions supported by ND, PASOK and the Communist Party	Strong and lengthy protests against both the PASOK and New Democracy governments	
Lawyers	Medium-low	Strong	Mainly ND but occasionally PASOK in big cities	Moderate to strong protests against both the PASOK and New Democracy governments	
Military	Medium	Very weak	ND	Small	No
Exporters	Low	Strong	ND	Small	No
Government subcontractors	Low	Medium/ strong	Association through collusion with politicians and civil servants	n/a	No

construction sector (Moschovis and Servera 2009). Growth was boosted by increasing borrowing and the inflow of EU funds (cohesion funds, structural funds and CAP transfers), but Greece throughout that period basically experienced jobless growth (with official unemployment rates persistently at 10%) exactly because the main source of investment was public infrastructure and procurement that was propping up domestic consumption but was also crowding out private export-oriented activities.

The higher returns from rent seeking through participation in public procurement and public investment, as well as increasing domestic consumption, led to a diversion of investment away from export-oriented activities into business that catered to public and private consumption. Highly regulated markets in the service sector and substantial wage and price inflation under a hard currency undermined Greece's export competitiveness throughout the 2000s. Adding to this problem, the increase in public-sector wages pushed for an increase in private-sector wages above the rate of productivity growth. As a result, the current account deficit rose from 0.8% of GDP in 1995 to 18% in 2008 (European Commission 2012: 14).[11] The vicious circle of debt, consumption and declining competitiveness created a bubble economy highly dependent on the ongoing inflow of cheap credit from abroad – predominantly through government borrowing and spending. The result was a high level of debt, lack of competitiveness and a large trade account deficit. Both Greece's debt dependency and its structural rigidities were problems that had to be managed simultaneously.

From a political and institutional perspective it can be argued that, although Greek governments found themselves under pressure to reform the economy, they took advantage of loose institutional constraints and new funding opportunities to revamp rather than reform the distributional system. Driven by the desire to preserve and renew patronage supply to their client groups, the key actors of the party system in the period between 1985 and 2009 manufactured a pattern of gradual and uneven policy adaptation instead of a radical revision or replacement of Greece's highly distributional model. With few notable exceptions, this policy choice reflected political calculations on the impact of reforms on the party's cohesion and mobilization capacity and its implication for electoral success. The political response to exogenous pressures was a creative effort of *clientelist bias* aimed at renewing and updating supply to client groups. This at times involved austerity measures in view of pressing conditions, but it adjusted structural reforms in order to protect the governing party's core client groups and took advantage of opportunities to delay reform and exploit new available resources for distribution.

11 The share of imports in the Greek GDP increased from 26.9% to 38.6%, and the share of exports in GDP stayed between 20% and 25%. Regulatory burdens such as lengthy export procedures, licenses, permits and approvals further burdened the business environment. In 2009, Greece ranked 96th out of 181 countries in the World Bank 'Doing Business' Report. Between 2000 and 2009, the real effective exchange rate relative to the Eurozone rose by 24.0% in terms of unit labor costs (European Commission 2012: 14).

It is noteworthy that until the 2009 fiscal crisis the Greek clientelist system was remarkably resilient and its key actors were creative and astute in employing strategies that fine-tuned the reform effort. This allowed them to continue to distribute privileges and state resources to their supporters. Economic adjustment was consistent with the Greek political model, which gave political parties a dominant position in the economy and society. Core properties of Greece's political economy survived despite external pressures, and a patchy record of reforms preserved party commitments under a clientelist structure. This reform pattern reflected, to a considerable extent, the degree to which external pressures for reform were binding and urgent, and much less so whether these policies were unpopular with the general population. This is obvious because Greek governments did not shy away from rising taxation and imposing new taxes and rounds of wage restraint for more than a decade between 1985 and 1999. Moreover, in policy areas outside the reach of direct EU policy prescriptions, the two main political parties abstained from implementing substantial reforms that could have decreased the politicization of government and social activities, such as the universities, the justice system, the police force and the operation of public utility enterprises. It is also worth mentioning that consecutive Greek governments took advantage of existing and new opportunities offered by EU membership to renew the resources by which they could meet their commitments to client groups in the form of subsidies, funding and fiscal credibility. In that context, until 2009, despite pressures for reforms, the Greek governments managed to design and implement a strategy of incremental and targeted reforms that avoided the destabilizing effect of rapidly changing external circumstances.

11 The Greek crisis (2009–2015)

The practice of clientelism requires fiscally expansionary policies that have an adverse effect on public finances and the economy itself. As the previous chapters have indicated, fiscal profligacy is nested in the clientelist game between two main political parties in which clientelist supply is the political equilibrium that 'overgrazes' fiscal and economic resources. This could eventually lead to a 'tragedy-of-the-commons' situation, when the resources for patronage supply are ultimately depleted. This outcome happens when the government loses access to resources for redistribution because a sharp economic recession reduces tax revenue and considerably increases the cost of public borrowing. A fiscal crisis could then evolve into a critical juncture for the clientelist system, as in the case of Greece after 2009.

The onset of the Greek crisis

In September 2009, PASOK, led by George Papandreou, won the parliamentary election with 43.92% of the votes and formed a government at a time when Greece's fiscal and economic condition was rapidly deteriorating. Although Greece was not the only country running a large public deficit in the aftermath of a global financial crisis, it stood out because of the scale of its fiscal imbalances, the uncertainty over the integrity of its fiscal data, the already high level of public debt and its fundamental problems with competitiveness and endemic corruption. Not surprisingly, by the end of 2009 private lenders were becoming increasingly skeptical about Greece's creditworthiness. Following further revision of Greece's budget deficit upwards in late 2009 to approximately 15% of GDP, Greece faced a barrage of credit downgrades by international rating agencies and, consequently, borrowing rates for its bonds skyrocketed. In response, the government announced two packages of major cuts in public-sector pay and an increase in consumption taxes in February and March 2010. The prime minister pledged to reform the public sector and establish an independent national statistics authority. However, these announcements failed to placate speculations in private bond markets that Greek default was possible.[1] In view of the newly revised fiscal data for Greece, credit agencies ultimately downgraded Greek bonds to 'junk status'. On 5 April 2010, the government made a final effort to sell a 7-year bond with a yield of 6% amidst rumors that Greece could soon go bankrupt.

Unable to borrow at reasonable prices, the Greek government filed a request for a loan of 45 billion euros from the European Union and the International Monetary Fund (IMF) on April 23. Few days later, on May 8, Greece signed with the EU authorities and the IMF an agreement for a loan of 110 billion euros under a 3-year program of economic adjustment (IMF 2010).[2] Greece's Economic Adjustment Program – the first in a series of other programs implemented in Ireland, Portugal and Cyprus – had noticeable similarities with the structural adjustment programs supervised by the IMF and the World Bank in developing and transition economies during the 1980s and 1990s (Greer 2013). What became popularly known as 'the Memorandum' ('*Mnimonio*') was a detailed plan of action that was governed by strict conditionality and surveillance by the three creditor institutions (the 'troika') as a prerequisite for the continuation of funding (Ladi 2014; Theodoropoulou 2014). The program aimed at a combined and fast-track effort for fiscal consolidation and structural reform, but its targets and predictions were very ambitious and unrealistic.[3] The Greek government had to take measures to reduce public spending by 7 percentage points of GDP until 2013 and cut the deficit below 3% of GDP by 2014. It also had to implement reforms that would open its production and service market and was expected to return to growth in 2011 (European Commission 2010a). Fiscal consolidation involved sharp rises in taxation and large reductions in wages in the public sector and pensions. It also included cuts in public investment and the reorganization of tax collection authorities.

The first review of the progress achieved by August 2010 was reticently positive, particularly regarding the degree of fiscal consolidation (European Commission 2010b). However, there was limited progress with the implementation of structural reforms, which led the European Commission to set up a task force in July 2011 to guide the Greek government towards streamlining the prescribed policy reforms and privatizations. Soon the Memorandum became the central topic of political confrontation. PASOK was a center-left party in charge of a

1 A number of public statements by the prime minister and the minister of finance reinforced the view abroad that the Greek economy was in deep trouble. Speaking at the European Council, Papandreou confessed that Greece's public administration was riddled with corruption (*Financial Times*, 11/12/2009). Greek Finance Minister George Papaconstantinou compared his efforts to restore Greece's finances to 'changing the course of the Titanic' (*Economist*, 03/03/2010).

2 There were formally two agreements: the Memorandum of Understanding on Specific Economic Policy Conditionality signed by Greece, the European Commission and the European Central Bank, and the Memorandum of Economic and Financial Policies signed between Greece and the IMF. These two agreements were known as the 'First Memorandum' signed between Greece and the so-called 'troika' institutions, which were responsible for evaluating the implementation of the program: the IMF, the European Commission and the European Central Bank (ECB).

3 The IMF later admitted that it had calculated the effect of austerity on growth using the wrong fiscal multipliers (IMF 2013).

program of sweeping reforms and deep austerity whose implementation was breaking the party's distributional links to its core support groups. Many Greek politicians and part of the press saw the Memorandum, both its content and its tight surveillance mechanisms, as an intrusion into Greece's political sovereignty and an assault on the Greek welfare state. The implementation of the bailout program damaged the relationship between several party unionists and PASOK. The party's cohesion was at stake.[4] Papandreou confronted criticism from several PASOK MPs but claimed that he had no other viable option but to sign and implement the bailout agreement. He presented his critics both inside and outside his party with the dilemma: 'you either vote the agreement or the country will go bankrupt' (*Kathimerini*, 30/06/2011). The prime minister was repeatedly calling for a broader interparty consensus on implementing the bailout agreement. Papandreou did not want to bear the full cost of the reform process and wanted to include New Democracy in the implementation of the program.

New Democracy, under the leadership of Antonis Samaras, voted against Greece's bailout agreement and rejected its policy direction on the grounds that the program's deep austerity and overreliance on taxes would exacerbate the recession and would bring Greece closer to bankruptcy (*Naftemporiki*, 22/04/2012).[5] Several prominent New Democracy politicians were suggesting that the party should adopt a milder stance on the Memorandum. Samaras' EU counterparts were also putting pressure on the New Democracy leader to accept the agreement (*Kathimerini*, 02/06/2011: 09/06/2011; 12/06/2011). However, Antonis Samaras consistently refused to sign up for what he proclaimed to be a flawed policy and firmly insisted that future fiscal and economic developments would vindicate his stance (*Kathimerini*, 29/05/2011; 11/06/2011). Samaras announced his own economic plan for fiscal consolidation and growth, with a focus on curbing wasteful public spending and lowering taxation to promote investment. Notwithstanding his substantive arguments against the first Memorandum, Samaras' anti-Memorandum stance made sense as a political strategy, given the fact that Papandreou's agreement on a bailout package had already offset the risk of systemic collapse. His rejection of the Memorandum meant that Papandreou and PASOK alone would bear the cost of the ensuing tough measures, whereas New Democracy might profit from the unpopularity of its measures and, possibly, their early failure to stabilize the economy. Indeed, New Democracy took a lead in the polls against PASOK in the beginning of the summer of 2011 (*Kathimerini*, 12/06/2011; 15/06/2011).

An analytic outlook

The stance which Papandreou and Samaras took on Greece's first bailout agreement can be understood in light of the clientelist game, which reached a point

4 Instead, Papandreou reshuffled the Cabinet, and Samaras asked Papandreou to resign and call for a new election.

5 See Samaras' parliamentary speech on 28/06/2011.

where foreign institutional creditors offered Greece a loan under strict conditionality to prevent Greece's default. For Papandreou, the rejection of the package was thought to lead to systemic collapse and probably Greece's exit from the Eurozone. In an ordinal scale that indicates his preference ranking over possible outcomes from best to worst (Table 11.1), Papandreou believed that accepting

Table 11.1 Order of preferences for the governing party

Order	*The governing party's stance*	*The opposition's stance*	*Payoffs*	*Explanation*
1	Accept reform package	Accept reform package	4	• Prevents systemic collapse • Both parties share the political cost of implementation with a 'there is no alternative' argument • Triggers reactions inside the party that can undermine party unity but at least will not lead to defections to the main opposition party
2	Accept reform package	Reject reform package	3	• Prevents systemic collapse • Only the government bears the political cost of implementation while coming under fire from the opposition that presents a milder policy alternative as viable • The government can accuse the opposition of being irresponsible and unrealistic • Triggers reactions inside the party that can undermine party unity and lead to defections to other opposition parties
3	Reject reform package	Reject reform package	2	• Provokes systemic collapse • Both parties share responsibility for the systemic collapse • The collapse of the distributional system will undermine party unity, but the party's rejection of reform may not necessarily lead to massive defections to the main opposition party
4	Reject reform package	Accept reform package	1	• Provokes systemic collapse • The government will be accused by the opposition of being the main culprit behind the collapse • The collapse of the distributional system will undermine party unity, but the party's rejection of reform may not lead to sizeable defections to the main opposition party • However, criticism of the government may allow the opposition to claim that 'it would have done it differently', and the opposition is better positioned to appeal to those heavily hurt by systemic collapse

the bailout agreement was the only reasonable option. Samaras, however, could criticize Papandreou for not negotiating an alternative program, whereas his stance could not cause Greece's default and euro exit, given Papandreou's signature on the agreement (Table 11.2).

Table 11.2 Order of preferences for the main opposition party

Order	*The opposition's stance*	*The governing party's stance*	*Payoffs*	*Explanation*
1	Reject reform package	Accept reform package	4	• Government prevents systemic collapse • The opposition party does not share the political cost of implementation • Response inside the governing party will undermine its unity • The opposition party can profit from defections from the governing party
2	Accept reform package with criticism over its details	Accept reform package	3	• Government prevents systemic collapse • The opposition party shares the political cost of implementation, but can still criticize the government over specific decisions • Does not profit directly from defections from the governing party, yet the government's cohesion is weakened
3	Accept reform package	Reject reform package	2	• Government provokes systemic collapse that will hurt the opposition party's capacity to credibly promise and offer future benefits • The opposition party accuses the government of being responsible for the systemic collapse • Does not bear any potential cost from the reform package it has endorsed, as this will not be implemented • The collapse of the distributional system will undermine both parties' cohesion
4	Reject reform package	Reject reform package	1	• Government provokes systemic collapse • The opposition party shares responsibility for rejecting the rescue package and has to build a new narrative of blame against the government • The collapse of the distributional system will undermine both parties' cohesion, but will not lead to defections to the governing party

Table 11.3 Game between the government and the opposition in the face of imminent systemic collapse

		Opposition	
		Accept with criticism O1	*Reject with criticism O2*
Government	Accept G1	4, 3	3, 4
	Reject G2	1, 2	2, 1

Table 11.3 indicates that when fiscal profligacy leads to deep fiscal or economic crisis, the government must take measures for economic reform that break with clientelist bias in order to prevent systemic collapse. The opposition will be better off criticizing government policy (G1O2: 3, 4). This outcome will only change to mutual acceptance of a reform package (G1O1:, 4, 3) when financial 'aid' (in the form of loans) to prevent a systemic crisis is offered on condition that both parties sign up for reforms or agree to implement the agreement, as the next session shows.

Interparty collaboration (2011–2015)

Contrary to the optimistic projections of the bailout program, the economic recession was deep and pushed deficit spending upwards as a percentage of a shrinking GDP. This forced the government to enact new rounds of austerity with higher taxes and deeper spending cuts. Consumption plummeted, driving many businesses to bankruptcy or pushing them to lay off staff. Official unemployment soared to around 25%, hitting the young and women the hardest. Total household income in Greece dropped by a third between 2007 and 2012 (OECD 2014). People from all walks of life – particularly pensioners and private-sector employees, small and medium entrepreneurs and the recently unemployed – experienced a major upheaval in their personal fiscal and employment circumstances. The economic depression, tough austerity measures and the deep-cutting reforms of the pension system, the labor market and the public sector caused increasing political and social unrest. The cost of fiscal austerity, new taxes and falling incomes were strong enough to mobilize public reaction and protest even from people with no prior engagement in collective action. Impromptu public rallies, mostly coordinated via social media, gave rise to the Greek 'indignados' movement ('*aganaktismenoi*'), which lacked a specific partisan affiliation but had an active presence in frequent rallies before the Greek Parliament. Their main cause of distress was that low-income and average-income people were usually the worst hit by the financial and social costs of the crisis and by the ensuing reforms.

On June 15, the day the Parliament was discussing the ratification of the medium-term upgrade of the fiscal adjustment program, the Parliament building was surrounded by vocal crowds rallying against the 'political class' and the austerity measures which it was about to impose in response to a crisis it was largely responsible for. On the same day, Papandreou contacted Samaras to tell him that he would step down as prime minister if Samaras agreed to join PASOK in a coalition government. It was reported that Samaras accepted the proposal on the condition that the new government would renegotiate the terms of the bailout agreement, repeal PASOK's immigration law and call for elections once the negotiations were completed (*Vima*, 15/06/2011), but Papandreou did not accept these terms and withdrew his proposal just a few hours later.[6] New Democracy attributed Papandreou's withdrawal of the proposal to intense pressures from his own political entourage to stay in power (*Kathimerini*, 16/06/2011; 19/09/2011). A few months later, Papandreou invited Samaras to join him at the negotiating table over a second bailout program, an invitation which Samaras rejected on the grounds that there had been no prior talks and no agreement on a joint position (*Kathimerini*, 20/10/2011). Papandreou still wanted to find a way to share the political cost of a tough bailout program. New speculations emerged that the government would submit the new agreement of October 2011 for parliamentary approval under the qualified majority process that required 180 votes instead of 151, out of a total of 300, in order to compel New Democracy to vote in favor of the agreement or risk taking responsibility for Greece's default. There were also rumors that Papandreou might call for a referendum over the new agreement (*Kathimerini*, 17/07/2011; 26/10/2011).

Greece's creditors also put pressure on the leader of New Democracy to sign up for the forthcoming Second Memorandum (*Kathimerini*, 02/07/2011; 23/10/2011). Samaras again refused to endorse Greece's bailout program despite increasing pressures from prominent New Democracy politicians (*Kathimerini*, 21/06/2011; 29/10/2011). He defended his policy proposals for an alternative path to growth and stabilization, which included privatizations and spending cuts instead of higher taxes, and expressed his belief that, if he was elected prime minister, he would be able to start new negotiations with European Union leaders to agree on different terms and conditions (*Kathimerini*, 30/06/2011).

On 26 October 2011, Papandreou signed a second bailout agreement with Greece's creditors, which included a new loan and the decision to move towards a partial write-off of the Greek debt in return for new structural reforms and more fiscal austerity. Right after his return to Greece, Papandreou announced his decision to call for a referendum that would allow the Greek voters to accept or reject the second bailout plan. It was thought that a 'yes' outcome would strengthen his position and would enable Papandreou to quiet down the reactions

6 PASOK's version of these events was that Papandreou could not accept Samaras' maximalist terms for a short-lived government to launch a renegotiation process and that Samaras did not genuinely want to join a coalition government (*Kathimerini*, 17/06/2011).

of its own party members. However, several PASOK politicians and his European counterparts saw this decision as a risky initiative (*Kathimerini*, 02.11.2011). Papandreou claimed that he had previously notified European leaders of this decision. But when he was called to attend the G20 Summit in Cannes, France, he faced a hostile reception led by French President Sarkozy. It was reported that Papandreou was warned that funding (of around 30 to 40 billion euros) would be suspended until Greece decided on a new referendum question whether to keep or leave the euro (*Kathimerini*, 02/11/2011; *Vima*, 16/07/2012). Both the recently signed bailout agreement and the debt-restructuring plan were then to be exposed to the uncertainties of the popular vote.

When Papandreou returned to Greece, he faced strong reactions against his decision to call the referendum from several Cabinet ministers and prominent PASOK politicians. After the resignation of an MP from PASOK's parliamentary team, the government's majority in the Parliament fell to only two seats. Papandreou called for a vote of confidence, which he won. Soon after, amidst fears of a possible bank run and government default, he cancelled the referendum. On the same day, Samaras stated that his party would vote in favor of the loan agreement, provided that the government would resign and a new technocratic government would be formed with the support of both PASOK and New Democracy. Papandreou accepted this proposition and decided to step down (*Kathimerini*, 04/11/2011). The press reported that Greece's creditors had exerted strong pressure on both parties to form a new coalition government and ratify the bailout agreement in its entirety (not just the loan agreement, but also the terms and conditions attached). They had reportedly warned that in the event that there would be no stable government in Greece to pass the agreement, Greece could find itself ousted from the Eurozone (*Kathimerini*, 05/11/2011; 07/11/2011). Regardless of whether this threat was real or not, Samaras agreed to join a coalition government and back up the bailout plan on the condition that, once the new government ratified the Second Memorandum and completed the debt-restructuring process, it would then call for a new general election.[7]

On November 11, PASOK, New Democracy and LAOS (an extreme right-wing party) formed a government under the former vice-governor of the European Central Bank and former Bank of Greece Governor Lucas Papademos with the mandate to complete the debt-restructuring process and implement structural reforms that would restructure the broader public sector and the pensions system. New Democracy's ministers were given Cabinet positions that were not related to the implementation of the Memorandum. A few days later, Samaras yielded to pressures from Greece's creditors and sent a letter with a signed pledge that

7 Under pressure from their European counterparts and some of its top ranking party cadres, the two leaders moved back and forth for a few days before agreeing to form a coalition government. Samaras wanted a short-lived government staffed by technocrats alone, whereas Papandreou insisted on a government consisting of politicians, and many of his Cabinet ministers expressed their desire to preserve their portfolios (*Kathimerini*, 08/11/2011; 13/11/2011).

he would help implement the bailout agreement (*Nea*, 24/11/2011). By signing a new Memorandum New Democracy would now share the cost of its implementation and would also have to change its political rhetoric and narrative of blame.[8] Samaras' U-turn can be explained by reference to the threat of Greece's euro exit and the imminent collapse of the Greek financial system, which had changed New Democracy's payoffs regarding its best stance towards the Second Memorandum and the question of whether to join a coalition government or not. This time, it was Samaras' decision that was to determine whether Greece would head towards a disorderly default and possibly exit from the euro.[9]

The formation of a government by two traditional opponents, PASOK and New Democracy, was an unprecedented development in Greece's political history. Under difficult economic and social circumstances, the coalition government marked the beginning of a political division in Greek politics between the pro-Memorandum and the anti-Memorandum political forces, possibly reflecting the socioeconomic division between those who lost heavily because of the crisis and those who retained some of their pre-crisis standing. The remaining opposition forces (SYRIZA, the Coalition of the Radical Left and the Communists of KKE) could now attack both parties as a single political bloc. SYRIZA assumed the role of the main opposition party with an anti-Memorandum stance, and it would attract center-left voters, including dissenters from PASOK and its affiliated unions. New Democracy's cohesion was undermined when several politicians who belonged to its so-called 'popular right' faction left the party and formed a new anti-Memorandum party, the 'Independent Greeks' (ANEL).

The second rescue package of 130 billion euros was completed in February 2012 and the partial restructuring ('haircut') of Greece's debt was finalized in March and April 2012. In return, the government undertook the obligation to pass new spending cuts in wages and pensions and a new round of structural reforms (IMF 2012). At the same time, economic and social conditions severely deteriorated. The Greek economy entered its fourth year of recession in 2012, unemployment rose to 23.6% in the second quarter of 2012 (compared with 16.3% a year earlier), wages fell considerably and the economic downturn in Greece was much deeper than anticipated when the first adjustment program was adopted in May 2010, following a sharp drop in domestic demand and public consumption (European Commission 2012: 9).

In late spring 2012, the Papademos government resigned, and new elections were held in May 2012. The electoral result recorded the dramatic shift in political preferences among Greek voters that ended the bipartisan hegemony of PASOK and New Democracy in Greek politics, which had lasted since 1977.

8 Samaras told his parliamentary team: 'We are supporting the work of the transitional government. We are not offering forgiveness to anyone. We are not bearing responsibility for what the Papandreou government had done' (*Kathimerini*, 15/11/2011).

9 Samaras publicly justified his U-turn: 'I have explained many times and [a] long time ago that implementing the decision of the 27th of October is inevitable to protect the Greek economy and the euro' (*Kathimerini*, 09/11/2011).

New Democracy came in first place, but its share of votes slipped from 33.5% in 2009 to 18.9%, whereas PASOK, under a new leader, plummeted to third place, from 43% to just over 13%. SYRIZA (the Coalition of the Radical Left that evolved from the Coalition of the Left, Synaspismos), led by a former youth political activist Alexis Tsipras, came in second place with a surprising 16.8% of the vote, just below New Democracy's share, and was ahead among younger and middle-aged voters (18 to 54) and in all Athens constituencies.[10] Two thirds of the Greek voters chose parties that were opposed to the EU/IMF bailout. For the first time, Golden Dawn, an ultra-nationalist party, was elected to Parliament with 6.9% of the vote. Its narrative of blame capitalized on growing disillusionment and anger with traditional political parties (Halikiopoulou and Vasilopoulou 2015).[11] New political entries to Parliament also included the right-wing anti-Memorandum party 'Independent Greeks' (ANEL) and the Democratic Left party (DIMAR) on the center-left that mostly included politicians who left SYRIZA in 2010. No political party secured a parliamentary majority, and a new election was scheduled for June 2015.

The electoral period took place amidst warnings from EU leaders that the electoral result could decide whether Greece would stay in the Eurozone.[12] New Democracy leader Antonis Samaras described the choice between New Democracy and SYRIZA as one between 'the euro and its safety and the drachma with [its] isolation and instability' (*Vima*, 14/06/2012). SYRIZA's leader Alexis Tsipras reassured everyone that his government would guarantee Greece's position in the Eurozone, but he would fight to put an end to the Memorandum and its 'neoliberal' policies, and presumed that the EU leaders would not risk a Greek exit from the Eurozone (*Vima*, 14/06/2012).

The second legislative election of 17 June 2012 led to the electoral victory of New Democracy with 29.7% of the votes. SYRIZA increased its vote share to 26.9%, whereas PASOK fell to 12.3%. A new coalition government led by Antonis Samaras was formed with the support of New Democracy, PASOK and

10 See the opinion polls (February to May 2012) by Public Issue (2012). New Democracy was more popular with pensioners, farmers and housewives and low-education voters, whereas SYRIZA was more popular with salaried private and public employees, students, higher-education graduates and the unemployed (*Ethnos*, 13/5.2012; Public Issue 2012).

11 The party's popularity skyrocketed from 0.29% in the 2009 election to double-digit figures in the opinion polls of 2013.

12 German Chancellor Angela Merkel stated that the Greek debt reforms were of 'utmost importance'. European Commission spokeswoman Pia Ahrenkilde Hansen said that Brussels expected the future government of Greece to respect the engagement that Greece had entered into (*BBC News*, 07/05/12). EU President Herman Van Rompuy added: 'We want Greece to remain in the euro area while respecting its commitments' (*Al Jazeera*, 24/05/2012). See also: BBC News, 'Greek socialist leader Venizelos warns of mass poverty' (05/05/2012); *Los Angeles Times*, 'Greek conservatives get boost from Eurozone exit warnings' (01/06/2012). There were speculations that the Greek government could run out of funds, Greek banks could run out of liquidity and the position of Greece in the Eurozone would be questioned unless there was a stable government after the election of June 2015 (*Vima*, 27/05/2012).

the Democratic Left party. The prolonged electoral period of the summer of 2012 caused delays in the implementation of Greece's second adjustment program and further economic uncertainty. Soon after, the new government accelerated the implementation of structural reforms. Prime Minister Samaras launched two new packages of austerity measures in October 2012 and in July 2013 and came under fire from the opposition, who accused him of reneging on his earlier promises that he would renegotiate the first Memorandum's policies.

By the end of 2012, a deteriorating macroeconomic situation and delays in program implementation worsened the outlook for Greece's debt sustainability (European Commission 2012: 5). Although the government managed to tighten budgetary spending, it made little progress towards market liberalization and tax reforms. Greece improved its ranking in the 2013 World Bank Doing Business Indicator, mainly thanks to labor market reforms that pushed down wage costs, but it continued to score low in competitiveness. It had to implement further reforms, such as the liberalization of its energy sector and transport system, and move on with privatization whose proceeds had so far been 'disappointing' (European Commission 2012: 4).

A year later, in the beginning of 2014, Greece's public finances were showing signs of stabilization. For the first time after 6 years of deep recession, the country registered a small growth rate – the highest among Eurozone countries in the third quarter of 2014. In April 2014, the European Commission acknowledged that Greece's degree of fiscal consolidation in recent years was 'impressive', exceeding its target in 2013 and recording a primary surplus.[13] The Commission claimed that economic recovery was about to result from the reforms Greece had introduced in the areas of revenue administration, taxation, public financial management, public administration, healthcare, pensions, social welfare, education and the fight against corruption (European Commission 2014a: 1).[14] It also reported that Greece's competitiveness had been improved thanks to labor market reforms and declining wage costs. Greece was dubbed 'a very active reformer' in lifting job protection and restrictions on working time (European Commission 2014a: 51). The creditors' institutions hailed the progress the Greek government had achieved in terms of the reallocation of personnel via mandatory mobility, the dismissal of people illegally appointed or receiving disciplinary

13 The Commission's report on the implementation of the Greek program in April 2014 noted: 'Wages better aligned with productivity dynamics and falling unit labor costs are improving cost competitiveness, although the performance of exports will improve visibly only when reforms in other parts of the economy are fully implemented. Key structural reforms in the areas of product markets and business environment have been recently undertaken or are now being taken by the authorities to increase competition and reduce administrative burden. Still very sizeable challenges remain in many areas' (European Commission 2014a: 1).

14 It is still uncertain whether this small recovery can be attributed to the implemented structural reforms, improved business confidence, higher tourist revenue or the fact that no new rounds of austerity measures were passed after the spring of 2014.

penalties, the performance evaluation of managers and staff and better financial management (European Commission 2014a: 3).

Nevertheless, the rate of growth was anemic and not widely seen as an indication of a strong recovery (IMF 2014). At the end of 2014, the overall economic outlook in Greece still looked uncertain. Greece improved its current account, but this improvement was led by a sharp drop in imports, whereas export levels stagnated in everything but oil products. Growth was small, and official unemployment levels were persistently high at 20%, and youth unemployment reached 60%. The credit crunch continued to hit Greek business, further undermining job creation. The Greek government was still not able to borrow from private markets at reasonable rates. Finally, arrears towards the government increased, and the banking system faced a rising number of nonperforming loans – the combined result of recession, unemployment and contraction in personal finances (Hellenic Parliament 2015).

Greece's failure to restore growth with a strong export record was partly attributed to the country's persistent structural problems associated with the distortions caused by the prevalence of highly distributional/clientelist economic activities in the previous years. During that time, many resources had been geared towards public investment and public and private consumption – due to the generally higher and safer returns that business investors could expect from engaging with government procurement or by simply catering to Greece's rising private consumption in the 1990s and 2000s. As a result, Greece found itself trapped in a vicious circle of having a production base dependent on consumption that was largely fueled by government spending. Tackling the deficit problem with sharp austerity measures seriously disturbed those economic activities that were dependent on domestic demand. The sharp drop in public expenditure and higher taxes led to a sudden bust of the economy. Falling consumption and a credit crunch was exacerbated by the deflation of wages and asset prices, and this deepened the output downfall. Important structural reforms were delayed, and those that were implemented were insufficient to lead to a rapid restructuring of Greece's productive base. Reforms did not offset the immediate shock on domestic demand.

The program's mistakes, contradictions and 'unintended' consequences were the topic of debate in academic circles worldwide and the turf in which different economic views clashed. Some economic views partly blamed euro membership for exacerbating the buildup to the crisis, leading to increased borrowing and price bubbles, as well as the depth of the crisis, due to prolonged austerity,[15] or the absence of automatic transfers (Krugman 2012). The policy of 'internal devaluation' of wage and asset prices was tried as a substitute for currency devaluation, aimed at primarily lowering unit labor costs (Åslund and Dombrovskis 2011; Wolf 2011). This belief was criticized as procyclical and detrimental for the Greek banking system, too, because nonperforming loans increased due to general prices depreciation. Internal devaluation was said to

15 For instance, 'Bank of England Governor Attacks Eurozone Austerity' (*Guardian*, 29/01/2015).

depress growth and ultimately require further austerity for the government to regain its fiscal credibility, thus generating a vicious circle (Armingeon and Baccaro 2012; Stockhammer and Sotiropoulos 2014).[16] The ensuing credit crunch further harmed economic activity.

The depth and extent of austerity aimed at unrealistic primary deficits – with higher taxes paying for a debt denominated in a hard currency and owed to foreigners. Fiscal consolidation at the very start, when structural rigidities remained unreformed, was estimated to have led to a sharp fall in consumption and investment (Weisbrot and Montecino 2012). This drained the economy and had a counterproductive impact on Greece's growth and unemployment rates. A self-reinforcing cycle of austerity and recession was triggered, while the rhetoric of Grexit, political turmoil and workforce emigration prompted capital flight and disinvestment, further undermining fiscal consolidation and debt sustainability. Moreover, structural reforms, although implemented to a considerable extent, did not lead to a rapid export boom that could have offset the fall of demand-led output; hence both consumption and investment collapsed (Hazakis and Kyrkilis 2014: 17).

Notwithstanding the economic causes of the crisis, job redundancies, persistent joblessness and the sharp drop in incomes unsettled the livelihoods and life plans of millions of Greeks, in particular families and businesses that, before the crisis, had undertaken loans and mortgages under higher asset prices and wages and made investment and consumption decisions with a different financial forecast. The crisis hardly left anyone unscathed but it hit the poor and the unemployed worst. There were concerns that an increasing number of people did not have full access to healthcare services and primary care (European Commission 2013: 35). On the political sphere, economic hardship ignited a climate of increasing social discontent and political resentment. There was a widespread feeling that the political establishment had not been held accountable for Greece's economic failure, and there was anger against the political impunity which politicians enjoyed when they were accused of engagement in corruption cases. Anti-austerity protests, rounds of strikes, occupation of public buildings, clashes with the police and the heckling of politicians in public and private events became recurrent themes in Greece's political life.

The pattern of reform: traces of clientelist bias

The effort to fight middle- and low-level corruption

Throughout the period of the economic crisis, revelations about past corruption scandals cast a heavy shadow on the Greek political system, most notably, the transfer of bribes allegedly reaching 130 million German marks by Siemens to

16 See Jeffrey Sommers and Michael Hudson, 'Latvia and the Disciples of Internal Devaluation', *Guardian* (16/09/20110 September 2011. Anders Åslund held a different view and argued that a longer period was needed to assess the effectiveness of internal devaluation: 'Why Internal Devaluation Is Advantageous', at piie.com, 6/06/2012.

a chain of political actors over a period of 20 years.[17] At the beginning of the Greek economic crisis, Greek public opinion was shocked when a former minister of transport and communication under the Simitis government, and a former advisor to the prime minister himself, confessed that they had received 'donations' by Siemens, yet they could not be prosecuted due to strict time limitations governing the penal liability of former ministers and members of parliament.[18] Consecutive Greek governments had not repealed the special penal liability status which former ministers and members of parliament enjoyed, even if it was obvious that this had blocked the investigation of high-profile cases of corruption. A new judicial investigation also disclosed that the previously appointed legal investigator mishandled the case and charged him with infringement of duty and abuse of power (*Vima*, 20/12/2009). The ongoing impunity raised suspicions of broader complicity from the political class to protect high-ranking politicians who were left untouched by the justice system.[19] In few cases, retired politicians, such as former Defense Minister Tsohatzopoulos, were prosecuted and sentenced to long prison sentences for money laundering, which penal law regards as a continuous violation of the law and, therefore, not subject to the strict statute of limitations.

New investigations revealed extensive corruption in many public agencies: in the tax collection service (*Eleftherotypia*, 25/04/2009), the urban planning authority (*Eleftherotypia*, 15/03/2011), the police and the prison system, the social benefits system, the justice system (*Eleftherotypia*, 26/09/2010), local administration, forest protection agencies, the land registry and the Ministry of Transport (*Eleftherotypia*, 03/03/2010; 12/07/2013). Widespread corruption was also associated with soaring levels of spending in healthcare, especially social security spending in private hospitals and diagnostic centers, medical supplies and pharmaceutical products whose costs continued to rise during the first years of the crisis (European Commission 2013: 34). In its annual report, the General Inspector of Public Administration noted that, despite the government's pledge to fight

17 Siemens had been involved in procurement procedures by several government-controlled organizations for equipment in telecommunications, the Olympic Games security system, railways and urban transport machinery, military telecommunications and defense and hospitals.

18 Although the Parliament had concluded in 2010 that the Siemens scandal cost the Greek state approximately 2 billion euros, PASOK and New Democracy voted for a law in May 2012 that passed a 'settlement' agreement according to which Siemens would pay the Greek government 270 million euros in compensation.

19 George Katrougalos, a professor of constitutional law who will later served as a Cabinet minister in the SYRIZA government, made the comment that 'in the past, the political system secured the impunity of selected politicians through ties of complicity connecting the two main parties that were alternating in power. We are now witnessing the disclosure of some cases for which we previously had suspicions but no proof, because the political system is collapsing and is incapable of imposing a complete "*omertà*" through and through. However, even today, punishment has not touched the core of the old party system. Those politicians who are on the dock are, essentially, dead horses who are being used as scapegoats in order to appease the popular call for justice' (*Eleftherotypia*, 21/01/2014).

corruption, the control mechanisms were still insufficient and there were delays in the justice system regarding the prosecution of corruption cases (*Eleftherotypia*, 07/06/2011; General Inspector of Public Administration 2013). Corruption was fueled by complicated legislation ('polynomia') and regulatory uncertainty (*Eleftherotypia*, 25/05/2009).[20] A research survey from the University of Athens showed that 71% of respondents attributed corruption to 'illegality' and a sense that 'everything is permitted' (*Eleftherotypia*, 16/09/2010). Many of these corruption cases involved politically appointed state officials and party cliques in key administrative positions. Throughout the period of economic adjustment under the Memoranda, Greece was ranked as the most corrupt country among the old 15 EU member states in the Transparency International's corruption index, with an estimated cost of corruption around 632 million euros (Transparency International, Greece: 2010).

The Greek government took some steps to increase transparency. Most notably, the Papandreou government passed a law in 2010 that placed all public institutions under the obligation to publish their decisions online, including those involving public procurement (European Commission 2014b: 5). In late 2012, Greek authorities agreed to launch an anticorruption strategy (a 'road map') and devise a specific action plan to tackle widespread corruption by early 2013. Most of the effort, however, focused on petty corruption.[21] The effort by Greek authorities to fight petty corruption led to new revelations of how extensive this phenomenon had been. Between 2011 and 2013, citizens' reports of corruption concerning employees of the public sector increased by 94.64% (*Eleftherotypia*, 03/04/2013). An astounding case was the extortion of bribes in exchange for project approval by fund management officials in the infamous 'fourth floor' of the Ministry of Development between 2005 and 2012 (European Commission 2014b: 6; *Ethnos*, 21/3/2014). Another case of cigarette smuggling by coastguards revealed that there had been a hierarchy of officials within the criminal group and that the administrative prosecution had led to only one disciplinary penalty and four dismissals (European Commission 2014b: 9). This was one of many cases that revealed that internal control mechanisms in the civil service were ineffective, to say the least (European Commission 2014b: 5). Disciplinary councils consisted of politically appointed members and unionists who were reluctant to impose penalties

20 The 2014 Eurobarometer survey on corruption revealed that 76% of Greek respondents believed that public procurement was imbued with corruption: it was reported that special preconditions were tailor-made to favor particular companies, and the favored bidders were at times involved in the design of the preconditions and specifications. Among the patterns noted was the abuse of negotiated procedures, collusive bidding, unclear selection or evaluation criteria, the abuse of emergency grounds to avoid competitive procedures and several amendments of contractual terms after the conclusion of the contract (Eurobarometer 2014).

21 A report by the European Commission on the problem of corruption in the EU stated that Greece had achieved progress towards reducing widespread corruption of middle-ranking and lower-ranking state officials despite Greece's fragmented and complex legislation (*Eleftherotypia*, 03/02/2014).

on civil servants charged with violating the civil service code.[22] Amendments to the civil service code adopted in 2012 and 2013 sped up disciplinary proceedings and changed the composition of disciplinary councils to include judges who could ensure greater impartiality (European Commission 2014b: 6). Between July and September 2013, a record number of 26 civil servants were dismissed on disciplinary grounds.

At the same time, the opposition and part of the press criticized the government for passing new legislation further protecting state officials from penal prosecutions. SYRIZA published a brochure dubbed 'Black Bible' that accused New Democracy and PASOK of complicity in preventing the investigation of corruption cases. These accusations concerned the formal settlement of the Siemens scandal, the obstruction of criminal cases involving former PASOK and New Democracy ministers,[23] the enactment of several 'impunity clauses' in the penal law protecting state officials,[24] lack of transparency regarding the workings of the privatizations fund (TAIPED)[25] and the alleged protection of high-income tax evasion.[26] SYRIZA's leader Alexis Tsipras publicly accused the government of breeding corruption:

22 It may be the case that many of the accused were active members of the labor organization or had the protection of senior officials. It may also be that the members of disciplinary committees were afraid of retaliation either from the accused themselves or their patrons.

23 Between 2012 and 2014, the Parliament took no action to allow criminal justice to investigate 89 pending criminal files and, consequently, the penal liability of former ministers was erased due to the short statute of limitations governing their cases. Moreover, government MPs voted against SYRIZA's proposal that the Parliament would investigate accusations of fraud and embezzlement concerning the never-completed building of four military submarines by a German conglomerate in the Skaramangas Shipyard following a contract signed in 1998 by the Simitis government (*Vima*, 18/12/2013). This was one of the cases for which former Minister Tsohatzopoulos was sentenced to 20 years in prison for money laundering allegedly related to bribes (*Vima*, 07/10/2013).

24 SYRIZA's anticorruption brochure 'Black Bible' used the term 'criminal laundering' to describe legislation passed by the Parliament that altered the criminal liability status (by either suspending or stopping penal procedures or erasing future criminal liability) of certain penal law offences if they were committed by a number of state officials as part of their duties. This covered the managers of companies under privatization, bank executives for decisions when approving loans to political parties or companies of the broader public sector, members of the state's Legal Council when giving a formal opinion in favor of government actions which the courts of justice would later nullify as illegal or unconstitutional, the managers of farming cooperatives, the managers of special Funds and the Privatization Fund (TAIPED) and local administration officials (Mayors and Regional Governors). SYRIZA also attacked the government for favoritism towards media owners regarding outstanding tax liabilities.

25 SYRIZA's leader, Alexis Tsipras, promised that, once elected Prime Minister, he would investigate the legality of all contracts signed by TAIPED (*Nea*, 12/12/2014). In July 2015, the Public Prosecutor for Corruption filed charges of embezzlement against members of TAIPED (*Kathimerini*, 20/07/2015).

26 A prominent case was the infamous 'Lagarde list', which contained the names of approximately 2000 Greeks who were potentially involved in tax evasion. The list was named after French Finance Minister Christine Lagarde who had reportedly passed this list on to the Greek government to help in its efforts with curbing tax evasion.

> Whose political child is spending waste, corruption and state inefficiency? Who benefited from preferential tax credits, from bribes and the overpricing of public works?
>
> (*Eleftherotypia*, 13/03/2010)

Protecting the status of professional groups

In February 2011, the Papandreou government passed legislation to establish general free access to professional activities and abolish, at least in principle, fixed prices, compulsory minimum fees and administrative licenses for professional activities. The scope of the law was left unspecified, and its implementation was both delayed and partial because there was no secondary legislation that would abolish each of the specific restrictions in force by previous regulations. Direct implementation would have abrogated the protected status of a number of professions: auditors, audit firms, accountants and tax consultants, lawyers, notaries, energy inspectors, travel agents, tourist guides, private labor consultancy offices, custom brokers, pharmacists, lorry owners, real estate agents, actuaries, chartered valuers and geo-technicians. Moreover, the law gave Cabinet ministers the authority to reinstate these restrictions by decree within 4 months after the law's enactment. This loophole allowed professional associations to secure derogations and the revision of regulations. The result was only the partial liberalization of professions such as notaries, lawyers and law firms, engineers and auditors, whereas separate laws were later passed for pharmacists, technical professions and truck and transportation companies (European Commission 2014a: 55). The delay in the opening of professional services can be associated with the electoral and political clout that these groups had, particularly for the government's main party, New Democracy.

Under intense pressure from the troika, the Samaras government later specified the list of over 150 professions in June 2013 and promised to implement all measures that would liberalize professional activities as recommended by the OECD's Competition Assessment Review of March 2014 (European Commission 2014a: 285). Several measures that cut red tape but did not directly affect the status of professional groups were also introduced.[27] Still, by the end of the Second Adjustment Program, Greece had relatively strict product market regulations (European Commission 2014a: 5).

Social reactions and shifting alliances

The scale of austerity and the range of the structural reforms under way came as a shock to private and public employees alike. For the first time, Greece was

27 These measures included lowering the property transfer tax, easing licensing procedures for retail outlets, reducing the minimum duration of commercial rental contracts, simplifying licensing and customs procedures, streamlining rules for land use and adopting legislation to simplify administrative procedures for business (European Commission 2014a: 5–6).

Table 11.4 Greece: employment and projected employment in the public sector (number of persons)

	2009	*2010*	*2011*	*2012*	*2013*	*2014*	*2015*	*2016*
General Government				707,609	653,746	635,227	623,219	606,170
Ordinary staff	692,907	667,374	646,657	629,114	599,207	581,886	570,271	553,619
Other staff	175,550	132,877	72,333	56,588	36,372	36,037	36,037	36,037
Total public sector	907,351	834,505	747,356	726,212	671,111	651,717	639,311	621,860
ESPA and self-financed other staff				15,343	47,570	44,946	44,946	44,946

Source: European Commission 2014a: 38.

Public sector is defined as the general government, as well as legal entities of private law supervised by local government and the state.

introducing reforms that lifted embedded protections in the labor market at a pace faster than any other OECD country, making wage formation and redundancies more flexible. The proposed plans for wide-ranging privatizations caused great anxiety among public-sector employees.[28] In addition, after the signing of the second Memorandum, the government was expected to reduce general government employment by 150,000 employees ahead of 2015 and had to implement measures of 'mobility' (i.e. paid 'redundancy') affecting 25,000 employees (European Commission 2014a: 10. See Table 11.4). Although this target was to be largely met by the application of the 1:5 attrition rule (only one employee was to be hired for every five who retire), for the very first time, the prospect of job redundancies was on the table (European Commission 2014a: 10). Plans for performance evaluation in the public sector were met with skepticism by those who were apprehensive that the process would not be fair, but could be driven by the same clientelist considerations that traditionally governed promotions, new placements and appointments in the public sector (*Kathimerini*, 12/01/2013; *Avgi*, 30/04/2014).[29] There was anxiety that clientelism, once the politics of co-option,

28 The privatization program included the Greek Energy Company (DEI), the electricity distribution network operator (ADMIE) (European Commission 2014a: 5–6), OTE (telecommunications), the Hellenic Football Prognostics Organization (OPAP) and state lotteries. The scheduled privatizations also included the regional airports and the sale of shares in Athens Water (EYDAP), Thessaloniki Water (EYATH), train operations (TRAINOSE), railway maintenance (ROSCO), Pireaus Port, Thessaloniki Port, Athens Airport, Hellenic Post (ELTA), Egnatia Motorway, natural gas (DEPA) and public electricity (DEI) (European Commission 2014a: 5–6, 29, 61, 289).

29 Former ADEDY unionist (in the public sector), Giorgos Petropoulos, raised concerns about the possible use of performance evaluation 'as a mechanism for control and [gaining] consensus on the policies under way and as an effort to restore the dismantled clientelist mechanisms which would now build on the anxiety and fear of redundancy' (*Avgi*, 30/04/2014).

would degenerate into tactics of fear: 'you either support me or you can lose your job'. Moreover, the prospect of lower salaries, lower pension schemes, the imminent change of their employment status and the threatening prospect of redundancy were all interventions so strong this time that they departed from the logic of horizontal diffusion of adjustment costs (in the form of higher taxes or pay freezes) which previous governments had implemented without major friction.

Amidst mounting social discontent and anxiety, leading PASOK unionists and mostly middle-ranking politicians were increasingly uncomfortable with this policy direction. Many unionists and union members affiliated with PASOK and New Democracy felt that these measures were beyond their threshold of tolerance and left the party. Several trade unionists formed independent groups or joined the ranks of SYRIZA-backed labor organizations (see *TVXS*, 29/05/2012; *Kathimerini* 27/10/2012; *Vima*, 10/03/2013; *Iefimerida*, 12/10/2014; *Enikos.gr*, 13/10/2014).[30] These defections gradually but steadily contributed to a realignment of political loyalties towards the anti-Memorandum political forces and SYRIZA, in particular.[31] SYRIZA voiced the anger and frustration of the social and professional groups that suffered significant losses from the implementation of the program and the crisis itself, mostly civil servants and employees of the broader public sector, but also low-income pensioners, the unemployed and several professionals hit by the crisis.

This shift in political alignments was manifested in the results of the 2012 elections and continued with the electoral rise and, ultimately, victory of SYRIZA in the parliamentary election of January 2015, which took place after the Parliament failed to elect a new president of the republic. SYRIZA received 36.3% of the popular vote, New Democracy retained its popularity but fell to second place with 27.8% and PASOK plummeted to seventh place with 4.7%, barely succeeding in gaining seats in the Parliament.[32] The extreme right-wing party Golden Dawn kept its support base despite the fact that its leader and several of its prominent politicians were awaiting trial for several criminal offences. The electoral results revealed the deep impact that social unrest and political anger had on political preferences under a prolonged crisis. Five years of economic crisis and two tough adjustment programs (2010–2015) led to a dramatic

30 Former PASOK minister and deputy prime minister under George Papandreou, Theodoros Pangalos, described the labor unionists who had defected PASOK to join SYRIZA as the 'worst species of unionist vagrancy that were the ones who had prevented PASOK from governing properly and the ones who led the country to disaster' (*ANT1*, 23/06/2015).

31 Political realignment was gradual, and many union leaders stood for re-election as independent candidates. For instance, a center-left independent candidate was elected as the president of the Athens Bar Association (*SKAI*, 25/02/2014). Independents also won the election in the pharmacists' professional organization (*onmed.gr*, 14/06/2014).

32 Golden Dawn came third with 6.3%; a new centrist party, Potami, led by journalist Stavros Theodorakis, received 6.1%; the Communists (KKE) gained 5.5%; and the Independent Greeks (ANEL) received 4.8%. In Athens, lower- and middle-income regions voted for SYRIZA, whereas the 'affluent' northern and southern suburbs voted for New Democracy (*Nea*, 31/01/2015).

reshuffling in Greece's party politics and brought about the collapse of the bipartisan system and the rise of anti-Memorandum parties, most notably, SYRIZA.

United by their anti-Memorandum stance, SYRIZA and the 'Independent Greeks' formed a new government led by Alexis Tsipras in February 2015 with the aim of renegotiating the terms of the Greek bailout and achieving debt relief.[33] SYRIZA's pre-electoral pledge to put an end to austerity was reframed in the context of this negotiation as an effort to secure a milder pathway to fiscal consolidation and exclude 'neoliberal' structural reforms that SYRIZA considered unjust and counterproductive, namely labor market flexibility, full liberalization of certain professions and 'fire sale' privatizations of Greece's infrastructure. The government declared as its priority the fight against tax evasion by high incomes and the preferential treatment of Greece's 'economic oligarchy'. Change in the direction of Greece's adjustment effort, in the view of SYRIZA, had to include debt restructuring and stronger social and humanitarian policies to tackle the social problems that the prolonged recession had caused. The government also pledged to implement reforms that would increase the transparency and quality of public administration, curb red tape, break the state-protected private monopolies and cartels and reform labor market relations by returning to collective agreements as the framework for a coordinated adjustment. The SYRIZA-led government asked that the requirement for primary surpluses be lowered to allow the government to relax fiscal austerity which, in its view, had created a 'recessionary trap'. Several renowned economists raised objections to deep austerity as a viable policy for Greece, and they instead, supported debt relief.[34]

Nevertheless, Greece's creditors found the Greek government's anti-austerity stance and its refusal to accept reforms in the labor and product markets unacceptable and raised issues of trust. SYRIZA's militant rhetoric against the 'neoliberal' status quo in the European Union challenged the economic orthodoxy, both in macroeconomic policy and in the choice of structural reforms, and, as a result, fueled mistrust among Eurozone politicians, who repeatedly urged Greece to 'play by the rules' and stick to the previous reform pattern. Greece's creditors were not willing to finance a milder pace of fiscal adjustment under the policy mix proposed by SYRIZA, and the EMU countries were hostile to the idea of restructuring the nominal level of Greek debt. This negative stance was fueled by their deep

33 See Alexis Tsipras' letter to *Financial Times* 'End Austerity Before Fear Kills Greek Democracy' (20/01/2015). For a negative view see Sean O'Grady '9 Reasons Greece's Experiment with the Radical Left Is Doomed to Failure' (*Independent*, 28/01/2015).

34 See 32 economists with a letter titled 'Greece Needs Debts Cancelled and Growth' published in *The Guardian* on 20/01/2015. Also Paul Krugman in *New York Times* ('Ending Greece's Nightmare, 26/01/2015 and 'Weimer on the Aegean', 16/02/2015), Joseph Stiglitz in *The Guardian* ('A Greek Morality Tale', 04/02/2015), Jeffery Sachs in *The Guardian* ('Let Greece Profit from German History, 21/01/2015). Different views by Kenneth Rogoff ('What is Plan B for Greece, *Project Syndicate*, 05/02/2015) and Edmund Phelps in *The World Post* ('Why Debt Relief Won't Solve Greece's Problem, 13/07/2015).

disagreement with SYRIZA's ideology and interpretation of what had caused the Greek crisis, what was causing Europe's economic troubles in general and what type of policies were necessary to address the Greek crisis and the structural problems associated with the Eurozone as a monetary union.[35]

The failure of the negotiations to reach an agreement on a future program for Greece over a period of 5 months led to a major fiscal and political crisis in July 2015, when the previous economic adjustment program expired. Greece was unable to refinance its debt and went into arrears with an IMF loan payment. Prime Minister Alexis Tsipras called a referendum so that the Greeks could decide on the Commission's informal note proposing a new round of austerity and structural reforms. The announcement was followed by a bank run in Greece which, under tight liquidity provision by the European Central Bank, forced the government to declare a bank holiday until after the referendum and introduce capital controls on domestic bank deposits. In a very polarized and heated climate, Alexis Tsipras won the referendum on July 5 with a resounding 62% of the vote, but, facing the threat of a disorderly Greek exit (the notorious 'Grexit') and the collapse of the Greek banks, he agreed to sign a Third Memorandum a week later, on 13th July 2015, which included new austerity measures and structural reforms under tight surveillance and conditionality.

Conclusion: clientelist politics and the economic and political implications of crisis

The Greek crisis was the combined outcome of an exogenous shock hitting a country with long-standing macroeconomic imbalances and structural rigidities. Among Eurozone countries, Greece stands out for years of fiscal mismanagement and reform inertia that made its economy vulnerable to exogenous shocks, foreign capital fluctuation and a domestic consumption–led boom-and-bust cycle. As previously stated, resistance to comprehensive policy reforms came from inside the governing parties themselves. Prior to the crisis, it was politically irrational for consecutive Greek governments to implement radical reforms that could jeopardize their ties with client groups. Accumulated growing fiscal imbalances and structural distortions laid the foundations of the subsequent Greek crisis, which broke up in the aftermath of the 2008 global financial crisis, first as a recession and a liquidity crisis (leading to a solvency crisis), and then as a deeper depression.

The general model of distributional and clientelist politics presented in the previous chapters captures important dynamics and events during the crisis period too: both the opposition to the Memoranda from the main opposition party (New Democracy until 2012 and SYRIZA until 2015) and the stance of all Greek governments in face of imminent fiscal and economic collapse. It also explains

35 The case of Greece became part of broader political discussions regarding the future of the Eurozone and the architecture of European integration.

the pattern of reform performance under strict conditionality: the emphasis on fiscal consolidation and less progress with structural reforms during the first years.

The prospect of systemic collapse changed the payoffs that PASOK as the governing party expected to get from refusing to accept the terms of the bailout agreement. PASOK was later joined by New Democracy in taking measures that departed from the previously 'optimal' mode of adjustment that had been governed by clientelist bias. The threat of euro exit tied the hands of the Greek governments, including SYRIZA, in 2015, which, despite its strong ideological opposition to the Memoranda, signed up for tough reforms. The pace, intensity and recorded delays in Greece's economic adjustment program and the reactions and re-alignments in the Greek party system are consistent with our expectations, given the historical dynamics in Greece's distributional system. Clientelist bias did not just drive the growth and development of the clientelist party system over the previous 4 decades; it can also be traced in the dramatic political developments that took place after the Greek crisis in 2009 under a very tight range of policy options. There were efforts to tailor and pace the reforms. Emphasis was placed on fiscal consolidation, and there were delays in privatization and structural reform. However, this time under a binding adjustment program guided by strict conditionality and the threat of a disorderly exit from the Eurozone, the Greek governments were left with no other viable choice – at least in their perception of events – but to modify important parameters of Greece's distributional system.

The prolonged crisis caused the collapse of Greece's distributional system. Rising public discontent, deep mistrust of the political elite in view of revelations of widespread corruption and impunity and the dissolution of clientelist alliances led to the political realignment of social and professional groups and, consequently, the breakup of Greece's two-party system that had heavily relied on patronage politics. The scale and nature of Greece's economic adjustment since 2009 harmed many party-affiliated groups and inflicted considerable political damage on both PASOK and New Democracy. PASOK experienced an exodus of middle-ranking politicians and union leaders and was heavily discredited by corruption scandals. New Democracy also struggled with a withering internal cohesion but retained its core supporters.

Finally, growing popular discontent allowed SYRIZA to articulate an anti-austerity rhetoric. SYRIZA led a social coalition of forces that were harmed by economic adjustment, including public-sector employees who wanted to protect the 'public' character of key companies and safeguard their employment status. However, SYRIZA's initial policy proposals were sharply at odds with the policy orthodoxy in the European Union and were considered by their opponents unrealistic and 'populist'. This agenda set the government on a collision path with its creditors during its first months. Following a liquidity crisis, a bank run and the threat of a disorderly Greek exit from the Eurozone, the SYRIZA-led government signed a new Memorandum in July 2015 that contradicted the expectations it had generated in the previous election. Soon after, Prime Minister Tsipras confronted a rebellion from a bloc of MPs and party members, which eventually led to the effective loss of his parliamentary majority. Alexis Tsipras called for an early parliamentary election in September 2015, which SYRIZA won with 35.3% of the votes and formed a new government, together with the Independent Greeks (ANEL). The electoral victory of SYRIZA – with a lead in votes that was unexpected given what the opinion polls predicted before the election – was a sign of Tsipras' enduring popularity at that time, despite his noteworthy political U-turn after signing the Third Memorandum.

12 Conclusion

A new insight into the clientelist system

The book has sought to address a theoretical question: Is there something distinctive in clientelist politics that has not been adequately captured by the analytical framework of interest-group competition or by the view that party politics are primarily sensitive to the general preferences of the voters? The book's focus on Greece sheds light on the distinct properties of a clientelist system of interest intermediation and its impact on the design and implementation of economic reforms. By identifying the strong linkage between client groups and political parties – namely, the role of client groups as key campaign resources for political mobilization and their importance for the patrons' political success – the book's main finding is that client groups are *privileged groups* in the sense that their demands are given priority by the clientelist parties in power. Even when there are strong pressures for reform, as in the case of Greece, policy making will exhibit a *clientelist bias* and will accommodate primarily the interests of political clients who constitute the political parties' 'core' supporters. Consequently, clientelist linkages endure very difficult economic conditions and withstand strong institutional pressures for reform, even if this leads to persisting structural weaknesses that make a national economy susceptible to exogenous shocks.

Delving into the historical development of Greece's political and economic system has given us a number of other theoretically interesting findings. The Greek story is a warning against the danger of following a model of state-sponsored economic growth intended to accelerate development and steer investment in 'economically and socially desirable' directions. In the real world of politics, such a model will tend to degenerate into a system of extensive rent seeking and corruption. The Greek clientelist system was the consequence of the failure of a post-war system of elite-level rent seeking to secure political stability by means of political exclusion and discrimination. When full political participation was established in 1974 (during the *metapolitefsi*), the distributional system opened up to engulf a larger group of beneficiaries. This allowed the two main parties, New Democracy and PASOK, to build strong party structures and reduce within-party and interparty volatility. In response, both supply and demand for clientelism increased. When the oil crisis of the 1970s exposed the structural weaknesses of the Greek economic model and led to rising unemployment in the late 1970s and 1980s, the policy response was consistent with the existing demand for state protection and government jobs.

Chapter 3 has highlighted how the supply and demand of patronage intersect. For party leaders, political campaigns and, ultimately, electoral success require the mobilization of a critical number of party members and supporters, which clientelism secures thanks to the strong incentivizing power of clientelist benefits to activate political engagement and loyalty. Clientelist politics is therefore the rational choice of political leaders. Clientelism becomes a prominent method of party organization that serves as a solution to a collective mobilization problem facing political parties. It offers a strong mechanism to discipline party members and secure party cohesion by threatening dissenters with exclusion from selective benefits. As an aggregate effect, the practice of clientelism affects the distribution of campaign resources across political parties. Patronage politics makes it more difficult for new autonomous political organizations and new political competitors to emerge outside the clientelist system. In Greece, extensive patronage helped the main parties, PASOK and New Democracy, build large and active support bases and establish a hegemonic position in politics which permeated all spheres of social and economic activity, from labor unions and professional organizations to schools, universities and the army. Their political and societal dominance significantly reduced the degree of contestability they faced from outsiders and created a lock-in effect that reproduced a remarkably stable pattern of political alignments from the early 1980s up until the Greek economic crisis in 2009.

Refining the initial hypotheses

Although the typical view of rent seeking is that autonomous groups or corporate interests lobby the government to enact policies that will serve their interests, rent seeking in a clientelist system is primarily incorporated into party structures and transforms political parties into large rent-extracting networks. In a clientelist system, *the political party is the main rent-seeking organization.* Clientelist supply becomes the prominent form of interest accommodation, which secures the unity of divergent and heterogeneous interests inside a vast party network consisting of individual clients and affiliated social organizations. This creates a symbiotic relationship between the patron party and its client groups. Patrons and political parties undertake the obligation towards their clients to ensure the ongoing supply of patronage in return for their consistent support and loyalty.

This view may challenge the assertion that in a democracy the proportion of public goods provided will outweigh private goods because of the large size of the winning coalition the leader needs in order to get elected and the high cost of providing private goods to this group (cf. the 'selectorate' in the language of Bueno de Mesquita et al. 2003). In a clientelist system, *the political party is the first selecting group* which politicians must win before they occupy the leadership position from which they can appeal to general voters. For party politicians, both entry into party politics and career advancement largely depend on their capacity to provide clientelist benefits. This context generates informal norms of behavior which actors situated in the party's clientelist network must follow. As the empirical part of the book confirms, this dense web of patron–client interdependences inside the party generates strong incentives for the uninterrupted reproduction and expansion of clientelist supply and skews policy making towards a clientelist bias, as the initial hypothesis expected:

> H1. *Clientelist bias in policy making:* clientelism as a method of political mobilization creates a strong preference for a political party in government to preserve economic policies that cater to clientelist demands and avoid policies that could limit the allocation of resources to their clients.

This bias is manifested in the workings of a political system dominated by two parties. As Chapter 3 has demonstrated, the two main parties in Greece were locked in a *clientelist equilibrium* (H2):

> H2. In a bipartisan clientelist party system, patronage supply is a Nash equilibrium for the two parties. Any unilateral move by the party in government to implement reforms that reduce the scope and intensity of clientelism will give a competitive advantage to the opposition party in terms of political organization and electoral mobilization. This equilibrium lays the foundation for a fiscal crisis that could affect the overall sustainability of the clientelist system at some point in the future.

Because the supply of clientelism is the 'equilibrium' strategy for the two main parties, this tends to generate fiscal profligacy and macroeconomic imbalances. In terms of its future systemic impact, clientelism leads the party system and its main actors to 'a tragedy-of-the-commons' effect (Cf. Wagner 2012a). In Greece, extensive patronage and fiscal profligacy paved the way for consecutive crisis events since 1985. At those moments, the sustainability of the clientelist party system was at stake. As Chapter 4 indicates, in the context of strong party competition over the supply of patronage, the political leadership will be reluctant to abandon clientelism.[1] In response to deteriorating fiscal and economic conditions, the government can delay the onset of the 'tragedy-of-the-commons' effect through external borrowing that helps it maintain or even increase the same level of spending by replacing tax revenue with public debt.

However, economic reform becomes unavoidable when accumulated macroeconomic imbalances and structural weaknesses are likely to bring about the collapse of the distributional system itself within the life span of a government. The systemic risk from policy inertia pushes the government to launch reforms in order to stabilize public finances and revamp the economy. In this situation, the governing party is still trapped in a 'clientelist equilibrium', whereby

1 For the opposite view, see Grzymala-Busse 2007, Kitschelt and Wilkinson 2007a.

implementing reforms that reduce the scope and intensity of clientelism will risk undermining the governing party's cohesion and could offer the main opposition party an advantage in political mobilization. At that point, the government can try and diffuse the cost of fiscal consolidation across the population through measures such as new taxes or a general wage freeze and protect its client groups.

Chapter 4 sheds light on this pattern as it happened in 1985 when the Greek government faced a fiscal crisis that could have been a critical juncture for Greece's highly clientelist system of distribution. The government responded quite artfully to the challenge it faced, avoiding a radical shift in economic policy towards market liberalization and privatization policies that could have caused permanent damage to its relations with its client groups in the broader public sector. The stabilization program that was implemented between 1985 and 1987 and the following events until 1989 indicate the resilience of clientelist politics. The observed pattern of reforms can be viewed as a case of 'reproduction by adaptation' for Greece's clientelist system and adds empirical support to the book's hypothesis according to which:

> H2a. In response to external pressures for reform, politicians in a highly clientelist system will seek to mitigate the cost of its policies on client groups and will design a reform package that preserves clientelist supply as much as possible (*clientelist bias in economic reform*).

Chapter 5 addresses another interesting question: Is it possible that a party with weaker ties to client groups in particular sectors has more of an incentive to launch economic reform and more success in implementing it? Between 1990 and 1993, New Democracy attempted to implement an ambitious program of structural reforms and privatization. The findings here relax the determinism of the initial hypothesis and indicate the possible input of ideology and the role of political miscalculations in view of limited information and uncertainty about other actors' preferences and strategies. Mitsotakis' agenda triggered a general revolt by the labor unions under the sponsorship of PASOK, as well as a within-party rebellion. This negative experience with a bold and comprehensive reform agenda offers additional information regarding the political impact of government policies that depart from the clientelist equilibrium. The governing party with weaker ties to client groups will still suffer political losses because the affected client groups will rally around the opposition party or will support a within-party opposition. These observations help formulate a new hypothesis about the political implications of policy reform that diverges significantly from the clientelist equilibrium:

> H2c. Reforms that primarily inflict political losses on the clients of the opposition party could strengthen the political mobilization capacity of the opposition that sponsors the protests and could weaken the capacity of the government by alienating its own clients. In that case, this reform agenda remains a departure from the equilibrium strategy.

The fate of the Mitsotakis government gave rise to a critical political question: What can a government do when economic and institutional pressures make structural reform inevitable? In Greece, the signing of the Maastricht Treaty in 1992 committed Greece to a path towards entry to the European Monetary Union (EMU) that required measurable progress in the country's macroeconomic performance by 1999. This challenge was particularly pressing for the third period of the PASOK government between 1993 and 2004, which faced challenging macroeconomic conditions but had previously made promises to its client groups in the state sector that it would protect their status. Chapters 6 and 7 review policy making under the PASOK government at a time when Greece's economic and political system faced the prospect of systemic crisis in the event it failed to meet the benchmarks specified by the Maastricht Treaty. Quite interestingly, Chapter 6 observes that the government made a significant effort for fiscal stabilization and indicates that the reform effort by the government of Costas Simitis was closely associated with the timing of an anticipated 'sanction', that is entry into or exclusion from the Eurozone.

The timing and gravity of a benchmark such as EMU led to a change of direction in monetary and fiscal policy under Papandreou and Simitis. The same policy shift, however, dispersed the costs of macroeconomic consolidation, exhibiting clientelist bias. This suggests that, to the extent that there are policies which could stabilize the economy without concentrating losses to party clients, the government will opt for these policies:

> H2d. If nonreform is likely to impose a heavier cost on the leadership of the governing party than the envisaged reform (the *crisis-in-tenure* prediction), the party in government will launch the reform and try to fine-tune it to protect its client groups.

In that context, reform inertia, delay and omissions are not indications of weak state capacity, but of clientelist bias. The government is an active reformer to the extent that it will effectuate a pattern of 'reproduction by adaptation' for the clientelist system as a whole. Although falling short in the provision of public goods, the state remains capable of performing *the functions in which the political parties had chosen to make it strong* in the context of clientelist politics.

Chapter 8 illustrates how these considerations affected the design of macroeconomic policies by the Simitis government. Client–patron interactions were endogenous to the party structure, and the party was the most important setting that conditioned preference formation and constrained reactions from unionists, party politicians and the party leadership. As both Chapters 4 and 8 have highlighted, clientelist ties between the party and its affiliated unions and other client groups limited the scope for collective action. Most union leaders with overlapping roles in the trade unions and the party valued their party linkages. The party leadership took advantage of the vested interest of all members in the party's electoral success, which was, after all, the desired outcome that secured their preferential access to clientelist resources. By invoking the need for party unity as a necessary prerequisite for electoral success, it was able to ask its members to be complacent with its policies. Union leaders were rewarded for their mild stance vis-à-vis the party's policies with placements and promotions in the public sector as Cabinet ministers, MPs and state officials. This strategy for mitigating reactions occasionally failed to prevent episodes of confrontation and deter defections, but it generally kept reactions at bay. This setting of party–union relations allowed the leadership of PASOK to contain collective action through the 'co-optation' of leading unionists and the 'exclusion' from the party system of the rebellious unionists. These findings from Chapter 8 indicate that:

> H3. Clientelist bias in policy making can be complemented by a strategy of co-optation by which clientelist ties mitigate the risk of defection and favor moderation and mutual accommodation by both patrons and clients in their collective action.

Clientelist ties between the central party and the unions delineate the upper boundaries for the actions of the government and the reactions of the unions. Client groups in the public sector can use trade unions as platforms for collective action, but the scale and intensity of their collective action is constrained by interpersonal clientelist ties and collective interdependences.

Moreover, as the government tries to safeguard its clientelist commitments and, at the same time, prevent the crisis that could bring about the 'breakdown' of the clientelist system, it must design its reforms under conditions of uncertainty and incomplete information regarding the possible effect of different policy options. A clientelist party in government must carefully craft a pattern of reforms on the basis of information drawn from past experience with reforms and on the basis of feedback from ongoing interactions with its client groups – in the case of Greece, for instance, the clients in the labor unions of the public sector. Chapter 8 illustrates the fact that the relationship between patrons and clients evolves in a context of incomplete information. The Simitis government had to establish an open and informal communication link with its affiliated unions to trace their preferences and track possible reactions. Incomplete information and opportunistic behavior led to occasional clashes when government proposals went too far and threatened to hurt the interests of key stakeholders. However, when conflicts break up, both the leadership and the party unionists are better off striking compromises because they both value the unity of the party, and their career aspirations depend on the party's electoral success. Here, incomplete information further relaxes the rational-choice prediction for the politically optimal design of reform:

> H3a. Strategic behavior between patrons and organized client groups confronts the problem of incomplete information, which could lead to reform decisions that trigger conflict. However, communication between the leadership and the client groups is possible and will reconfirm that mutual-interest accommodation is the preferable strategy for all.

Chapter 9 gives further evidence that governments could also respond to exogenous pressures by searching for new resources to revitalize the supply of rents. In Greece, entry into the EMU and the inflow of Community funds revamped its distributional model. Lower inflation and currency stability following the country's entry into the EMU lowered the cost of borrowing and, consequently, increased the moral hazard regarding the level of borrowing and consumption. The cheaper cost of borrowing allowed the government to sustain the rising cost of the broader public sector. Community funds, new pricing policies and privatization proceeds helped lower the government's direct transfers to public-sector firms and the level of debt assumption. In this environment, structural reforms were delayed or postponed. Following Greece's entry into the EMU, the government yielded to pressures from trade unions to abandon some of its initial proposals for reforms in the social security system and avoided further privatization and the restructuring of the deficit-running state companies:

> H4. In a clientelist system undergoing economic restructuring, patrons will search for new resources to revitalize patronage supply. (*creative adjustment*)

As the case of both the Simitis and Karamanlis governments indicate, external borrowing and funding are sources that facilitate the systemic reproduction of the clientelist system. However, while political entrepreneurship shall search for new resources for rent seeking, the nature of these new resources may be less amenable to typical patronage politics and may open new opportunities for lobbying and collusion between corporate interests and government officials in the typical corporate interest-group schema.

Moreover, even though borrowing instead of taxation gives a temporary boost to public finances and domestic demand that does not immediately burden the taxpayers, it generates intertemporal externalities. As the fiscal burden is moved further ahead in time, government spending can be in tune with the electoral cycle and the demand for patronage. Insofar as governments are able to issue new bonds to finance previous liabilities (*debt recycling*), the sustainability of the system as a whole is secured, although it may undergo periods of revision or gradual transformation. This trend may not continue indefinitely, particularly when an exogenous shock exposes the structural weaknesses of the clientelist economy and derails the already imbalanced state of public finances. The onset of deep fiscal and economic crisis can bring about significant domestic upheaval that will necessitate a more comprehensive change of economic policy, depending on its gravity and the range of policy options available:

> H5. Political leaders will undertake reforms that break up ties with client groups only if the severity of the imminent crisis is such that they will believe that these measures will be less costly for them than the possible losses from a systemic collapse.

If the program of radical reforms introduces policies that significantly depart from the clientelist bias, this shift will alienate client supporters and will trigger defections, causing serious cracks in the stability of the clientelist system, as Chapter 11 indicates. We can associate the electoral collapse of PASOK and the shrinking of New Democracy with the depth of austerity and the nature of the proposed or implemented deep-cutting reforms which the two parties had to undertake as part of Greece's huge bailout programs. The result was a shift in political alignments amidst the labor unions and other professional organizations, as well as great popular discontent in the aftermath of a deep and prolonged economic and social crisis, which led to the rise of SYRIZA as the main opposition party and, a few years later, as the party in government.

The Greek case leads to a refinement of the general premise that economic reforms are shaped by the government's calculations of the relative political benefits and costs of different policy options in interaction with external pressures and domestic interests. It highlights that government calculations in a clientelist system are shaped in the context of interparty and intraparty competition and lead to a more limited range of policy options. The general expectation still holds: a government is more likely to enact reforms if the political cost of nonreform outweighs the political cost that the government will incur by implementing it. But for this expectation to work against a clientelist system, there must be an extreme economic crisis, binding commitments and the threat of sanctions that essentially bring the government in front of the dilemma 'you either comply and try to survive politically in a new unfavorable political environment or systemic collapse is likely to wipe out your support base and destroy your career altogether'. For radical policy reforms to be introduced, the impending political cost must be that of an imminent systemic collapse, and the type of sanction that will force domestic political actors to comply with external institutional prescriptions must be a rescue package offered by external organizations under strict conditionality. Even under these strong pressures, it is reasonable to argue that the party in government will implement the recommended reforms up to the point that they will not inflict losses higher than the expected cost of noncompliance. It is also plausible to predict that, once the economy stabilizes and the external pressures are relaxed, the political parties will find it rational to reboot distributional politics and again return to patronage supply.

Bibliography

Afonso, Alexandre, Sotirios Zartaloudis and Yannis Papadopoulos, 2015, 'How Party Linkages Shape Austerity Politics: Clientelism and Fiscal Adjustment in Greece and Portugal during the Eurozone Crisis', *Journal of European Public Policy* 22(3): 315–334.

Alesina, Alberto and Allan Drazen, 1998, 'Why Are Stabilizations Delayed', in Sturzenegger, Federico and Mariano Tommasi (eds.), *The Political Economy of Reform*, Cambridge, MA and London: MIT Press, pp. 77–103.

Alogoskoufis, George, 1995, 'Greece. The Two Faces of Janus: Institutions, Policy Regimes and Macroeconomic Performance', *Economic Policy* 10(20): 149–184.

Allison, Graham T., and Kalypso Nicolaidis (eds.), 1997, *The Greek Paradox: Promise vs. Performance*, Cambridge, MA: John F. Kennedy School of Government, Center for Science and International Affairs.

Alpha Bank, 2005, *Economic Bulletin*, December 2005, Athens.

Andreou, George and Nikos Koutsiaras, 2002, 'The Greek Welfare System in the European Context', in P.C. Ioakimidis (ed.), *Greece in the European Union: The New Role and the New Agenda*, Athens: Ministry of Press and Mass Media, pp. 156–168.

Antoniades, Andreas, 2003, 'Epistemic Communities, Epistemes and the Construction of (World) Politics', *Global Society* 17(1): 21–38.

Antoniades, Andreas and Vassilis Monastiriotis, 2009, 'Reform that! Greece's Failing Reform Technology: Beyond "Vested Interests" and "Political Exchange" ', GreeSE Paper No 28, Hellenic Observatory Papers on Greece and Southeast Europe, October 2009.

Armingeon, Klaus and Lucio Baccaro, 2012, 'Political Economy of the Sovereign Debt Crisis: The Limits of Internal Devaluation' *Industrial Law Journal* 41(3): 254–275.

Arsenis, Gerasimos, 1987, *Political Statement* (in Greek, *Πολιτική Κατάθεση*), Athens: Odysseas.

Arsenis, Gerasimos, 1992, 'Address to the Dialogue of Political Agents' (in Greek, «Παρέμβαση στο Διάλογο Πολιτικών Φορέων»), in Yannis Tolios (ed.), *Progressive Modernization as a Response to the Privatization Policy* (in Greek, *Προοδευτικός Εκσυγχρονισμός Απάντηση στην Πολιτική των Ιδιωτικοποιήσεων*), Athens: Economic Policy Council (Συμβούλιο Οικονομικής Πολιτικής), pp. 21–29.

Åslund, Anders and Valdis Dombrovski, 2011, *How Latvia Came through the Financial Crisis*, Washington, DC: Peterson Institute for International Economics.

Bank of Greece, *Report of the Governor of Bank of Greece* (several years), Athens.

Bates, Robert and Anne O. Krueger (eds.), 1993, 'Introduction', in Robert Bates and Anne O. Krueger (eds.), *Political and Economic Interactions in Economic Policy Reform: Evidence from Eight Countries*, Oxford: Basil Blackwell, pp. 1–26.

Bates, Robert, Ayner Greif, Margaret Levi, Jean-Laurent Rosenthal and Barry R. Weingast (eds.), 1998, 'Introduction', in Bates, Robert H., Avner Grief, Margaret Levi and Jean-Laurent Rosenthal (eds.), *Analytic Narratives*. Princeton, NJ: Princeton University Press, pp. 1–22.

Becker, Gary, 1983, 'A Theory of Competition among Pressure Groups for Political Influence', *Quarterly Journal of Economics* 98(3): 371–400.

Bitros Georgios, 1992, 'From Economic Crisis to Economic Policy Crisis' (in Greek, «Από την Κρίση της Οικονομίας στην Κρίση της Οικονομικής Πολιτικής»), in Tryfon Kolintzas and Georgios Bitros (eds.), *In Search of Hope for the Greek Economy* (in Greek, *Αναζητώντας την Ελπίδα για την Ελληνική Οικονομία*), Athens: Institute of Economic Policy Studies (Ινστιτούτο Μελετών Οικονομικής Πολιτικής), pp. 41–55.

Boettke, Peter J., 2000, 'Book Review: Analytical Narratives ed. by Bates, Greif, Levi, Rosenthal and Weingast', *Constitutional Political Economy* 11: 377–379.

Boettke, Peter J., Christopher J. Coyne and Peter T. Leeson, 2005, 'The New Comparative Political Economy', *The Review of Austrian Economics* 18(3/4): 281–304.

Boettke, Peter J. and Rosolino Candela, 2015, 'Rational Choice as If the Choosers Were Human', *GMU Working Paper in Economics* published in SSRN, July 3, 2015.

Börsch-Supan, Axel and Platon Tinios, 2001, 'The Greek Pension System: Strategic Framework for Reform', in Ralph C. Bryant, Nicholas C. Garganas and George S. Tavlas (eds.), *Greece's Economic Performance and Prospects*, Athens and Washington, DC: Bank of Greece and The Brookings Institution, pp. 361–452.

Börzel, Tanja, 1999, 'Towards Convergence in Europe? Institutional Adaptation to Europeanisation in Germany and Spain', *Journal of Common Market Studies* 37(4): 573–596.

Bosworth, Barry and Tryphon Kollintzas, 2001, 'Economic Growth in Greece: Past Performance and Future Prospects', in Ralph C. Bryant, Nicholas C. Garganas and George S. Tavlas (eds.), *Greece's Economic Performance and Prospects*, Athens and Washington, DC: Bank of Greece and The Brookings Institution, pp. 153–210.

Botsiou Katerina, 2002, 'Greece in the EU: A Historical Account', in P.C. Ioakimidis (ed.), *Greece in the EU: The New Role and the New Agenda*, Athens and Brussels: EKEM/Greek Ministry of Press/European Commission, pp. 17–36.

Brusco, Valeria, Marcelo Nazareno and Susan C. Stokes, 2004, 'Vote Buying in Argentina', *Latin American Research Review* 39(2): 66–88.

Bryant, Ralph C., Nicholas C. Garganas and George S. Tavlas, 2001, 'Introduction', in Ralph C. Bryant, Nicholas C. Garganas and George S. Tavlas (eds.), *Greece's Economic Performance and Prospects*, Athens and Washington, DC: Bank of Greece and The Brookings Institution, pp. 1–42.

Buchanan, James M., Tollison Robert D., and Tullock Gordon (eds.), 1980, *Towards a Theory of the Rent-Seeking Society*, College Station, TX: A & M Press.

Bueno de Mesquita, Bruce, Alastair Smith, Randolph M. Siverson and James D. Morrow, 2003, *The Logic of Political Survival*, Cambridge, MA: MIT Press.

Bulmer, Simon, 2007, 'Theorizing Europeanization', in Paolo Graziano and Maarten P. Vink (eds.), *Europeanization: New Research Agendas*, Basingstoke, Hampshire: Palgrave Macmillan, pp. 46–58.

Burtless, Gary, 2001, 'The Greek Labor Market', in Ralph C. Bryant, Nicholas C. Garganas and George S. Tavlas (eds.), *Greece's Economic Performance and Prospects*, Athens and Washington, DC: Bank of Greece and The Brookings Institution, pp. 453–498.

Callaghy, Thomas M., 1990, 'Lost Between State and Market: The Politics of Economic Adjustment in Ghana, Zambia and Nigeria, in Joan M. Nelson (ed.), *Economic Crisis and Policy Choice: The Politics of Adjustment in the Third World*, Princeton, NJ: Princeton University Press, pp. 257–319.

Calvo, Ernesto and Maria Victoria Murillo, 2004, 'Who Delivers? Partisan Clients in the Argentine Electoral Market', *American Journal of Political Science* 48(4): 742–757.

Chubb, Judith, 1982, *Patronage, Power and Poverty in Southern Italy: A Tale of Two Cities*, Cambridge: Cambridge University Press.

Clogg, Richard, 1987, *Parties and Elections in Greece: The Search for Legitimacy*, Durham, NC: Duke University Press.

Commission for the Review of Macroeconomic Policy (Spraos Committee, in Greek, Επιτροπή για την Αναθεώρηση της Μακροοικονομικής Πολιτικής), 1997, *Economy and Pensions: Contribution to Social Dialogue* (in Greek, *Οικονομία και Συντάξεις: Συνεισφορά στον Κοινωνικό Διάλογο)*, Athens, October 1997.

Council of the European Union, 2003, *Annex to the Communication from the Commission on the implementation of the 2002 Broad Economic Policy Guidelines* (Implementation Report), Brussels, 14.1.2003, SEC(2003) 33.

Court of Audit (in Greek, Ελεγκτικό Συνέδριο), 2003, *Annual Report of the Court of Audit to the Greek Parliament* (in Greek, Ετήσια Έκθεση του Ελεγκτικού Συνεδρίου στη Βουλή των Ελλήνων) Athens.

Christodoulakis, Nikos and Sarantis Kalyvitis, 1998, 'A Four-Sector Macroeconomic Model for Greece and the Evaluation of the Community Support Framework 1994–99', *Economic Modelling* 15(4): 572–620.

Denzau, Arthur T. and Michael C. Munger, 1986, 'Legislators and Interest Groups: How Unorganized Interests Get Represented', *American Political Science Review* 80(1): 89–106.

Diamandouros, Nikiforos, 1994, *Cultural Dualism and Political Change in Post-Authoritarian Greece*. Madrid: Centro Juan March de Estudios Avanzados en Ciencias Sociales' Estudio 50.

Diamandouros, Nikiforos P., 1997, 'Greek Politics and Society in the 1990s', in Graham T. Allison and Kalypso Nicolaidis (eds.), *The Greek Paradox: Promise vs. Performance*, Cambridge, MA: John F. Kennedy School of Government, Center for Science and International Affairs, pp. 23–37.

Eckstein, Harry, 1975/1992, 'Case Study and Theory in Political Science, in Fred I. Greenstein and Nelson W. Polsby (eds.), *Handbook of Political Science*, Vol. 7, Reading, MA: Addison-Wesley, pp. 79–137.

Eichengreen, Barry and Heather D. Gibson, 2001, 'Greek Banking at the Dawn of the New Millennium', in Ralph C. Bryant, Nicholas C. Garganas and George S. Tavlas (eds.), *Greece's Economic Performance and Prospects*, Athens and Washington, DC: Bank of Greece and The Brookings Institution, pp. 545–602.

Eisenstadt, Shmuel Noah and Luis Roniger, 1984, *Patrons, Clients and Friends: Interpersonal Relations and the Structure of Trust in Society*, Cambridge: Cambridge University Press.

Elefantis Angelos, 1981, 'PASOK and the Elections of 1977: The Rise of the Populist Movement', in Howard R. Penniman (ed.), *Greece at the Polls: The National Elections of 1974 and 1977*, Washington, DC: American Enterprise Institute, pp. 105–125.

Eleftheriadis, Pavlos, 2005, 'Constitutional Reform and the Rule of Law in Greece', *West European Politics* 28(2): 317–334.

Elster, Jon, 2000, 'Book Review: Rational Choice History: A Case of Excessive Ambition', *American Political Science Review* 94(3): 685–695.

Epstein, Leon D., 1986, *Political Parties in the American Mold*, Madison, WI: University of Wisconsin Press.

Esping-Andersen, Gøsta, 1990, *The Three Worlds of Welfare Capitalism*, Cambridge: Polity.
Evans, Peter, 1992, 'The State as Problem and Solution: Predation, Embedded Autonomy, and Structural Change', in Stephan Haggard and Robert R. Kaufman (eds.), *International Constraints, Distributive Conflicts and the State*, Princeton, NJ: Princeton University Press, pp. 139–181.
Evans, Peter B., Dietrich Rueschemeyer and Theda Skocpol (eds.), 1985, *Bringing the State Back In*, Cambridge: Cambridge University Press.
Eurobarometer, 2014, 'Businesses' Attitudes Towards Corruption in the EU', Report Fieldwork, 374, Brussels.
European Central Bank, 2000, 'Convergence Report 2000', Frankfurt: European Central Bank.
European Commission, Directorate-General for Economic and Financial Affairs, 1999, 'European Economy', No. 68. Brussels.
European Commission, Directorate-General for Economic and Financial Affairs, 2000a, 'European Economy', No. 70. Brussels.
European Commission, Directorate-General for Economic and Financial Affairs, 2000b, 'European Economy', No. 71. Brussels.
European Commission, Directorate General for Economic and Fiscal Affairs, 2001, 'European Economy', No. 3. Brussels.
European Commission, Directorate General for Economic and Fiscal Affairs, 2002, 'European Economy', No. 1. Brussels.
European Commission, Directorate General for Economic and Fiscal Affairs, 2003a, 'European Economy', No. 1. Brussels.
European Commission Directorate-General for Economic and Fiscal Affairs, 2003b, 'European Economy', No. 4. Brussels.
European Commission, Directorate General for Economic and Fiscal Affairs, 2004a, 'European Economy', No. 1. Brussels.
European Commission, Directorate General for Economic and Fiscal Affairs, 2004b, 'European Economy', No. 3. Brussels.
European Commission, Directorate General for Economic and Fiscal Affairs, 2010a, 'The Economic Adjustment Program for Greece', Occasional Papers 61, Brussels, May 2010, Brussels.
European Commission, Directorate-General for Economic and Financial Affairs, 2010b, 'The Economic Adjustment Program for Greece, First Review – Summer 2010', Occasional Paper 68, August 2010, Brussels.
European Commission, Directorate General for Economic and Fiscal Affairs, 2012, 'The Second Economic Adjustment Program for Greece, First Review', Occasional Paper 123, December 2012, Brussels.
European Commission, Directorate-General for Economic and Financial Affairs, 2013, 'The Second Economic Adjustment Program for Greece, Third Review', Occasional Paper 159, July 2013, Brussels.
European Commission, Directorate-General for Economic and Financial Affairs, 2014a, 'The Second Economic Adjustment Program for Greece, Fourth Review, Occasional Papers 192, April 2014, Brussels.
European Commission, Directorate General for Economic and Fiscal Affairs, 2014b, 'Annex Greece to the EU Anti-Corruption Report from the Commission to the Council and the European Parliament', Com/2014/038 final, February 2014, Brussels.
Featherstone, Kevin, 2005a, 'Introduction: "Modernization" and the Structural Constraints of Greek Politics', *West European Politics* 28(2): 223–241.

Featherstone, Kevin, 2005b, 'Soft' Co-ordination Meets 'Hard' Politics: The European Union and Pension Reform in Greece', *Journal of European Public Policy* 12(4): 733–750.

Featherstone, Kevin, 2008, 'Varieties of Capitalism' and the Greek Case: Explaining the Constraints on Domestic Reform?', GreeSE Paper No 11. February 2008, London: Hellenic Observatory, LSE.

Featherstone, Kevin and George Kazamias, 1997, 'In the Absence of Charisma: The Greek Elections of September 1996, *West European Politics* 20(2): 157–164.

Featherstone, Kevin, Georgios Kazamias and Dimitris Papadimitriou, 2001, 'The Limits of External Empowerment: EMU, Technocracy and Reform of the Greek Pension System', *Political Studies* 49(3): 462–480.

Featherstone, Kevin and Dimitris Papadimitriou, 2008, *The Limits of Europeanization: Reform Capacity and Policy Conflict in Greece*, London: Palgrave Macmillan.

Featherstone, Kevin and Dimitris Papadimitriou, 2012, 'Assessing Reform Capacity in Greece: Applying Political Economy Perspectives', in Stathis Kalyvas, George Pagoulatos and Haridimos Tsoukas (eds.), *From Stagnation to Forced Adjustment: Reforms in Greece, 1974–2010*, London: Hurst and Co, pp. 31–46.

Ferrera, Maurizio, 1996, 'The "Southern Model" of Welfare in Social Europe', *Journal of European Social Policy* 6(1): 13–37.

Fouskas, Vassilis K., 2013, 'Whatever Happened to Greece?', *Political Quarterly* 84(1): 132–138.

Gatsios, Konstantinos, 1993, 'The Workings of the Market, Competition and State Intervention in Greece' (in Greek, «Η Λειτουργία της Αγοράς, Ανταγωνισμός και Κρατική Παρέμβαση στην Ελλάδα»), in Loukas Tsoukalis (ed.), *Greece in the European Community: The Challenge of Adjustment* (in Greek, *Η Ελλάδα στην Ευρωπαϊκή Ένωση: Η Πρόκληση της Προσαρμογής*), Athens: EKEM, pp. 192–197.

Geddes, Barbara, 1994, *Politician's Dilemma: Building State Capacity in Latin America*, Berkeley, CA: University of California Press.

General Inspector of Public Administration (Γενικός Επιθεωρητής Δημόσιας Διοίκησης), 2013, *Annual Report*, Athens, July 2013.

George, Alexander and Andrew Bennett, 2005, *Case Studies and Theory Development in the Social Sciences*, Cambridge, MA: MIT Press.

Gerring, John, 2004, 'What Is a Case Study and What Is It Good for?', *American Political Science Review* 98(2): 341–354.

Giannitsis, Tassos, 2007, *The Case of the Pension System and a Way Out* (in Greek, *Το Ασφαλιστικό και μια Διέξοδος*), Athens: Polis.

Graziano, Luigi, 1978, 'Centre-periphery Relations and the Italian Crisis: The Problem of Clientelism', in Sidney Tarrow, Peter J. Katzenstein and Luigi Graziano (eds.), *Territorial Politics in Industrial Nations*, New York: Praeger, pp. 290–326.

Greek Ombudsman (Συνήγορος του Πολίτη), 2004, *Report: Procedures for Appointments to the Citizens' Service Centers (KEP)* (in Greek, *Πόρισμα: Διαδικασίες Στελέχωσης των Κέντρων Εξυπηρέτησης Πολιτών (ΚΕΠ)*), June 2004, Athens.

Greer, Scott, 2013, 'Structural Adjustment Comes to Europe: Lessons from the Eurozone from the Conditionality Debates', *Global Social Policy*, 1: 1–21.

Grzymała-Busse, Anna, 2007, 'Encouraging Effective Democratic Competition', *East European Politics and Societies* 21(1): 91–110.

Grzymala-Busse, Anna, 2008, 'Beyond Clientelism: Incumbent State Capture and State Formation', *Comparative Political Studies* 41(4–5): 638–673.

Hacker, Jacob S., 2004, 'Privatizing Risk without Privatizing the Welfare State: The Hidden Politics of Social Policy Retrenchment in the United States', *American Political Science Review*, 98(2): 243–260.

Haggard, Stephan, Richard N. Cooper and Chung-in Moon, 1993, 'Policy Reform in Korea', in Robert H. Bates and Anne O. Krueger (eds.), *Political and Economic Interactions in Economic Policy Reform: Evidence from Eight Countries*, Oxford and Cambridge, MA: Blackwell, pp. 294–332.

Haggard, Stephan and Robert R. Kaufman, 1992, 'Introduction', in Stephan Haggard and Robert R. Kaufman (eds.), *International Constraints, Distributive Conflicts and the State*, Princeton, NJ: Princeton University Press, pp. 3–37.

Halikiopoulou, Daphne and Sophia Vasilopoulou, 2015, *The Golden Dawn's 'Nationalist Solution' Explaining the Rise of the Far Right in Greece*, London: Palgrave Macmillan.

Hall, Peter, 1986, *Governing the Economy. The Politics of State Intervention in Britain and France*, New York: Oxford University Press.

Hall, Peter and David Soskice, 2001, *Varieties of Capitalism: The Institutional Foundations of Comparative Advantage*, Oxford: Oxford University Press.

Hall, Peter and Rosemary C.R. Taylor, 1996, 'Political Science and the Three New Institutionalisms', Max Planck Institut für Gesellschaftsforschung (MPIFG) Discussion Paper 96/6, June 1996.

Hallin, Daniel C. and Stylianos Papathanassopoulos, 2002, 'Political Clientelism and the Media: Southern Europe and Latin America in Comparative Perspective', *Media, Culture and Society* 24(2): 175–195.

Harris, Douglas B., 2012, 'Behavioral Reality and Institutional Change', in Scott A. Frisch, Douglas B. Harris, Sean G. Kelly and David C.W. Parker (eds.), *Doing Archival Research in Political Science*, Amherst, NY: Cambria Press, pp. 59–98.

Hazakis, Konstantinos J. and Dimitris Kyrkilis, 2014, 'The Impact of Economic Adjustment Programs on Greek Competitiveness', South and East European Development Conference 'The Greek Economy from Crisis to Development', 4–5 April 2014, Volos, Greece.

Hellenic Parliament (Βουλή των Ελλήνων), 2015, 'Trimester Report of the Government Budget Office' (Τριμηνιαία Έκθεση του Γραφείου Προϋπολογισμού του Κράτους), October–December 2013, Athens, January 2015.

Hellenic Statistical Authority (ELSTAT), 1991, Public Finance Statistics (in Greek, Στατιστική Δημοσίων Οικονομικών), Athens.

Helmke, Gretchen and Steven Levitsky, 2006, 'Introduction', in Gretchen Helmke and Steven Levitsky (eds.), *Informal Institutions and Democracy: Lessons from Latin America*, Baltimore: Johns Hopkins University Press, pp. 1–32.

Hindmoor, Andrew and Iain Hampsher-Monk, 2010, 'Rational Choice and Interpretive Evidence: Caught between a Rock and a Hard Place?', *Political Studies* 58(1): 47–65.

Ikenberry, John G., 1988, 'Conclusion: An Institutional Approach to American Foreign Economic Policy', in John G. Ikenberry, David A. Lake and Michael Mastanduno (eds.), *The State and American Foreign Economic Policy*, Ithaca, NY: Cornell University Press, pp. 219–243.

Iliadou, Ekaterini N., 2009, 'Electricity Sector Reform in Greece', *Utilities Policy* 17(1): 76–87.

IMF (International Monetary Fund), 2010, 'Letter of Intent, Memorandum of Economic and Financial Policies, Technical Memorandum of Understanding, and Memorandum of Understanding on Specific Economic Policy Conditionality', Athens, 6 August 2010.

IMF, 2012, 'Letter of Intent, Memorandum of Economic and Financial Policies, Technical Memorandum of Understanding, and Memorandum of Understanding on Specific Economic Policy Conditionality', Athens, 9 March 2012.

IMF, 2013, 'Greece: Ex Post Evaluation of Exceptional Access under the 2010 Stand-By Arrangement', Country Report No. 13/156, June 2013, Washington, DC: International Monetary Fund.

IMF, 2014, 'Country Report, Greece', No. 14/151, June 2014, Washington, DC: International Monetary Fund.

Kaempfer, William H. and Anton D. Lowenberg, 1992, *International Economic Sanctions: A Public Choice Perspective*, Boulder: Westview.

Kanellopoulos, Athanasios, 1984, 'The Role of Public Enterprises in the Greek Economy: Problems and Ways to Address Them' (in Greek, «Ο Ρόλος των Δημόσιων Επιχειρήσεων στην Ελληνική Οικονομία: Προβλήματα και Μέθοδοι Αντιμετώπισης τους»), Presentation in the OEE Conference on the Public Sector, 22–24 October 1984.

Kassimeris, George, 2004, 'The 2004 Greek Election: PASOK's Monopoly Ends', *West European Politics* 27(5): 943–953.

Katsoudas, Dimitris K., 1987, 'The Conservative Movement and New Democracy: From Past to Present', in Kevin Featherstone and Dimitrios K. Katsoudas (eds.), *Political Change in Greece: Before and After the Colonels*, London and Sydney: Croom Helm, pp. 85–111.

Kazakos, Panos, 1993, 'The Regulatory Role of the State in the Economy: Problems and Prospects of Privatization Policy in Greece' (in Greek, «Ο Ρυθμιστικός Ρόλος του Κράτους στην Οικονομία: Προβλήματα και Προοπτικές της Πολιτικής Αποκρατικοποιήσεων στην Ελλάδα»), in Loukas Tsoukalis (ed.), *Greece in the European Community: The Challenge of Adjustment* (in Greek, *Η Ελλάδα στην Ευρωπαϊκή Ένωση: Η Πρόκληση της Προσαρμογής*), Athens: EKEM, pp. 129–171.

Kazakos, Panos, 2003, 'Greece: Stabilization and Reform in the 90s', in Panagiotis C. Ioakimidis (ed.), *Greece in the European Union: The New Role and the New Agenda*, Athens: Ministry of Press and Mass Media, pp. 133–155.

Kemahlıoğlu, Özge, 2012, *Agents or Bosses? Patronage and Intra-Party Politics in Argentina and Turkey*, Colchester: ECPR Press.

Kitschelt, Herbert, 2000, 'Linkages Between Citizens and Politicians in Democratic Polities', *Comparative Political Studies* 33(6/7): 845–879.

Kitschelt, Herbert, Kirk A. Hawkins, Juan Pablo Luna, Guillermo Rosas and Elizabeth J. Zechmeister, 2010, *Latin American Party Systems*, Cambridge: Cambridge University Press.

Kitschelt, Herbert and Steven I. Wilkinson (eds.), 2007, *Patrons, Clients, and Policies: Patterns of Democratic Accountability and Political Competition*, Cambridge: Cambridge University Press.

Kofas, Jon V., 1989, *Intervention and Underdevelopment: Greece during the Cold War*, University Park, PA: Pennsylvania State University Press.

Kotzias, Nikos, 1984, *The Third Road of PASOK* (in Greek, *Ο Τρίτος Δρόμος του ΠΑΣΟΚ*), Athens: Synhroni Epohi.

Koutsogeorgopoulou, Vassiliki and Ziegelschmidt, Helmut, 2005, 'Raising Greece's Potential Output Growth', Working Paper No. 452, OECD Economics Department, OECD Publishing, Paris.

Kouzis, Yannis, 1996, 'Trade Unionism and Labor Relations: From Democratization to Party Interference' (in Greek, «Συνδικαλισμός-Εργασιακές Σχέσεις: Από τον Εκδημοκρατισμό στις Κομματικές Παρεμβάσεις»), in Spilios Papaspiliopoulos (ed.),

PASOK. *Conquest and Exercise of Power* (in Greek, *ΠΑΣΟΚ. Κατάκτηση και Άσκηση της Εξουσίας*), Athens: I. Sideris, pp. 153–158.

Krueger, Anne O., 1974, 'The Political Economy of the Rent-Seeking Society', *American Economic Review* 64(3): 291–303.

Krugman, Paul, 2012, 'Revenge of the Optimum Currency Area', *NBER Macroeconomics Annual*, 27(1): 439–448.

Kuran, Timur, 1995, *Private Truths, Public Lies: The Social Consequences of Preference Falsification*, Cambridge, MA: Harvard University Press.

Labán, Raúl and Federico Sturzenegger F., 1994, 'Distributional Conflict, Financial Adaptation and Delayed Stabilization', *Economics and Politics* 6(3): 257–76.

Labán, Raúl and Federico Sturzenegger, 1998, 'Fiscal Conservatism as a Response to the Debt Crisis', in Federico Sturzenegger and Mariano Tommasi (eds.), *The Political Economy of Reform*. Cambridge, MA and London: MIT Press, pp. 105–126.

Ladi, Stella, 2005, 'Policy Learning and the Role of Expertise in the Reform Process in Greece', *West European Politics* 28(2): 279–296.

Ladi, Stella, 2014, 'Austerity Politics and Administrative Reform: The Eurozone Crisis and Its Impact upon Greek Public Administration', *Comparative European Politics*, 12(2): 184–208.

Lambropoulou, Effi, Theodoros Iosifidis, Nikos Papapamanolis, Eleftheria Bakali, Stella Ageli, Erifyli Bakirli and Garyfalia Massouri, 2008, 'Corruption in Greece or Corruption of Greece? The "Modern" Triumphalism', Discussion Paper Series 'Crime as a Cultural Problem. The Relevance of Perceptions of Corruption to Crime Prevention: A Comparative Cultural Study in the EU-Accession States Bulgaria and Romania, the EU-Candidate States Turkey and Croatia and the EU-States Germany, Greece and United Kingdom', No. 23.

Lanza, Orazio and Kostas A. Lavdas, 2000, 'The Disentanglement of Interest Politics: Business Associability, the Parties and Policy in Italy and Greece', *European Journal of Political Research* 37(2): 203–235.

LaPalombara, Joseph, 1964, *Interest Groups in Italian Politics*, Princeton, NJ: Princeton University Press.

Lavdas, Kostas A., 1998, *The Europeanization of Greece: Interest Politics and Crises of Integration*, London: Palgrave Macmillan.

Lavdas, Kostas A., 2005, 'Interest Groups in Disjointed Corporatism: Social Dialogue in Greece and European Competitive Corporatism', *West European Politics* 28(2): 297–316.

Lemarchand, René and Keith Legg, 1972, 'Political Clientelism and Development: A Preliminary Analysis', *Comparative Politics* 4(2): 149–172.

Liargovas, Panagiotis, 2007, *Foreign Direct Investment and Competitiveness: The Experience of Greece and Other European Countries* (in Greek, *Ξένες Άμεσες Επενδύσεις και Ανταγωνιστικότητα. Η Εμπειρία της Ελλάδος και Άλλων Ευρωπαϊκών Χωρών*) Athens: Papazisis.

Lindberg, Staffan I. and Minion K.C. Morrison, 2008, 'Are African Voters Really Ethnic or Clientelistic? Survey Evidence from Ghana', *Political Science Quarterly* 123(10): 95–122.

Lolos, Sarantis E.G., 2005, 'The Role of European Integration in the Reform Process: The Greek Experience', in Mats Lundahl and Michael L. Wyzan (eds.), *The Political Economy of Reform Failure*, Oxford and New York: Routledge, pp. 70–88.

Loulis, John C., 1981, 'New Democracy: The Face of Conservatism'. In Howard R. Penniman (ed.), *Greece at the Polls: The National Elections of 1974 and 1977*, Washington, DC: American Enterprise Institute, pp. 49–83.

Lyberaki, Antigone and Euclid Tsakalotos, 2002, 'Reforming the Economy without Society: Social and Institutional Constraints to Economic Reform in post-1974 Greece', *New Political Economy* 7(1): 93–114.

Lyne, Mona M., 2008, *The Voter's Dilemma and Democratic Accountability: Latin America and Beyond*, University Park, PA: Pennsylvania State University Press.

Lyrintzis, Christos, 1982, 'The Rise of Pasok: The Greek Election of 1981', *West European Politics* 5(3): 308–313.

Lyrintzis, Christos, 1984, 'Political Parties in Post-Junta Greece: A Case of Bureaucratic Clientelism', *West European Politics* 7(2): 99–118.

Lyrintzis, Christos, 1987, 'The Power of Populism: The Greek Case', *European Journal of Political Research* 15(6): 667–686.

Lyrintzis, Christos, 2002, Greek Civil Society in the 21st Century, in P.C. Ioakimidis (ed.), *Greece in the European Union: The New Role and the New Agenda*, pp. 90–99.

Lyrintzis, Christos, 2005, 'The Changing Party System: Stable Democracy, Contested "Modernization"', *West European Politics* 28(2): 242–259.

Mair, Peter, 2000, 'The Limited Impact of Europe on National Party Systems', *West European Politics* 23(4): 27–51.

Manessiotis, Vassilios G. and Robert D. Reischauer, 2001, 'Greek Fiscal and Budget Policy and EMU', in Ralph C. Bryant, Nicholas C. Garganas and George S. Tavlas (eds.), *Greece's Economic Performance and Prospects*, Athens and Washington, DC: Bank of Greece and The Brookings Institution, pp. 103–152.

Maravall, José María, 1993, 'Politics and Policy: Economic Reforms in Southern Europe', in Luis Carlos Bresser Pereira, José María Maravall and Andrew Przeworsky (eds.), *Economic Reforms in New Democracies: A Social Democratic Approach*, Cambridge: Cambridge University Press, pp. 77–131.

Markoglou, Emmanouil, 1963, *The Truman Doctrine* (in Greek, *Το Δόγμα Τρούμαν*), Athens: Etaireia Meletis Ellinikis Istorias.

Marks, Gary, 1992, 'Structural Policy in the European Community' in Alberta Sbragia (ed.), *Euro-politics: Institutions and Policy Making in the New European Community*, Washington, DC: Brookings Institutions, pp. 191–224.

Martini, Roger, 2007, 'The Role of Compensation in Policy Reform', OECD Food, Agriculture and Fisheries Working Papers, No. 5, Paris: OECD Publishing.

Massavetas, Giorgis, 1996, *Topple Down Mitsotakis: The Chronicles of a Political Conspiracy* (in Greek, *Ανατρέψατε Μητσοτάκη: το Χρονικό μιας Πολιτικής Συνωμοσίας*), Athens: Elliniki Evroekdotiki.

Matsaganis, Manos, 2002, 'Yet Another Piece of Pension Reform in Greece', *South European Society and Politics* 7(3): 109–122.

Mavrogordatos, Giorgos, 1984, 'The Greek Party System: A Case of Limited but Polarized Pluralism?', *West European Politics* 7(4): 156–69.

Mavrogordatos, Giorgos, 1988, *Between Pytiokamptes and Procroustes: Occupational Interest Groups in Greece* (in Greek, *Μεταξύ Πιτυοκάμπτη και Προκρούστη. Οι Επαγγελματικές Οργανώσεις στην Ελλάδα*), Athens: Odysseas.

Mavrogordatos, Giorgos, 1997, 'From Traditional Clientelism to Machine Politics: The Impact of PASOK Populism in Greece', *South European Society and Politics* 3(2): 1–26.

Medina, Luis Fernando and Susan C. Stokes, 2007, 'Monopoly and Monitoring: An Approach to Political Clientelism', in Herbert Kitschelt and Steven I. Wilkinson (eds.), *Patrons, Clients and Policies: Patterns of Democratic Accountability and Political Competition*, Cambridge: Cambridge University Press, pp. 68–83.

Mitsopoulos, Michael and Theodore Pelagidis, 2006, *Analysis of the Greek Economy: Rent-Seeking and the Reforms* (in Greek, *Ανάλυση της Ελληνικής Οικολογίας: Η Προσοδοθηρία και οι Μεταρρυθμίσεις*), Athens: Papazisis.

Mitsopoulos, Michael and Theodore Pelagidis, 2011, *Understanding the Crisis in Greece: From Boom to Bust,* London: McMillan Palgrave.

Moschonas, Gerassimos, 2001, 'The Path of Modernization: PASOK and European Integration', *Journal of Southern Europe and the Balkans* 3(1): 11–24.

Moschovis, George and Mateo Capo Servera, 2009, "External Imbalances of the Greek Economy: The Role of Fiscal and Structural Policies." ECFIN Country Focus 6, No. 6 (July 10).

Mossialos, Elias and Sara Allin, 2005, 'Interest Groups and Health System Reform in Greece', *West European Politics* 28(2): 420–444.

Moutos, Thomas and Christos Tsitsikas, 2010, 'Wither Public Interest: The Case of Greece's Public Finances, *FinanzArchiv: Public Finance Analysis* 66(2): 170–206.

Mouzelis, Nikos, 1978, *Greece: Facets of Underdevelopment*, London: Macmillan and Holmes & Meier.

Mouzelis, Nikos, 1986, *Politics in the Semi-Periphery*, London: Macmillan.

Mouzelis, Nikos, 1993, 'Political System and Modernization' (in Greek, «Πολιτικό Σύστημα και Εκσυγχρονισμός»), in Loukas Tsoukalis (ed.), *Greece in the European Community: The Challenge of Adjustment* (in Greek, *Η Ελλάδα στην Ευρωπαϊκή Ένωση: Η Πρόκληση της Προσαρμογής*), Athens: EKEM, pp. 289–310.

Mylonas, Paul and George Papaconstantinou, 2001, 'Product Market Reform in Greece: Policy Priorities and Prospects', in Ralph C. Bryant, Nicholas C. Garganas and George S. Tavlas (eds.), *Greece's Economic Performance and Prospects*, Athens and Washington, DC: Bank of Greece and The Brookings Institution, pp. 499–544.

OECD, 1983, 'Economic Surveys: Greece 1983/1984', OECD Publishing, Paris.

OECD, 1986, 'Economic Surveys: Greece 1985/1986', OECD Publishing, Paris.

OECD, 1987, 'Economic Survey of Greece: 1987', OECD Publishing, Paris.

OECD, 1990, 'Economic Surveys: Greece 1989/1990', OECD Publishing, Paris.

OECD, 1993, 'Economic Surveys: Greece 1993', OECD Publishing, Paris.

OECD, 1997, 'Economic Surveys: Greece 1997', OECD Publishing, Paris.

OECD, 1998, 'Economic Surveys, Greece 1998', OECD Publishing, Paris.

OECD, 1999, 'Main Economic Indicators', Volume 4, May 1999, OECD Publishing, Paris.

OECD, 2000, 'Employment Outlook', OECD Publishing, Paris.

OECD, 2001, 'Regulatory Reform in Greece', OECD Publishing, Paris.

OECD, 2002, 'Etudes Economiques de l'OCDE', OECD Publishing, Paris.

OECD, 2005, 'Economic Survey of Greece 2005', OECD Publishing, Paris.

OECD, 2007, 'Economic Policy Reforms: Going for Growth', OECD Publishing, Paris.

OECD, 2014, 'Society at a Glance 2014 Highlights: Greece, The Crisis and Its Aftermath', OECD Publishing, Paris.

Oikonomou, Georgios E., 1992, *The Greek Economy before the 1992 Prospect* (in Greek, *Η Ελληνική Οικονομία στην Προοπτική του 1992*), Athens: IOBE.

Olson, Mancur, 1971/1965, *The Logic of Collective Action: Public Goods and the Theory of Groups* (Revised edition ed.), Cambridge, MA: Harvard University Press.

Ostrom, Elinor, 1998, 'A Behavioral Approach to the Rational Choice of Collective Action'. *American Political Science Review* 92(1): 1–22.

Pagoulatos, George, 2003, *Greece's New Political Economy: State, Finance, and Growth from Postwar to EMU*, Houndsmills and New York: Palgrave Macmillan.

Pagoulatos, George, 2005, 'The Politics of Privatization: Redrawing the Public-Private Boundary', *West European Politics* 28(2): 358–80.

Pantazidis, Stelios N., 2002, *Macroeconomic Developments and Economic Policy in Greece: From the Metapolitefsi to the Entry to EMU* (1975–2002) (in Greek, *Μακροοικονομικές Εξελίξεις και Οικονομική Πολιτική στην Ελλάδα: από τη Μεταπολίτευση στην Ένταξη στην ΟΝΕ*), Athens: Kritiki.

Pantazopoulos, Andreas, 1987, 'Η Κοινωνική Σύνθεση του Στελεχικού Δυναμικού του ΠΑΣΟΚ (1974–1981)' (in Greek, 'The Social Composition of PASOK Cadres (1974–1981)'), *O Politis* 83(11): 17–21.

Papadimitriou, Dimitris, 2005, 'The Limits of Engineering Collective Escape: The 2000 Reform of the Greek Labor Market', *West European Politics* 28(2): 381–401.

Papandreou, Andreas, 1977, *Transition to Socialism* (in Greek, *Μετάβαση στο Σοσιαλισμό*), Athens: Aihmi.

Papandreou, Andreas, 1989, 'Declaration of the Prime Minister Andreas Papandreou' (in Greek, «Δήλωση του Πρωθυπουργού, Ανδρέα Παπανδρέου»), in Costas Simitis, Nikos Garganas, Takis Thomopoulos, Yannis Spraos (eds.), *The Politics of Economic Stabilization* (in Greek, *Η Πολιτική της Οικονομικής Σταθεροποίησης*), Athens: Gnossi, pp. 43–50.

Papaspiliopoulos, Spilios, 1996, 'Confusion and Disorientation Around the State of Our Economy' (in Greek, «Συγχύσεις και Αποπροσανατολισμοί Γύρω από την Κατάσταση της Οικονομίας Μας»), in Spilios Papaspiliopoulos (ed.), *PASOK: Conquest and Exercise of Power* (in Greek, *ΠΑΣΟΚ. Κατάκτηση και Άσκηση της Εξουσίας*), Athens: I Sideris, pp. 209–211.

Papathanassopoulos, Stylianos, 1999, 'The Effects of Media Commercialization on Journalism and Politics in Greece', *The Communication Review* 3(4): 379–402.

Papathanassopoulos, Stylianos, 2001, 'Media Commercialization and Journalism in Greece', *European Journal of Communication* 16(4): 505–521.

Pappas, Takis S., 1999, *Making Party Democracy in Greece*, London: Macmillan.

Pappas, Takis S., 2009, 'Patrons Against Partisans: The Politics of Patronage in Mass Ideological Parties', *Party Politics* 15(3): 315–334.

Pappas, Takis S., 2013, *Populism and Crisis Politics in Greece*. Basingstoke, Houndmills: Palgrave Macmillan.

Pappas, Takis S. and Zina Assimakopoulou, 2012, 'Party Patronage in Greece and Political Entrepreneurship in a Party Patronage Democracy', in Petr Kopecký, Peter Mair and Maria Spirova (eds.), *Party Patronage and Party Government: Public Appointments and Political Control in European Democracies*, Oxford: Oxford University Press, pp. 144–162.

PASOK, 1977, *For a Socialist Society: Socialization, Self-management, Decentralization and Local Administration* (in Greek, *Για μια Σοσιαλιστική Κοινωνία: Κοινωνικοποίηση, Αυτοδιαχείριση, Αποκέντρωση, Τοπική Αυτοδιοίκηση*, Συνδικαλισμός), Athens: PASOK.

PASOK, 1981, *Contract with the People* (in Greek, *Συμβόλαιο με το Λαό*) PASOK leaflet, Athens: PASOK.

Petmesidou, Maria, 2000, 'Social Protection in Greece in the Nineties: Reforming the "Weak" Welfare State', in Achilleas Mitsos and Elias Mossialos (eds.), *Contemporary Greece and Europe*, Aldershot: Ashgate, pp. 303–330.

Piattoni, Simona (ed.), 2001, *Clientelism, Interests, and Democratic Representation: The European Experience in Historical and Comparative Perspective*, Cambridge: Cambridge University Press.

Pierson, Paul, 2000, 'Not Just What, but When: Timing and Sequence in Political Processes', *Studies in American Political Development* 14(1): 72–92.

Polychroniou, C.J., 2011, 'An Unblinking Glance at a National Catastrophe and the Potential Dissolution of the Eurozone: Greece's Debt Crisis in Context', The Levy Economics Institute Working Paper No. 688, Levy Economics Institute of Bard College.

Public Issue, 2012, 'Cumulative Archive of the Pre-electoral Barometer February–May 2012' (in Greek: Αθροιστικό Αρχείο Προεκλογικού Βαρομέτρου, Φεβρουάριος-Μάιος 2012), Athens, Greece.

Ragin, Charles C., 1997, 'Turning the Tables: How Case-Oriented Research Challenges Variable-Oriented Research', *Comparative Social Research* 16: 27–42.

Rapanos, Vassilis, 2009, *Size and Range of Public Sector Activities* (in Greek *Μέγεθος και Εύρος Δραστηριοτήτων του Δημόσιου Τομέα*), Athens: IOVE, Foundation for Economic and Industrial Research.

Robinson, J. A. and Thierry Verdier, 2002, 'The Political Economy of Clientelism', Centre for Economic Policy Research Discussion Papers Series No. 3205.

Rodrik, Dani, 1996, 'Understanding Economic Policy Reform', *Journal of Economic Literature* 34(1): 9–41.

Roniger, Luis and Ayşe Güneş-Ayata, 1994, *Democracy, Clientelism and Civil Society*, Boulder: Lynne Rienner.

Root, Hilton L., 2013, Dynamics among Nations: The Evolution of Legitimacy and Development in Modern States, Cambridge, MA: The MIT Press.

Rueschemeyer, Dietrich and John D. Stephens, 1997, 'Comparing Historical Sequences: A Powerful Tool for Causal Analysis', *Comparative Social Research* 16: 55–72.

Saint-Paul, Gilles, 1996, 'Exploring the Political Economy of Labor Market Institutions', *Economic Policy* 11(23): 265–315.

Sandholtz, Wayne, 1996, 'Membership Matters: Limits of the Functional Approach to European Institutions', *Journal of Common Market Studies* 34(3): 403–429.

Schamis, Hector E., 1999, 'Distributional Coalitions and the Politics of Economic Reform in Latin America', *World Politics* 51(2): 236–268.

Scharpf, Fritz W., 1990, 'Games Real Actors Could Play: The Problem of Mutual Predictability', *Rationality and Society* 2(4): 471–494.

Scharpf, Fritz W., 1992, *Crisis and Choice in Social Democracy*, Ithaca: Cornell University Press.

Schmidt, Vivien A., 2007, 'Bringing the State Back into the Varieties of Capitalism and Discourse Back into the Explanation of Change', CES Germany & Europe Working Papers, No. 07.3.

Schmitter, Philippe C., 1979, 'Still the Century of Corporatism?', in Philippe C. Schmitter and Gerhard Lehmbruch (eds.), *Trends Toward Corporatist Intermediation,* Beverly Hills, CA: Sage, pp. 7–52.

Scott, James, 1972, *Comparative Political Corruption*, Englewood Cliffs, NJ: Prentice Hall.

Shonfield, Andrew, 1965, *Modern Capitalism: The Changing Balance of Public and Private Power*, Oxford: Oxford University Press.

Simitis, Costas, 1989, A first Assessment' (in Greek, «Μια Πρώτη Εκτίμηση»), in Costas Simitis, Nikos Garganas, Takis Thomopoulos, Yannis Spraos (eds.), *The Politics of Economic Stabilization* (in Greek, *Η Πολιτική της Οικονομικής Σταθεροποίησης*), Athens: Gnossi, pp. 11–30.

Simitis, Costas, 2005, *Politics for a Creative Greece 1996–2004* (in Greek, *Πολιτική για μια Δημιουργική Ελλάδα 1996–2004*), Athens: Polis.

Simon, Herbert, 1985, 'Human Nature in Politics: The Dialogue of Psychology with Political Science', *American Political Science Review* 79(2): 293–304.

Smith, Howard K, 1950, *The State of Europe*, New York: Alfred A. Knopf.

Sotiropoulos, Dimitri A., 1996, *Populism and Bureaucracy: The Case of Greece Under PASOK, 1981–1989*, Notre Dame and London: University of Notre Dame Press.

Sotiropoulos, Dimitri, 2001, *The Peak of the Clientelist State* (in Greek, *Η Κορυφή του Πελατειακού Κράτους*), Athens: Potamos.

Sotiropoulos, Dimitri A., 2004a, 'Democratization, Administrative Reform and the State in Greece, Italy, Portugal and Spain: Is There a 'Model' of South European Bureaucracy?', The Hellenic Observatory The European Institute, The London School of Economics and Political Science, April 2004.

Sotiropoulos, Dimitri A., 2004b, 'The EU's Impact on the Greek Welfare State: Europeanization on Paper?', *Journal of European Social Policy*, 14(3): 267–284.

Sotiropoulos, Dimitri A., 2012, 'The Paradox of Non-Reform in a Reform-Ripe Environment: Lessons from Post-Authoritarian Greece', in Stathis Kalyvas, George Pagoulatos, and Haridimos Tsoukas (eds.), *From Stagnation to Forced Adjustment: Reforms in Greece, 1974–2010*, London: Hurst and Co, pp. 9–30.

Spanou, Calliope, 2001, '(Re)shaping the Politics-Administration Nexus in Greece: The Decline of a Symbiotic relationship?', in Guy B. Peters and Jon Pierre (eds.), *Politicians, Bureaucrats and Administrative Reform*, London: Routledge, pp. 106–15.

Spanou, Calliope, 2008, State Reform in Greece: Responding to Old and New Challenges', *International Journal of Public Sector Management* 21(2): 150–173.

Spanou, Calliope, 2012, 'The Quandary of Administrative Reform: Institutional and Performance Modernization', in Stathis Kalyvas, George Pagoulatos and Haridimos Tsoukas (eds.), 2012, *From Stagnation to Forced Adjustment: Reforms in Greece, 1974–2010*, London: Hurst and Co, pp. 171–194.

Spourdalakis, Michalis, 1988a, *PASOK: Structure, Within-party Assessments and Power Concentration* (in Greek, *ΠΑΣΟΚ: Δομή, Εσωκομματικές Κρίσεις και Συγκέντρωση Εξουσίας*), Athens: Exantas.

Spourdalakis, Michalis, 1988b, *The Rise of the Greek Socialist Party*, London: Routledge.

Spourdalakis, Michalis, 1998, *PASOK: Party–State-Society* (in Greek, *ΠΑΣΟΚ: Κόμμα – Κράτος – Κοινωνία*), Athens: Patakis.

Spraos, Yannis, 1993, 'Macroeconomic Policy for an Open Economy' (in Greek, «Μακροοικονομική Πολιτική για μια Ανοικτή Οικονομία»), in Loukas Tsoukalis (ed.), *Greece in the European Community: The Challenge of Adjustment* (in Greek, *Η Ελλάδα στην Ευρωπαϊκή Κοινότητα: η Πρόκληση της Προσαρμογής*), Athens: EKEM, pp. 57–103.

Stallings, Barbara, 1990, 'Politics and Economic Crisis: A Comparative Study of Chile, Peru, and Colombia', in Joan M. Nelson, (ed.), *Economic Crisis and Policy Choice: The Politics of Adjustment in the Third World*, Princeton, NJ: Princeton University Press, pp. 113–168.

Stergiou, Dimitris L., 2002, *The Great Bubble of the Economy 1981–2002* (in Greek, *Η Μεγάλη Φούσκα της Οικονομίας*), Athens: Papazisis.

Stockhammer, Engelbert and Dimitris P. Sotiropoulos, 2014, 'Rebalancing the Euro Area: The Costs of Internal Devaluation', *Review of Political Economy*, 26(2): 210–233.

Streeck, Wolfgang and Kathleen Thelen, 2005, 'Introduction: Institutional Change in Advanced Political Economies', in Wolfgang Streeck and Kathleen Thelen (eds.), *Beyond Continuity: Institutional Change in Advanced Political Economies*, Oxford: Oxford University Press, pp. 1–39.

Stigler, George J., 1971, 'The Theory of Economic Regulation', *Bell Journal of Economics and Management Sciences* 2(1): 3–21.

Stokes, Susan C., 2005, 'Perverse Accountability: A Formal Model of Machine Politics with Evidence from Argentina' *American Political Science Review* 99(3): 315–325.

Stokes, Susana C., 2007, 'Political Clientelism', in Carles Bois and Susan C. Stokes (eds.), *The Oxford Handbook of Political Science*, Oxford: Oxford University Press, pp. 602–627.

Telloglou, Tassos, 2009, *The Network: The Siemens File* (in Greek, *Το Δίκτυο: Ο Φάκελος Siemens*), Athens: SKAI.

Themelis, Nikos, 1998, *I Have Finished the Course* (in Greek, *Τον Δρόμον Τετέλεκα*), Athens: Sideris.

Theodoropoulou, Sotiria, 2014, 'Has the EU Become More Intrusive in Shaping National Welfare State Reforms?', Working Paper, Brussels: European Trade Union Institute.

Thomadakis, Stavros B., 1997, 'The Greek Economy: Performance, Expectations, and Paradoxes', in Graham T. Allison and Kalypso Nicolaidis (eds.), *The Greek Paradox: Promise vs. Performance*, Cambridge, MA: John F. Kennedy School of Government, Center for Science and International Affairs, pp. 39–60.

Thomadakis, Stavros, 2011, *State and Growth in Greece* (in Greek, *Κράτος και Ανάπτυξη στην Ελλάδα*), Athens: Alexandria.

Tinios, Platon, 2005, 'Pension Reform in Greece: "Reform by Instalments" – A Blocked Process?' *West European Policy* 28(2): 402–419.

Tornell, Aaron, 1995, 'Are Economic Crises Necessary for Trade Liberalization and Fiscal Reform? The Mexican Experience', in Rudiger Dornbusch and Sebastian Edwards (eds.), *Reform, Recovery, and Growth: Latin America and the Middle East*, Chicago: University of Chicago Press, pp. 53–73.

Transparency International, Greece – Public Issue, 2010, 'National Survey on Corruption in Greece', Athens, March 2010.

Trantidis, Aris, 2012, *The Dominant Party System: Clientelism, Pluralism and Limited Contestability*, MPhil thesis, The London School of Economics and Political Science (LSE).

Trantidis, Aris, 2013, 'Clientelism and the Classification of Dominant Party Systems', *Democratization* 22(1): 113–133.

Trantidis Aris, 2014, 'Reforms and Collective Action in a Clientelist System: Greece during the Mitsotakis Administration (1990–93)', *South European Society and Politics* 19(2): 215–234.

Trantidis Aris, 2015, 'Clientelism and Economic Policy: Hybrid Characteristics and Collective Action in Greece', *Journal of European Public Policy*, DOI: 10.1080/13501763.2015.1088564, November 2015.

Triantafyllou, Anna, Ruby Gropas and Hara Kouki (eds.), 2013, *The Greek Crisis and European Modernity*, London: Palgrave Macmillan.

Tsakalotos, Euclid, 1991, *Alternative Economic Strategies: The Case of Greece*, Aldershot: Avebury.

Tsakalotos, Euclid, 1998, 'The Political Economy of Social Democratic Economic Policies: The PASOK Experiment in Greece', *Oxford Review of Economic Policy* 14(1): 114–138.

Tsatsos, Dimitris T, 1993, *Constitutional Law, Volume B* (in Greek, *Συνταγματικό Δίκαιο, Τόμος Β*), Athens, Komotini: Ant. N. Sakkoulas.

Tsakiris, Athanasios, 2003, 'The Janus-faced Political Intervention of Greek Socialists (PASOK) in the Trade-unions in the 1990s: The Case of PASKE in OTOE', 1st LSE PhD Symposium on Social Science Research on Greece, Hellenic Observatory, European Institute, LSE London, June 21, 2003.

Tsaveas, Nicholas T., 2001, 'Greece's Balance of Payments and Competitiveness', in Ralph C. Bryant, Nicholas C. Garganas and George S. Tavlas (eds.), *Greece's Economic Performance and Prospects*, Athens and Washington, DC: Bank of Greece and The Brookings Institution, pp. 323–360.

Tsebelis, George, 1990, *Nested Games: Rational Choice in Comparative Politics*, Berkeley and Los Angeles, CA: University of California Press.

Tsoukalas, Konstantinos, 1993, '"Free-riders" in Wonderland: On the Greeks in Greece' (in Greek, «Τζαμπατζήδες» στη Χώρα των Θαυμάτων. Περί Ελλήνων στην Ελλάδα»), *Greek Review of Political Science* (*Ελληνική Επιθεώρηση Πολιτικής Επιστήμης*) 1: 9–52.

Tsoukalis, Loukas, 1993, 'Introduction: European Adjustment and National Particularities' (in Greek, «Εισαγωγή: Ευρωπαϊκή Προσαρμογή και Εθνικές Ιδιαιτερότητες), in Loukas Tsoukalis, (ed.), *Greece in the European Community: The Challenge of Adjustment* (in Greek, *Η Ελλάδα στην Ευρωπαϊκή Κοινότητα: Ο Χαρακτήρας της Προσαρμογής*), Athens: EKEM, pp. 17–29.

Tsoukalis, Loukas, 1997, 'Beyond the Greek Paradox', in Graham T. Allison and Kalypso Nicolaidis (eds.), *The Greek Paradox: Promise vs. Performance*, Cambridge, MA: John F. Kennedy School of Government, Center for Science and International Affairs, pp. 163–174.

Tullock, Gordon, 1965, 'Entry Barriers in Politics', *American Economic Review* 55(1/2): 458–466.

Tullock, Gordon, 1993, *Rent-Seeking*, Aldershot: Edward Elgar.

Tullock, Gordon, 2005, *The Rent-Seeking Society: The Selected Works of Gordon Tullock*, Vol. 5, Indianapolis: Liberty Fund.

Vassiliadis, Damianos, 2002, 'Andreas Papandreou, PASOK and the Causes of Greece's Political Crisis' (in Greek, «Ο Ανδρέας Παπανδρέου, το ΠΑΣΟΚ και τα Αίτια της Πολιτικής Κρίσης στην Ελλάδα»), *Tetradia Politikou Dialogou, Erevnas kai Kritikis* 47: 35–55.

Velasco, Andrés, 1993, 'A Model of Endogenous Fiscal Deficits, and Delayed Fiscal Reforms', C.V. Starr Center Report 93–94, New York University.

Vergopoulos, Kostas, 1992, 'The Dark Side of Modernization' (in Greek, «Η Σκοτεινή Πλευρά του Εκσυγχρονισμού»), *Theseis* 39 (April–June), retrieved online on 27.1.2011.

Verney, Susannah, 1997, 'Greece: A New Era', *Mediterranean Politics* 2(1): 193–200.

Vink, Maarten P. and Paolo Graziano, 2007, 'Challenges of a New Research Agenda', in Paolo Graziano and Maarten P. Vink (eds.), *Europeanization: New Research Agendas*, Basingstoke, Hampshire: Palgrave Macmillan, pp. 3–20.

Vourloumis, Panagis, 2002, *Social Security in Plain Words* (in Greek, *Το Ασφαλιστικό με Απλά Λόγια*), Athens: Potamos.

Wagner, Richard E., 2012a, *Deficits, Debt, and Democracy: Wrestling with Tragedy on the Fiscal Commons*, Northampton: Edward Elgar.

Wagner, Richard E., 2012b, 'Public Choice, Past and Present', Studies in Political Choice 28: 65–79.

Walle, Nicolas van de, 2001, *African Economies and the Politics of Permanent Crisis, 1979–1999*, Cambridge: Cambridge University Press.

Wantchekon, Leonard, 2003, 'Clientelism and Voting Behavior Evidence from a Field Experiment in Benin', *World Politics* 55(3): 399–422.

Waterbury, John, 1992, 'The Heart of the Matter? Public Enterprise and the Adjustment Process', in Stephan Haggard and Robert R. Kaufman (eds.), *International Constraints, Distributive Conflicts and the State*, Princeton, NJ: Princeton University Press, pp. 182–217.

Weingrod, Alex, 1968, 'Patrons, Patronage, and Political Parties', *Comparative Studies in Society and History* 10(4): 377–400.

Weisbrot, Mark and Juan Antonio Montecino, 2012, 'More Pain, No Gain for Greece: Is the Euro Worth the Costs of Pro-Cyclical Fiscal Policy and Internal Devaluation', Washington, DC: Center for Economic and Policy Research.

World Economic Forum, 2003, *The Global Competitiveness Report 2003*, Geneva: World Economic Forum.

Wolf, Holger, 2011, 'Internal Devaluation in a Monetary Union', *International Economics and Economic Policy* 8(1): 3–6.

Xanthakis, Manolis, 1989, *The Crisis of the Greek Industry and State Intervention* (in Greek, *Η Κρίση της Ελληνικής Μεταποίησης και η Παρέμβαση του Κράτους*), Athens: Papazisis.

Zambarloukou, Stella, 1997, *State and the Labor Union Movement in Greece, 1936–90*, (in Greek, *Κράτος και Εργατικός Συνδικαλισμός*), Athens: Sakkoulas [in Greece].

Zartaloudis, Sotirios, 2014, *The Impact of European Employment Strategy in Greece and Portugal: Europeanization in a World of Neglect*, London: Palgrave Macmillan.

Index

Page numbers in italic format indicate figures and tables.

www.ingramcontent.com/pod-product-compliance
Lightning Source LLC
LaVergne TN
LVHW011121300926
849160LV00008B/468
* 9 7 8 1 1 3 8 4 8 8 2 3 6 *